Sea Power In Its Relations To The War Of 1812 - Volume II

ALFRED THAYER MAHAN

London 1899

TABLE OF CONTENTS

THE WINTER OF 1812 TO 1813

The War, Continued

Bainbridge's Squadron: Actionsbetween "Constitution" And "Java," "Hornet" And"Peacock"—Increasing Pressure On Atlantic Coast

The squadron under Commodore William Bainbridge, the third which sailed from the United States in October, 1812, started nearly three weeks after the joint departure of Rodgers and Decatur. It consisted of the "Constitution" and sloop of war "Hornet," then in Boston, and of the "Essex," the only 32-gun frigate in the navy, fitting for sea in the Delaware. The original armament of the latter, from which she derived her rate, had been changed to forty 32-pounder carronades and six long twelves; total, forty-six guns. It is noticeable that this battery, which ultimately contributed not merely to her capture, but to her almost helplessness under the fire of an enemy able to maintain his distance out of carronade range, was strongly objected to by Captain Porter. On October 14 he applied to be transferred to the "Adams," giving as reasons "my insuperable dislike to carronades, and the bad sailing of the "Essex," which render her, in my opinion, the worst frigate in the service."[1] The request was not granted, and Porter sailed in command of the ship on October 28, the two other vessels having left Boston on the 26th.

In order to facilitate a junction, Bainbridge had sent Porter full details of his intended movements.[2] A summary of these will show his views as to a well-planned commerce-destroying cruise. Starting about October 25, he would steer first a course not differing greatly from the general direction taken by Rodgers and Decatur, to the Cape Verde Islands, where he would fill with water, and by November 27 sail for the island Fernando de

Noronha, two hundred and fifty miles south of the Equator, and two hundred miles from the mainland of Brazil, then a Portuguese colony, of which the island was a dependency. The trade winds being fair for this passage, he hoped to leave there by December 15, and to cruise south along the Brazilian coast as far as Rio de Janeiro, until January 15. In the outcome the meeting of the "Constitution" with the "Java" cut short her proceedings at this point; but Bainbridge had purposed to stay yet another month along the Brazilian coast, between Rio and St. Catherine's, three hundred miles south. Thence he would cross the South Atlantic to the neighborhood of St. Helena, remaining just beyond sight of it, to intercept returning British Indiamen, which frequently stopped there. Porter failed to overtake the other vessels, on account of the bad sailing of the "Essex." He arrived at Fernando de Noronha December 14, one day before that fixed by Bainbridge as his last there; but the "Constitution" and "Hornet" had already gone on to Bahia, on the Brazilian mainland, seven hundred miles to the southwest, leaving a letter for him to proceed off Cape Frio, sixty miles from the entrance of Rio. He reached this rendezvous on the 25th, but saw nothing of Bainbridge, who had been detained off Bahia by conditions there. The result was that the "Essex" never found her consorts, and finally struck out a career for herself, which belongs rather to a subsequent period of the war. We therefore leave her spending her Christmas off Cape Frio.

The two other vessels had arrived off Bahia on December 13. Here was lying a British sloop of war, the "Bonne Citoyenne," understood to have on board a very large amount of specie for England. The American vessels blockaded her for some days, and then Captain Lawrence challenged her to single combat; Bainbridge acquiescing, and pledging his honor that the "Constitution" should remain out of the way, or at least not interfere. The British captain, properly enough, declined. That his ship and her reported value were detaining two American vessels from wider depredations was a reason more important than any fighting-cock glory to be had from an arranged encounter on equal terms, and should have sufficed him without expressing the doubt he did as to Bainbridge's good faith.[3] On the 26th the Commodore, leaving Lawrence alone to watch the British sloop, stood out to sea with the "Constitution," cruising well off shore; and thus on the 29th, at 9 A.M., being then five miles south of the port and some miles from land, discovered two strange sail, which were the British frigate "Java," Captain Henry Lambert, going to Bahia for water, with an American ship, prize to her.

Upon seeing the "Constitution" in the south-southwest, the British captain shaped his course for her, directing the prize to enter the harbor. Bainbridge, watching these movements, now tacked his ship, and at 11.30 A.M. steered away southeast under all plain sail, to draw the enemy well away from neutral waters; the Portuguese authorities having shown some sensitiveness on that score. The "Java" followed, running full ten miles an hour, a great speed in those days, and gaining rapidly. At 1.30, being now as far off shore as desired, Bainbridge went about and stood toward the enemy, who kept away with a view to rake, which the "Constitution" avoided by the usual means of wearing, resuming her course southeast, but under canvas much reduced. At 2.10 the "Java," having closed to a half mile, the "Constitution" fired one gun ahead of her; whereupon the British ship hoisted her colors, and the American then fired two broadsides. The "Java" now took up a position to windward of the "Constitution," on her port side, a little forward (2.10); "within pistol-shot," according to the minutes submitted by the officer who succeeded to the command; "much further than I wished," by Bainbridge's journal. It is not possible entirely to reconcile the pretty full details of further movements given by each;[4] but it may be said, generally, that this battle was not mainly an artillery duel, like those of the "Constitution" and "Guerrière," the "Wasp" and "Frolic," nor yet one in which a principal manœuvre, by its decisive effect upon the use of artillery, played the determining part, as was the case with the "United States" and "Macedonian." Here it was a combination of the two factors, a succession of evolutions resembling the changes of position, the retreats and advances, of a fencing or boxing match, in which the opponents work round the ring; accompanied by a continual play of the guns, answering to the thrusts and blows of individual encounter. In this game of manœuvres the "Constitution" was somewhat handicapped by her wheel being shot away at 2.30. The rudder remained unharmed; but working a ship by relieving tackles, the substitute for the wheel, is for several reasons neither as quick nor as accurate.

Certain salient incidents stand out in both accounts, marking the progress of the engagement. Shortly before three o'clock the head of the "Java's" bowsprit was shot away, and with it went the jib-boom. At this time, the fore and main masts of the British frigate being badly wounded, with all the rigging cut to pieces, Captain Lambert looked upon the day as lost unless he could board. The sailing master having been sent below wounded, the first lieutenant, whose account is here followed, was directed to run the ship alongside the enemy; but the helm was hardly put up when the foremast went overboard, at five minutes past three, a time in which both accounts agree. The British narrative states that the stump of their bowsprit caught in the mizzen rigging of the "Constitution" (3.35). This Bainbridge does not mention; but, if correct, the contact did not last long, for the "Constitution" immediately wore across the "Java's" bow, and the latter's maintopmast followed the foremast. The British frigate was now beaten beyond recovery; nevertheless the flag was kept flying, and it was after this that Captain Lambert fell, mortally wounded. Resistance was continued until 4.05, by the American accounts; by the British, till 4.35. Then, the enemy's mizzenmast having fallen, and nothing left standing but the main lower mast, the "Constitution" shot ahead to repair damages. There was no more firing, but the "Java's" colors remained up till 5.25,—5.50 by the British times,—when they were hauled down as the "Constitution" returned. The American loss was nine killed and twenty-five wounded; that of the British, by their official accounts, twenty-two killed, one hundred and two wounded.

The superiority in broadside weight of fire of the "Constitution" over the "Java" was about the same as over the "Guerrière." The "Java's" crew was stronger in number than that of the "Guerrière," mustering about four hundred, owing to having on board a hundred supernumeraries for the East India station, to which the ship was ultimately destined. On the other hand, the material of the ship's company is credibly stated to have been extremely inferior, a condition frequently complained of by British officers at this late period of the Napoleonic wars. It has also been said, in apparent extenuation of her defeat, that although six weeks out from England, having sailed November 12, and greater part of that time necessarily in the trade winds, with their usual good weather, the men had not been exercised in firing the guns until December 28, the day before meeting the "Constitution," when six broadsides of blank cartridges were discharged. Whatever excuse may exist in the individual instance for such neglect, it is scarcely receivable in bar of judgment when disaster follows. No particular reason is given, except "the many services of a newly fitted ship, lumbered with stores;" for in such latitudes the other allegation, "a succession of gales of wind since the day of departure,"[5] is incredible. On broad general grounds the "Java" needed no apology for being beaten by a ship so much heavier; and the "Constitution's" loss in killed and wounded was over double that suffered from the "Guerrière" four months before, when the American ship had substantially the same crew.[6] Further, Bainbridge reported to his Government that "the damage received in the action, but more especially the decayed state of the "Constitution," made it necessary to return to the United States for repairs." Although Lieutenant Chads, who succeeded Lambert, was mistaken in supposing the American ship bound to the East Indies, he was evidently justified in claiming that the stout resistance of the "Java" had broken up the enemy's cruise, thus contributing to the protection of the British commerce.

The "Java" was considered by Bainbridge too much injured to be worth taking to the United States. She was therefore set on fire December 31, and the "Constitution" went back to Bahia, where the prisoners were landed under parole. Thence she sailed for home January 6, 1813, reaching Boston February 27. Before his departure the Commodore directed Lawrence to blockade Bahia as long as seemed advisable, but to beware of a British seventy-four, said to be on the coast. When it became expedient, he was to quit the position and move northward; first off Pernambuco, and thence to the coast of Cayenne, Surinam, and Demerara, a favorite cruising ground for American commerce-destroyers. The "Hornet" was to be in Boston in the first fortnight of April.

In pursuance of these discretionary orders Lawrence remained off Bahia for eighteen days, till January 24, when the expected seventy-four, the "Montagu," appeared, forcing him into the harbor; but the same night he came out, gave her the slip, and proceeded on his cruise. On February 24, off the Demarara River, he encountered the British brig of war "Peacock," a vessel of the same class as the "Frolic," which was captured a few months before by the "Wasp," sister ship to the "Hornet." There was no substantial difference in size between these two approaching antagonists; but, unfortunately for the equality of the contest, the "Peacock" carried 24-pounder carronades, instead of the 32's which were her proper armament. Her battery power was therefore but two thirds that of the "Hornet." The vessels crossed on opposite tacks, exchanging broadsides within half pistol-shot, the "Hornet" to windward(1). The "Peacock" then wore; observing which, Lawrence kept off at once for her and ran on board her starboard quarter (2). In this position the engagement was hot for about fifteen minutes, when the "Peacock" surrendered, hoisting a flag union down, in signal of distress. She had already six feet of water in the hold. Being on soundings, in less than six fathoms, both anchored, and every effort was made to save the British vessel; but she sank, carrying down nine of her own crew and three of the "Hornet's." Her loss in action was her commander and four men killed, and twenty-nine wounded, of whom three died; that of the American vessel, one killed and two wounded. The inequality in armament detracts inevitably from glory in achievement; but the credit of readiness and efficiency is established for Lawrence and his crew by prompt action and decisive results. So, also, defeat is not inglorious under such odds; but it remains to the discredit of the British commander that his ship did no more execution, when well within the most effective range of her guns. In commenting upon this engagement, after noticing the dandy neatness of the "Peacock," James says, "Neglect to exercise the ship's company at the guns prevailed then over two thirds of the British navy; to which the Admiralty, by their sparing allowance of powder and shot for practice, were in some degree instrumental."

With the survivors of the "Peacock," and prisoners from other prizes, Captain Lawrence found himself now with two hundred and seventy-seven souls on board and only thirty-four hundred gallons of water. There was at hand no friendly port where to deposit his captives, and [9]provisions were running short. He therefore steered for the United States, and arrived at Holmes' Hole on March 19.[7]

The capture of the "Peacock" was the last of five naval duels, three between frigates and two between sloops, all favorable in issue to the United States, which took place in what may justly be considered the first of the three periods into which the War of 1812 obviously divides. Great Britain, long reluctant to accept the fact of war as irreversible, did not begin to put forth her strength, or to exercise the measures of repression open to her, until the winter of 1812-13 was drawing to a close. On October 13, convinced that the mere news of the revocation of the Orders in Council would not induce any change in the American determination, the hitherto deferred authority for general reprisals was given; but accompanying them was an express provision that they were not to be understood as recalling the declaration which Warren had been commissioned to make, in order to effect a suspension of hostilities.[8] On November 27, however, hopes from this source having apparently disappeared, directions were sent the admiral to institute a rigorous commercial blockade of Delaware and Chesapeake bays,[9] the usual public notification of the fact to neutral Powers, for the information of their shipping affected by it, being issued December 26, three days before the action between the "Constitution" and "Java." On February 21, three days before the "Hornet" sank the "Peacock," Warren wrote that in compliance with the orders of November 27 this blockade had been put in force. The ship "Emily," from Baltimore for Lisbon, under a British license, with a cargo of flour, was turned back when attempting to go to sea from the Chesapeake, about February 5; Warren indorsing on her papers that the bay had been placed under rigorous blockade the day before.[10] Captain Stewart, the senior United States officer at Norfolk, notified his Government of these facts on February 10.[11] Soon after, by an Order in Council dated March 30, the measure was extended to New York, Charleston, Port Royal, Savannah, and the Mississippi River.[12] Later in the year Warren, by a sweeping proclamation, dated November 16,[13] widened its scope to cover Long Island Sound, inside of Montauk and Black Point; the latter being on the Connecticut shore, eight miles west of New London. From thence it applied not only to the ports named, but to all inlets whatsoever, southward, as far as the Florida boundary. Narragansett Bay and the rest of New England remained still exempt.

These restrictions, together with the increase of Warren's force and the operations of 1813 in the Chesapeake, may be considered as initiating the second stage of the war, when Great Britain no longer cherished hopes of any other solution than by the sword, but still was restrained in the exercise of her power by the conflict with Napoleon. With the downfall of the latter, in April, 1814, began the third and final act, when she was more at liberty to let loose her strength, to terminate a conflict at once weakening and exasperating. It is not without significance that the treaty of peace with the restored Bourbon government of France was signed May 30, 1814,[14] and that on May 31 was issued a proclamation placing under strict and rigorous blockade, not merely specified places, but "all the ports, harbors, bays, creeks, rivers, inlets, outlets, islands, and sea-coasts of the United States," from the border of New Brunswick to that of Florida.[15] In form, this was only the public notification of a measure already instituted by Warren's successor, Cochrane, embracing Newport, Boston, and the East under restrictions heretofore limited to New York—including Long Island Sound—and the coast southward; but it was not merely the assertion of a stringent resolution. It was a clear defiance, in the assurance of conscious power, of a principal contention of the United States, that the measure of blockades against neutrals was not legitimately applicable to whole coasts, but only to specified ports closely watched by a naval force competent to its avowed purpose.

Despite the gathering of the storm, the full force of which was to be expected in the spring, the United States ships of war that reached port in the early and middle winter of 1812-13 remained. There is, perhaps, an unrecognized element of "hindsight" in the surprise felt at this fact by a seaman of to-day, knowing the views and wishes of the prominent officers of the navy at that period. Decatur, with the "United States," reached New York in December, accompanied by the "Macedonian." Neither of these vessels got to sea again during the war. By the time they were ready, both outlets to the port were effectually blocked. Rodgers, with the "President" and "Congress," entered Boston December 31, but did not sail again until April 23. The "Constellation," Captain Stewart, was reported, perhaps erroneously, as nearly ready for sea at Washington, November 26, waiting only for a few additional hands. Later in the winter she went to Annapolis, to examine her powder, leaving there for Hampton Roads February 1, on account of the ice. On the 4th, approaching her destination, she discovered two ships of the line, three frigates, and two smaller British vessels, working up from the Capes for the Roads. In the face of such a force there was nothing to do but to escape to Norfolk, where she remained effectually shut up for the rest of the war. Bainbridge, as already known, brought the "Constitution" back for repairs in February. Even from Boston she was unable to escape till the following December.

That there were satisfactory reasons for this seeming dilatoriness is assured by the character of the officers. Probably the difficulty of keeping up the ship's companies, in competition with the superior attractions of privateering and the very high wages offered by the merchants for their hazardous but remunerative commercial voyages accounted for much. Hull wrote from New York, October 29, 1812, that the merchants fitting out their vessels gave such high wages that it was difficult to get either seamen or workmen.[16] Where no system of forced enrolment—conscription or impressment—is permitted, privateering has always tended to injure the regular naval service. Though unquestionably capable of being put by owners on a business basis, as a commercial undertaking, with the individual seaman the appeal of privateering has always been to the stimulants of chance and gain, which prove so attractive in the lottery. Stewart, an officer of great intelligence and experience in his profession, found a further cause in the heavy ships of the enemy. In the hostilities with France in 1798-1800, he said, "We had nearly four thousand able seamen in the navy. We could frequently man a frigate in a week. One reason was because the enemy we were then contending with had not afloat (with very few exceptions) vessels superior in rate to frigates. The enemy we are fighting now have ships of the line, and our sailors know the great difference between them and frigates, and cannot but feel a degree of reluctance at entering the service from the disparity of force."[17] The reason seems to prove too much; pressed to an extreme, no navy would be able to use light vessels, because the enemy had heavier which might—or might not—be encountered. Certain it is, however, that when the government in the following winter, in order to stop the license trade with the enemy, embargoed all vessels in home ports, much less difficulty was experienced in getting seamen for the navy.

Whatever the reasons, the only frigates at sea during the first four months of 1813 were the "Essex" and the "Chesapeake." The former, after failing to meet Bainbridge, struck off boldly for the Pacific Ocean on Porter's own motion; and on March 15, 1813, anchored at Valparaiso, preparatory to entering on a very successful career of a year's duration in those seas. The "Chesapeake" had sailed from Boston December 17, making for the Cape Verde Islands. In their neighborhood she captured two of a British convoy, which, thinking itself beyond danger, had dispersed for South American destinations. The frigate then proceeded to her cruising ground near the equator, between longitudes 24° and 30° west, where she remained for about a month, taking only one other merchantman. Leaving this position, she was off the coast of Surinam from March 2 to 6, when she returned to the United States; passing sixty miles east of the Caribbean Islands and thence north of Porto Rico and Santo Domingo, as far west as longitude 75°, whence she ran parallel to the American coast, reaching Boston April 9. Having seen nothing between February 5 and March 19, she then began to meet sails, speaking eight between the latter date and her arrival. Most of these were Americans, homeward bound from the Spanish peninsula; the others neutrals.[18] The conclusion is evident, that the British were keeping their trade well shepherded in convoys. If a ship like the "Chesapeake" struck one of them, she would probably have to fight the escorting vessel, as the "Wasp" did the "Frolic," while the merchantmen escaped; but the chances were against her seeing anything. Another evident conclusion, corresponding to the export returns already quoted, is that the enemy had not yet shut down upon the access of American merchant ships to their own coast.

This process was gradual, but steady. It is necessary to keep in mind the distinction between a blockade, in the loose use of the term, which closes a port only to the ships of the hostile nation, and the commercial blockade which forbids neutrals as well. The former may be intermittent, for the mere fact of war authorizes the capture of the belligerent's shipping, wherever found; hence to intercept them at the mouths of their own harbors is merely a more effectual method of carrying out the measure. A blockade against neutrals requires the permanent presence, before the blockaded port, of a force adequate to make the attempt to enter or leave dangerous. For this many more ships are needed. The British ministry, desirous chiefly to compel the United States to peace, and embarrassed by the gigantic continental strife in which it was engaged, sought at the outset to inflict such harassment on the American coast as would cost the least diversion of strength from the European contest. An ordinary blockade might be tightened or relaxed as convenience demanded; and, moreover, there were as yet, in comparison with American vessels, few neutrals to be restrained. Normally, American shipping was adequate to American commerce. The first move, therefore, was to gather upon the coast of the United States all cruisers that could be spared from the Halifax and West India stations, and to dispose along the approaches to the principal ports those that were not needed to repress the privateers in the Bay of Fundy and the waters of Nova Scotia. The action of these privateers, strictly offensive in character, and the course of Commodore Rodgers in sailing with a large squadron, before explained, illustrate exactly how offensive operations promote defensive security. With numbers scanty for their work, and obliged to concentrate instead of scattering, the British, prior to Warren's arrival, had not disposable the cruisers with which greatly to harass even the hostile shipping, still less to institute a commercial blockade. The wish to sk the Spanish peninsula and the West Indies with provisions contributed further to mitigate the pressure.

These restraining considerations gradually disappeared. Re-enforcements arrived. Rodgers' squadron returned and could be watched, its position being known. The license trade filled up Lisbon, Cadiz, and the West Indies. Hopes of a change of mind in the American Government lessened. Napoleon's disaster in Russia reversed the outlook in European politics. Step by step the altered conditions were reflected in the measures of the British ministry and navy. For months, only the maritime centres of the Middle States were molested. The senior naval officer at Charleston, South Carolina, wrote on October 14, four months after war was declared, "Till to-day this coast has been clear of enemy's cruisers; now Charleston is blockaded by three brigs, two very large, and they have captured nine sail within three miles of the bar."[19] The number was increased shortly; and two months later he expressed surprise that the inland navigation behind the sea islands had not been destroyed,[20] in consequence of its defenceless state. In January, 1813, the mouth of the Chesapeake was watched by a ship of the line, two frigates, and a sloop; the commercial blockade not having been yet established. The hostile divisions still remained outside, and American vessels continued to go out and in with comparative facility, both there and at Charleston. A lively trade had sprung up with France by letters-of-marque; that is, by vessels whose primary object is commerce, and which therefore carry cargoes, but have also guns, and a commission from the Government to make prizes. Without such authorization capture is piracy. By February 12 conditions grow worse. The blockaders have entered the Chesapeake, the commercial blockade has been proclaimed, vessels under neutral flags, Spanish and Swedish, are being turned away, and two fine letter-of-marque schooners have been captured inside, one of them after a gallant struggle in which her captain was killed. Nautical misadventures of that kind became frequent. On April 3 three letters-of-marque and a privateer, which had entered the Rappahannock, were attacked at anchor by boats from Warren's fleet. The letters-of-marque, with smaller crews, offered little resistance to boarding; but the privateer, having near a hundred men, made a sharp resistance. The Americans lost six killed and ten wounded; the enemy, two killed and eleven wounded.[21]

In like manner the lower Delaware was occupied by one or more ships of the line. Supported thus by a heavy squadron, hostile operations were pushed to the upper waters of both bays, and in various directions; the extensive water communications of the region offering great facilities for depredation. Dismay and incessant disquietude spread through all quarters of the waterside. Light cruisers make their way above Reedy Island, fifty miles from the Capes of the Delaware; coasting vessels are chased into the Severn River, over a hundred miles above Hampton Roads; and a detachment appears even at the mouth of the Patapsco, twelve miles from Baltimore. The destruction of bay craft, and interruption of water traffic, show their effects in the rise of marketing and fuel to double their usual prices. By May 1, all intercourse by water was stopped, and Philadelphia was also cut off from the lower Delaware. Both Philadelphia and Baltimore were now severed from the sea, and their commerce destroyed, not to revive till after the peace; while alarms, which the near future was to justify, were felt for the land road which connected the two cities. As this crossed the head waters of the Chesapeake, it was open to attack from ships, which was further invited by deposits of goods in transit at Elkton and Frenchtown. Fears for the safety of Norfolk were felt by Captain Stewart, senior naval officer there. "When the means and force of the enemy are considered, and the state of this place for defence, it presents but a gloomy prospect for security."[22] Commodore Murray from Philadelphia reports serious apprehensions, consternation among the citizens, a situation daily more critical, and inadequate provision for resistance.[23] There, as everywhere, the impotence of the General Government has to be supplemented by local subscription and local energy.

At the same time, both northward and southward of these two great estuaries, the approach of spring brought ever increasing enemies, big and little, vexing the coasting trade; upon which, then as now, depended largely the exchange of products between different sections of the country. What it meant at that day to be reduced to communication by land may be realized from a contemporary quotation: "Four wagons loaded with dry goods passed to-day through Georgetown, South Carolina, for Charleston, forty-six days from Philadelphia."[24] Under the heading "New Carrying Trade" a Boston paper announces on April 28 the arrival of "a large number of teams from New Bedford with West India produce, and four Pennsylvania wagons, seventeen days from Philadelphia."[25] "The enemy has commenced his depredations on the coasting trade of the Eastern States on a very extensive scale, by several ships and sloops-of-war, and five or six active privateers. The United States brig "Argus" cruises at the entrance of Long Island Sound for the protection of trade, latterly jeopardized;"[26] a position from which she was soon driven by an overwhelming force. Hull, now commanding at Portsmouth, reports April 9, "several privateers on the Eastern coast, which have been successful in cutting coasters out of several harbors east." May 7: "A small force is indeed needed here; the enemy appear off the harbor nearly every day. A few days since, a little east of this, they burnt twelve coasters and chased several into this port."[27] The town is defenceless. The Governor of Rhode Island laments to the Legislature "the critical and exposed situation of our fellow-citizens in Newport, who are frequently menaced by the ships and vessels about Point Judith"; mentioning beside, "the burning of vessels in Narragansett Bay, and the destruction of our coasting trade, which deprives us of the usual and very necessary supplies of bread stuffs from other States."[28] The ship "Maddox," blockaded for two or three months in the Chesapeake, escaped in May, and reached Newport with five thousand barrels of flour. This is said to have reduced the price by $2.50 in Boston, where it was ranging at $17 to $18; while at Cadiz and Lisbon, thanks to British licenses and heavy sking in anticipation of war, it stood at $12 to $13. The arrival at Machias of a captured British vessel, laden with wheat, was hailed "as a seasonable supply for the starving inhabitants of the eastward."[29]

Ships returning from abroad necessarily had to pass through the cruisers which interrupted the coasting trade. "Many valuable vessels arrive, making at times hairbreadth escapes." The trade of Baltimore and Philadelphia is thrown back upon New York and Boston; but both of these, and the eastern entrance of Long Island Sound, have hostile squadrons before them. The letter-of-marque schooner "Ned" has transmitted an experience doubtless undergone by many. Bound to Baltimore, she arrived off the Chesapeake April 18, and was chased away; tried to get into the Delaware on the 19th, but was headed off; made for Sandy Hook, and was again chased. Finally, she tried the east end of the Sound, and there made her way through four or five ships of war, reaching New York April 24.[30] Of course, under such circumstances trade rapidly dwindled. Only very fast and weatherly vessels could hope to cope with the difficulties. Of these the conspicuous type was the Baltimore schooner, which also had not too many eggs in one basket. In the general deprivation of commerce a lucky voyage was proportionately remunerative; but the high prices of the successful venture were but the complement and reflection of suffering in the community. The harbors, even of New York, became crowded with unemployed shipping.

This condition of things coastwise, supplemented by the activity of American privateers, induced abnormal conditions of navigation in the western Atlantic. The scanty success of Rodgers, Bainbridge, and the "Chesapeake" have been noted; and it may be observed that there was a great similarity in the directions taken by these and others. The Cape Verdes, the equator between 24° and 30° west, the Guiana coast, the eastern West Indies, Bermuda to Halifax, indicate a general line of cruising; with which coincides substantially a project submitted by Stewart, March 2, 1813, for a cruise by the "Constellation." These plans were conceived with intelligent reference to known British trade-routes; but, being met by the enemy with a rigid convoy system, it was often hard to find a sail. The scattered American traders were rapidly diminishing in numbers, retained in port as they arrived; and it is noted that a British division of four vessels, returning to Halifax after a four months' cruise between the Banks of Newfoundland and Bermuda, have captured only one American.[31] An American privateer, arriving at Providence after an absence of nearly four months, "vexing the whole Atlantic," reports not seeing a single enemy's merchant ship. Niles' return of prizes[32] to American cruisers, national as well as privateers, gives three hundred and five as the total for the first six months of the war; of which seventy-nine only seem to have been taken distant from the home shores. For the second six months, to June 30, 1813, the aggregate has fallen to one hundred and fifty-nine, of which, as far as can be probably inferred, ninety-one were captured in remote waters. Comparing with the preceding and subsequent periods, we find here evidently a time of transition, when American enterprise had not yet aroused to the fact that British precaution in the Western Hemisphere had made it necessary to seek prizes farther afield.

In view of the incompleteness of the data it is difficult to state more than broad conclusions. It seems fairly safe, however, to say that after the winter of 1812-13 American commerce dwindled very rapidly, till in 1814 it was practically annihilated; but that, prior to Napoleon's downfall, the necessities of the British Government, and the importunity of the British mercantile community, promoted a certain collusive intercourse by licenses, or by neutrals, real or feigned, between the enemy and the Eastern States of the Union, for the exportation of American produce. This trade, from the reasons which prompted it, was of course exempt from British capture. Subsidiary to it, as a partial relief to the loss of the direct American market, was fostered an indirect smuggling import from Great Britain, by way of Halifax and Montreal, which conduced greatly to the prosperity of both these places during the war, as it had during the preceding periods of commercial restriction. It was to maintain this contraband traffic, as well as to foster disaffection in an important section of the Union, that the first extension of the commercial blockade, issued by Warren from Bermuda, May 26, 1813, stopped short of Newport; while the distinction thus drawn was emphasized, by turning back vessels even with British licenses seeking to sail from the Chesapeake. By this insidious action the commercial prosperity of the country, so far as any existed, was centred about the Eastern States. It was, however, almost purely local. Little relief reached the Middle and South, which besides, as before mentioned, were thus drained of specie, while their products lay idle in their stores.

As regards relative captures made by the two belligerents, exact numbers cannot be affirmed; but from the lists transmitted a fairly correct estimate can be formed as to the comparative injury done in this way. It must be remembered that such losses, however grievous in themselves, and productive of individual suffering, have by no means the decisive effect produced by the stoppage of commerce, even though such cessation involves no more than the retention in harbor of the belligerent's ships, as the Americans were after 1812, or as had been the case during Jefferson's embargo of 1808. As that measure and its congeners failed in their object of bringing the British Government to terms, by deprivation of commerce, the pecuniary harm done the United States by them was much greater than that suffered in the previous years from the arbitrary action of Great Britain. She had seized, it was alleged, as many as nine hundred and seventeen American vessels,[33] many of which were condemned contrary to law, while the remainder suffered loss from detention and attendant expenses; but despite all this the commercial prosperity was such that the commercial classes were averse to resenting the insults and injury. It was the agricultural sections of the country, not the commercial, which forced on the war.

Niles' Register has transmitted a careful contemporary compilation of American captures, in closing which the editor affirmed that in the course of the war he had examined not less than ten, perhaps twelve, thousand columns of ship news, rejecting all prizes not accounted for by arrival or destruction. It is unlikely that data complete as he used are now attainable, even if an increase of accuracy in this point were worth the trouble of the search. Up to May 1, 1813, he records four hundred and eleven captures, in which are included the British ships of war as well as merchantmen; not a very material addition. The British Naval Chronicle gives the prize lists of the various British admirals. From these may be inferred in the same period at least three hundred seizures of American merchant vessels. Among these are a good many Chesapeake Bay craft, very small. This excludes privateers, but not letters-of-marque, which are properly cargo ships. Both figures are almost certainly underestimates; but not improbably the proportion of four to three is nearly correct. Granting, however, that the Americans had seized four British ships for every three lost by themselves, what does the fact establish as regards the effect upon the commerce of the two peoples? Take the simple report of a British periodical in the same month of May, 1813: "We are happy to announce the arrival of a valuable fleet from the West Indies, consisting of two hundred and twenty-six sail, under convoy of the "Cumberland," seventy-four, and three other ships of war."[34] This one fleet among many, safely entering port, numbers more than half of their total losses in the twelvemonth. Contrast this relative security with the experience of the "Ned," cited a few pages back, hunted from headland to headland on her home coast, and slipping in—a single ship by dexterous management—past foes from whom no countryman can pretend to shield her.

Even more mortifying to Americans, because under their very eyes, in sharp contrast to their sufferings, was the prosperity of Halifax and Canada. Vexed though British commerce was by the daring activity of American cruisers, the main streams continued to flow; diminished in volume, but not interrupted. The closure of American harbors threw upon the two ports named the business of supplying American products to the British forces, the British West Indies, and in measure to Great Britain itself. The same reason fixed in them the deposit of British goods, to be illicitly conveyed into the United States by the smuggling that went on actively along the northern seacoast and land frontier; a revival of the practices under the embargo of 1808. This underground traffic was of course inadequate to compensate for that lost by the war and the blockade; but it was quite sufficient to add immensely to the prosperity of these places, the communications of which with the sea were held open and free by the British navy, and in which centred what was left from one of the most important branches of British trade in the days of peace. Halifax, from its position on the sea, was the chief gainer. The effects of the war on it were very marked. Trade was active. Prices rose. Provisions were in great demand, to the profit of agriculture and fisheries. Rents doubled and trebled. The frequent arrival of prizes, and of ships of war going and coming, added to the transactions, and made money plentiful.[35]

Recalling the generalization already made, that the seacoast of the United States was strictly a defensive frontier, it will be recognized that the successive institution of the commercial blockades, first of the Chesapeake and Delaware in March, and afterward of the whole coast south of Newport, in May, were the offensive operations with which the British initiated the campaign of 1813. These blockades were supported, and their effects sustained and intensified, by an accumulation of naval force entirely beyond the competition of the American navy. In view of such overwhelming disparity, it was no longer possible, as in 1812, by assembling a squadron, to impose some measure of concentration upon the enemy, and thus to facilitate egress and ingress. The movements of the British had passed wholly beyond control. Their admiral was free to dispose his fleet as he would, having care only not to hazard a detachment weaker than that in the port watched. This was a condition perfectly easy of fulfilment with the numbers under his command. As a matter of fact, his vessels were distributed over the entire seacoast; and at every point, with the possible exception of Boston, the division stationed was so strong that escape was possible only by evasion, under cover of severe weather conditions.

Under such circumstances, the larger the ship the more difficult for her to get out. As early as the middle of April, Captain Jones, formerly of the "Wasp," and now commanding the "Macedonian" in New York, reports that "both outlets are at present strongly blocked, but I believe at dark of the moon we shall be able to pass without much risk."[36] May 22, when a moon had come and gone, Decatur, still on board the "United States," in company with which the "Macedonian" was to sail, thinks it will be better to try the Sound route. "The last gale, which promised the fairest opportunity for us to get out, ended in light southerly winds, which continued till the blockading ships had regained their stations."[37] A few days later, the attempt by the Sound resulted in the two being driven into New London, where they remained to the close of the war. The only offensive operation by sea open to the United States, the destruction of the enemy's commerce, fell therefore to the smaller cruisers and privateers, the size and numbers of which combined to make it impossible to restrain them all.

For defensive measures the seaboard depended upon such fortifications as existed, everywhere inadequate, but which either the laxness or the policy of the British commander did not attempt to overcome in the case of the seaports, narrowly so called. The wide-mouthed estuaries of the Chesapeake and Delaware, entrance to which could not thus be barred, bore, therefore, the full brunt of hostile occupation and widespread harassment. In this there may have been deliberate intention, as well as easy adoption of the readiest means of annoyance. The war, though fairly supported in the middle section of the Union, was essentially a Southern and Western measure. Its most strenuous fomenters came from those parts, and the administration was Virginian. The President himself had been identified with the entire course of Jefferson's commercial retaliation, and general policy toward Great Britain during twelve years past. It is impossible for land forces alone to defend against naval aggression a region like the Chesapeake, with its several great, and numerous small, streams penetrating the country in every direction; and matters are not helped when the defendants are loosely organized militia. The water in such a case offers a great central district, with interior lines, in the hands of a power to which belongs the initiative, with an overpowering mobile force, able at any moment to appear where it will in superior strength.

No wonder then that the local journals of the day speak of continual watchfulness, which from the present organization of the militia is exceedingly toilsome, and of no little derangement to the private affairs of the people.[38] The enemy spreads in every direction; and, although the alarm caused much exceeds the injury done, disquietude is extreme and universal. "Applications from various quarters are constantly pouring in upon us," wrote a Governor of Maryland to the President; "and as far as our very limited means will enable us we are endeavoring to afford protection. But we have not arms and ammunition to supply the demands of every section of the State; the unavoidable expense of calling out the militia for its protection would greatly exceed the ability of the State government. The capital of the State [which was three miles from the bay, on a navigable river] has not sufficient force for its protection. By the Constitution of the United States, the common defence is committed to the National Government, which is to protect each State against invasion, and to defray all necessary expenses of a national war; and to us it is a most painful reflection that after every effort we have made, or can make, for the security of our fellow-citizens and of their property, they have little to rely on but the possible forbearance of the enemy."[39] The process of reaping what has been sowed is at times extremely unpleasant.

FOOTNOTES:

[1] Captains' Letters. Navy Department.

[2] Ibid., Bainbridge, Oct. 13, 1812.

[3] Niles' Register, vol. iv. p. 25.

[4] Bainbridge's report is in the Captains' Letters. Navy Department, Jan. 3, 1813. It will be found also in Niles' Register, vol. iii. p. 410. Both give extracts from Bainbridge's journal, which is very full on the subject of manœuvres and times. The British account will be found in the Naval Chronicle, vol. xxix. pp. 403-408, from which the plan of the battle is

copied.

[5] James' Naval History, edition 1824, vol. v. p. 313.

[6] Bainbridge in a private letter speaks of the men looking forward to prize money for the "Guerrière" on their return. Niles' Register, vol. iii. p. 411.

[7] Lawrence's Report of these transactions is in Captains' Letters, March 19, 1813. It will be found also in Niles' Register, vol. iv. p. 84.

[8] Naval Chronicle, vol. xxviii. p. 305.

[9] Admiralty to Warren, British Records Office.

[10] Niles' Register, vol. iii. p. 383.

[11] Captains' Letters.

[12] Niles' Register, vol. iv. p. 159. The Admiralty's letter to Warren to institute this blockade is dated March 25. British Records Office.

[13] Niles' Register, vol. v. p. 264.

[14] Naval Chronicle, vol. xxxi. p. 464.

[15] Naval Chronicle, vol. xxxi. p. 475.

[16] Captains' Letters.

[17] American State Papers, Naval Affairs, vol. i. p. 280.

[18] Captain Evans' Report, April 10, 1813. Captains' Letters.

[19] Captains' Letters.

[20] Ibid, Dec. 17, 1812.

[21] Niles' Register, vol. iv. p. 119. Naval Chronicle, vol. xxix. p. 501.

[22] March 17, 1813. Captains' Letters.

[23] March 17, 18, and 21. Ibid.

[24] Niles' Register, vol. iv. p. 222.

[25] Columbian Centinel.

[26] Niles' Register, vol. iv. p. 117.

[27] Captains' Letters.

[28] Message of the Governor of Rhode Island, May 5, 1813.

[29] Niles' Register, vol. iv. pp. 200, 209. There were reported in Cadiz at this time 160,000 barrels of flour, unsold. The Columbian Centinel (Feb. 17) speaks of the Lisbon market as deplorable.

[30] Niles' Register, vol. iv. p. 150.

[31] Niles' Register, vol. iv. p. 101.

[32] Ibid., p. 117.

[33] American State Papers, Foreign Relations, vol. iii. p. 584. France in the same period had seized five hundred and fifty-eight.

[34] Naval Chronicle, vol. xxix. p. 497. The following extract from an American journal may have interest as indicating the extent of the British convoy movement. "American brig 'Hazard,' arrived at New York from Madeira, June 5, reports: 'April 11, arrived at Funchal the outward bound East India and Brazil fleets, forty sail, under convoy. Sailed April 12. April 21, arrived outward bound Cork fleet, one hundred and eighty sail convoyed by a seventy-four, a frigate, and a sloop.' April 30, sailed from

Jamaica, three hundred merchantmen, under convoy of a seventy-four, two frigates and a sloop." (Columbian Centinel, of Boston, June 9, 1813.)

[35] Murdoch's History of Nova Scotia, vol. iii. p. 351.

[36] Captains' Letters, April 13, 1813.

[37] Ibid., May 22.

[38] Niles' Register, vol. iv. p. 134.

[39] Letter of Governor Winder, April 26, 1813. Niles' Register, vol. iv. p. 204.

CAMPAIGN OF 1813 ON THE LAKE FRONTIER

In April, 1813, on the land frontier of the north and west, no substantial change had taken place in the conditions which gave to the United States the power of the offensive. Such modification as Chauncey's energy had effected was to strengthen superiority, by promising ultimate control of the upper and lower lakes. The British had not been idle; but the greater natural difficulties under which they labored, from less numerous population and less advanced development of the country and its communications, together with a greater severity of climate, had not been compensated by a naval direction similar to that exercised by the American commodore and his efficient second, Perry. Sir John Warren had been ordered to pay attention to the lakes, the naval service of which was placed under his charge. This added to his responsibilities, and to the drain upon his resources of men and materials; but, with an oversight already extending from Halifax to Jamaica and Barbados, he could do little for the lakes, beyond meeting requisitions of the local authorities and furnishing a draft of officers. Among those sent from his fleet was Captain Barclay, who commanded the British squadron in Perry's action.

The Admiralty, meantime, had awaked to the necessity of placing preparations and operations under competent naval guidance, if command of the water was to be secured. For that purpose they selected Captain Sir James Lucas Yeo, a young officer of much distinction, just turned thirty, who was appointed to the general charge of the lake service, under Warren. Leaving England in March, accompanied by a body of officers and seamen, Yeo did not reach Kingston until May 15, 1813, when the campaign was already well under way; having been begun by Dearborn and Chauncey April 24. His impressions on arrival were discouraging. He found the squadron in a weak state, and the enemy superior in fact and in promise. They had just succeeded in burning at York a British vessel intended for thirty guns, and they had, besides, vessels building at Sackett's Harbor. He had set to work, however, getting his force ready for action, and would go out as soon as possible to contest the control of Ontario; for upon that depended the tenure of Upper Canada.[40] Barclay, upon the arrival of his superior, was sent on to Amherstburg, to fulfil upon Erie the same relation to Yeo that Perry did to Chauncey.

It had been clearly recognized by the American authorities that any further movement for the recapture of Detroit and invasion of Canada would depend upon the command of Lake Erie; and that that in turn would depend largely upon mastery of Ontario. In fact, the nearer the sea control over the water communications could be established, the more radical and far-reaching the effect produced. For this reason, Montreal was the true objective of American effort, but the Government's attention from the first had centred upon the northwestern territory; upon the extremity of the enemy's power, instead of upon its heart. Under this prepossession, despite adequate warning, it had persisted in the course of which Hull's disaster was the outcome; and now, though aroused by this stunning humiliation, its understanding embraced nothing beyond the Great Lakes. Clear indication of this narrow outlook is to be found in the conditions on Lake Champlain, the natural highway to Canada. Only the scantiest mention is to be found of naval preparation there, because actually little was being done; and although the American force was momentarily superior, it was so simply because the British, being in Canada wholly on the defensive, and therefore obliged to conform to American initiative, contemplated no use of this lake, the mastery of which, nevertheless, was soon afterward thrown into their hands by a singularly unfortunate occurrence.

Dearborn, who still remained in chief command of the armies on the New York frontier, was therefore directed to concentrate his effort upon Ontario, starting from Sackett's Harbor as a base. Chauncey, whose charge extended no farther than the upper rapids of the St. Lawrence, had of course no other interest. His first plan, transmitted to the Navy Department January 21, 1813,[41] had been to proceed immediately upon the opening of navigation, with the fleet and a land force of a thousand picked troops, against Kingston, the capture of which, if effected, would solve at a single stroke every difficulty in the upper territory. No other harbor was tenable as a naval station; with its fall, and the destruction of shipping and forts, would go the control of the lake, even if the place itself were not permanently held. Deprived thus of the water communications, the enemy could retain no position to the westward, because neither re-enforcements nor supplies could reach them. To quote Chauncey's own words, "I have no doubt we should succeed in taking or destroying their ships and forts, and, of course, preserve our ascendency on this lake."

This remark, though sound, was narrow in scope; for it failed to recognize, what was perfectly knowable, that the British support of the Lake Erie stations and the upper country depended on their power to control, or at worst to contest, Ontario. Of this they themselves were conscious, as the words of Yeo and Brock alike testify. The new American Secretary of War, Armstrong, who was a man of correct strategical judgment and considerable military information, entered heartily into this view; and in a letter dated February 10 communicated to Dearborn the orders of the President for his operations, based upon the Secretary's recommendation.[42] Four thousand men were to be assembled at Sackett's, and three thousand at Buffalo. The former, under convoy of the fleet, was to proceed first against Kingston, then against York (Toronto). After this the two corps should co-operate in an attack to be made upon the British Niagara frontier, which rested upon Fort George on the Ontario shore, and Fort Erie upon Lake Erie. This plan was adopted upon the assumption, which was probably correct, that the enemy's entire military force upon Ontario did not exceed twenty-one hundred regular troops, of whom six hundred were at Kingston and twelve hundred at Niagara. Armstrong, who recognized the paramount importance of Montreal, had received the exaggerated impression that there might be in that neighborhood eight to ten thousand regulars. There were not yet nearly that number in all Canada;[43] but he was perhaps correct in thinking that the provision for the offensive, which he had found upon taking office a few weeks before, was insufficient for an advance in that quarter.

Dearborn very soon discovered objections to proceeding against Kingston, in his own estimates of the enemy's numbers, based upon remarkable reports received from sources "entitled to full credit." On March 3 he was satisfied that from six to eight thousand men had been assembled there from Quebec, Montreal, and Upper Canada; while the presence of Sir George Prevost, the Governor General, and commander-in-chief in Canada, who had seized an opportunity to make a hurried visit to Kingston to assure himself as to the progress of the ships building, convinced the American general that an attack upon Sackett's was contemplated.[44] From that time forward Dearborn realized in his own person the process of making pictures to one's self concerning a military situation, against which Napoleon uttered a warning. Chauncey was more sceptical, although he could not very well avoid attention to the reports brought in. He expresses himself as believing that a considerable number of men had been assembled in Kingston, but that their real object was to proceed against Harrison in the Far West.[45]

There seems to have been no foundation for any of these alarms. Prevost was a soldier of good reputation, but wanting in initiative, audacity, and resolution, as the current war was to prove. His presence at Kingston at this moment was simply one incident in a rapid official visit to the upper military posts, extending as far as Niagara, and accomplished in four weeks; for, leaving Quebec February 17, he was again writing from there on the 17th of March. As far as can be deduced from his correspondence, four companies of regulars had preceded him from Montreal to Kingston, and there may very well have been a gathering of local forces for inspection or otherwise; but no re-enforcements of regulars, other than that just mentioned, reached Kingston from down the river before May. Dearborn never renounced his belief in the meditated attack, though finally satisfied that it was abandoned; and his positive reports as to the enemy's numbers wrung from Armstrong acquiescence in a change of plan, by which York, and not Kingston, should be the first object of the campaign.[46]

Chauncey, who had some sound military ideas, as his first plan showed, was also brought round to this conclusion by a process of reasoning which he developed in a second plan of operations, submitted March 18,[47] but evidently long since matured. It apparently antedates Dearborn's apprehensions, and is not affected by them, though the two worked together to a common mistaken decision. The commodore's letter presents an interesting study, in its demonstration of how an erroneous first conception works out to false conclusions, and in the particular instance to ultimate military disaster. The capture of Kingston, his first plan, and its retention, which Armstrong purposed, would have settled the whole campaign and affected decisively the issue of the war. Chauncey's new project is dominated throughout by the view, which was that of the Government, that the great object of the war was to control the northwestern territory by local operations, instead of striking at the source of British power in its communication with the sea. At this moment, the end of March, the British naval force on Ontario was divided between York and Kingston; in each were vessels afloat and vessels building. An attack upon Kingston, Chauncey said, no doubt would be finally successful—an initial admission which gave away his case; but as the opposing force would be considerable, it would protract the general operations of the campaign—the reduction of the northwest—longer than would be advisable, particularly as large re-enforcements would probably arrive at Quebec in the course of two months. On the other hand, to proceed against York, which probably could be carried immediately, would result in destroying at once a large fraction of the British fleet, greatly weakening the whole body. Thence the combined Americans would turn against Fort George and the Niagara line. If successful here, the abandonment of Fort Erie by the British would release the American vessels which by its guns were confined at Black Rock. They would sail forth and join their consorts at Erie; which done, Chauncey, leaving his Ontario fleet to blockade Yeo at Kingston, would go to the upper lake and carry against the British the squadron thus concentrated there, would co-operate with the army under General

Harrison, recover Detroit, and capture Malden. Lake Erie and its surroundings would thus become an American holding. After this, it would be but a step to reconquer Michilimackinac, thereby acquiring an influence over the Indians which, in conjunction with military and naval preponderance, would compel the enemy to forsake the upper country altogether, and concentrate his forces about Kingston and Montreal.

It is interesting to see an elaborate piece of serious reasoning gradually culminate in a reductio ad absurdum; and Chauncey's reasoning ends in a military absurdity. The importance of Kingston is conceded by him, and the probability of capturing it at the first is admitted. Thereupon follows a long project of operation, which ends in compelling the enemy to concentrate all his strength at the very points—Kingston and Montreal—which it is most important for the Americans to gain; away from which, therefore, they should seek to keep the enemy, and not to drive him in upon them. This comes from the bias of the Government, and of the particular officer, regarding the Northwestern territory as the means whereby success was to be accomplished instead of merely the end to be attained. To make the Western territory and control of the Indians the objects of the campaign was a political and military motive perfectly allowable, and probably, in view of recent history, extremely necessary; but to make these things the objective of operations was to invert the order of proceedings, as one who, desiring to fell a tree, should procure a ladder and begin cutting off the outermost branches, instead of striking at the trunk by the ground.

Eighteen months later Chauncey wrote some very wise words in this spirit. "It has always been my opinion that the best means to conquer Canada was to cut off supplies from Lower to Upper by taking and maintaining some position on the St. Lawrence. That would be killing the tree by girdling; the branches, dependent on ordinary supplies, die of necessity. But it is now attempted to kill the tree by lopping off branches" [he is speaking of the Niagara campaign of 1814]; "the body becomes invigorated by reducing the demands on its resources."[48] By this time Chauncey had been chastened by experience. He had seen his anticipated glory reaped on Lake Erie by his junior. He had seen the control of Ontario contested, and finally wrung from him, by vessels built at Kingston, the place which he had failed to take when he thought it possible. He had been blockaded during critical months by a superior squadron; and at the moment of writing, November 5, 1814, Sir James Yeo was moving, irresistible, back and forth over the waters of Ontario, with his flag flying in a ship of 102 guns, built at Kingston. In short, the Canadian tree was rooted in the ocean, where it was nourished by the sea power of Great Britain. To destroy it, failing the ocean navy which the United States had not, the trunk must be severed; the nearer the root the better.

Demonstration of these truths was not long in coming, and will be supplied by the narrative of events. When Chauncey penned the plan of operations just analyzed, there were in York two vessels, the "Prince Regent" of twenty guns, the "Duke of Gloucester," sixteen, and two—by his information—on the sks. On April 14 the ice in Sackett's Harbor broke up, though large floes still remained in the lake. On the 19th these also had disappeared. Eighteen hundred troops were embarked by the squadron, and on the 24th the expedition started, but was driven back by heavy weather. The next day it got away finally, and on the early morning of the 27th appeared off York. The troops were landed westward of the town, and proceeded to attack, supported by the shipping. The enemy, inferior in number, retired; the small regular force making its escape, with the exception of fifty who surrendered with the militia present. The American loss, army and navy, was a little over three hundred; among whom was General Pike, an excellent soldier, who commanded the landing and was mortally wounded by the explosion of a magazine. The "Duke of Gloucester" schooner was taken, but the "Prince Regent" had gone to Kingston three days before; the weather which drove Chauncey back had enabled her to join her fleet as soon as released by the ice. By her escape the blow lost most of its effect; for York itself was indefensible, and was taken again without difficulty in the following July. A 30-gun vessel approaching completion was found on the sks and burned, and a large quantity of military and naval stores were either destroyed or brought away by the victorious squadron. These losses were among the news that greeted Yeo's arrival; but, though severe, they were not irreparable, as Chauncey for the moment imagined. He wrote: "I believe that the enemy has received a blow that he cannot recover, and if we succeed in our next enterprise, which I see no reason to doubt, we may consider the upper province as conquered."[49] The mistake here was soon to be evident.

No time was wasted at York. The work of destruction, and of loading what was to be carried away, was completed in three days, and on May 1 the troops were re-embarked, to sail for Fort George on the morrow. The wind, which for some days had been fair and moderate from the eastward, then came on to blow a gale which would make landing impossible off Niagara, and even navigation dangerous for the small vessels. This lasted through the 7th, Chauncey writing on that day that they were still riding with two anchors ahead and lower yards down. So crowded were the ships that only half the soldiers could be below at one time; hence they were exposed to the rain, and also to the fresh-water waves, which made a clean breach over the schooners. Under such circumstances both troops and seamen sickened fast. On the 8th, the weather moderating, the squadron stood over to Fort Niagara, landed the troops for refreshment, and then returned to Sackett's; it being thought that the opportunity for surprise had been lost, and that no harm could come of a short further delay, during which also re-enforcements might be expected.

Soon after his return Chauncey sent a flag of truce to Kingston. This made observations as to the condition of the enemy which began to dispel his fair illusions.[50] His purpose to go in person to Niagara was postponed; and despatching thither the squadron with troops, he remained at Sackett's to protect the yard and the ships building, in co-operation with the garrison. His solicitude was not misplaced. Niagara being a hundred and fifty miles from Sackett's, the fleet and army had been committed to a relatively distant operation, depending upon a main line of communication,—the lake,—on the flank and rear of which, and close to their own inadequately protected base, was a hostile arsenal, Kingston, harboring a naval force quite able to compete with their own. The danger of such a situation is obvious to any military man, and even to a layman needs only to be indicated. Nevertheless the enterprise was launched, and there was nothing for it now but to proceed on the lines laid down.

Chauncey accordingly sailed May 22, re-enforcements of troops for the defence of Sackett's having meantime arrived. He did not reach Niagara until the 25th. The next day was spent in reconnoissances, and other preparations for a landing on the lake shore, a short mile west of Fort George. On the 27th, at 9 A.M., the attack began, covered by the squadron. General Vincent, in command of the British Niagara frontier, moved out to meet his enemy with the entire force near Fort George, leaving only a small garrison of one hundred and thirty men to hold the post itself. There was sharp fighting at the coast-line; but Vincent's numbers were much inferior, and he was compelled steadily to give ground, until finally, seeing that the only alternatives were the destruction of his force or the abandonment of the position, he sent word to the garrison to spike the guns, destroy the ammunition, and to join his column as it withdrew. He retreated along the Niagara River toward Queenston, and thence west to Beaver Dam, about sixteen miles from Fort George. At the same time word was sent to the officers commanding at Fort Erie, and the intermediate post of Chippewa, to retire upon the same place, which had already been prepared in anticipation of such an emergency. The three divisions were thus in simultaneous movement, converging upon a common point of concentration, where they all assembled during the night; the whole, as reported by Vincent to his superior, now not exceeding sixteen hundred.[51] The casualties during the day's fighting had been heavy, over four hundred killed and wounded; but in the retreat no prisoners were lost except the garrison of the fort, which was intercepted. Dearborn, as before at York, had not landed with his troops; prevented, doubtless, by the infirmities of age increasing upon him. Two days later he wrote to the Department, "I had presumed that the enemy would confide in the strength of his position and venture an action, by which an opportunity would be afforded to cut off his retreat."[52] This guileless expectation, that the net may be spread not in vain before the eyes of any bird, provoked beyond control such measure of equanimity as Armstrong possessed. Probably suspecting already that his correct design upon Kingston had been thwarted by false information, he retorted: "I cannot disguise from you the surprise occasioned by the two escapes of a beaten enemy; first on May 27, and again on June 1. Battles are not gained, when an inferior and broken enemy is not destroyed. Nothing is done, while anything that might have been done is omitted."[53] Vincent was unkind enough to disappoint his opponent. The morning after the engagement he retired toward a position at the head of the lake, known then as Burlington Heights, where the town of Hamilton now stands. Upon his tenure here the course of operations turned twice in the course of the next six months.

While Vincent was in retreat upon Burlington, Captain Barclay arrived at his headquarters, on the way to take charge of the Lake Erie squadron;[54] having had to coast the north shore of Ontario, on account of the American control of the water. The inopportuneness of the moment was prophetic of the numberless disappointments with which the naval officer would have to contend during the brief three months preceding his defeat by Perry. "The ordnance, ammunition, and other stores for the service on Lake Erie," wrote Prevost on July 20, with reference to Barclay's deficiencies, "had been deposited at York for the purpose of being transported to Amherstburg, but unfortunately were either destroyed or fell into the enemy's hands when York was taken by them; and the subsequent interruption to the communication, by their occupation of Fort George, has rendered it extremely difficult to afford the supplies Captain Barclay requires, which, however, are in readiness to forward whenever circumstances will permit it to be done with safety."[55] The road from Queenston to Fort Erie, around Niagara Falls, was the most used and the best line of transportation, because the shortest. To be thrown off it to that from Burlington to Long Point was a serious mishap for a force requiring much of heavy and bulky supplies. To add to these more vital embarrassments, the principal ship, the "Queen Charlotte," which had been lying at Fort Erie, had been ordered by Vincent to leave there when the place was evacuated, and to go to Amherstburg, thus giving Barclay the prospect of a land journey of two hundred miles through the wilderness to his destination. Fortunately for him, a vessel turned up at Long Point, enabling him to reach Amherstburg about June 7.

The second step in Chauncey's programme had now been successfully taken, and the vessels at Black Rock were free to move. With an energy and foresight which in administration seldom forsook him, he had prepared beforehand to seize even a fleeting opportunity to get them out. Immediately upon the fall of York, "to put nothing to hazard, I directed Mr.

Eckford to take thirty carpenters to Black Rock, where he has gone to put the vessels lying there in a perfect state of repair, ready to leave the river for Presqu' Isle the moment we are in possession of the opposite shore." Perry also was on hand, being actively engaged in the landing at Fort George; and the same evening, May 27, he left for Black Rock to hasten the departure. The process involved great physical labor, the several vessels having to be dragged by oxen against the current of the Niagara, here setting heavily toward the falls. It was not until June 12 that they were all above the rapids, and even this could not have been accomplished but for soldiers furnished by Dearborn.[56] The circumstance shows how hopeless the undertaking would have been if the enemy had remained in Fort Erie. Nor was this the only peril in their path. Barclay, with commendable promptitude, had taken the lake in superior force very shortly after his arrival at Amherstburg, and about June 15 appeared off Erie [Presqu' Isle]. Having reconnoitred the place, he cruised between it and Black Rock, to intercept the expected division; but the small vessels, coasting the beach, passed their adversary unseen in a fog,[57] and on June 18 reached the port. As Chauncey had reported on May 29 that the two brigs building there were launched, affairs on that lake began to wear a promising aspect. The Lakes station as a whole, however, was still very short of men; and the commodore added that if none arrived before his approaching return to Sackett's, he would have to lay up the Ontario fleet to man that upon Erie.

To do this would have been to abandon to the enemy the very important link in the communications, upon which chiefly depended the re-enforcement and supplies for both armies on the Niagara peninsula. The inherent viciousness of the plan upon which the American operations were proceeding was now quickly evident. At the very moment of the attack upon Fort George, a threatening but irresolute movement against Sackett's was undertaken by Prevost, with the co-operation of Yeo, by whom the attempt is described as a diversion, in consequence of the enemy's attack upon Fort George. Had the place fallen, Chauncey would have lost the ship then building, on which he was counting to control the water; he would have had nowhere to rest his foot except his own quarter-deck, and no means to repair his fleet or build the new vessels continually needed to maintain superiority. The case of Yeo dispossessed of Kingston would have been similar, but worse; for land transport in the United States was much better than in Canada. The issue of the war, as regarded the lakes and the Northwestern territory, lay in those two places. Upon them depended offensive and defensive action.

At the time of the attack upon Sackett's only two vessels of the squadron were there, the senior officer of which, Lieutenant Chauncey, was in momentary command of the navy yard as well. The garrison consisted of four hundred regular troops, the coming of whom a week before had enabled Chauncey to leave for Niagara. Dearborn had already written to Major-General Jacob Brown, of the New York militia, asking him to take command of the station; for which his local knowledge particularly fitted him, as he was a resident of some years' standing. He had moreover manifested marked military capacity on the St. Lawrence line, which was under his charge. Brown, whose instincts were soldierly, was reluctant to supersede Colonel Backus, the officer of regulars in command; but a letter from the latter received on the 27th, asking him to take charge, determined his compliance. When he arrived five hundred militia had assembled.

The British expedition left Kingston with a fine fair wind on the early morning of May 27—the same day that the Americans were landing at Fort George. The whole fleet accompanied the movement, having embarked troops numbering over seven hundred; chiefly regulars. At noon they were off Sackett's Harbor. Prevost and Yeo stood in to reconnoitre; but in the course of an hour the troops, who were already in the boats, ready to pull to the beach, were ordered to re-embark, and the squadron stood out into the lake. The only result so far was the capture of twelve out of nineteen American barges, on their way from Oswego to the Harbor. The other seven gained the port.

During the next thirty-six hours militia kept coming in, and Brown took command. Sackett's Harbor is an indentation on the south side of a broad bay, called Black River Bay, into which the Black River empties. The harbor opens eastward; that is, its back is toward the lake, from which it is distant a little over a mile; and its north side is formed by a long narrow point, called Navy Point, on which was the naval establishment. Where Black River Bay meets the lake, its south shore is prolonged to the west by a projection called Horse Island, connected with the land by a fordable neck. Brown expected the landing to be made upon this, and he decided to meet the attack at the water's edge of the mainland, as the enemy crossed the neck. There he disposed his five hundred militia, placing the regulars under Backus in a second line; a steadying point in case the first line of untrained men failed to stand firm. It was arranged that, if the enemy could not be resisted, Lieutenant Chauncey was to set fire to the naval stores and shipping, and cross with his crews to the south side of the harbor, east of a work called Fort Volunteer, where Brown proposed to make his final stand. From there, although an enemy at the yard could be molested, he could not certainly be prevented from carrying off stores or ships; hence the necessity for destruction.

The British landed upon Horse Island soon after daylight of May 29, and from there advanced. The militia met them with a volley, but then broke and fled, as had been foreseen by Brown, himself yet a militia officer. Their colonel behaved gallantly, and was killed in trying to rally his men; while Brown in person, collecting a hundred of the fugitives, worked round with them to the left flank of the approaching British. These, moving through the woods, now encountered Backus and his regulars, who made upon them an impression of overwhelming numbers, to which the British official report bears a vivid testimony. The failure to carry the place is laid by this paper upon the light and adverse winds, which prevented the co-operation of the squadron's heavy guns, to reduce the batteries and blockhouse. Without this assistance, it was impracticable to carry by assault the works in which the Americans had taken refuge. The gunboats alone could get within range, and their small carronades were totally inadequate to make any impression on the forts and blockhouses. "The troops were reluctantly ordered to leave a beaten enemy." Brown makes no mention of this retreat into the works, though it appears clear that the Americans fell gradually back to their support; but he justifies Prevost's withdrawal, bitterly criticised by writers of his own nation, in the words, "Had not General Prevost retreated most rapidly under the guns of his vessels, he would never have returned to Kingston."[58]

In the midst of the action word was brought to Lieutenant Chauncey that the battle was lost, and that the yard must be fired. Brown, in his official report, expressly acquitted him of blame, with words of personal commendation. The two schooners in commission had retreated up Black River; but the prize "Duke of Gloucester," and the ship approaching completion, were fired. Fortunately, the flames were extinguished before serious damage was done; but when Commodore Chauncey returned on June 1, he found that among a large quantity of materials consumed were the stores and sails of the new ship. The loss of these he thought would delay the movements of the squadron three weeks; for without her Yeo's force was now superior.[59]

The defence of Sackett's Harbor obtained immediately for Brown, who was just thirty-eight, the commission of brigadier general in the army; for the new Secretary, Armstrong, was looking round anxiously for men to put in command, and was quick to seize upon one when he found him. To Chauncey, on the other hand, the affair in its consequences and demonstration of actualities was a rude awakening, to which his correspondence during the succeeding six weeks bears witness by an evident waning of confidence, not before to be noted. On June 4 he tells the Secretary of the Navy that he has on Ontario, exclusive of the new ship not yet ready, fourteen vessels of every description, mounting sixty-two guns; whereas Yeo has seven, which, with six gunboats, carry one hundred and six. "If he leave Kingston, I shall meet him. The result may be doubtful, but worth the trial." This resolution is not maintained. June 11 he hears, with truth, that Yeo was seen at the head of the lake on the 7th, and that the Americans at Fort George had taken his squadron to be Chauncey's. By the same channel he learns of a disastrous engagement of the army there, which was likewise true. His impulse is to go out to meet the British squadron; but he reflects that the enemy may then again find an opportunity to descend upon Sackett's, and perhaps succeed in burning the new ship. Her size and armament will, he thinks, give him the decisive superiority. He therefore resolves to put nothing to hazard till she is finished.[60]

The impression produced by the late attack is obvious, and this decision was probably correct; but Yeo too is building, and meantime he has possession of the lake. On June 3 he left Kingston with a squadron, two ships and four schooners, carrying some three hundred troops for Vincent. On the evening of the 7th, about six o'clock, he was sighted by the American army, which was then at Forty Mile Creek on the Ontario shore; a position to which it had retired after a severe reverse inflicted by the enemy thirty-six hours before. Vincent's retreat had been followed as far as Stony Creek, ten miles west of Forty Mile Creek, and somewhat less distant from Burlington Heights, where the British lay. The situation of the latter was extremely perilous; for, though strongly placed, they were greatly outnumbered. In case of being driven from their lines, they must retreat on York by a long and difficult road; and upon the same poor communications they were dependent for supplies, unless their squadron kept control of the lake. Recognizing that desperate conditions call for desperate remedies, Vincent resolved to risk an attack with seven hundred men under Colonel Harvey, in whose suggestion the movement originated. These fell upon the American advance corps at two o'clock in the morning of June 6. An hour of fighting ensued, with severe loss on both sides; then Harvey, considering sufficient effect produced, drew off his men before daylight revealed the smallness of their numbers.

There was in this affair nothing intrinsically decisive, scarcely more than a business of outposts; but by a singular coincidence both American generals present were captured in the confusion. The officer who succeeded to the command, a colonel of cavalry, modestly distrustful of his own powers, could think of nothing more proper than to return to Forty Mile Creek, sending word to Fort George. Dearborn, still too weak to go to the front, despatched thither General Morgan Lewis. On his way Lewis was overtaken by two brief messages from the commander-in-chief announcing the appearance of Yeo's fleet, and indicating apprehension that by means of it Vincent might come upon Fort George before the main army could fall back there. It was most improbable that the British general, with the command of the lake in doubt would thus place himself again in the position from which he had with difficulty escaped ten days before; but Dearborn's fears for the safety of the forts prevailed, and he ordered a retreat. The movement began by noon of June 8, and in a few days the army was back at Niagara River, having lost or abandoned a quantity of stores. The British followed to within ten miles of the fort, where they took up a position. They also reoccupied Beaver Dam; and a force of six hundred Americans sent to dislodge them, under Colonel Boerstler, was compelled to surrender on June 24.[61] Dearborn, who had already reported to the Department that he personally was "so reduced in strength as to be incapable of any command," attributed his embarrassments "to the temporary loss of command of the lake. The enemy has availed himself of the advantage and forwarded re-enforcements and supplies." The effect of controlling the water cannot be contested; but the conditions at Stony Creek were such that it should have been possible to drive Vincent away from any hold on the south shore of Ontario. Creditable as had been the enterprise of Colonel Harvey, it had accomplished no change in material conditions. Dearborn was soon afterward relieved. His officers, including Scott, joined in a letter of regret and esteem, prompted doubtless by sympathy for the sufferings and miscarriage of an aged officer who had served gallantly in his youth during the War of Independence.

To Colonel Harvey's attack, on the morning of June 6, a British military critic has with justice assigned the turning of the tide in the affairs of Upper Canada.[62] It is perfectly true that that well-judged movement, admirable in conception and execution, checked the progress of the American arms at a moment most favorable to them, and put an end to conditions of advantage which never there recurred. That this effect was produced, however, is attributable to the inefficiency of the American officers in command. If Harvey had divined this, from the previous operations, and made it a part of his calculations, it is so much more to his credit; the competency of the opponent is a chief factor to be considered in a military enterprise. It detracts nothing from Harvey's merit to say that there was no occasion for the American retreat, nor for the subsequent paralysis of effort, which ended in expulsion from the Niagara peninsula at the end of the year. "For some two months after this," wrote a very competent eye-witness, afterward General Scott, "the army of Niagara, never less than four thousand strong, stood fixed in a state of ignominy, under Boyd, within five miles of an unintrenched enemy, with never more than three thousand five hundred men."[63] Scott seems not to have known that this inactivity was enjoined by the War Department till Chauncey could resume control of the lake.[64] From this time, in fact, the Niagara army and its plans disappear from the active operations.

Yeo remained in undisputed mastery of the water. That the British at this time felt themselves the stronger in effective force, may be reasonably inferred from their continuing to keep the lake after Chauncey's new ship was out. She was launched June 12, and named the "General Pike," in honor of the officer killed at the taking of York. Her armament was to be twenty-six long 24-pounders, which under some circumstances would make her superior, not only to any single vessel, but to any combination of vessels then under the British flag. If it was still possible, by use of favoring conditions, to contend with the American fleet after the addition to it of this ship, by so much more was Yeo able to deal successfully with it before her coming. A comparison of the armaments of the opposing forces also demonstrates that, whatever Chauncey's duty might have been without such prospect, he was justified, having this decisive advantage within reach, in keeping his fleet housed waiting for its realization. The British new vessel, the "Wolfe," with the "Royal George"[65] and the "Melville," together threw a broadside weight of nine hundred and twenty pounds,[66] to which the "Madison" and "Oneida" could oppose only six hundred; and the batteries of all five being mainly carronades, there are no qualifications to be made on the score of differing ranges. The American schooners, though much more numerous than the British, in no way compensated for this disparity, for reasons which will be given when the narrative of operations begins. Unknown to Chauncey, the vindication of his delay was to be found in Yeo's writing to the Admiralty, that he was trying to induce the enemy to come out before his new ship was ready.

Disappointed in this endeavor, the British commodore meantime employed his vessels in maintaining the communications of the British and harassing those of the Americans, thus observing the true relation of the lake to the hostilities. Mention has been made of the effect upon Dearborn; morally, in the apprehension created, actually, in the strength contributed to Vincent's army. "The enemy's fleet is constantly hovering on the coast and interrupting our supplies," wrote General Lewis, during Dearborn's incapacity. Besides incidental mentions by American officers, Yeo himself reports the capture of two schooners and boats loaded with stores June 13; and between that date and the 19th he landed parties at the Genesee River and Great Sodus, capturing or destroying a quantity of provisions. Transit between Oswego and Sackett's was also in constant danger of an unexpected interference by the British squadron. On June 20 it appeared off Oswego, with apparent disposition to attack; but Yeo, who in his exercise of chief command displayed a degree of caution remarkable in view of his deservedly high reputation for dash acquired in less responsible positions, did not pass beyond threat. All the same, the mere uncertainty exercised a powerful influence on the maintenance of intercourse. "If the schooners 'Lark' and 'Fly' are not now in Sackett's," wrote Lieutenant Woolsey from Oswego, "they must have been taken yesterday by the British boats. They were loaded with powder, shot, and hospital stores for the army." He has also cordage, powder, guns, cables, to send, and boats in which to ship them; but "under existing circumstances I dare not take upon myself to send them farther than to Sandy Creek, under strong guard. I think it would be unsafe to venture round Stony Point [a projecting headland twelve miles from Sackett's] without convoy or a good guard."[67] On July 2, having ranged the lake at will since June 1, Yeo returned to Kingston, and Chauncey again began to hear rumors. "The fleet has taken on board two thousand men, and two thousand more are to embark in boats; an attack upon this place is the object. The plan is to make a desperate push at our fleet before the 'General Pike' can be got ready.... His real object may be to land re-enforcements near Fort George, to act with General Vincent against Dearborn. If this be his object, he will succeed in obliging our army to recross the Niagara River;"[68] a damaging commentary on the American plan of campaign. This fear, however, was excessive, for the reason that an effective American army on the Niagara had a land line of communication, bad but possible, alternative to the lake. The British had not. Moreover, the Niagara peninsula had for them a value, as a land link between Ontario and Erie, to which nothing corresponded on the United States side. Had Vincent been driven from Burlington Heights, not only would he have lost touch with the lake, and been forced back on York, but Ontario would for the British have been entirely cut off from Erie.

The "General Pike" was ready for service on July 20, and the following evening Chauncey sailed. With this begins a period, extending over ten or twelve weeks, which has no parallel in the naval lake history of the war. It was unproductive of decisive results, and especially of the one particular result which is the object of all naval action—the destruction of the enemy's organized force, and the establishment of one's own control of the water; nevertheless, the ensuing movements of Yeo and Chauncey constituted a naval campaign of considerable interest. Nothing resembling it occurred on either Lake Champlain or Erie, and no similar condition recurred on Ontario. The fleets were frequently in presence of each other, and three times came to blows. On Erie and on Champlain the opposing forces met but once, and then without any prolonged previous attempts at manœuvring. They fought immediately; the result in each case being an American victory, not only complete but decisive, which has kept their remembrance alive to this day in the national memory. On Ontario, after the close of the season of 1813, the struggle resolved itself into a race of ship-building; both parties endeavoring to maintain superiority by the creation of ever-increasing numbers, instead of by crushing the enemy. Such a contest sufficiently befits a period of peace; it is, for instance, at this moment the condition of the great naval nations of the world, each of which is endeavoring to maintain its place in the naval scale by the constant production and development of material. In war, however, the object is to put an end to a period of national tension and expense by destroying the enemy; and the failure of the commanders to effect this object calls for examination.

The indecisive result on Ontario was due to the particular composition of the two squadrons; to the absence of strong compelling conditions, such as made fighting imperative on Barclay upon Erie, and perhaps also on Downie upon Champlain; and finally, to the extreme wariness of the commanders, each of whom was deeply impressed with the importance of preserving his own fleet, in order not to sacrifice control of the lake. Chauncey has depicted for us his frame of mind in instructions issued at this very moment—July 14—to his subordinate, Perry. "The first object will be to destroy or cripple the enemy's fleet; but in all attempts upon the fleet you ought to use great caution, for the loss of a single vessel may decide the fate of the campaign."[69] A practical commentary of singular irony was passed upon this utterance within two months; for by sacrificing a single ship Perry decided his own campaign in his own favor. Given the spirit of Chauncey's warning, and also two opponents with fleets so different in constitution that one is strong where the other is weak, and vice versa, and there is found the elements of wary and protracted fighting, with a strong chance that neither will be badly hurt; but also that neither will accomplish much. This is what happened on Ontario.

The relative powers of the two fleets need to be briefly explained; for they constituted, so to say, the hands in the game which each commander had to play. The British had six vessels, of varying sizes and rigs, but all built for war, and sailing fairly well together. They formed therefore a good manœuvring squadron. The Americans had three vessels built for war, and at the beginning ten schooners also, not so designed, and not sailing well with the armaments they bore. Whatever the merits of this or that vessel, the squadron as a whole manœuvred badly, and its movements were impeded by the poorer sailors. The contrast in armaments likewise had a very decisive effect. There were in those days two principal classes of naval cannon,—long guns, often called simply "guns," and carronades. The guns had long range with light weight of shot fired; the carronades had short range and heavy shot. Now in long guns the Americans were four times as strong as the British, while in carronades the British were twice as strong as the Americans. It follows that the American commodore should prefer long range to begin with; whereas the British would be careful not to approach within long range, unless with such a breeze as would carry him rapidly down to where his carronades would come into play.

There was another controlling reason why short range favored the British against the Americans. The schooners of the latter, not being built for war, carried their guns on a deck unprotected by bulwarks. The men, being exposed from the feet up, could be swept away by canister, which is a quantity of small iron balls packed in a case and fired from a cannon. When discharged, these separate and spread like buckshot, striking many in a group. They can maim or kill a man, but their range is short and penetrative power small. A bulwarked vessel was, so to say, armored against canister; for it makes no difference whether the protection is six inches of wood or ten of iron, provided it keeps out the projectile. The American schooners were in this respect wholly vulnerable.

Over-insistence upon details of advantage or disadvantage is often wearisome, and may be pushed to pettifogging; but these quoted are general and fundamental. To mention them is not to chaffer over details, but to state principles. There is one other which should be noted, although its value may be differently estimated. Of the great long-gun superiority of the Americans more than one half was in the unprotected schooners; distributed, that is, among several vessels not built for war, and not capable of acting well together, so as to concentrate their fire. There is no equality between ten guns in five such vessels and the same ten concentrated on one deck, under one captain. That this is not special pleading, to contravene the assertion advanced by James of great American superiority on Ontario, I may quote words of my own, written years ago with reference to a British officer: "An attempt was made to disparage Howe's conduct (in 1778), and to prove that his force was even superior to that of the French, by adding together the guns in all his ships, disregarding their classes, or by combining groups of his small vessels against D'Estaing's larger units. For this kind of professional arithmetic Howe felt and expressed just and utter contempt."[70] So Nelson wrote to the commander of a British cruising squadron, "Your intentions of attacking the 'Aigle'"—a seventy-four— "with your three frigates are certainly very laudable, but I do not consider your force by any means equal to it." The new American ship, the "General Pike," possessed this advantage of the seventy-four. One discharge of her broadside was substantially equal to that of the ten schooners, and all her guns were long; entirely out-ranging the batteries of her antagonists. Under some circumstances—a good breeze and the windward position—she was doubtless able to encounter and beat the whole British squadron on Ontario. But the American schooners were mere gunboats, called to act in conditions unfavorable to that class of vessel, the record of which for efficiency is under no circumstances satisfactory.

After leaving Sackett's, Chauncey showed himself off Kingston and then went up the lake, arriving off Niagara on the evening of July 27. An abortive attempt, in conjunction with the army, was made upon a position of the enemy at Burlington Heights, then far in rear of his main line; but it being found too strong, the fleet, with the troops still on board, bore over to York and there retaliated the injury done by Yeo at Genesee and Sodus. There was no opposition; many stores were destroyed or brought away, some military buildings burned, and the vessels then returned to Niagara. They were lying there at daybreak of August 7 when the British appeared: two ships, two brigs, and two large schooners. Chauncey had substantially his whole force: two ships, the "Pike" and "Madison," the brig "Oneida," and ten schooners. He got under way shortly and put out into the lake. Various manœuvres followed, his principal object being to get to windward of the enemy; or, when the wind failed, to sweep[71] the schooners close enough for their long guns to reach; the only useful function they possessed. These efforts were unsuccessful, and night shut in with the two opponents sailing in parallel lines, heading north, with the wind at west; the Americans to leeward and in rear of the British. At two in the morning, in a heavy squall, two schooners upset, with the loss of all on board save sixteen souls. Chauncey reckoned these to be among his best, and, as they together mounted nineteen guns, he considered that "this accident gave the enemy decidedly the superiority"; another instance of faulty professional arithmetic, omitting from the account the concentration of power in the "General Pike."

Yeo did not estimate conditions in the same way, and persisted warily in keeping the weather gage, watching for a chance to cut off schooners, or for other favoring opportunity; while Chauncey as diligently sought to gain the advantage of the wind, to force action with his heavy ships. Manœuvring continued all day of the 8th, 9th, and 10th. The winds, being light and shifting, favored now one, now the other; but in no case for long enough to insure a meeting which the American with good reason desired, and his antagonist with equal propriety would accept only under conditions that suited him. At nine in the evening of August 10 the American squadron was standing northwest, with the wind at southwest, when the British, which was then following to windward, wore and stood south. Chauncey made no change in direction, but kept his vessels in two lines; this being the order of battle by which, not being able to attack himself, he hoped to induce Yeo to engage incautiously. The six smallest schooners, of the eight now left to him, were put in the weather line; therefore toward the enemy, if he persisted in keeping to windward. The lee line, abreast of the other, and six hundred yards from it, was composed of the "Pike," "Madison," and "Oneida," astern of which were the two heaviest schooners. The smaller vessels were displayed as a tempting bait, disposed, as it were, in such manner that the opponent might hope to lay hands on one or more, without coming too much under the "Pike's" heavy guns; for her two larger consorts, carrying carronades chiefly, might be neglected at the distance named. If such an attempt were made, the schooners' orders were to edge imperceptibly to leeward, enticing the enemy to follow in his eagerness; and when he was near enough they were to slip cleverly through the intervals in the lee line, leaving it to finish the business. The lure was perhaps a little too obvious, the enemy's innocent forgetfulness of the dangers to leeward too easily presumed; for a ship does not get out of the hold of a clear-headed captain as a mob of troops in hot pursuit may at times escape the control of their officers. In view, however, of Yeo's evident determination to keep his "fleet in being," by avoiding action except on his own terms, nothing better was open to Chauncey, unless fortune should favor him.

At half-past ten the British again wore, now standing northwest after the American squadron, the rear vessels of which opened fire at eleven (A). At quarter-past eleven the cannonade became general between the enemy and the weather line (B). Fifteen minutes later, the four rear schooners of the latter, which were overmatched when once within carronade range, bore up and ran to leeward; two taking position on the other side of the main division, and two astern of it (c, c). So far all went according to plan; but unhappily the leading two American schooners, instead of keeping away in obedience to orders, tacked—went about towards the enemy—keeping to windward (d). Chauncey, seeing the risk involved for them, but prepossessed with the idea of luring Yeo down by the appearance of flight set by the schooners, made what can scarcely be considered other than the mistake of keeping away himself, with the heavy ships; "filled the maintopsail, and edged away two points, to lead the enemy down, not only to engage him to more advantage, but to lead him away from the 'Growler' and 'Julia'" (C). Yeo, equally dominated by a preconceived purpose not to bring his ships under the guns of the "Pike," acted much as a squirrel would do with two nuts in sight; he went for the one safely distant from suspected danger. "He kept his wind," reported Chauncey, "until he had completely separated those two vessels from the rest of the squadron, exchanged a few shot with the 'Pike,' as he passed, without injury to us, and made sail after the two schooners" (e). Some time after midnight these surrendered to odds plainly irresistible.[72]

The tacking of the two schooners was an act as ill-judged as it was insubordinate, for which Chauncey was in no wise responsible. His bearing up was certainly an error, which unfortunately lent itself to the statement, contemporaneously made by an American paper, that he retreated, leaving the two vessels to their fate. It was possible, therefore, for Sir James to word the transaction as he airily did: "At eleven we came within gunshot of their line of schooners, which opened a heavy fire, their ships keeping off the wind to prevent our closing. At half-past twelve this ship came within gunshot of the 'Pike' and 'Madison,' when they immediately bore up, fired their stern chase-guns, and made sail for Niagara, leaving two of their schooners astern, which we captured."[73] This gives a more victorious and dashing air to the success than it quite deserves. As it stood, it was real enough, though trivial. To take two vessels from a superior fleet, within range of its commander-in-chief, is a handsome business, which should not need to be embellished by the implication that a greatly desired fight could not be had. To quote Marryat, "It is very hard to come at the real truth of this sort of thing, as I found out during the time that I was in his Majesty's service." Chauncey's version is perfectly probable. Seeing that the enemy would not follow, "tacked and stood after him. At twelve (midnight), finding that I must either separate from the rest of the squadron, or relinquish the hope of saving the two which had separated, I reluctantly gave up the pursuit." His reading of Yeo's conduct is plausible. "From what I have been able to discover of the movements of the enemy, he has no intention of engaging us, except he can get decidedly the advantage of wind and weather; and as his vessels in squadron sail better than our squadron, he can always avoid an action.... He thinks to cut off our small dull sailing schooners in detail." Here and always Chauncey's conduct reflects the caution prescribed in his instructions to Perry, rather than the resolute determination the latter showed to bring matters to an issue. On the other hand, it is to be remembered that, owing to the nearly equal facilities for ship-building—for replacing ships lost—possessed by Kingston and Sackett's, a decisive naval victory would not have the finality of result to be expected on Lake Erie. Contrary to the usual conditions of naval war, the two ports, not the fleets dependent on them, were the decisive elements of the Ontario campaign; and the ignoring of that truth was the fundamental, irremediable, American error.

Chauncey returned to Sackett's on August 13, provisioned the squadron for five weeks, and sailed the same evening. On the 16th he was back off Niagara, and there again sighted the enemy; but a heavy westerly gale drove both squadrons to the lower end of the lake, where each entered its own harbor on the 19th. August 29 the American put out again, having an additional newly built schooner, named the "Sylph," large and fast, carrying three or four long 32-pounders. Chauncey reported that he had now nine vessels with ninety-one guns, but that the enemy was still superior. In number of guns, possibly; but it is difficult to accept the statement otherwise, except in the one very important particular of squadron manœuvring power. This enabled Yeo to avoid action, except when it suited him to fight; or unless Chauncey was willing to engage first with part only of his squadron, following it with the rest. Such advantage in manœuvring greatly increases the ability of the inferior to serve his own cause, but it does not constitute superiority. The delusion of measuring force by guns, irrespective of the ships that carry them, has been explained.

Yeo's intermediate movements do not appear, but on September 7 the antagonists again met off the Niagara River. From that day till the 12th the American fleet endeavored to force a general action, which the other steadily, and properly, refused. The persistent efforts of the one to close, and of the other to avoid, led to a movement round the lake, ending by the British entering Amherst Bay, five miles west of Kingston. On one occasion, off the Genesee on September 11, a westerly breeze carried the United States squadron within three-quarters of a mile of the enemy, before the latter felt it. A cannonade and pursuit of some hours followed, but without decisive result. There seems traceable throughout Chauncey's account a distinct indisposition to what is called technically "a general chase;" to press on with part of the squadron, trusting to the slower vessels coming up soon enough to complete the work of the faster. He was unwilling thus to let his fleet loose. "This ship" (the "General Pike"), "the 'Madison,' and the 'Sylph,' have each a schooner constantly in tow, yet the others cannot sail as fast as the enemy's squadron, which gives him decidedly the advantage, and puts it in his power to engage me when and how he chooses." In such a situation success can be had only by throwing the more rapid upon the enemy as an advance guard, engaging as they get within range, relying upon their effecting such detention that the others can arrive in time to their support. To this recourse, though in halting fashion, Chauncey finally came on what proved to be his last collision with Yeo, September 28.

FOOTNOTES:

[40] Yeo to Croker, May 26, 1813. Admiralty In-Letters, Records Office.
[41] Captains' Letters, Navy Department.
[42] American State Papers, Military Affairs, vol. i. p. 439.
[43] Between July, 1812, and March 25, 1813, Prevost received re-enforcements amounting in all to 2,175 regulars. His total force then, for all Canada, excluding militia, was 9,177; of which 2,000 were provincial corps. British Records Office.
[44] American State Papers, Military Affairs, vol. i. p. 441.
[45] Chauncey to Navy Department, March 8, 12, and 16, 1813. Captains' Letters.
[46] American State Papers, Military Affairs, vol. i. p. 442.
[47] Captains' Letters.
[48] Captains' Letters, Nov. 5, 1814.
[49] Captains' Letters, May 7, 1813.
[50] Ibid., May 15.
[51] Canadian Archives. C. 678, p. 332.
[52] American State Papers, Military Affairs, vol. i. p. 445.
[53] Ibid., p. 449. Armstrong's italics.
[54] Barclay's Narrative before the British Court Martial on the Battle of Lake Erie. British Records Office.
[55] Prevost to Bathurst, Canadian Archives.
[56] Mackenzie's Life of Perry, vol. i. p. 148.
[57] Barclay's Narrative.
[58] Brown's and Prevost's Reports of this affair may be found in Niles' Register, vol. iv. pp. 260, 261. That of Yeo is in the Canadian Archives; M.

389, 6, p. 22.

[59] Captains' Letters, June 11, 1813.

[60] Captains' Letters.

[61] The account of these transactions is summarized from American State Papers, Military Affairs, vol. i. pp. 445-449. For Vincent's report of the Stony Creek affair see Cruikshank's Documentary History of the Campaign on the Niagara Frontier, 1813, Part II, p. 8.

[62] Smyth's Précis of Wars in Canada, p. 137.

[63] Scott's Memoirs, vol. i. p. 94.

[64] American State Papers, Military Affairs, vol. i. pp. 450, 451.

[65] Formerly the "Prince Regent."

[66] Yeo's Report of the Vessels on the Lakes, July 15, 1813. British Records Office.

[67] Woolsey to Chauncey, June 20 and 21, 1813. Captains' Letters.

[68] Chauncey to the Department, July 5, 1813. Captains' Letters.

[69] Captains' Letters. Navy Department MSS.

[70] "History of the Royal Navy," edited by Sir W.L. Clowes, vol. iii. p. 411.

[71] That is,—row

[72] Chauncey's Report of this cruise is in Captains' Letters, Aug. 13, 1813. Also, in Niles' Register, vol. iv. p. 421.

[73] James, Naval Occurrences. Appendix, p. lxxiv.

THE CAMPAIGN OF 1813 ON THE LAKES AND NORTHERN FRONTIER

The Battle Of Lake Erie

While the movements last related in the preceding chapter were in progress, the contest for Lake Erie was brought to a final decision. After the successful transfer of the vessels from Black Rock to Erie, June 18, Perry remained upon the upper lake superintending all administrative work; but in particular pressing the equipment of the two brigs ordered by Chauncey the previous winter. To one of these, on which Perry intended to embark his own fortunes, was given the name of "Lawrence," the captain of the "Chesapeake," whose death, heroic in defeat, occurred at this period. The other was called the "Niagara." They were sister vessels, of five hundred tons, constructed for war, and brig-rigged; that is, with two masts, and carrying square sails on both. Their armaments also were alike; eighteen 32-pounder carronades, and two long 12-pounder guns. They were thus about equivalent in fighting force to the ocean sloops-of-war, "Wasp" and "Hornet," which, however, were three-masted. The remainder of the force would now be called a scratch lot. Three were schooner-rigged gunboats, built for the navy at Erie; the remainder were the vessels brought from Black Rock. Of these, one was the brig "Caledonia," formerly British, captured by Elliott the previous autumn; the others were purchased lake craft. When finally taking the lake, August 6, the squadron consisted of the two brigs, of the Black Rock division,—"Caledonia," "Somers," "Tigress," "Ohio," and "Trippe,"—and of three other schooners,—"Ariel," "Scorpion," and "Porcupine,"—apparently those built at Erie; ten sail, all of which, except the "Ohio," were in the final decisive battle.

On July 23 the vessels were rigged, armed, and ready for service, but there were not men enough to man them. How little exacting Perry was in this matter, and how eager to enter upon active operations, is shown by a letter from his superior, Chauncey, to the Secretary of the Navy, dated July 8: "I am at a loss," he says, "to account for the change in Captain Perry's sentiments with respect to the number of men required for the little fleet at Presqu' Isle; for when I parted with him on the last of May, we coincided in opinion perfectly as to the number required for each vessel, which was one hundred and eighty for each of the new brigs, sixty for the 'Caledonia,' and forty for each of the other vessels, making in all seven hundred and forty officers and men. But if Captain Perry can beat the enemy with half that number, no one will feel more happy than myself."[74] Chauncey having supreme control over both lakes, all re-enforcements from the seaboard were sent to him; and as he had his own particular enemy on Ontario to confront, it was evident, and natural, that Perry would be least well served. Hence, after successive disappointments, and being of more venturous temper than his superior, it is not surprising that he soon was willing to undertake his task with fewer men than his unbiased judgment would call necessary.

The clash of interests between the two squadrons, having a common superior but separate responsibilities, is seen by a comparison of dates, which shows operations nearly simultaneous. On July 23 the Erie squadron was reported "all ready to meet the enemy the moment they are officered and manned;" on July 20 the "General Pike" was ready, and on the 21st the Ontario squadron sailed from Sackett's Harbor. On August 5 Perry had his vessels across the bar at Erie, and next day stood out into the lake. On the 7th Chauncey and Yeo met for their first encounter. On the 8th the two Ontario schooners, "Hamilton" and "Scourge," were lost with nearly all on board; and on the 10th the "Julia" and "Growler" were captured. After this, it may be imagined that Chauncey with difficulty parted with men; and in the midst of his second collision with Yeo the battle of Lake Erie occurred. In it, of the one hundred and eighty men deemed necessary by Chauncey, Perry's brig had one hundred and forty-two, of whom thirty were sick; while the squadron, with nearly all its vessels present, instead of the intended seven hundred and forty, had but four hundred and ninety. Of this total, nearly one hundred were received from the army on August 31, only nine days before the action. For the most part these were strangers to shipboard. Barring them, Perry's fighting force was barely more than half that required by Chauncey's estimate.

Indirectly, and notwithstanding Perry's disposition to make the best of his difficulty, this condition came near causing his withdrawal from the lake service; a loss which, had it occurred, might have reversed the issues, for in few general actions has the personality of the commander counted for so much, after the battle joined. In a letter of July 26 to Chauncey, he had written: "The men that came by Mr. Champlin are a motley set, blacks, soldiers, and boys. I cannot think you saw them after they were selected."[75] Chauncey replied, somewhat testily, "I regret you are not pleased with the men sent you; for, to my knowledge, a part of them are not surpassed by any seamen we have in the fleet; and I have yet to learn that the color of the skin, or the cut and trimmings of the coat, can affect a man's qualifications or usefulness." To this he added a warning not much short of a reproof: "As you have assured the secretary that you should conceive yourself equal or superior to the enemy, with a force in men so much less than I had deemed necessary, there will be a great deal expected from you by your country, and I trust they will not be disappointed in the high expectations formed of your gallantry and judgment. I will barely make an observation, which was impressed upon my mind by an old soldier; that is, 'Never despise your enemy.'"[76]

This advice was sound, rightly weighed. Yet it is not too much to say that the confidence which carried Perry on to decisive victory has in it inevitably something of that assurance of success which is akin to contempt of the enemy, and that it was the precise quality in which Chauncey, throughout his own career on the lakes, showed himself deficient, and consequently failed. His plan at that moment, as he himself said in a letter to Perry of July 14, was "to seek a meeting with Sir James Yeo as soon as possible, in order to decide the fate of this lake, and join you immediately after." This was an intelligent project: to beat one enemy first, and then carry his force over to beat the other; but never, when in presence of his antagonist, could he despise him sufficiently to cut his gunboats adrift, and throw one or two vessels into the midst of the fire, as Perry rushed his own ship in, had her cut to pieces,—and won. It is even worse to respect your enemy too greatly than to despise him. Said Farragut, speaking of an officer he highly valued: "Drayton does not know fear, but he believes in acting as if the enemy never can be caught unprepared; whereas I believe in judging him by ourselves, and my motto in action is, 'L'audace, et encore de l'audace, et toujours de l'audace!'" This described Perry in battle.

Although Chauncey closed with expressions of confidence which might be considered conciliatory, Perry experienced an annoyance which was natural, though excessive. He was only twenty-eight, quick of temper, though amiable, and somewhat prone to see more offence than was intended. When the letter reached him, the squadron had just crossed the bar; the most critical movement of the campaign, had the enemy been duly watchful. Having accomplished this, he had before him only the common vicissitudes of naval warfare. Nevertheless, under his first impulse of resentment, he applied to be removed from the station,[77] giving as his reason, not the quality of men sent, concerning which indeed he had said, "I am pleased to see anything in the shape of a man," but that "I cannot serve under an officer who has been so totally regardless of my feelings." He then summarized the difficulties with which he had contended, and added, "The critical state of General Harrison was such that I took upon myself the responsibility of going out with the few young officers you had been pleased to send me," (Elliott, the second in command, did not arrive till the squadron was over the bar), "with the few seamen I had, and as many volunteers as I could muster from the militia. I did not shrink from this responsibility; but, Sir, at that very moment I surely did not anticipate the receipt of a letter in every line of which is an insult." He then renewed his request. "I am willing to forego that reward which I have considered for two months past almost within my grasp." Fortunately for the renown of the service, from which one of its finest actions might have been lost, it was impossible to grant his application until after the battle had made the question of the command on Lake Erie one of very minor importance. The secretary replied to him with words in which rebuke and appreciation were aptly blended. "A change of commander, under existing circumstances, is equally inadmissible as it respects the interest of the service and your own reputation. It is right that you should reap the harvest which you have sown."[78]

After the Frenchtown disaster[79] of January 22, 1813, the Army of the Northwest under General Harrison had remained strictly on the defensive throughout the spring and summer. The tenure of its position on the Maumee River depended upon Fort Meigs, built during the winter just above the Rapids, some twenty miles from the lake. Thirty miles east of Meigs was Fort Stephenson at the mouth of the Sandusky River, protecting the approaches to Sandusky Bay, near which were Harrison's headquarters at the time Perry's squadron was ready to move. Fort Stephenson by its situation contributed also to secure the communications of the Maumee line with Central Ohio, and was an obstacle to an enemy's approach by land to Erie, a hundred and fifty miles further east. It was not, however, a work permanent in character, like Meigs; and neither post could be considered secure, because inadequately garrisoned. Fortunately, the general tenor of the instructions received by Procter from Prevost conspired with his own natural character to indispose him to energetic measures. His force of regulars was small; and he had not the faculty, which occasional white men have shown, to arouse vigorous and sustained activity in the Indians, of whom he had an abundance at call. The use of them in desultory guerilla warfare, which was prescribed to him by Prevost, became in his hands ineffective. Nevertheless, from the number known to be under his command, and the control of the water enabling him to land where he would, the threat of savage warfare hung over the frontier like a pall, until finally dissipated by Perry's victory.

The danger to British control of the water, and thereby to the maintenance of their position in the northwest, if the American fleet now building should succeed in getting upon the lake, was perfectly apparent, and made Erie a third and principal point of interest. At the time of Perry's arrival, March 27, the place was entirely defenceless, and without any organization for defence, although the keels of the two brigs were laid, and the three gunboats well advanced in construction. By a visit to Pittsburgh he obtained from an army ordnance officer four small guns, with some muskets; and upon his application the local commander of Pennsylvania militia stationed at Erie five hundred men, who remained till the vessels crossed the bar. Under this slender protection went on the arduous work of building and equipping a squadron in what was substantially a wilderness, to which most of the mechanics and material had to be brought half a thousand miles from the seaboard, under the difficulties of transport in those days. The rapid advance in the preparations aroused the disquietude of the British, but Procter had not the enterprising temper to throw all upon the hazard, for the sake of destroying an armament which, if completed, might destroy him; while the British inferiority of force on Lake Ontario and the Niagara peninsula, together with the movement of Chauncey and Dearborn resulting in the capture of York, April 27, effectually prevented intervention from that quarter in the affairs of Lake Erie. At this time Procter made his first effort of the season, directed against Fort Meigs, which he held besieged for over a week,—from May 1 to May 9. Although unable to capture it, the mismanagement of an American relief force enabled him to inflict a very severe loss; a corps of eight hundred and sixty-six men being cut to pieces or captured, only one hundred and seventy escaping. The chief points of interest in this business are the demonstration of the weakness of the American frontier,—the principal defence of which was thus not merely braved but threatened,—and the effect of control of the water. By it Procter brought over gunboats which ascended the river, and guns of a weight not to be transported by land. The lake also secured his communications.

After the failure before Meigs, Procter turned his attention more seriously to the situation at Erie, and demanded re-enforcements to enable him to attack the place.[80] Prevost, being commander-in-chief for all Canada, recognized the expediency of the move, and wrote him, June 20, that he had directed General De Rottenburg at Niagara, to push on re-enforcements and supplies; but Prevost was in Kingston, and De Rottenburg, immediately responsible for Niagara, wrote declining to weaken his force. He was already inferior to the United States army under Boyd, which was then confronting him, resting upon Fort George; and there was the prospect also that Chauncey might regain control of the lake. Instead of co-operation for offence, he transmitted arrangements for retreat in case of a disaster to Yeo on Ontario. Procter enclosed this letter to the commander-in-chief, remarking pathetically that he was fully confident of receiving aid from him, but intentions were of no avail. Had the force ordered been sent, he felt sure of destroying the fleet at Erie, thus securing the command of the lake, which would have benefited also the centre division. He should now, he said, make an attempt upon Sandusky; Erie was impossible without re-enforcements. At the same time, July 13, Captain Barclay was about to sail for Long Point, on the Canada shore directly opposite Erie, to embark one hundred troops, and then to endeavor to retain the American fleet in port until the required assistance could be sent. The new British ship "Detroit" was nearly ready for launching at Amherstburg, and could be equipped and gunned there; but seamen were absolutely needed.

In accordance with these plans Barclay went with his squadron to Long Point. There the desired soldiers were refused him; and, as also no seamen were forthcoming, he wrote on July 16 a letter directly to Sir George Prevost, "lest Sir James Yeo should be on the lake," representing the critical state of affairs, owing to the inadequate equipment of his vessels, the want of seamen, and the advanced preparations of the Americans to put afloat a force superior to his. July 20 he appeared off Erie, where Perry's fleet was still in the harbor, waiting for men. How imminent the exposure of the American flotilla at that moment, and how great the British opportunity, appears from the recently published memoirs of a prominent resident.[81] "An English fleet of five vessels of war was at that time cruising off the harbor, in full view. That fleet might at any time have sent in its boats during a dark night, and the destruction of the whole American fleet was almost inevitable; for Perry's force was totally inadequate to its defence, and the regiment of Pennsylvania militia, stationed at Erie expressly for the defence of the fleet, refused to keep guard at night on board. 'I told the boys to go, Captain,' said the worthless colonel of the regiment, 'but the boys won't go.'" Like American merchant ships, American militia obeyed or disobeyed as they pleased. Two hundred soldiers, loaned by Dearborn when the Black Rock flotilla came round, had been recalled July 10. On the 23d and 30th re-enforcements were received from Chauncey, in all one hundred and thirty men. With these, and some landsmen enlisted on the spot for four months, the force of the squadron, estimated to require seven hundred and forty men, was raised to three hundred; but having lately received two pressing letters from the Navy Department, urging General Harrison's critical need of co-operation, Perry determined to go out. Most opportunely for his purpose, Barclay disappeared on the 30th, Friday, which thus for him made good its title to "unlucky." He was absent until August 4, and was by the Americans believed to have gone to Long Point. Before his Court Martial he merely stated that "I blockaded as closely as I could, until I one morning saw the whole of the enemy's force over the bar, and in a most formidable state of preparation." The Court did not press inquiry on the point, which perhaps lay beyond its instructions; but the double failure, to intercept the Black Rock division on its way to Erie,[82] and to prevent the crossing of the bar, were serious strategic misadventures when confronting superior numbers. Perry's preparations for the passage had been for some time completed, but information of contemplated movements travelled so easily from shore to shore that he gave no indication of immediate action until Sunday. On that day the officers were permitted to disperse in town as usual, but afterwards were hastily summoned back, and the vessels moved down to the bar, on which the depth ordinarily was from five to seven feet, much less than needed for the "Lawrence" and "Niagara." This obstacle, hitherto a protection against naval attack, now imposed an extremely critical operation; for to get over, the brigs must be lightened of their guns and their hulls lifted upon floats. So situated, they were helplessly exposed to destruction, as far as their own powers went.

From point to point the mouth of the harbor, where the outer bar occurs, was eight tenths of a mile wide. As shown by a sketch of the period, the distance to be travelled on the floats, from deep water within to deep water without, was a mile; rather less than more. On Monday morning, August 2, the movement of the vessels began simultaneously. Five of the smaller, which under usual conditions could pass without lightening, were ordered to cross and take positions outside, covering the channel; a sixth, with the "Niagara," were similarly posted within. The protection thus afforded was re-enforced by three 12-pounder long guns, mounted on the beach, abreast the bar; distant not over five hundred yards from the point where the channel issued on the lake. While these dispositions were being made, the "Lawrence's" guns were hoisted out, and placed in boats to be towed astern of her; the floats taken alongside, filled, sunk, and made fast, so that when pumped out their rising would lift the brig. In the course of these preparations it was found that the water had fallen to four feet, so that even the schooners had to be lightened, while the transit of the "Lawrence" was rendered more tedious and difficult. The weather, however, was propitious, with a smooth lake; and although the brig grounded in the shoalest spot, necessitating a second sinking of the burden-bearing floats,—appropriately called "camels,"—perseverance protracted through that night and the day of the 3d carried her outside. At 8 A.M. of the 4th she was fairly afloat. Guns, singly light in weight as hers were, were quickly hoisted on board and mounted; but none too soon, for the enemy appeared almost immediately. The "Niagara's" passage was more easily effected, and Barclay offered no molestation. In a letter to the Department, dated August 4, 1813, 9 P.M., Perry reported, "I have great pleasure in informing you that I have succeeded in getting over the bar the United States vessels, the 'Lawrence,'

'Niagara,' 'Caledonia,' 'Ariel,' 'Scorpion,' 'Somers,' 'Tigress,' and 'Porcupine.'" He added, "The enemy have been in sight all day." The vessels named, with the schooner "Ohio" and the sloop "Trippe," constituted the entire squadron.

While Perry was thus profitably employed, Procter had embarked on another enterprise against the magazines on the American front of operations. His intention, as first reported to Prevost, was to attack Sandusky; but the conduct of the Indians, upon the co-operation of whom he had to rely, compelled him to diverge to Fort Meigs. Here the savages began to desert, an attempt to draw the garrison into an ambush having failed; and when Procter, after two days' stay, determined to revert to Sandusky, he was accompanied by "as many hundred of them as there should have been thousands." The white troops went on by water, the Indians by the shore. They appeared before Fort Stephenson on Sunday, August 1. The garrison was summoned, with the customary intimation of the dire consequences to be apprehended from the savages in case of an assault. The American commander, Major Croghan, accepted these possibilities, and the following day, during which the "Lawrence" was working her way over Erie bar, the artillery and the guns of the gunboats were busy battering the northwest angle of the fort. At 4 P.M. an assault was made. It was repelled with heavy loss to the assailants, and little to the besieged. That night the baffled enemy withdrew to Malden.

The American squadron having gained the lake and mounted its batteries, Barclay found himself like Chauncey while awaiting the "General Pike." His new and most powerful vessel, the ship "Detroit," was approaching completion. He was now too inferior in force to risk action when he might expect her help so soon, and he therefore retired to Malden. Perry was thus left in control of Lake Erie. He put out on August 6; but, failing to find the enemy, he anchored again off Erie, to take on board provisions, and also stores to be carried to Sandusky for the army. While thus occupied, there came on the evening of the 8th the welcome news that a re-enforcement of officers and seamen was approaching. On the 10th, these joined him to the number of one hundred and two. At their head was Commander Jesse D. Elliott, an officer of reputation, who became second in command to Perry, and took charge of the "Niagara."

On August 12 the squadron finally made sail for the westward, not to return to Erie till the campaign was decided. Its intermediate movements possess little interest, the battle of Lake Erie being so conspicuously the decisive incident as to reduce all preceding it to insignificance. Perry was off Malden on August 25, and again on September 1. The wind on the latter day favoring movement both to go and come, a somewhat rare circumstance, he remained all day reconnoitring near the harbor's mouth. The British squadron appeared complete in vessels and equipment; but

Barclay had his own troubles about crews, as had his antagonist, his continual representations to Yeo meeting with even less attention than Perry conceived himself to receive from Chauncey. He was determined to postpone action until re-enforcements of seamen should arrive from the eastward, unless failure of provisions, already staring him in the face, should force him to battle in order to re-establish communications by the lake.

The headquarters of the United States squadron was at Put-in Bay, in the Bass Islands, a group thirty miles southeast of Malden. The harbor was good, and the position suitable for watching the enemy, in case he should attempt to pass eastward down the lake, towards Long Point or elsewhere. Hither Perry returned on September 6, after a brief visit to Sandusky Bay, where information was received that the British leaders had determined that the fleet must, at all hazards, restore intercourse with Long Point. From official correspondence, afterwards captured with Procter's baggage, it appears that the Amherstburg and Malden district was now entirely dependent for flour upon Long Point, access to which had been effectually destroyed by the presence of the American squadron. Even cattle, though somewhat more plentiful, could no longer be obtained in the neighborhood in sufficient numbers, owing to the wasteful way in which the Indians had killed where they wanted. They could not be restrained without alienating them, or, worse, provoking them to outrage. Including warriors and their families, fourteen thousand were now consuming provisions. In the condition of the roads, only water transport could meet the requirements; and that not by an occasional schooner running blockade, but by the free transit of supplies conferred by naval control. To the decision to fight may have been contributed also a letter from Prevost, who had been drawn down from Kingston to St. David's, on the Niagara frontier, by his anxiety about the general situation, particularly aroused by Procter's repulse from Fort Stephenson. Alluding to the capture of Chauncey's two schooners on August 10, he wrote Procter on the 22d, "Yeo's experience should convince Barclay that he has only to dare and he will be successful."[83] It was to be Sir George's unhappy lot, a year later, to goad the British naval commander on Lake Champlain into premature action; and there was ample time for the present indiscreet innuendo to reach Barclay, and impel him to a step which Prevost afterwards condemned as hasty, because not awaiting the arrival of a body of fifty seamen announced to be at Kingston on their way to Malden.

At sunrise of September 10, the lookout at the masthead of the "Lawrence" sighted the British squadron in the northwest. Barclay was on his way down the lake, intending to fight. The wind was southwest, fair for the British, but adverse to the Americans quitting the harbor by the channel leading towards the enemy. Fortunately it shifted to southeast, and there steadied; which not only enabled them to go out, but gave them the windward position throughout the engagement. The windward position, or weather gage, as it was commonly called, conferred the power of initiative; whereas the vessel or fleet to leeward, while it might by skill at times force action, or itself obtain the weather gage by manœuvring, was commonly obliged to await attack and accept the distance chosen by the opponent. Where the principal force of a squadron, as in Perry's case, consists in two vessels armed almost entirely with carronades, the importance of getting within carronade range is apparent.

Looking forward to a meeting, Perry had prearranged the disposition of his vessels to conform to that which he expected the enemy to assume. Unlike ocean fleets, all the lake squadrons, as is already known of Ontario, were composed of vessels very heterogeneous in character. This was because the most had been bought, not designed for the navy. It was antecedently probable, therefore, that a certain general principle would dictate the constitution of the three parts of the order of battle, the centre and two flanks, into which every military line divides. The French have an expression for the centre,—corps de bataille,—which was particularly appropriate to squadrons like those of Barclay and Perry. Each had a natural "body of battle," in vessels decisively stronger than all the others combined. This relatively powerful division would take the centre, as a cohesive force, to prevent the two ends—or flanks—being driven asunder by the enemy. Barclay's vessels of this class were the new ship, "Detroit," and the "Queen Charlotte;" Perry's were the "Lawrence" and "Niagara." Each had an intermediate vessel; the British the "Lady Prevost," the Americans the "Caledonia." In addition to these were the light craft, three British and six Americans; concerning which it is to be said that the latter were not only the more numerous, but individually much more powerfully armed.

The same remark is true, vessel for vessel, of those opposed to one another by Perry's plan; that is, measuring the weight of shot discharged at a broadside, which is the usual standard of comparison, the "Lawrence" threw more metal than the "Detroit," the "Niagara" much more than the "Queen Charlotte," and the "Caledonia," than the "Lady Prevost." This, however, must be qualified by the consideration, more conspicuously noticeable on Ontario than on Erie, of the greater length of range of the long gun. This applies particularly to the principal British vessel, the "Detroit." Owing to the difficulties of transportation, and the demands of the Ontario squadron, her proper armament had not arrived. She was provided with guns from the ramparts of Fort Malden, and a more curiously composite battery probably never was mounted; but, of the total nineteen, seventeen were long guns. It is impossible to say what her broadside may have weighed. All her pieces together fired two hundred and thirty pounds, but it is incredible that a seaman like Barclay should not so have disposed them as to give more than half that amount to one broadside. That of the "Lawrence," was three hundred pounds; but all her guns, save two twelves, were carronades. Compared with the "Queen Charlotte," the battery of the "Niagara" was as 3 to 2; both chiefly carronades.

From what has been stated, it is evident that if Perry's plan were carried out, opposing vessel to vessel, the Americans would have a superiority of at least fifty per cent. Such an advantage, in some quarter at least, is the aim of every capable commander; for the object of war is not to kill men, but to carry a point: not glory by fighting, but success in result. The only obvious dangers were that the wind might fail or be very light, which would unduly protract exposure to long guns before getting within carronade range; or that, by some vessels coming tardily into action, one or more of the others would suffer from concentration of the enemy's fire. It was this contingency, realized in fact, which gave rise to the embittered controversy about the battle; a controversy never settled, and probably now not susceptible of settlement, because the President of the United States, Mr. Monroe, pigeonholed the charges formulated by Perry against Elliott in 1818. There is thus no American sworn testimony to facts, searched and sifted by cross-examination; for the affidavits submitted on the one side and the other were ex parte, while the Court of Inquiry, asked by Elliott in 1815, neglected to call all accessible witnesses—notably Perry himself. In fact, there was not before it a single commanding officer of a vessel engaged. Such a procedure was manifestly inadequate to the requirement of the Navy Department's letter to the Court, that "a true statement of the facts in relation to Captain Elliott's conduct be exhibited to the world." Investigation seems to have been confined to an assertion in a British periodical, based upon the proceedings of the Court Martial upon Barclay, to the effect that Elliott's vessel "had not been engaged, and was making away,"[84] at the time when Perry "was obliged to leave his ship, which soon after surrendered, and hoist his flag on board another of his squadron." The American Court examined two officers of Perry's vessel, and five of Elliott's; no others. To the direct question, "Did the 'Niagara' at any time during the action attempt to make off from the British fleet?" all replied, "No." The Court, therefore, on the testimony before it, decided that the charge "made in the proceedings[85] of the British Court Martial ... was malicious, and unfounded in fact;" expressing besides its conviction "that the attempts to wrest from Captain Elliott the laurels he gained in that splendid victory ... ought in no wise to lessen him in the opinion of his fellow citizens as a brave and skilful officer." At the same time it regretted that "imperious duty compelled it to promulgate testimony which appears materially to differ in some of its most important points."

In this state the evidence still remains, owing to the failure of the President to take action, probably with a benevolent desire to allay discord, and envelop facts under a kindly "All's well that ends well." Perry died a year after making his charges, which labored under the just imputation that he had commended Elliott in his report, and again immediately afterwards, though in terms that his subordinate thought failed to do him justice. American naval opinion divided, apparently in very unequal numbers. Elliott's officers stood by him, as was natural; for men feel themselves involved in that which concerns the conduct of their ship, and see incidents in that light. Perry's officers considered that the "Lawrence" had not been properly supported; owing to which, after losses almost unparalleled, she had to undergo the mortification of surrender. Her heroism, her losses, and her surrender, were truths beyond question.

The historian to-day thus finds himself in the dilemma that the American testimony is in two categories, distinctly contradictory and mutually destructive; yet to be tested only by his own capacity to cross-examine the record, and by reference to the British accounts. The latter are impartial, as between the American parties; their only bias is to constitute a fair case for Barclay, by establishing the surrender of the American flagship and the hesitancy of the "Niagara" to enter into action. This would indicate victory so far, changed to defeat by the use Perry made of the vessel preserved to him intact by the over-caution of his second. Waiving motives, these claims are substantially correct, and constitute the analysis of the battle as fought and won.

Barclay, finding the wind to head him and place him to leeward, arranged his fleet to await attack in the following order, from van to rear: The schooner "Chippewa," "Detroit," "Hunter," "Queen Charlotte," "Lady Prevost," "Little Belt."[86] This, he said in his official letter, was "according to a given plan, so that each ship [that is, the "Detroit" and "Queen Charlotte"] might be supported against the superior force of the two brigs opposed to them." The British vessels lay in column, in each other's wake, by the wind on the port tack, hove-to (stopped) with a topsail to the mast, heading to the southwest (position 1). Perry now modified some details of his disposition. It had been expected that the "Queen Charlotte" would precede the "Detroit," and the American commander had therefore placed the "Niagara" leading, as designated to fight the "Charlotte," the "Lawrence" following the "Niagara." This order was now reversed, and the "Caledonia" interposed between the two; the succession being "Lawrence," "Caledonia," "Niagara." Having more schooners than the enemy, he placed in the van two of the best, the "Scorpion" and the "Ariel"; the other four behind the "Niagara." His centre, therefore, the "Lawrence," "Caledonia," and "Niagara," were opposed to the "Detroit," "Hunter," and "Queen Charlotte." The long guns of the "Ariel," "Scorpion," and "Caledonia" supplied in measure the deficiency of gun power in the "Lawrence," while standing down outside of carronade range; the "Caledonia," with the rear schooners, giving a like support to the "Niagara." The "Ariel," and perhaps also the "Scorpion," was ordered to keep a little to windward of the "Lawrence." This was a not uncommon use of van vessels, making more hazardous any attempt of the opponent to tack and pass to windward, in order to gain the weather gage with its particular advantages (position 1).

The rear four schooners, as is frequently the case in long columns, were straggling somewhat at the time the signal to bear down was made; and they had difficulty in getting into action, being compelled to resort to the sweeps because the wind was light. It is not uncommon to see small vessels with low sails thus retarded, while larger are being urged forward by their lofty light canvas. The line otherwise having been formed, Perry stood down without regard to them. At quarter before noon the "Detroit" opened upon the "Lawrence" with her long guns. Ten minutes later the Americans began to reply. Finding the British fire at this range more destructive than he had anticipated, Perry made more sail upon the Lawrence. Word had already been passed by hail of trumpet to close up in the line, and for each vessel to come into action against her opponent, before designated. The "Lawrence" continued thus to approach obliquely, using her own long twelves, and backed by the long guns of the vessels ahead and astern, till she was within "canister range," apparently about two hundred and fifty yards, when she turned her side to the wind on the weather quarter of the "Detroit," bringing her carronade battery to bear (position 2). This distance was greater than desirable for carronades; but with a very light breeze, little more than two miles an hour, there was a limit to the time during which it was prudent to allow an opponent's raking fire to play, unaffected in aim by any reply. Moreover, much of her rigging was already shot away, and she was becoming unmanageable. The battle was thus joined by the commander-in-chief; but, while supported to his satisfaction by the "Scorpion" and "Ariel" ahead, and "Caledonia" astern, with their long guns, the "Niagara" did not come up, and her carronades failed to do their share. The captain of her opponent, the "Queen Charlotte," finding that his own carronades would not reach her, made sail ahead, passed the "Hunter," and brought his battery to the support of the "Detroit" in her contest with the "Lawrence" (Q2). Perry's vessel thus found herself under the combined fire of the "Detroit," "Queen Charlotte," and in some measure of the "Hunter"; the armament of the last, however, was too trivial to count for much.

Elliott's first placing of the "Niagara" may, or may not, have been judicious as regards his particular opponent. The "Queen Charlotte's" twenty-fours would not reach him; and it may be quite proper to take a range where your own guns can tell and your enemy's cannot. Circumstance must determine. The precaution applicable in a naval duel may cease to be so when friends are in need of assistance; and when the British captain, seeing how the case stood, properly and promptly carried his ship forward to support his commander, concentrating two vessels upon Perry's one, the situation was entirely changed. The plea set up by Cooper, who fought Elliott's battle conscientiously, but with characteristic bitterness as well as shrewdness, that the "Niagara's" position, assigned in the line behind the "Caledonia," could not properly be left without signal, practically surrenders the case. It is applying the dry-rot system of fleet tactics in the middle of the eighteenth century to the days after Rodney and Nelson, and is further effectually disposed of by the consentient statement of several of the American captains, that their commander's dispositions were made with reference to the enemy's order; that is, that he assigned a special enemy's ship to a special American, and particularly the "Detroit" to the "Lawrence," and the "Queen Charlotte" to the "Niagara." The vessels of both fleets being so heterogeneous, it was not wise to act as with units nearly homogeneous, by laying down an order, the governing principle of which was mutual support by a line based upon its own intrinsic qualities. The considerations dictating Perry's dispositions were external to his fleet, not internal; in the enemy's order, not in his own. This was emphasized by his changing the previously arranged stations of the "Lawrence" and the "Niagara," when he saw Barclay's line. Lastly, he re-enforced all this by quoting to his subordinates Nelson's words, that no captain could go very far wrong who placed his vessel close alongside those of the enemy.

Cooper, the ablest of Elliott's champions, has insisted so strongly upon the obligation of keeping the station in the line, as laid down, that it is necessary to examine the facts in the particular case. He rests the certainty of his contention on general principles, then long exploded, and further upon a sentence in Perry's charges, preferred in 1818, that "the commanding officer issued, 1st, an order directing in what manner the line of battle should be formed ... and enjoined upon the commanders to preserve their stations in the line" thus laid down.[87] This is correct; but Cooper omits to give the words immediately following in the specification: "and in all cases to keep as near the commanding officer's vessel [the "Lawrence"] as possible."[88] Cooper also omits that which next succeeds: "2d, An order of attack, in which the 'Lawrence' was designated to attack the enemy's new ship (afterwards ascertained to have been named the 'Detroit'), and the 'Niagara' designated to attack the 'Queen Charlotte,' which orders were then communicated to all the commanders, including the said Captain Elliott, who for that purpose ... were by signal called together by the said commanding officer ... and expressly instructed that 'if, in the expected engagement, they laid their vessels close alongside of those of the enemy, they could not be out of the way.'"[89] An officer, if at once gallant and intelligent, finding himself behind a dull sailing vessel, as Cooper tells us the "Caledonia" was, could hardly desire clearer authority than the above to

imitate his commanding officer when he made sail to close the enemy:—
"Keep close to him," and follow up the ship which "the 'Niagara' was
designated to attack."

Charges preferred are not technical legal proof, but, if duly scrutinized, they
are statements equivalent in value to many that history rightly accepts; and,
at all events, that which Cooper quotes is not duly scrutinized if that which
he does not quote is omitted. He does indeed express a gloss upon them, in
the words: "Though the 'Niagara' was ordered to direct her fire at the
'Queen Charlotte,' it could only be done from her station astern of the
'Caledonia,' ... without violating the primary order to preserve the line."[90]
This does not correctly construe the natural meaning of Perry's full
instructions. It is clear that, while he laid down a primary formation, "a line
of battle," he also most properly qualified it by a contingent instruction, an
"order of attack," designed to meet the emergency likely to occur in every
fleet engagement, and which occurred here, when a slavish adherence to the
line of battle would prevent intelligent support to the main effort. If he
knew naval history, as his quotation from Nelson indicates, he also knew
how many a battle had been discreditably lost by "keeping the line."

With regard to the line, however, it is apt to remark that in fleet battle,
unless otherwise specially directed, the line of the assailant was supposed to
be parallel to that of the defence, for the obvious reason that the attacking
vessels should all be substantially at the same effective range. This distance,
equal for all in fleets as usually constituted, would naturally be set, and in
practice was set, by the commander-in-chief; his ship forming the point
through which should be drawn the line parallel to the enemy. This rule,
well established under Rodney, who died in 1792, was rigidly applicable
between vessels of the same force, such as the "Lawrence" and "Niagara;"
and whatever deductions might be made for the case of a light-framed
vessel, armed with long guns, like the "Caledonia," keeping out of
carronade distance of an opponent with heavy scantling, would not in the
least apply to the "Niagara." For her, the standard of position was not, as
Cooper insists, a half-cable's length from her next ahead, the "Caledonia;"
but abreast her designated opponent, at the same distance as the
"Lawrence" from the enemy's line. Repeated mishaps had established the
rule that position was to be taken from the centre,—that is, from the
commander-in-chief. Ships in line of battle, bearing down upon an enemy
in like order, did not steer in each other's wake, unless specially ordered;
and there is something difficult to understand in the "Niagara" with her
topsail sharp aback to keep from running on board the "Caledonia,"
although the fact is in evidence. The expression in Perry's report of the
action, "at 10 A.M. ... formed the line and bore up," would by a person
familiar with naval battles be understood to mean that the line was first
formed parallel to the enemy, the vessels following one another, after which

they steered down for him, changing course together; they would then no longer be in each other's wake, but in echelon, or as the naval phrase then went, in bow and quarter line. Barclay confirms this, "At 10 the enemy bore up under easy sail, in a line abreast."[91] Thus, when the distance desired by the commander-in-chief was reached,—a fact more often indicated by his example than by signal,—the helm would bring them again in line of battle, their broadsides bearing upon the enemy.

The technical point at issue is whether Perry, finding the long-gun fire of the "Detroit" more destructive than he had anticipated, and determining in consequence to shorten the period of its duration by changing his original plan, increasing sail beyond the speed of such slower vessels as the "Caledonia," had a right to expect that his subordinates would follow his example. In the opinion of the writer, he had, in the then condition of the theory and practice of fleet battles; his transfer of his own position transferred the line of battle in its entirety to the distance relative to the enemy which he himself was seeking to assume. Were other authority lacking, his action was warrant to his captains; but the expression in his report, "I made sail, and directed the other vessels to follow, for the purpose of closing with the enemy," causes increased regret that the exact facts were not ascertained by cross-examination before a Court-Martial.

Elliott's place therefore was alongside the "Queen Charlotte," so to engage her that she could attend to nothing else. This he did not do, and for failure the only possible excuse was inability, through lack of wind. The wind was light throughout, yet not so light but that the "Lawrence" closed with the "Detroit," and the "Queen Charlotte" with her flagship when she wished. None of Elliott's witnesses before the Court of Inquiry state that he made sail before the middle of the action, but they attribute the failure to get down to the lightness of the wind. They do state that, after the "Lawrence" was disabled, a breeze springing up, sail was made; which indicates that previously it had not been. Again, it is alleged by the testimony in favor of Elliott that much of the time the maintopsail was sharp aback, to keep from running into the "Caledonia;" a circumstance upon which Cooper dwells triumphantly, as showing that the "Niagara" was not by the wind and was in her place, close astern of the "Caledonia." Accepting the statements, they would show there was wind enough to fan the "Niagara" to—what was really her place—her commodore's aid; for in those days the distance between under fire and out of fire for efficient action was a matter of half a mile.[92] Perry's formulated charge, addressed to the Navy Department, and notified to Elliott, but never brought to trial, was that when coming into action an order was passed by trumpet for the vessels astern to close up in the line; that a few moments previously to the enemy's opening fire the "Niagara" had been within hail of the "Lawrence," and nevertheless she was allowed to drop astern, and for two hours to remain at such distance from the enemy as to render useless all her battery except the two long guns. Perry himself made sail at the time the hail by trumpet was passed. The "Niagara" did not.

There is little reason for doubt that the tenor of Perry's instructions required Elliott to follow the "Queen Charlotte," and no doubt whatever that military propriety imperiously demanded it of him. The question of wind must be matter of inference from the incidents above stated: the movement of the "Lawrence" and "Queen Charlotte," and the bracing aback of the "Niagara's" topsail. A sentence in Perry's report apparently, but only apparently, attenuates the force of these. He said, "At half-past two, the wind springing up, Captain Elliott was enabled to bring his vessel, the 'Niagara,' gallantly into close action." Alluding to, without insisting on, Perry's subsequent statement that he endeavored to give as favorable a color as possible to Elliott's course, it is clear enough that these words simply state that Captain Elliott at 2.30 reached the range at which the "Lawrence" had fought since a little after noon.

Quitting now the discussion of proprieties, the order of events seems to have been as follows: Perry having taken the initiative of bearing down, under increased sail, Elliott remained behind, governed by, or availing himself of—two very different motives, not lightly to be determined, or assumed, by the historian—the technical point, long before abandoned in practice, that he could not leave his place in the line without a signal. Thus his action was controlled by the position of his next ahead in the line, the dull-sailing "Caledonia," a vessel differing radically from his own in armament, having two long and for that day heavy guns, quite equal in range and efficiency to the best of the "Detroit's,"[93] and therefore capable of good service, though possibly not of their best, from the distance at which Perry changed his speed. Elliott's battery was the same as Perry's. He thus continued until it became evident that, the "Queen Charlotte" having gone to the support of the "Detroit," the "Lawrence" was heavily overpowered. Then, not earlier than an hour after Perry bore down, he realized that his commander-in-chief would be destroyed under his eyes, unless he went to his support, and he himself would rest under the imputation of an inefficient spectator. He ordered the "Caledonia" to bear up, in order that he might pass (position 3; C1, C2). Though not demonstrably certain, it seems probable that the wind, light throughout, was now so fallen as to impede the retrieval of his position; the opportunity to close, used by Perry, had passed away. At all events it was not till between 2 and 2.30 that the "Niagara" arrived on the scene, within effective range of the carronades which constituted nine tenths of her battery.

With this began the second stage of the battle (3). Perry's bearing down, receiving only the support of the long guns of the "Caledonia" and of the schooners ahead of him, had brought the "Lawrence" into hot engagement with the "Detroit," supported a half hour later by the "Queen Charlotte." By a little after two o'clock both flagships were well-nigh disabled, hull and battery; the "Lawrence" most so, having but one gun left out of ten on the broadside. "At 2.30," wrote Barclay, "the Detroit was a perfect wreck, principally from the raking fire of the gunboats." Which gunboats? Evidently the "Ariel" and "Scorpion," for all agree that the rear four were at this hour still far astern, though not absolutely out of range. To these last was probably due the crippling of the "Lady Prevost," which by now had gone to leeward with her rudder injured. Up to this time, when the first scene closed, what had been the general course of the action? and what now the situation? Assuming, as is very probable, that Barclay did not open with his long 24's until Perry was a mile, two thousand yards, from him,—that distance requiring six degrees elevation for those guns,—an estimate of speeds and courses, as indicated by the evidence, would put the "Lawrence" in action, at two hundred and fifty yards, at 12.10. This calculation, made independently, received subsequent confirmation in consulting Barclay's report, which says 12.15.[94] The same time, for the duller "Caledonia" and the "Niagara," would place them one thousand yards from the British line. This range, for the 32-pounder carronades of the "Niagara," and the 24's of the "Queen Charlotte," required an elevation of from four to six degrees. Coupling this with the British statement, that the carronades of the "Charlotte" could not reach the "Niagara," we obtain probable positions, two hundred and fifty yards and one thousand yards, for the principal two American vessels at quarter-past noon.

From the general lightness and occasional failure of the wind up to 2 P.M., it is more than likely that no great change took place before that hour. What air there was might touch all alike, but would affect least the "Lawrence," "Detroit," and "Queen Charlotte," because their sails were being rent; and also they were in the centre of the cannonade, which is believed usually to kill the breeze. The tendency of the "Caledonia," "Niagara," and American vessels in rear of them, between 12.30 and 2 P.M., during which period, to use Barclay's report, "the action continued with great fury," would therefore be to approach slowly the scene where the "Lawrence," supported by the long guns of the "Ariel," "Scorpion," and "Caledonia," maintained the day against the "Detroit" and "Queen Charlotte," backed by the schooner "Chippewa" and the 6 and 4 pounder pop-guns of the "Hunter." How near they drew is a mere matter of estimate. Taking all together, it may be inferred that the "Niagara" had then been carried as close as five hundred to six hundred yards to the British line, but it would appear also towards its rear; rather, probably, that the British had advanced relatively to her, owing to her course being oblique to theirs.

The situation then was as follows: The "Lawrence," disabled, was dropping astern of the "Detroit," "Queen Charlotte," and "Hunter." More than half her ship's company lay dead or wounded on her decks. Her loss, 83 killed and wounded out of a total of 142,—sick included,[95]—was mostly incurred before this. With only one gun left, she was a beaten ship, although her colors were up. The "Detroit" lay in the British line almost equally mauled. On her lee quarter,—that is, behind, but on the lee side,— and close to her, was the "Queen Charlotte." Her captain, second to Barclay, had been killed,—the first man hit on board,—and her first lieutenant knocked senseless; being succeeded in command by an officer whom Barclay described as of little experience. The first lieutenant of the "Detroit" was also wounded mortally; and Barclay himself, who already had been once hit in the thigh, was now a second time so severely injured,— being his eighth wound in battle, though now only thirty-two,—that he was forced at this critical instant to go below, leaving the deck with the second lieutenant. The "Hunter" was astern of her two consorts. The "Lady Prevost," fifth in the British order, had fallen to leeward with her rudder crippled. The position of the leading and rear British schooners is not mentioned, and is not important; the reliance of each being one long 9-pounder gun.

Before this, taking advantage of the breeze freshening, the "Niagara" had gone clear of the "Caledonia," on her windward side, and had stood to the southwest, towards the "Detroit." She had not at first either foresail or topgallantsails set; and since she passed the "Lawrence" to windward, she was then almost certainly over two hundred and fifty yards from the British line, for there is no conclusive proof that the "Lawrence" was nearer than that. Combining the narrative of the British commodore with that of his second lieutenant, who now took charge, it appears that Barclay, before going below, saw a boat passing from the "Lawrence" to the "Niagara," and that the second lieutenant, Inglis, after relieving him, found the "Niagara" on the weather beam of the "Detroit." Perry, seeing the "Lawrence" incapable of further offensive action, had decided to leave her and go on board the "Niagara," and in this brief interval was making his passage from one vessel to the other. After leaving the "Lawrence" astern, the "Niagara" had made sail; the foresail having been set, and the topgallantsails "in the act of being set, before Captain Perry came on board."[96] This necessarily prolonged the time of his passage, and may have given rise to the opprobrious British report that she was making off. Her making sail as she did indicated that she had suffered little aloft; she had been out of carronade range, while her consort, still in fighting condition, was bearing the brunt; it was natural to conclude that she would not alone renew the action, now that the "Lawrence" was hopelessly disabled. The wish, too, may possibly have helped the thought. The "Lawrence," in fact, having kept her colors flying till Perry reached the "Niagara," struck immediately afterwards. Had she surrendered while he was on board, he could not honorably have quitted her; and the record was clearer by his reaching a fresh ship while the flag of the one he left was still up.

What next happened is under no doubt so far as the movements of the "Niagara" are concerned, though there is irreconcilable difference as to who initiated the action. Immediately after Perry came on board, Elliott left her, to urge forward the rear gunboats. Her helm was put up, and she bore down ahead of the "Detroit" to rake her; supported in so doing by the small vessels, presumably the "Ariel," "Scorpion," and "Caledonia." The British ship tried to wear, both to avoid being raked and to get her starboard battery into action; many of the guns on the broadside heretofore engaged being disabled. The "Charlotte" being on her lee quarter, and ranging ahead, the two fell foul, and so remained for some time. This condition gave free play to the American guns, which were soon after re-enforced by those of the rear gunboats; enabled, like the "Niagara," to close with the freshening breeze. After the two British vessels got clear, another attempt was made to bring their batteries to bear; but the end was inevitable, and is best told in the words of the officer upon whom devolved the duty of surrendering the "Detroit." "The ship lying completely unmanageable, every brace cut away, the mizzen-topmast and gaff down, all the other masts badly wounded, not a stay left forward, hull shattered very much, a number of guns disabled, and the enemy's squadron raking both ships ahead and astern, none of our own in a position to support us, I was under the painful necessity of answering the enemy to say we had struck, the 'Queen Charlotte' having previously done so."[97] A Canadian officer taken prisoner at the battle of the Thames saw the "Detroit," a month later, at Put-in Bay. "It would be impossible," he wrote, "to place a hand upon that broadside which had been exposed to the enemy's fire without covering some portion of a wound, either from grape, round, canister, or chain shot."[98] Her loss in men was never specifically given. Barclay reported that of the squadron as a whole to be forty-one killed, ninety-four wounded. He had lost an arm at Trafalgar; and on this occasion, besides other injuries, the one remaining to him was so shattered as to be still in bandages a year later, when he appeared before the Court Martial which emphatically acquitted him of blame. The loss of the American squadron was twenty-seven killed, ninety-six wounded; of whom twenty-two killed and sixty-one wounded were on board the "Lawrence."

Thus was the battle of Lake Erie fought and won. Captain Barclay not only had borne himself gallantly and tenaciously against a superior force,— favored in so doing by the enemy attacking in detail,—but the testimony on his trial showed that he had labored diligently during the brief period of his command, amid surroundings of extreme difficulty, to equip his squadron, and to train to discipline and efficiency the heterogeneous material of which his crews were composed. The only point not satisfactorily covered is his absence when Perry was crossing the bar. In his defence his allusion to this incident is very casual,—resembles somewhat gliding rapidly over thin ice; but the Court raised no question, satisfied, probably, with the certainty that the honor of the flag had not suffered in the action. On the American side, since the history of a country is not merely the narrative of principal transactions, but the record also of honor reflected upon the nation by the distinguished men it produces, it is proper to consider the question of credit, which has been raised in this instance. There can be no doubt that opportunity must be seized as it is offered; for accident or chance may prevent its recurrence. Constituted as Perry's squadron was, the opportunity presented to him could be seized only by standing down as he did, trusting that the other vessels would follow the example of their commander. The shifting of the wind in the morning, and its failure during the engagement, alike testify to the urgency of taking the tide as it serves. There was no lagging, like Chauncey's, to fetch up heavy schooners; and the campaign was decided in a month, instead of remaining at the end of three months a drawn contest, to lapse thenceforth into a race of ship-building. Had the "Niagara" followed closely, there could have been no doubling on the "Lawrence"; and Perry's confidence would have been justified as well as his conduct. The latter needs no apology. Without the help of the "Niagara," the "Detroit" was reduced to a "defenceless state," and a "perfect wreck,"[99] by the carronades of the "Lawrence," supported by the raking fire of the "Ariel" and "Scorpion." Both the expressions quoted are applied by the heroic Barclay to her condition at 2.30, when, as he also says, the "Niagara" was perfectly fresh. Not only was the "Detroit" thus put out of action, but the "Charlotte" was so damaged that she surrendered before her. To this the "Caledonia's" two long twenty-fours had contributed effectively. The first lieutenant of the "Queen Charlotte" testified that up to the time he was disabled, an hour or an hour and a quarter after the action began, the vessel was still manageable; that "the 'Niagara' engaged us on our quarter, out of carronade range, with what long guns she had; but our principal injury was from the 'Caledonia,' who laid on our beam, with two long 24-pounders on pivots, also out of carronade-shot distance."[100]

Is it to Perry, or to Elliott, that is due the credit of the "Niagara's" action in bearing up across the bows of the "Detroit"? This is the second stage of the battle; the bringing up the reserves. An absolute reply is impossible in the face of the evidence, sworn but not cross-examined. A probable inference, which in the present writer amounts to conviction, is attainable. Before the Court of Inquiry, in 1815, Captain Elliott put the question to several of his witnesses, "Was not the 'Niagara's' helm up and she standing direct for the 'Detroit' when Captain Perry came on board?" They replied, "Yes." All these were midshipmen. By a singular fatality most of the "Niagara's" responsible officers were already dead, and the one surviving lieutenant had been below, stunned, when Perry reached the deck. It may very possibly be that this answer applied only to the first change of course, when Elliott decided to leave his position behind the "Caledonia"; but if it is claimed as covering also the subsequent bearing up eight points (at right angles), to cross the bows of the "Detroit," it is to be observed that no mention of this very important movement is made in a letter addressed to the Secretary of the Navy, October 13, 1813, one month after the battle, drawn up for the express purpose of vindicating Elliott, and signed by all the lieutenants of the "Niagara," and by the purser, who formerly had been a lieutenant in the navy. Their account was that Perry, on reaching the ship, said he feared the day was lost; that Elliott replied it was not, that he would repair on board the rear schooners, and bring them up; that he did so, and "the consequence was that in ten minutes the 'Detroit' and 'Queen Charlotte' with the 'Lady Prevost,' struck to us, and soon after the whole of the enemy's squadron followed their example."[101] This attributes the victory to the half-dozen long guns of the four schooners, mostly inferior in caliber to the nine carronades on board a single vessel, the "Niagara," raking within pistol-shot of antagonists already in the condition described by Barclay. Such a conclusion traverses all experience of the tactical advantage of guns massed under one captain over a like number distributed in several commands, and also contravenes the particular superiority of carronades at close quarters. An officer of the "Detroit," who was on deck throughout, testified that the "Lawrence" had engaged at musket-shot, the "Niagara," when she bore down under Perry, at pistol-shot. Barclay, and his surviving lieutenant, Inglis, both lay most weight upon this action of the "Niagara," from which arose also the fouling of the two largest British ships.

Perry's charges of 1818 against Elliott formulated deliberate statements, under the responsible expectation of cross-examination under oath. This is his account: "When the commanding officer went on board the 'Niagara,' Captain Elliott was keeping her on a course by the wind, which would in a few minutes have carried said vessel entirely out of action, to prevent which, and in order to bring the said vessel into close action with the enemy, the said commanding officer was under the necessity of heaving-to, stopping and immediately wearing said vessel, and altering her course at least eight points"; that is, perpendicular to the direction before steered. Against this solemn and serious charge is unquestionably to be placed the commendatory mention and letter given by Perry to Elliott immediately after the battle. Upon these also he had to expect the sharpest interrogation, to the mortification attendant upon which he could only oppose evidence extenuative of, but in no case justifying, undeniable self-contradiction. If the formal charge was true, no excuse can be admitted for the previous explicit commendation. As a matter of historical inquiry, however, such contradictions have to be met, and must be weighed in the light of all the testimony. The author's conclusion upon the whole is that, as Perry's action in first standing down insured decisive action, so by him was imparted to the "Niagara" the final direction which determined victory. The influence of the rear gunboats brought up by Elliott was contributive, but not decisive. In short, the campaign of Lake Erie was brought to an immediate successful issue by the ready initiative taken by Perry when he found the British distant fire more destructive than he expected, and by his instant acceptance of necessary risk, in standing down exposed to a raking cannonade to which he for a long while could not reply. If, as the author holds, he was entitled to expect prompt imitation by the "Niagara," the risk was actual, but not undue. As it was, though the "Lawrence" surrendered, it was not until she had, with the help of gunboats stationed by Perry for that object, so damaged both her opponents that they were incapable of further resistance. In the tactical management of the "Lawrence" and her supports was no mere headlong dash, but preparation adequate to conditions. Had the "Niagara" followed, the "Lawrence" [99]need never have struck. The contemporary incidents on Erie and Ontario afford an instructive commentary upon Napoleon's incisive irony, that "War cannot be waged without running risks." There has been sufficient quotation from Chauncey to indicate why the campaign on Ontario dragged through two seasons, and then left the enemy in control. Small as the scale and the theatre of these naval operations, they illustrate the unvarying lesson that only in offensive action can defensive security be found.

The destruction of the British naval force decided the campaign in the Northwest by transferring the control of the water. Its general military results were in this respect final. Nothing occurred to modify them during the rest of the war. Detroit and Michigan territory fell back into the hands of the United States; and the allegiance of the Indians to the British cause, procured by Brock's sagacious daring a twelvemonth before, but rudely shaken by the events narrated, was destroyed by the death of their great leader, Tecumseh, a month later in the battle of the Thames, itself the direct consequence of Perry's success. The frontier was henceforth free from the Indian terror, which had hitherto disquieted it from the Maumee to Cleveland.

A more far-reaching political issue was also here definitely settled. A sense of having betrayed the Indian interests in the previous treaties of 1783 and 1794 was prevalent in British official circles, and in their counsels a scheme had been circulated for constituting an independent Indian territory, under joint guarantee of the two nations, between their several dominions. This would be locally within the boundaries of the United States; the sole jurisdiction of which was thus to be limited and trammelled, because open to continual British representation and reclamation, based upon treaty stipulations.[102] This infringement upon the perfect sovereignty of the nation inside its own borders, in favor of savage communities and under foreign guarantee, was one of the propositions formally brought forward as a sine quâ non by the British negotiators at Ghent. Although by that time the United States stood alone face to face with Great Britain, at whose full disposal were now the veterans of the Peninsular War, and the gigantic navy, which the abdication of Napoleon had released from all other opponents, the American commissioners refused with dignity to receive the proposition even for reference. "It is not necessary," they replied, "to refer such demands to the American Government for its instructions. They will only be a fit subject for deliberation when it becomes necessary to decide upon the expediency of an absolute surrender of national independence."[103]

The envoys of the United States were able to be firm, because secure of indignant support by their people; but it is beyond question that two naval victories had arrayed upon their side, at the moment, the preponderance of military argument, which weighs so heavily in treaties of peace. New Orleans was yet in the future, with adverse chances apparent; but, owing to the victory of Perry, the United States was in firm military tenure of the territory, the virtual cession of which was thus demanded. A year after Perry, McDonough's equally complete success on Lake Champlain, by insuring control of the water route for invasion, rolled back the army of Peninsular veterans under Prevost, at a season of the year which forbade all hope of renewing the enterprise until another spring. Great Britain was too eager to end twenty years of continued war to brook further delay. The lake campaigns of 1813 and 1814 thus emphasized the teaching of history as to the influence of control of the water upon the course of events; and they illustrate also the too often forgotten truth, that it is not by brilliant individual feats of gallantry or skill, by ships or men, but by the massing of superior forces, that military issues are decided. For, although on a small scale, the lakes were oceans, and the forces which met on them were fleets; and as, on a wider field and in more tremendous issues, the fleets of Great Britain saved their country and determined the fortunes of Europe, so Perry and McDonough averted from the United States, without further fighting, a rectification of frontier—as it is euphemistically styled,—the effecting of which is one of the most fruitful causes and frequent results of war in every continent and at every period.

Note.—For the battle of Lake Erie, the most important original data are the Court Martial upon Barclay (British Records Office), and the Court of Inquiry held at Elliott's request, in April, 1815. The proceedings and testimony of the latter are published in the appendix to a "Biographical Notice of Commodore Jesse D. Elliott," by Russell Jarvis, Philadelphia, 1835. Perry's Report of the battle, Sept. 13, 1813, is in American State Papers, Naval Affairs, vol. i. p. 295. Barclay's report is in Naval Chronicle, vol. xxxi. pp. 250-253, as well as in the record of the Court. Jarvis, and Mackenzie's Life of Perry (5th edition), give a large number of affidavits by officers present in the engagement, and Mackenzie gives also a copy of the charges preferred by Perry in 1818 against Elliott. In the controversy which arose over the battle, Mackenzie, in the appendix to the fifth edition of Perry's Life, Duer, and Tristam Burges, Battle of Lake Erie (Boston, 1839), are the principal champions on Perry's side; Jarvis (as above) and J. Fenimore Cooper, Battle of Lake Erie, on the side of Elliott; but the latter himself published several vindications of his conduct. The usual naval histories, American and British, may be consulted, and there are also incidental mentions and reports in Niles' Register and the British Naval Chronicle, which will be found useful.

FOOTNOTES:

[74] Captains' Letters, Navy Department MSS.
[75] Mackenzie's Life of Perry, vol. i. p. 166.
[76] Mackenzie's Life of Perry, vol. i. p. 186.
[77] Perry to the Secretary of the Navy, Aug. 10, 1813. Mackenzie's Life of Perry, vol. i. p. 191.
[78] Secretary's Letters, Aug. 18, 1813. Navy Department MSS.
[79] Otherwise known by the name of the River Raisin. Ante, vol. i. p. 370.
[80] The data of this paragraph are taken from the Report on Canadian Archives, 1896, Lower Canada, pp. 132, 138-140. Barclay in his Defence before the Court Martial mentions the designs on Erie.
[81] Harm Jan Huidekoper, by Nina Moore Tiffany and Francis Tiffany. 1904. p. 187. Mr. Huidekoper speaks admiringly of the unfaltering composure and cheerfulness which under these circumstances accompanied Perry's energy.
[82] See ante, p. 41.
[83] Report on Canadian Archives, 1896. Lower Canada, p. 133.
[84] This statement appeared in the course of a summary of the evidence before the British Court, given by the Naval Chronicle, vol. xxxii. pp. 241-242. The only support to it in the evidence, as recorded, is Barclay's official letter, which he appears to have confirmed under oath, that the "Niagara" kept out of carronade range, and "was perfectly fresh at 2.30," when Perry went on board her. The first lieutenant of the "Queen Charlotte," who remained in command, the captain being killed, corroborated Barclay as to her distance.
[85] In the finding—or verdict—of the British Court, as in the evidence, there is no expression of a charge that the "Niagara" was making away. The finding restricted itself to the matter before the Court, namely, Barclay's official conduct.

[86] There was a question whether the "Hunter" was ahead or astern of the "Queen Charlotte." In the author's opinion the balance of evidence is as stated in the text. Perry rearranged his line with reference to the British, upon seeing their array. Had the "Charlotte" been next the "Detroit," as James puts her, it seems probable he would have placed the "Niagara" next the "Lawrence."

[87] Cooper, Battle of Lake Erie, p. 63.

[88] See Mackenzie's Life of Perry, 5th edition, vol. ii. pp. 251-252. Perry's charges against Elliott, dated Aug. 8, 1818, are there given in full.

[89] See Mackenzie's Life of Perry, 5th edition, vol. ii. pp. 251-252.

[90] Cooper's Battle of Lake Erie, p. 63.

[91] Barclay's Report, Naval Chronicle, vol. xxxi. p. 251.

[92] The range of a 32 pdr. carronade, with which the "Niagara" was armed, throwing one solid shot, with ¼ degree elevation,—substantially point-blank,—was 260 yards; at 5 degrees, 1260 yards. The difference, 1000 yards, is just half a sea mile. A British professional writer of that day, criticising their commander's choice of position at Lake Champlain, says: "At 1000 or 1100 yards the elevation necessary to be given a carronade would have been so great that none but chance shots [from the Americans] could have taken effect; whereas, in closing, he gave up this advantage." Naval Chronicle, vol. xxxiii. p. 132.

[93] The "Caledonia" had two long 24-pounders, and one other lighter gun, variously stated. The "Detroit's" heaviest were also two long 24's; she had besides one long 18, six long 12's, etc.

[94] With reference to times, always very difficult to establish, and often very important as bases of calculation, the following extract from the Diary of Dr. Usher Parsons, surgeon of the "Lawrence," possesses value; the more so as it is believed to have been copied from the log of the vessel, which afterwards disappeared. The phraseology is that of a log and a seaman, not of a physician. "At 10 called all hands to quarters. A quarter before meridian the enemy began action at one mile distance. In a half hour came within musket-shot of the enemy's new ship.... At 1.30, so entirely disabled we could work the brig no longer. At 2 P.M., most of the guns were dismounted, breechings gone, or carriages knocked to pieces. At half-past two, when not another gun could be worked or fired, Captain Perry hauled down the fighting flag [not the national flag], which bore this motto 'Don't give up the ship,' and repaired on board the 'Niagara,' where he raised it again. In ten minutes after we struck." Publications of the Rhode Island Historical Society, vol. vii. p. 244. This was called to the author's attention after the account in the text was written.

[95] Mackenzie's Life of Perry, vol. ii. p. 283.

[96] Evidence of Midshipman Montgomery of the "Niagara," before the Court of Inquiry.

[97] Naval Chronicle, vol. xxxi. p. 252.

[98] Richardson, War of 1812, p. 243.

[99] Barclay's Report.

[100] British Court Martial Record.

[101] Navy Department, MSS. Miscellaneous Letters. My italics.

[102] This scheme appears outlined in a letter of Oct. 5, 1812, to Lord Bathurst from Sir George Prevost, who in support of it adduces Brock's opinion (Canadian Archives MSS). Bathurst replied, Dec. 9, 1812, "I so entirely concur in the expediency of the suggestions contained in your despatch, as to the necessity of securing the territories of the Indians from encroachment, that I have submitted it to His Majesty's Secretary for Foreign Affairs, in order that whenever negotiations for peace may be entered into, the security of their possessions may not be either compromised or forgotten." (British Colonial Office Records). Prevost transmitted a copy of the letter to Admiral Warren, in his early diplomatic capacity as a peace envoy. Gordon Drummond, the successor of Brock, and later of Prevost, expressed the same interest (Canadian Archives MSS., April 2, 1814).

[103] American State Papers, Foreign Affairs, vol. iii. pp. 710-713.

THE CAMPAIGN OF 1813 ON THE LAKES AND NORTHERN FRONTIER

After The Battle Of Lake Erie

Perry's victory was promptly followed up by himself and Harrison. Besides its ultimate influence on the general course of events, already mentioned, it produced immediate military consequences, the effect of which was felt throughout the lake frontier, from Detroit to Champlain. That success elsewhere did not follow was due to other causes than remissness on their part to improve the occasion. Although the "Lawrence" had to be sent back to Erie for extensive repairs, and the "Detroit" and "Queen Charlotte" rolled their masts overboard at anchor in Put-in Bay on the third day after the battle, Perry within a week had his squadron and four of the prizes sufficiently in repair to undertake the transport of the army. This timely facility, which betrayed the enemy's expectations, was due largely to the "Lawrence" having borne the brunt of the action. Had the injuries been more distributed, the delay of repairs must have been greater. The British Adjutant General at Niagara, Harvey, the hero of Stoney Creek, wrote on hearing of the battle, "After an action of three hours and a half, the enemy's vessels must have received so much damage as not to be in a situation to undertake anything for some time."[104] By September 26 Harrison had assembled his forces at an island in the lake, called Middle Sister, twelve miles from Malden. On the 27th they were conveyed to Malden, partly in vessels and partly in boats, the weather being fine. By September 30 Sandwich and Detroit were occupied; Procter retreating eastward up the valley of the Thames. Harrison pursued, and on October 5 overtook the British and Indians at a settlement called Moravian Town. Here they made a stand and were defeated, with the destruction or dispersal of the entire body, in an action known to Americans as the battle of the Thames. Procter himself, with some two hundred men, fled eastward and reached the lines at Burlington Heights, at the head of Ontario, whither Vincent had again retreated on October 9, immediately upon receiving news of the disaster at Moravian Town.

After this the Western Indians fell wholly away from the British alliance, and Harrison returned to Detroit, satisfied that it was useless to pursue the enemy by land. The season was thought now too far advanced for operations against Michilimackinac, which was believed also to be so effectually isolated, by the tenure of Lake Erie, as to prevent its receiving supplies. This was a mistake, there being a route, practicable though difficult, from Toronto to Georgian Bay, on Lake Huron, by which necessary stores were hurried through before the winter closed in. Mackinac remained in British hands to the end of the war.

At Detroit Harrison and Perry received orders to transport a body of troops down Lake Erie, to re-enforce the army on the general scene of operations centring round Lake Ontario. By the control of the Niagara peninsula, consequent upon Vincent's necessary retreat after the battle of the Thames, the American communications were complete and secure throughout from Detroit to Sackett's Harbor, permitting free movement from end to end. The two officers embarked together, taking with them thirteen hundred men in seven vessels. October 24 they reached Buffalo. Harrison went on to Niagara, but Perry was here detached from the lake service, and returned to the seaboard, leaving Elliott to command on Erie. In acknowledging the order for Perry's removal, Chauncey regretted the granting of his application as a bad precedent; and further took occasion to remark that when he himself was sent to the lakes the only vessel on them owned by the United States was the brig "Oneida." "Since then two fleets have been created, one of which has covered itself with glory: the other, though less fortunate, has not been less industrious." It may be questioned whether the evident difference of achievement was to be charged to fortune, or to relative quickness to seize opportunity, when offered.

The successes on Lake Erie had come very appositely for a change recently introduced into the plans of the Government, and then in process of accomplishment. Since the middle of the summer the Secretary of War, Armstrong, who at this time guided the military counsels, had become disgusted by the fruitlessness of the movements at the west end of Ontario, and had reverted to his earlier and sounder prepossession in favor of an attack upon either Kingston or Montreal. It had now been for some time in contemplation to transfer to Sackett's Harbor all the troops that could be spared from Niagara, leaving there only sufficient to hold Fort George, with Fort Niagara on the American side, as supports to a defensive attitude upon that frontier. Assured command of the lake was essential to the safety and rapidity of the concentration at Sackett's, and this led to the next meeting of the squadrons.

General James Wilkinson, an officer advanced in years, of extremely poor reputation, personal as well as professional, and of broken constitution, had been either selected by, or forced upon,[105] the Secretary of War to replace Dearborn in command of the New York frontier and conduct of the proposed operations. To his suggested doubts as to the direction of effort, whether westward or eastward, Armstrong had replied definitely and finally on August 8: "Operations westward of Kingston, if successful, leave the strength of the enemy unbroken. It is the great depot of his resources. So long as he retains this, and keeps open his communication with the sea, he will not want the means of multiplying his naval and other defences, and of re-enforcing or renewing the war in the West." He then explained that there were two ways of reducing the place; by direct attack, or, indirectly, by cutting its communications with the lower river. To accomplish the latter, a demonstration of direct attack should be made by part of the troops, while the main body should move rapidly down the St. Lawrence to Madrid (or Hamilton),[106] in New York, and cross there to the Canadian side, seizing and fortifying a bluff on the north bank to control the road and river. This done, the rest of the force should march upon Montreal. The army division on Champlain was to co-operate by a simultaneous movement and subsequent junction. The project, in general outline, had been approved by the President. In transmitting it Armstrong wrote to Wilkinson, "After this exposition, it is unnecessary to add, that, in conducting the present campaign, you will make Kingston your primary object, and that you will choose (as circumstances may warrant), between a direct and indirect attack upon that post."[107]

Contemporary and subsequent movements are to be regarded in their bearing on this plan. The first object was the concentration at Sackett's, for which some three thousand troops were to be withdrawn from the Niagara frontier. Wilkinson arrived at Sackett's from Washington, August 20. Chauncey was then in port, after the gale which had driven both him and Yeo down the lake. He sailed on the 29th. Wilkinson followed shortly, reaching Fort George September 4. On the 5th, Armstrong himself came to Sackett's, having established the War Department in northern New York for the campaign. On the 10th Perry destroyed the British squadron on Lake Erie, opening the way for Harrison's victorious entry to Upper Canada and subsequent transfer to Niagara.

Some days before the battle of the Thames the embarkation from Niagara for Sackett's Harbor took place under cover of the naval operations. After Yeo had gone into Amherst Bay on September 12, as already mentioned,[108] Chauncey remained cruising in the neighborhood till the

17th, when he went to Sackett's, the enemy having got into Kingston. On the 19th he sailed again for Niagara, to support the movement of the army. He arrived on the 24th, and found there a report of Perry's victory, which had been received on the 22d. On the 25th embarkation began, and Wilkinson hoped that the whole body, three thousand strong, would start on their coasting voyage along the south shore of the lake on the 27th; but after dark, to conceal the direction taken. At this juncture, on September 26, Chauncey heard that the British fleet was at York, which was confirmed by a lookout vessel despatched by him. As Yeo, unless checked, might molest the transportation of the troops, it became necessary first to seek him; but owing to a head wind the American squadron could not leave the river till the evening of the 27th.

As the schooner gun-vessels sailed badly, the "Pike," the "Madison," and the "Sylph" each took one in tow on the morning of the 28th, steering for York, where the British fleet was soon after sighted. As the Americans stood in, the British quitted the bay to gain the open lake; for their better manœuvring powers as a squadron would have scope clear of the land. They formed on the port tack, running south with the wind fresh at east (Positions 1). When about three miles distant, to windward, Chauncey put his fleet on the same tack as the enemy and edged down towards him (Positions 2). At ten minutes past noon, the Americans threatening to cut off the rearmost two of the British, Yeo tacked his column in succession, beginning with his own ship, the leader (a), heading north toward his endangered vessels, between them and the opponents. When round, he opened fire on the "General Pike." As this movement, if continued, would bring the leading and strongest British ships upon the weaker Americans astern, Chauncey put his helm up and steered for the "Wolfe" (b), as soon as the "General Pike" came abreast of her; the American column following in his wake. The "Wolfe" then kept away, and a sharp encounter followed between the two leaders, in which the rest of the squadrons took some share (Positions 3).

At the end of twenty minutes the "Wolfe" lost her main and mizzen topmasts, and main yard. With all her after sail gone, there was nothing to do but to keep before the wind, which was fair for the British posts at the head of the bay (Positions 4). The American squadron followed; but the "Madison," the next heaviest ship to the "Pike," superior in battery power to the "Wasp" and "Hornet" of the ocean navy, and substantially equal to the second British ship, the "Royal George," "having a heavy schooner in tow, prevented her commander from closing near enough to do any execution with her carronades."[109] The explanation requires explanation, which is not forthcoming. Concern at such instants for heavy schooners in tow is not the spirit in which battles are won or campaigns decided; and it must be admitted that Commodore Chauncey's solicitude to keep his schooners up with his real fighting vessels, to conform, at critical moments, the action of ships of eight hundred and six hundred tons, like the "Pike" and "Madison," to those of lake craft of under one hundred, is not creditable to his military instincts. He threw out a signal, true, for the fleet to make all sail; but as he held on to the schooner he had in tow, neither the "Madison" nor "Sylph" dropped hers. His flagship, individually, appears to have been well fought; but anxiety to keep a squadron united needs to be tempered with discretion of a kind somewhat more eager than the quality commonly thus named, and which on occasion can drop a schooner, or other small craft, in order to get at the enemy. As the dismasted "Wolfe" ran to leeward, "the 'Royal George,'" says the American naval historian Cooper, "luffed up in noble style across her stern to cover the English commodore" (c), and "kept yawing athwart her stern, delivering her broadsides in a manner to extort exclamations of delight from the American fleet (Positions 5). She was commanded by Captain Mulcaster." Her fighting mate, the "Madison," had a heavy schooner in tow. This interposition of the "Royal George" was especially timely if, as Yeo states, Chauncey was holding at a distance whence his long twenty-fours told, while the "Wolfe's" carronades did not reach.

At quarter before three Chauncey relinquished pursuit. Both squadrons were then about six miles from the head of the lake, running towards it before a wind which had increased to a gale, with a heavy sea. Ahead of them was a lee shore, and for the Americans a hostile coast. "Though we might succeed in driving him on shore, the probability was we should go on shore also, he amongst his friends, we amongst our enemies; and after the gale abated, if he could get off one or two vessels out of the two fleets, it would give him as completely the command of the lake as if he had twenty vessels. Moreover, he was covered at his anchorage by part of his army and several small batteries thrown up for the purpose." For these reasons, the commodore "without hesitation relinquished the opportunity then presenting itself of acquiring individual reputation at the expense of my country." The British squadron anchored without driving ashore. The American returned to Niagara, having received a certain amount of damage aloft, and one of the purchased schooners having lost her foremast; but the killed and wounded by the enemy amounted to only five, all on board the "General Pike." That vessel lost also twenty-two men by the bursting of a gun.

Chauncey had been in consultation with Armstrong at Sackett's, and understood perfectly the plans of the Government. On his return to Niagara he was requested by Wilkinson to keep watch over the hostile squadron in its present position under Burlington Heights, so as to cover the eastward movement of the troops, which began October 1. On the 2d the last transport had gone, and Wilkinson himself set out for Sackett's;

bringing, as he reported, thirty-five hundred men. On the 3d the British fleet was seen well towards the west end of the lake; but on the 4th a vessel sent especially to reconnoitre came back with the report that it was no longer there. This proved to be a mistake; but, as it came from a careful and competent officer, Chauncey inferred that the enemy had given him the slip and gone to the eastward. He therefore ran down the lake, to cover the arrival of the troops as he had their departure. On the afternoon of the 5th, near Kingston, he captured six out of seven transports bound thither with re-enforcements. Of these, two were the schooners taken by Yeo in the engagement of August 10, which the British had not thought fit to add to their fleet, but used simply as carriers; mounting their guns on the fortifications of Kingston. Cooper justly remarks, "This sufficiently proves the equivocal advantage enjoyed by the possession of these craft." Chauncey himself, at the end of the campaign, recommended the building of "one vessel of the size of the 'Sylph,'"—three hundred and forty tons,— "in lieu of all the heavy schooners; for really they are of no manner of service, except to carry troops or use as gunboats."[110] The reflection is inevitable,—Why, then, had he allowed them so to hamper his movements? It is to be feared that the long ascendency of the gunboat policy in the councils of the Government had sapped the professional intelligence even of some naval officers.

The capture of the detachment going from York to Kingston showed that the British had divined the general character of the American plans. In fact, as early as October 2, Major General de Rottenburg, who after an interval had succeeded to Brock's place in Upper Canada, as lieutenant governor and commander of the forces, had started with two regiments to re-enforce Kingston, leaving the Niagara peninsula again under the command of General Vincent. On October 6 Chauncey's squadron entered Sackett's, where Wilkinson had arrived on the 4th. The general began at once to remonstrate strenuously with Armstrong against an attempt upon Kingston, as delaying and possibly frustrating what he saw fit to style the chief object of the campaign, the capture of Montreal. The Secretary listened patiently, but overruled him.[111] Kingston had been the principal object from the beginning, and still so continued; but, if the garrison should be largely re-enforced, if the British fleet should enter the harbor, or if the weather should make navigation of the lake dangerous for the transports, then the troops should proceed direct for Montreal by the river. Yeo apparently returned to Kingston soon after this; but when Chauncey left port on October 16, to bring forward from the Genesee River a detachment under Colonel Winfield Scott, he still had the understanding that Kingston was first to be attacked.

On October 19, however, the Secretary reconsidered his decision. The concentration of the army at Sackett's had not been effected until the 18th.

On the 16th de Rottenburg, having coasted the north shore of the lake, reached Kingston with his two regiments, reckoned by Armstrong at fifteen hundred men. These raised to twenty-two hundred the garrison previously estimated at seven to eight hundred.[112] The numbers of the Americans were diminishing by sickness, and no further re-enforcement was to be expected, excepting by uniting with the Champlain division. This had been on the move from Plattsburg since September 19, and was now at Chateaugay, on the Chateaugay River; a local centre, whence roads running northeast, to the river's junction with the St. Lawrence, immediately opposite the island of Montreal, and west to St. Regis on the St. Lawrence, forty miles higher up, gave facilities for moving in either direction to meet Wilkinson's advance. By a letter of October 12 from its commander, General Wade Hampton, this corps numbered "four thousand effective infantry, with a well-appointed train." To bring it by land to Sackett's, over a hundred miles distant, was considered too protracted and laborious in the state of the roads; better utilize the current of the St. Lawrence to carry Wilkinson down to it. In view of these circumstances, and of the supposed increased strength of Kingston, Armstrong decided to abandon the attack upon the latter and to move against Montreal, which was believed to be much weaker, as well as strategically more important.[113] The movement was hazardous; for, as planned, ultimate success depended upon junction with another corps, which had natural difficulties of its own to contend with, while both were open to obstruction by an active enemy. As a distinguished military critic has said, "The Americans committed upon this occasion the same error that the British Government did in their plan for Burgoyne's march from the head of Champlain to Albany,—that of making the desired result of an important operation depend upon the success of all its constituent or component parts." It is one of the most common of blunders in war. Wilkinson and Hampton did not meet. Both moved, but one had retreated before the other arrived.

In fact, while Montreal, as the most important point in Canada for the British, except Quebec, and at the same time the one most accessible to the United States, was the true objective of the latter, concentration against it should have been made in territory entirely under American control, about Lake Champlain, and the advance begun early in the season. By its own choice the Government had relinquished this obvious and natural course, and throughout the summer had directed its efforts to the westward. When the change of operations from Niagara to the lower end of the lake was initiated, in the beginning of October, it was already too late to do more than attack Kingston, the strength of which appears to have been gravely over-estimated. Armstrong had good military ideas; but at this critical moment he seems to have faltered in the presence of an immediate difficulty, and to have sought escape from it by a hasty consent to a side measure, contrary to the soundest teachings of war.

Not the least of objections was the risk to which Sackett's Harbor, the naval base, was to be exposed. After October 16, Chauncey had remained cruising between there and Kingston, covering the approaches to the St. Lawrence. His intended trip to Genesee, to bring up Scott's eight hundred regulars, had been abandoned at the urgent demand of Wilkinson, who, while the troops were being transferred from Sackett's to Grenadier Island, at the outlet of the lake to the river, "would not allow any part of the fleet to be absent four days without throwing the responsibility, in case of a failure of his expedition, wholly on the navy."[114] The commodore did not learn of the new scheme until October 30, ten days after its adoption, when he was asked to cover the rear of the army from pursuit by water, by taking position inside the St. Lawrence. While objecting strongly to the change of plan, he of course consented to afford all the co-operation in his power; but he wrote to the Navy Department, "If Sir James Yeo knows the defenceless situation of Sackett's, he can take advantage of a westerly wind while I am in the river, run over and burn it; for to the best of my knowledge there are no troops left there except sick and invalids, nor are there more than three guns mounted."[115]

After many delays by rough water, Wilkinson's troops were assembled at Grenadier Island towards the end of October. On November 1 they began entering the river by detachments, collecting at French Creek, on the American side, fifteen miles from the lake. Being here immediately opposite one of the points considered suitable for advance on Kingston, the object of the movement remained still doubtful to the enemy. The detachments first arriving were cannonaded by four of Yeo's vessels that had come through the channel north of Long Island, which here divides the stream. On November 2 Chauncey anchored near by, preventing the recurrence of this annoyance. On the 4th the entire force was assembled, and next day started down the river with fine weather, which lasted until the 11th. Up to this date no serious difficulty was encountered; but immediately that the departure from French Creek proclaimed the real direction of the movement, de Rottenburg despatched a body of six hundred regular troops, under Lieutenant Colonel Morrison, accompanied by some gunboats under Captain Mulcaster, to harass the rear. For the purpose of being on hand to fall upon the American flotilla, should the attempt be made to cross the river to the north bank, Sir James Yeo on the 5th came out from Kingston with his fleet. He anchored on the north side of Long Island, only five miles from the American squadron, but separated by a reef, over which the "General Pike" could not pass without being lightened.[116] Steps were taken to effect this, and to buoy a channel; but on the 6th Yeo retired to Kingston. Chauncey's letters make no mention of Mulcaster's division, and after Yeo's withdrawal he moved down to Carleton Island.

Morrison and Mulcaster on the 8th reached Fort Wellington, opposite Ogdensburg. Here they paused and received re-enforcements from the garrison, raising their numbers to eight hundred, who continued to follow, by water and by land, until the 11th. Then they were turned upon by the rearguard of an American division, marching on the north bank to suppress the harassment to which the flotilla otherwise was liable in its advance. An action followed, known as that of Chrystler's Farm, in which the Americans were the assailants and in much superior numbers; but they were worsted and driven back, having lost one hundred and two killed and two hundred and thirty-seven wounded, besides one hundred prisoners. The troops engaged then embarked, and passed down the Long Saut Rapids to Cornwall, which is one hundred and twenty miles from Kingston and eighty-two from Montreal. Here they were rejoined on the 12th by the vanguard of the division, which had met little resistance in its progress.

At this time and place Wilkinson received a letter from General Hampton, to whom he had written that the provisions of his army were insufficient, and requested him to send "two or three months' supply by the safest route in a direction to the proposed scene of action."[117] He also instructed him to join the advance at St. Regis, opposite Cornwall, the point which had now been reached. As the two bodies were co-operating, and Wilkinson was senior, these instructions had the force of orders. In his reply, dated November 8,[118] Hampton said, "The idea of meeting at St. Regis was most pleasing, until I came to the disclosure of the amount of your supplies of provision." Actually, the disclosure about the supplies preceded in the letter the appointment to meet at St. Regis, which was the last subject mentioned. "It would be impossible," Hampton continued, "for me to bring more than each man could carry on his back; and when I reflected that, in throwing myself upon your scanty means, I should be weakening you in your most vulnerable point, I did not hesitate to adopt the opinion that by throwing myself back upon my main depot [Plattsburg], where all means of transportation had gone, and falling upon the enemy's flank, and straining every effort to open a communication from Plattsburg to ... the St. Lawrence, I should more effectually contribute to your success than by the junction at St. Regis."

Hampton then retired to Plattsburg, in the direction opposite from St. Regis. Wilkinson, upon receiving his letter, held a council of war and decided that "the attack on Montreal should be abandoned for the present season." The army accordingly crossed to the American side and went into winter quarters at French Mills, just within the New York boundary; on the Salmon River, which enters the St. Lawrence thirteen miles below St. Regis. Wilkinson was writing from there November 17, twelve days after he started from French Creek to capture Montreal. Thus two divisions, of eight thousand and four thousand respectively, both fell back helplessly, when within a few days of a junction which the enemy could not have prevented, even though he might successfully have opposed their joint attack upon Montreal. It is a delicate matter to judge the discretion of a general officer in Hampton's position; but the fact remains, as to provisions, that he was in a country where, by his own statement of a month before, "we have, and can have, an unlimited supply of good beef cattle."[119] A British commissary at Prescott wrote two months later, January 5, 1814, "Our supplies for sixteen hundred men are all drawn from the American side of the river. They drive droves of cattle from the interior under pretence of supplying their army at Salmon River, and so are allowed to pass the guards, and at night to cross them over to our side,"—the river being frozen. He adds, "I shall be also under the necessity of getting most of my flour from their side."[120] It is not necessary greatly to respect Wilkinson in order to think that in such a region Hampton might safely have waited for his superior to join, and to decide upon the movements of the whole. He was acting conjointly, and the junior.[121] Under all the circumstances there can be no reasonable doubt that his independent action was precipitate, unnecessary, contrary to orders, and therefore militarily culpable. It gave Wilkinson the excuse, probably much desired, for abruptly closing a campaign which had been ludicrously inefficient from the first, and under his leadership might well have ended in a manner even more mortifying.

Chauncey remained within the St. Lawrence until November 10, the day before the engagement at Chrystler's Farm. He was troubled with fears as to what might happen in his rear; the defenceless condition of Sackett's, and the possibility that the enemy by taking possession of Carleton Island, below him, might prevent the squadron's getting out.[122] None of these things occurred, and it would seem that the British had not force to attempt them. On the 11th the squadron returned to the Harbor, where was found a letter from Armstrong, requesting conveyance to Sackett's for the brigade of Harrison's army, which Perry had brought to Niagara, and which the Secretary destined to replace the garrison gone down stream with Wilkinson. The execution of this service closed the naval operations on Ontario for the year 1813. On November 21 Chauncey wrote that he had transported Harrison with eleven hundred troops. On the night of December 2 the harbor froze over, and a few days later the commodore learned that Yeo had laid up his ships for the winter.

There remains yet to tell the close of the campaign upon the Niagara peninsula, control of which had been a leading motive in the opening operations. Its disastrous ending supplies a vivid illustration of the military truth that positions are in themselves of but little value, if the organized forces of the enemy, armies or fleets, remain unimpaired. The regular troops were all withdrawn for Wilkinson's expedition; the last to go being the garrison of Fort George, eight hundred men under Colonel Winfield Scott, which left on October 13. The command of the frontier was turned over to Brigadier General George M'Clure of the New York Militia. Scott reported that Fort George, "as a field work, might be considered as complete at that period. It was garnished with ten pieces of artillery, which number might have been increased from the spare ordnance of the opposite fort"[123]—Niagara. The latter, on the American side, was garrisoned by two companies of regular artillery and "such of M'Clure's brigade as had refused to cross the river."

It was immediately before Scott's departure that the British forces under General Vincent, upon receipt of news of the battle of the Thames, had retreated precipitately to Burlington Heights, burning all their stores, and abandoning the rest of the peninsula. This was on October 9; a week after de Rottenburg had started for Kingston with two regiments, leaving only ten or twelve hundred regulars. De Rottenburg sent word for these also to retire upon York, and thence to Kingston; but the lateness of the season, the condition of the roads, and the necessity in such action to abandon sick and stores, decided Vincent, in the exercise of his discretion, to hold on. This resolution was as fortunate for his side as it proved unfortunate to the Americans. M'Clure's force, as stated by himself, was then about one thousand effective militia in Fort George, and two hundred and fifty Indians. Concerning the latter he wrote, "An exhibition of two or three hundred of them will strike more terror into the British than a thousand militia."[124] From time to time there were also bodies of "volunteers," who assembled on call and were subject to the orders of the national government for the period of their service. With such numbers, so constituted, it was as impossible for M'Clure to trouble Vincent as it was inexpedient for Vincent to attack Fort George.

A gleam of hope appeared for the American commander when Perry brought down the thirteen hundred of Harrison's victorious army, with the general himself. The latter, who was senior to M'Clure, lent a favorable ear to his suggestion that the two forces should be combined to attack Vincent's lines. Some four hundred additional volunteers gathered for this purpose; but, before the project could take effect, Chauncey arrived to carry Harrison's men to Sackett's, stripped of troops for Wilkinson's expedition. The urgency was real, and Chauncey pressing, on account both of Sackett's and the season. In reply to a very aggrieved remonstrance from M'Clure, Harrison expressed extreme sympathy with his disappointment and that of the volunteers, but said no material disadvantage was incurred, for he was convinced the British were removing as fast as they could from the head of the lake, and that an expedition thither would find them gone. Therewith, on November 16, he embarked and sailed.

The period of service for which the militia were "draughted" would expire

December 9. To M'Clure's representations the national government, which was responsible for the general defence, replied impotently by renewing its draught on the state government for another thousand militia. But, wrote Armstrong, if you cannot raise volunteers, "what are you to expect from militia draughts, with their constitutional scruples?"—about leaving their state. Armstrong was not personally responsible for the lack of organized power in the nation; but as the representative of the Government, which by a dozen years of inefficiency and neglect had laid open this and other frontiers, the fling was unbecoming. On December 10, the garrison of Fort George was reduced to "sixty effective regulars and probably forty volunteers. The militia have recrossed the river almost to a man."[125] M'Clure also learned "that the enemy were advancing in force." That night he abandoned the works, retiring to Fort Niagara, and carrying off such stores as he could; but in addition he committed the grave error of setting fire to the adjacent Canadian village of Newark, which was burned to the ground.

For this step M'Clure alleged the authority of the Secretary of War, who on October 4 had written him, "Understanding that the defence of the post committed to your charge may render it proper to destroy the town of Newark, you are directed to apprise its inhabitants of this circumstance, and to invite them to remove themselves and their effects to some place of greater safety." The general construed this to justify destruction in order to deprive the hostile troops of shelter near Fort George. "The enemy are now completely shut out from any hopes or means of wintering in the vicinity of Fort George." The exigency was insufficient to justify the measure, which was promptly disavowed by the United States Government; but the act imparted additional bitterness to the war, and was taken by the enemy as a justification and incentive to the retaliatory violence with which the campaign closed.

The civil and military government of Upper Canada at this time passed into the hands of Sir Gordon Drummond. For the moment he sent to Niagara General Riall, who took over the command from Vincent. On December 13, M'Clure reported the enemy appearing in force on the opposite shore; but, "having deprived them of shelter, they are marching up to Queenston." This alone showed the futility of burning Newark, but more decisive demonstration was to be given. Early on the 19th the British and Indians crossed the river before dawn, surprised Fort Niagara, and carried it at the point of the bayonet; meeting, indeed, but weak and disorganized resistance. At the same time a detachment of militia at Lewiston was attacked and driven in, and that village, with its neighbors, Youngstown and Manchester, were reduced to ashes, in revenge for Newark. On December 30 the British again crossed, burned Buffalo, and destroyed at Black Rock three small vessels of the Erie flotilla; two of which, the "Ariel" and

"Trippe," had been in Perry's squadron on September 10, while the third, the "Little Belt," was a prize taken in that action. Two thousand militia had been officially reported assembled on the frontier on December 26, summoned after the first alarm; but, "overpowered by the numbers and discipline of the enemy," wrote their commander, "they gave way and fled on every side. Every attempt to rally them was ineffectual."[126]

With this may be said to have terminated the northern campaign of 1813. The British had regained full control of the Niagara peninsula, and they continued to hold Fort Niagara, in the state of New York, till peace was concluded. The only substantial gain on the whole frontier, from the extreme east to the extreme west, was the destruction of the British fleet on Lake Erie, and the consequent transfer of power in the west to the United States. This was the left flank of the American position. Had the same result been accomplished on the right flank,—as it might have been,—at Montreal, or even at Kingston, the centre and left must have fallen also. For the misdirection of effort to Niagara, the local commanders, Dearborn and Chauncey, are primarily responsible; for Armstrong yielded his own correct perceptions to the representations of the first as to the enemy's force, supported by the arguments of the naval officer favoring the diversion of effort from Kingston to Toronto. Whether Chauncey ever formally admitted to himself this fundamental mistake, which wrecked the summer's work upon Lake Ontario, does not appear; but that he had learned from experience is shown by a letter to the Secretary of the Navy,[127] when the squadrons had been laid up. In this he recognized the uselessness of the heavy sailing schooners when once a cruising force of ships for war had been created, thereby condemning much of his individual management of the campaign; and he added: "If it is determined to prosecute the war offensively, and secure our conquests in Upper Canada, Kingston ought unquestionably to be the first object of attack, and that so early in the spring as to prevent the enemy from using the whole of the naval force that he is preparing."

In the three chapters which here end, the Ontario operations have been narrated consecutively and at length, without interruption by other issues,—except the immediately related Lake Erie campaign,—because upon them turned, and upon them by the dispositions of the Government this year were wrecked the fortunes of the war. The year 1813, from the opening of the spring to the closing in of winter, was for several reasons the period when conditions were most propitious to the American cause. In 1812 war was not begun until June, and then with little antecedent preparation; and it was waged halfheartedly, both governments desiring to nip hostilities. In 1814, on the other hand, when the season opened, Napoleon had fallen, and the United States no longer had an informal ally to divert the efforts of Great Britain. But in the intervening year, 1813, although the pressure upon the seaboard, the defensive frontier, was undoubtedly greater than before, and much vexation and harassment was inflicted, no serious injury was done beyond the suppression of commerce, inevitable in any event. In the north, on the lakes frontier, the offensive and the initiative continued in the hands of the United States. No substantial re-enforcements reached Canada until long after the ice broke up, and then in insufficient numbers. British naval preparations had been on an inadequate scale, receiving no proper professional supervision. The American Government, on the contrary, had had the whole winter to prepare, and the services of a very competent naval organizer. It had also the same period to get ready its land forces; while incompetent Secretaries of War and of the Navy gave place in January to capable men in both situations.

With all this in its favor, and despite certain gratifying successes, the general outcome was a complete failure, the full measure of which could be realized only when the downfall of Napoleon revealed what disaster may result from neglect to seize opportunity while it exists. The tide then ebbed, and never again flowed. For this many causes may be alleged. The imbecile ideas concerning military and naval preparation which had prevailed since the opening of the century doubtless counted for much. The intrusting of chief command to broken-down men like Dearborn and Wilkinson was enough to ruin the best conceived schemes. But, despite these very serious drawbacks, the strategic misdirection of effort was the most fatal cause of failure.

There is a simple but very fruitful remark of a Swiss military writer, that every military line may be conceived as having three parts, the middle and the two ends, or flanks. As sound principle requires that military effort should not be distributed along the whole of an enemy's position,—unless in the unusual case of overwhelming superiority,—but that distinctly superior numbers should be concentrated upon a limited portion of it, this idea of a threefold division aids materially in considering any given situation. One third, or two thirds, of an enemy's line may be assailed, but very seldom the whole; and everything may depend upon the choice made for attack. Now the British frontier, which the United States was to assail, extended from Montreal on the east to Detroit on the west. Its three parts were: Montreal and the St. Lawrence on the east, or left flank; Ontario in the middle, centring at Kingston; and Erie on the right; the strength of the British position in the last named section being at Detroit and Malden, because they commanded the straits upon, which the Indian tribes depended for access to the east. Over against the British positions named lay those of the United States. Given in the same order, these were: Lake Champlain, and the shores of Ontario and of Erie, centring respectively in the naval stations at Sackett's Harbor and Presqu' Isle.

Accepting these definitions, which are too obvious to admit of dispute, what considerations should have dictated to the United States the direction of attack; the one, or two, parts out of the three, on which effort should be concentrated? The reply, as a matter of abstract, accepted, military principle, is certain. Unless very urgent reasons to the contrary exist, strike at one end rather than at the middle, because both ends can come up to help the middle against you quicker than one end can get to help the other; and, as between the two ends, strike at the one upon which the enemy most depends for re-enforcements and supplies to maintain his strength. Sometimes this decision presents difficulties. Before Waterloo, Wellington had his own army as a centre of interest; on his right flank the sea, whence came supplies and re-enforcements from England; on his left the Prussian army, support by which was imminently necessary. On which flank would Napoleon throw the weight of his attack? Wellington reasoned, perhaps through national bias, intensified by years of official dependence upon sea support, that the blow would fall upon his right, and he strengthened it with a body of men sorely needed when the enemy came upon his left, in overwhelming numbers, seeking to separate him from the Prussians.

No such doubt was possible as to Canada in 1813. It depended wholly upon the sea, and it touched the sea at Montreal. The United States, with its combined naval and military strength, crude as the latter was, was at the beginning of 1813 quite able in material power to grapple two out of the three parts,—Montreal and Kingston. Had they been gained, Lake Erie would have fallen; as is demonstrated by the fact that the whole Erie region went down like a house of cards the moment Perry triumphed on the lake. His victory was decisive, simply because it destroyed the communications of Malden with the sea. The same result would have been achieved, with effect over a far wider region, by a similar success in the east.

FOOTNOTES:

[104] Canadian Archives MSS.

[105] Scott says, "The selection of this unprincipled imbecile was not the blunder of Secretary Armstrong." Memoirs, vol. i. p. 94, note.

[106] Both these names are used, confusingly, by Armstrong. Madrid was the township, Hamilton a village on the St. Lawrence, fifteen to twenty miles below the present Ogdensburg.

[107] American State Papers, Military Affairs, vol. i. p. 464. Armstrong's italics.

[108] Ante, p. 60.

[109] Chauncey's report, Oct. 1, 1813, Niles' Register, vol. v. p. 134. The extract has been verified from the original in the Captains' Letters. The report of Sir James Yeo (British Records Office) agrees substantially with Chauncey's accounts of the movements, but adds that upon the fall of the

"Wolfe's" topmasts the "Pike" immediately took a distance out of carronade range, whence her long 24's would tell. "I can assure you, Sir, that the great advantage the enemy have over us from their long 24-pounders almost precludes the possibility of success, unless we can force them to close action, which they have ever avoided with the most studied circumspection."

[110] Chauncey to Navy Department, Dec. 17, 1813. Captains' Letters.

[111] Armstrong, Oct. 5, 1813. American State Papers, Military Affairs, vol. i. p. 470.

[112] Ibid., p. 471.

[113] Armstrong, Oct. 20, 1813. American State Papers, Military Affairs, vol. i. p. 473.

[114] Scott's Memoirs, vol. i. p. 106. In consequence, though Scott personally succeeded in joining the movement from which so much was expected, this considerable number of regulars were withdrawn from it. They ultimately reached Sackett's, forming the nucleus of a garrison.

[115] Captains' Letters, Oct. 30, 1813.

[116] Chauncey to the Navy Department, Nov. 11, 1813. Captains' Letters.

[117] Wilkinson to Hampton. American State Papers, Military Affairs, vol. i. p. 462.

[118] Ibid.

[119] Hampton's Letters during this movement are in American State Papers, Military Affairs, vol. i. pp. 458-463.

[120] Ridout, Ten Years in Upper Canada, p. 269.

[121] American State Papers, Military Affairs, vol. i. p. 465.

[122] Chauncey to Navy Department, Nov. 11. Captains' Letters.

[123] American State Papers, Military Affairs, vol. i. p. 483.

[124] American State Papers, Military Affairs, vol. i. p. 484.

[125] American State Papers, Military Affairs, vol. i. p. 486.

[126] Report of General A. Hall, Niles' Register, vol. v. p. 394.

[127] December 17, 1813. Captains' Letters, Navy Department.

SEABOARD MARITIME OPERATIONS

Upon the Canada frontier the conditions of 1813 had permitted the United States an ample field for offensive operations, with good prospect of success. What use was made of the opportunity has now been narrated. Upon the seaboard, continuous illustration was afforded that there the country was widely open to attack, thrown wholly on the defensive, with the exception of preying upon the enemy's commerce by numerous small cruisers. As a secondary operation of war this has always possessed value, and better use of it perhaps never was made than by the American people at this time; but it is not determinative of great issues, and the achievements of the public and private armed vessels of the United States, energetic and successful as they were at this period, constituted no exception to the universal experience. Control of the highways of the ocean by great fleets destroys an enemy's commerce, root and branch. The depredations of scattered cruisers may inflict immense vexation, and even embarrassment; but they neither kill nor mortally wound, they merely harass. Co-operating with other influences, they may induce yielding in a maritime enemy; but singly they never have done so, and probably never can. In 1814 no commerce was left to the United States; and that conditions remained somewhat better during 1813 was due to collusion of the enemy, not to national power.

The needs of the British armies in the Spanish Peninsula and in Canada, and the exigencies of the West India colonies, induced the enemy to wink at, and even to uphold, a considerable clandestine export trade from the United States. Combined with this was the hope of embarrassing the general government by the disaffection of New England, and of possibly detaching that section of the country from the Union. For these reasons, the eastern coast was not included in the commercial blockade in 1813. But no motive existed for permitting the egress of armed vessels, or the continuance of the coasting trade, by which always, now as then, much of the intercourse between different parts of the country must be maintained, and upon which in 1812 it depended almost altogether. With the approach of spring in 1813, therefore, not only was the commercial blockade extended to embrace New York and all south of it, together with the Mississippi River, but the naval constriction upon the shore line became so severe as practically to annihilate the coasting trade, considered as a means of commercial exchange. It is not possible for deep-sea cruisers wholly to suppress the movement of small vessels, skirting the beaches from headland to headland; but their operations can be so much embarrassed as to reduce their usefulness to a bare alleviation of social necessities, inadequate to any scale of interchange deserving the name of commerce.

"I doubt not," wrote Captain Broke, when challenging Lawrence to a ship duel, "that you will feel convinced that it is only by repeated triumphs in even combat that your little navy can now hope to console your country for the loss of that trade it cannot protect."[128] The taunt, doubtless intended to further the object of the letter by the provocation involved, was applicable as well to coasting as to deep-sea commerce. It ignored, however, the consideration, necessarily predominant with American officers, that the conditions of the war imposed commerce destruction as the principal mission of their navy. They were not indeed to shun combat, when it offered as an incident, but neither were they to seek it as a mere means of glory, irrespective of advantage to be gained. Lawrence, whom Broke's letter did not reach, was perhaps not sufficiently attentive to this motive.

The British blockade, military and commercial, the coastwise operations of their navy, and the careers of American cruisers directed to the destruction of British commerce, are then the three heads under which the ocean activities of 1813 divide. Although this chapter is devoted to the first two of these subjects, brief mention should be made here of the distant cruises of two American vessels, because, while detached from any connection with other events, they are closely linked, in time and place, with the disastrous seaboard engagement between the "Chesapeake" and "Shannon," with which the account of sea-coast maritime operations opens. On April 30 Captain John Rodgers put to sea from Boston in the frigate "President," accompanied by the frigate "Congress," Captain John Smith. Head winds immediately after sailing detained them inside of Cape Cod until May 3, and it was not till near George's Bank that any of the blockading squadron was seen. As, by the Admiralty's instructions, one of the blockaders was usually a ship of the line, the American vessels very properly evaded them. The two continued together until May 8, when they separated, some six hundred miles east of Delaware Bay. Rodgers kept along northward to the Banks of Newfoundland, hoping, at that junction of commercial highways, to fall in with a West India convoy, or vessels bound into Halifax or the St. Lawrence. Nothing, however, was seen, and he thence steered to the Azores with equal bad fortune. Obtaining thereabouts information of a homeward-bound convoy from the West Indies, he went in pursuit to the northeast, but failed to find it. Not till June 9 did he make three captures, in quick succession. Being then two thirds of the way to the English Channel, he determined to try the North Sea, shaping his course to intercept vessels bound either by the north or south of Ireland. Not a sail was met until the Shetland Islands were reached, and there were found only Danes, which, though Denmark was in hostility with Great Britain, were trading under British licenses. The "President" remained in the North Sea until the end of July, but made only two prizes, although she lay in wait for convoys of whose sailing accounts were received. Having renewed her supply of water at Bergen, in Norway, she returned to the Atlantic, made three captures off the north coast of Ireland, and thence beat back to the Banks, where two stray homeward-bound West Indiamen were at last caught. From there the ship made her way, still with a constant head wind, to Nantucket, off which was captured a British man-of-war schooner, tender to the admiral. On September 27 she anchored in Narragansett Bay, having been absent almost five months, and made twelve prizes, few of which were valuable. One, however, was a mail packet to Halifax, the capture of which, as of its predecessors, was noted by Prevost.[129]

The "Congress" was still less successful in material result. She followed a course which had hitherto been a favorite with American captains, and which Rodgers had suggested as alternative to his own; southeast, passing near the Cape Verde Islands, to the equator between longitudes 24° and 31° west; thence to the coast of Brazil, and so home, by a route which carried her well clear of the West India Islands. She entered Portsmouth, New Hampshire, December 14, having spent seven months making this wide sweep; in the course of which three prizes only were taken.[130] It will be remembered that the "Chesapeake," which had returned only a month before the "Congress" sailed, had taken much the same direction with similar slight result.

These cruises were primarily commerce-destroying, and were pursued in that spirit, although with the full purpose of fighting should occasion arise. The paucity of result is doubtless to be attributed to the prey being sought chiefly on the high seas, too far away from the points of arrival and departure. The convoy system, rigidly enforced, as captured British correspondence shows, cleared the seas of British vessels, except in the spots where they were found congested, concentrated, by the operation of the system itself. It may be noted that the experience of all these vessels showed that nowhere was the system so rigidly operative as in the West Indies and Western Atlantic. Doubtless, too, the naval officers in command took pains to guide the droves of vessels entrusted to them over unusual courses, with a view to elude pursuers. As the home port was neared, the common disposition to relax tension of effort as the moment of relief draws nigh, co-operated with the gradual drawing together of convoys from all parts of the world to make the approaches to the English Channel the most probable scene of success for the pursuer. There the greatest number were to be found, and there presumption of safety tended to decrease carefulness. This was to be amply proved by subsequent experience. It had been predicted by Rodgers himself, although he apparently did not think wise to hazard in such close quarters so fine and large a frigate as the "President." "It is very generally believed," he had written, "that the coasts of England, Ireland, and Scotland are always swarming with British men of war, and that their commerce would be found amply protected. This, however, I well know by experience, in my voyages when a youth, to be incorrect; and that it has always been their policy to keep their enemies as far distant from their shores as possible, by stationing their ships at the commencement of a war on the enemy's coasts, and in such other distant situations, ... and thereby be enabled to protect their own commerce in a twofold degree. This, however, they have been enabled to do, owing as well to the inactivity of the enemy, as to the local advantages derived from their relative situations."[131]

The same tendency was observable at other points of arrival, and recognition of this dictated the instructions issued to Captain Lawrence for the cruise of the "Chesapeake," frustrated through her capture by the "Shannon." Lawrence was appointed to the ship on May 6; the sailing orders issued to Captain Evans being transferred to him on that date. He was to go to the mouth of the Gulf of St. Lawrence, seeking there to intercept the military store-ships, and transports with troops, destined to Quebec and Upper Canada. "The enemy," wrote the Secretary, "will not in all probability anticipate our taking this ground with our public ships of war; and as his convoys generally separate between Cape Race and Halifax, leaving the trade of the St. Lawrence to proceed without convoy, the chance of captures upon an extensive scale is very flattering." He added the just remark, that "it is impossible to conceive a naval service of a higher order in a national point of view than the destruction of the enemy's vessels, with supplies for his army in Canada and his fleets on this station."[132]

Lawrence took command of the "Chesapeake" at Boston on May 20. The ship had returned from her last cruise April 9, and had been so far prepared for sea by her former commander that, as has been seen, her sailing orders were issued May 6. It would appear from the statement of the British naval historian James,[133] based upon a paper captured in the ship, that the enlistments of her crew expired in April. Although there were many reshipments, and a nucleus of naval seamen, there was a large infusion of new and untrained men, amounting to a reconstitution of the ship's company. More important still was the fact that both the captain and first lieutenant were just appointed; her former first lying fatally ill at the time she sailed. The third and fourth lieutenants were also strange to her, and in a manner to their positions; being in fact midshipmen, to whom acting appointments as lieutenants were issued at Lawrence's request, by Commodore Bainbridge of the navy yard, on May 27, five days before the action. The third took charge of his division for the first time the day of the battle, and the men were personally unknown to him. The first lieutenant himself was extremely young.

The bearing of these facts is not to excuse the defeat, but to enforce the lesson that a grave military enterprise is not to be hazarded on a side issue, or on a point of pride, without adequate preparation. The "Chesapeake" was ordered to a service of very particular importance at the moment— May, 1813—when the Canada campaign was about to open. She was to act against the communications of the enemy; and while it is upon the whole more expedient, for the morale of a service, that battle with an equal should not be declined, quite as necessarily action should not be sought when it will materially interfere with the discharge of a duty intrinsically of greater consequence. The capture of a single enemy's frigate is not to be confounded with, or inflated to, that destruction of an enemy's organized force which is the prime object of all military effort. Indeed, the very purpose to which the "Chesapeake" was designated was to cripple the organized force of the British, either the army in Canada, or the navy on the lakes. The chance of a disabling blow by unexpected action in the St. Lawrence much exceeded any gain to be anticipated, even by a victorious ship duel, which would not improbably entail return to port to refit; while officers new to their duties, and unknown to their men, detracted greatly from the chances of success, should momentary disaster or confusion occur.

The blockade of Boston Harbor at this moment was conducted by Captain Philip Vere Broke of the "Shannon", a 38-gun frigate, which he had then commanded for seven years. His was one of those cases where singular merit as an officer, and an attention to duty altogether exceptional, had not yet obtained opportunity for distinction. It would probably be safe to say that no more thoroughly efficient ship of her class had been seen in the British navy during the twenty years' war with France, then drawing towards its close; but after Trafalgar Napoleon's policy, while steadily directed towards increasing the number of his ships, had more and more tended to husbanding them against a future occasion, which in the end never came. The result was a great diminution in naval combats. Hence, the outbreak of the American war, followed by three frigate actions in rapid succession, opened out a new prospect, which was none the less stimulative because of the British reverses suffered. Captain Broke was justly confident in his own leadership and in the efficiency of a ship's company, which, whatever individual changes it may have undergone, had retained its identity of organization through so many years of his personal and energetic supervision. He now reasonably hoped to demonstrate what could be done by officers and men so carefully trained. Captain Pechell of the "Santo Domingo," the flagship on the American station, wrote: "The 'Shannon's' men were better trained, and understood gunnery better, than any men I ever saw;" nevertheless, he added, "In the action with the 'Chesapeake' the guns were all laid by Captain Broke's directions, consequently the fire was all thrown in one horizontal line, not a shot going over the 'Chesapeake.'"[134]

The escape of the "President" and "Congress" early in May, while the "Shannon" and her consort, the "Tenedos," were temporarily off shore in consequence of easterly weather, put Broke still more upon his mettle; and, fearing a similar mishap with the "Chesapeake," he sent Lawrence a challenge.[135] It has been said, by both Americans and English, that this letter was a model of courtesy. Undoubtedly it was in all respects such as a gentleman might write; but the courtesy was that of the French duellist, nervously anxious lest he should misplace an accent in the name of the man whom he intended to force into fight, and to kill. It was provocative to the last degree, which, for the end in view, it was probably meant to be. In it Broke showed himself as adroit with his pen—the adroitness of Canning— as he was to prove himself in battle. Not to speak of other points of irritation, the underlining of the words, "even combat," involved an imputation, none the less stinging because founded in truth, upon the previous frigate actions, and upon Lawrence's own capture of the "Peacock." In guns, the "Chesapeake" and "Shannon" were practically of equal force; but in the engagement the American frigate carried fifty more men than her adversary. To an invitation couched as was Broke's Lawrence was doubly vulnerable, for only six months had elapsed since he himself had sent a challenge to the "Bonne Citoyenne." With his temperament he could scarcely have resisted the innuendo, had he received the letter; but this he did not. It passed him on the way out and was delivered to Bainbridge, by whom it was forwarded to the Navy Department.

Although Broke's letter did not reach him, Captain Lawrence made no attempt to get to sea without engagement. The "Shannon's" running close to Boston Light, showing her colors, and heaving-to in defiance, served the purpose of a challenge. Cooper, who was in full touch with the naval tradition of the time, has transmitted that Lawrence went into the action with great reluctance. This could have proceeded only from consciousness of defective organization, for the heroic temper of the man was notorious, and there is no hint of that mysterious presentiment so frequent in the annals of military services. The wind being fair from the westward, the "Chesapeake," which had unmoored at 8 A.M., lifted her last anchor at noon, June 1, and made sail. The "Shannon," seeing at hand the combat she had provoked, stood out to sea until on the line between Cape Ann and Cape Cod, where she hove-to on the starboard tack, heading to the southeast. The "Chesapeake" followed under all sail until 5 P.M., when she took in her light canvas, sending the loftier—royal—yards on deck; and at 5.30 hauled up her courses, thus reducing herself to the fighting trim already assumed by her adversary. The "Shannon," which had been lying stopped for a long time, at this same moment filled her sails, to regain headway with which to manœuvre, in case her opponent's action should require it; but, after gathering speed sufficient for this purpose, the British captain again slowed his ship, by so bracing the maintopsail that it was kept shaking in the wind. Its effect being thus lost, though readily recoverable, her forward movement depended upon the sails of the fore and mizzen masts (1). In this attitude, and steering southeast by the wind, she awaited her antagonist, who was running for her weather—starboard—quarter, and whose approach, thus seconded, became now very rapid. Broke made no further change in the ship's direction, leaving the choice of windward or leeward side to Lawrence, who took the former, discarding all tactical advantages, and preferring a simple artillery duel between the vessels.

Just before she closed, the "Chesapeake" rounded-to, taking a parallel course, and backing the maintopsail (1) to reduce her speed to that of the enemy. Captain Lawrence in his eagerness had made the serious error of coming up under too great headway. At 5.50, as her bows doubled on the quarter of the "Shannon" (1), at the distance of fifty yards, the British ship opened fire, beginning with the after gun, and continuing thence forward, as each in succession bore upon the advancing American frigate. The latter replied after the second British discharge, and the combat at once became furious. The previous history of the two vessels makes it probable that the British gunnery was the better; but it is impossible, seeing the course the action finally took, so far to disentangle the effects of the fire while they were on equal terms of position, from the totals afterwards ascertained, as to say where the advantage, if any, lay during those few minutes. The testimony of the "Chesapeake's" second lieutenant, that his division—the forward one on the gun deck—fired three rounds before their guns ceased to bear, agrees with Broke's report that two or three broadsides were exchanged; and the time needed by well-drilled men to do this is well within, yet accords fairly with, James' statement, that from the first gun to the second stage in the action six minutes elapsed. During the first of this period the "Chesapeake" kept moving parallel at fifty yards distance, but gaining continually, threatening thus to pass wholly ahead, so that her guns would bear no longer. To prevent this Lawrence luffed closer to the wind to shake her sails, but in vain; the movement increased her distance, but she still ranged ahead, so that she finally reached much further than abreast of the enemy. To use the nautical expression, she was on the "Shannon's" weather bow (2). While this was happening her sailing master was killed and Lawrence wounded; these being the two officers chiefly concerned in the handling of the ship.

Upon this supervened a concurrence of accidents, affecting her manageability, which initiated the second scene in the drama, and called for instantaneous action by the officers injured. The foretopsail tie being cut by the enemy's fire, the yard dropped, leaving the sail empty of wind; and at the same time were shot away the jib-sheet and the brails of the spanker. Although the latter, flying loose, tends to spread itself against the mizzen rigging, it probably added little to the effect of the after sails; but, the foresail not being set, the first two mishaps practically took all the forward canvas off the "Chesapeake." Under the combined impulses she, at 5.56, came up into the wind (3), lost her way, and, although her mainyard had been braced up, finally gathered sternboard; the upshot being that she lay paralyzed some seventy yards from the "Shannon" (3, 4, 5), obliquely to the latter's course and slightly ahead of her. The British ship going, or steering, a little off (3), her guns bore fair upon the "Chesapeake," which, by her involuntarily coming into the wind,—to such an extent that Broke thought she was attempting to haul off, and himself hauled closer to the wind in consequence (4),—lost in great measure the power of reply, except by musketry. The British shot, entering the stern and quarter of her opponent, swept diagonally along the after parts of the spar and main decks, a half-raking fire.

Under these conditions Lawrence and the first lieutenant were mortally wounded, the former falling by a musket-ball through his body; but he had already given orders to have the boarders called, seeing that the ship must drift foul of the enemy (5). The chaplain, who in the boarding behaved courageously, meeting Broke in person with a pistol-shot, and receiving a cutlass wound in return, was standing close by the captain at this instant. He afterwards testified that as Lawrence cried "Boarders away", the crews of the carronades ran forward; which corresponds to Broke's report that, seeing the enemy flinching from their guns, he then gave the order for boarding. This may have been, indeed, merely the instinctive impulse which drives disorganized men to seek escape from a fire which they cannot return; but if Cooper is correct in saying that it was the practice of that day to keep the boarders' weapons, not by their side, but on the quarter-deck or at the masts, it may also have been that this division, which had so far stuck to its guns while being raked, now, at the captain's call, ran from them to get the side-arms. At the Court of Inquiry it was in evidence that these men were unarmed; and one of them, a petty officer, stated that he had defended himself with the monkey tail of his gun. Whatever the cause, although there was fighting to prevent the "Chesapeake" from being lashed to the "Shannon", no combined resistance was offered abaft the mainmast. There the marines made a stand, but were overpowered and driven forward. The negro bugler of the ship, who should have echoed Lawrence's summons, was too frightened to sound a note, and the voices of the aids, who shouted the message to the gun deck, were imperfectly heard; but, above all, leaders were wanting. There was not on the upper deck an officer above the grade of midshipman; captain, first lieutenant, master, marine officer, and even the boatswain, had been mortally wounded before the ships touched. The second lieutenant was in charge of the first gun division, at the far end of the deck below, as yet ignorant how the fight was going, and that the fate of his superiors had put him in command. Of the remaining lieutenants, also stationed on the gun deck, the fourth had been mortally wounded by the first broadside; while the third, who had heard the shout for boarders, committed the indiscretion, ruinous to his professional reputation, of accompanying those who, at the moment the ships came together, were carrying below the wounded captain.

Before the new commanding officer could get to the spar deck, the ships were in contact. According to the report of Captain Broke, the most competent surviving eye-witness, the mizzen channels of the "Chesapeake" locked in the fore-rigging of the "Shannon." "I went forward," he continues, "to ascertain her position, and observing that the enemy were flinching from their guns, I gave orders to prepare for boarding." When the "Chesapeake's" second lieutenant reached the forecastle, the British were in possession of the after part of the ship, and of the principal hatchways by which the boarders of the after divisions could come up. He directed the foresail set, to shoot the ship clear, to prevent thus a re-enforcement to the enemy already on board; and he rallied a few men, but was himself soon wounded and thrown below. In brief, the fall of their officers and the position of the ship, in irons and being raked, had thrown the crew into the confusion attendant upon all sudden disaster. From this state only the rallying cry of a well-known voice and example can rescue men. "The enemy," reported Broke, "made a desperate but disorderly resistance." The desperation of brave men is the temper which at times may retrieve such conditions, but it must be guided and fashioned by a master spirit into something better than disorder, if it is to be effective. Disorder at any stage of a battle is incipient defeat; supervening upon the enemy's gaining a commanding position it commonly means defeat consummated.

Fifteen minutes elapsed from the discharge of the first gun of the "Shannon" to the "Chesapeake's" colors being hauled down. This was done by the enemy, her own crew having been driven forward. In that brief interval twenty-six British were killed and fifty-six wounded; of the Americans forty-eight were killed and ninety-nine wounded. In proportion to the number on board each ship when the action began, the "Shannon" lost in men 24 per cent; the "Chesapeake" 46 per cent, or practically double. Although a certain amount of national exultation or mortification attends victory or defeat in an international contest, from a yacht race to a frigate action, there is no question of national credit in the result where initial inequality is great, as in such combats as that of the "Chesapeake" and "Shannon," or the "Constitution" and "Guerrière." It is possible for an officer to command a ship for seven years, as Broke had, and fail to make of her the admirable pattern of all that a ship of war should be, which he accomplished with the "Shannon"; but no captain can in four weeks make a thoroughly efficient crew out of a crowd of men newly assembled, and never out of harbor together. The question at issue is not national, but personal; it is the credit of Captain Lawrence. That it was inexpedient to take the "Chesapeake" into action at all at that moment does not admit of dispute; though much allowance must be made for a gallant spirit, still in the early prime of life, and chafing under the thought that, should he get to sea by successful evasion, he would be open to the taunt, freely used by Broke,[136] of dodging, "eluding," an enemy only his equal in material force.

Having, however, undertaken a risk which cannot be justified, was Captain Lawrence also reckless, and vainly confident, in his conduct before and during the action? Was he foolhardy, or only rash? The reply, if favorable, is due to one of the most gallant and attractive personalities in the annals of the United States Navy.

From his action it is evident that Lawrence clearly recognized that a green crew can be more quickly formed to efficiency at the battery than to that familiarity with the rigging and the sails, and that habit of working together about decks, on which manœuvring power depends. He therefore chose an artillery duel, surrendering even the opportunity of raking permitted him by Broke, who awaited his approach without an attempt at molestation. How far was his expectation as to the results overstrained? The American crew lost double in proportion to their enemy; but it did not fail to inflict a very severe punishment, and it must be added under a very considerable disadvantage, which there has been a tendency recently to underestimate. The loss of the head sails, and all that followed, is part of the fortune of war; of that unforeseeable, which great leaders admit may derange even the surest calculations. It is not, therefore, to be complained of, but it is nevertheless to receive due account in the scales of praise and blame; for the man who will run no risks of accidents accomplishes nothing.

In the preceding narrative, and in the following analysis, the account of the British naval writer James is in essentials adopted; chiefly because, of all historians having contemporary sources of information, he has been at most pains to insure precision.[137] As told by him, the engagement divides into three stages. First, the combat side to side; second, the period during which the "Chesapeake" lay in the wind being raked; third, the boarding and taking possession. To these James assigns, as times: for the first, six minutes; for the second, four; for the third, five; this last being again subdivisible into a space of two minutes, during which the "Chesapeake" was being lashed to her opponent, and the actual fighting on her decks, which Broke states did not exceed three.

The brief and disorderly, though desperate, resistance to boarding proves that the "Chesapeake" was already beaten by the cannonade, which lasted, as above, ten minutes. During only six of these, accepting James' times, was she on equal gunnery terms. During four tenths—nearly one half—of the gunnery contest she was at a great disadvantage. The necessity of manœuvring, which Lawrence tried to avoid, was forced upon him; and the ship's company, or her circumstances, proved unequal to meeting it. Nevertheless, though little more than half the time on equal terms of position with her opponent, half her own loss was inflicted upon him. How great her subsequent disadvantage is best stated in the words of James, whom no one will accuse of making points in favor of Americans. "At 5.56, having had her jib-sheet and foretopsail tie shot away, and her helm, probably from the death of the men stationed at it, being at the moment unattended to, the 'Chesapeake' came so sharp to the wind as completely to deaden her way." How extreme this deviation from her course is shown by the impression made on Broke. "As the manœuvres of the 'Chesapeake' indicated an intention to haul away, Captain Broke ordered the helm to be put a-lee, as the 'Shannon' had fallen off a little." The "Chesapeake's" way being deadened, "the ship lay with her stern and quarter exposed to her opponent's broadside. The shot from the 'Shannon's' aftermost guns now took a diagonal direction along[138] the decks of the 'Chesapeake,' beating in her stern ports, and sweeping the men from their quarters. The shot from the 'Shannon's' foremost guns, at the same time, entering the 'Chesapeake's' ports from the mainmast aft, did considerable execution." This describes a semi-raking fire, which lasted four minutes, from 5.56 to 6 P.M., when the ships came together.

The manner of collision and the injuries received bear out the above account. The quarter of the "Chesapeake" came against the side of the "Shannon," the angle at the moment, as represented in James' diagram, being such as to make it impossible that any of the "Chesapeake's" guns, save one or two of the after ones, could then bear; and as she was already paying off, they had been in worse position before. "She was severely battered in the hull, on the larboard quarter particularly; and several shot entered the stern windows.... Her three lower masts were badly wounded, the main and mizzen especially. The bowsprit received no injury." All these details show that the sum total of the "Shannon's" fire was directed most effectively upon the after part of the ship, in the manner described by James; and coupled with the fact that the British first broadside, always reckoned the most deadly, would naturally take effect chiefly on the fore part of the "Chesapeake," as she advanced from the "Shannon's" stern to her bow,[139] we are justified in the inference that the worst of her loss was suffered after accident had taken her movements out of Lawrence's instant control. Under these circumstances it may be claimed for him that the artillery duel, to which he sought to confine the battle, was not so entirely a desperate chance as has been inferred.

It may therefore be said that, having resolved upon a risk which cannot be justified at the bar of dispassionate professional judgment, Captain Lawrence did not commit the further unpardonable error of not maturely weighing and judiciously choosing his course. That the crew was not organized and exercised at the guns, as far as his time and opportunity permitted, is disproved by incidental mention in the courts martial that followed, as well as by the execution done. Within ten minutes at the utmost, within six of equal terms, the "Chesapeake," an 18-pounder frigate, killed and wounded of the "Shannon's" ship's company as many as the "Constitution" with her 24's did of the "Guerrière's" in over twenty;[140] and the "Constitution" not only was a much heavier ship than her opponent, but had been six weeks almost continuously at sea. When her crew had been together four months longer, the loss inflicted by her upon the "Java," in a contest spread over two hours, did not greatly exceed in proportion that suffered by the "Shannon"; and the circumstances of that engagement, being largely manœuvring, justified Lawrence's decision, under his circumstances, to have none of it. His reliance upon the marksmanship of his men is further vindicated by Broke's report that neither vessel suffered much aloft. The American and best British tradition of firing low was sustained by both ships. Finally, although the organization of the "Chesapeake" was not matured sufficiently to hold the people together, without leaders, after a tremendous punishment by the enemy's battery, and in the face of well-trained and rapidly supported boarders, it had so far progressed in cohesion that they did not flinch from their guns through a severe raking fire. What further shows this is that the boatswain of the "Shannon," lashing the ships together in preparation for boarding, was mortally wounded, not by musketry only but by sabre. When thus attacked he doubtless was supported by a body of fighters as well as a gang of workers. In fact, Broke was himself close by.

Under thus much of preparation, certainly not sufficient, Lawrence chose for action a smooth sea, a royal breeze, an artillery duel, and a close range. "No manœuvring, but downright fighting," as Nelson said of his most critical battle; critical, just because his opponents, though raw tyros compared to his own crews, had nothing to do but to work their guns. The American captain took the most promising method open to him for achieving success, and carried into the fight a ship's company which was not so untrained but that, had some luck favored him, instead of going the other way, there was a fighting chance of victory. More cannot be claimed for him. He had no right, under the conditions, voluntarily to seek the odds against him, established by Broke's seven years of faithful and skilful command. Except in material force, the "Chesapeake" was a ship much inferior to the "Shannon," as a regiment newly enlisted is to one that has seen service; and the moment things went seriously wrong she could not retrieve herself. This her captain must have known; and to the accusation of his country and his service that he brought upon them a mortification which endures to this day, the only reply is that he died "sword in hand." This covers the error of the dead, but cannot justify the example to the living.

As is customary in such cases, a Court of Inquiry was ordered to investigate the defeat of the "Chesapeake," and sat from February 2 to February 8, 1814. Little can be gleaned from the evidence concerning the manœuvring of the ship; the only two commissioned officers surviving, having been stationed on the gun deck, could not see what passed above. Incidental statements by midshipmen examined confirm substantially the account above given. One mentions the particular that, when the head sheets were shot away, "the bow of the 'Shannon' was abreast of the 'Chesapeake's' midships, and she came into the wind;" he adds that the mizzen-topsail was a-back, as well as the main. This is the only important contribution to the determination of the relative positions and handling of the vessels. As far as it goes, it confirms a general impression that Lawrence's eagerness prevented his making due allowance for the way of the "Chesapeake," causing him to overshoot his aim; an error of judgment, which the accidents to the headsails converted into irretrievable disaster. The general testimony agrees that the crew, though dissatisfied at non-receipt of pay and prize money, behaved well until the moment of boarding. Four witnesses, all officers, stated as of their own observation that the "Shannon" received several shot between wind and water, and used her pumps continuously on the way to Halifax. Budd, the second lieutenant, "was informed by an officer of the 'Shannon' that she was in a sinking condition." "The 'Chesapeake' was not injured below her quarters, except by one or two shot." "The 'Chesapeake' made no water; but the 'Shannon' had hands at the pumps continually." A good deal of pumping in a ship seven years in commission did not necessarily indicate injuries in action; Midshipman Curtis, however, who was transferred to the "Shannon," testified that "the British officers were encouraging the men by cheering to work at the pumps," which looks more serious. The purser of the "Chesapeake" swore that she had shot plugs at the water-line, and that "her sailing master said she had three shot holes below." The repetition of remarks made by the "Shannon's" officers is of course only hearsay testimony; but as regards the shots below the water-line,—as distinguished from the general body of the ship,—this on the one hand shows that the "Shannon" had her share of bad luck, for in the smoke of the battle this result is not attributable to nice precision of aiming. On the other hand it strongly re-enforces the proof of the excellent marksmanship of the American frigate, deducible from the killed and wounded of her opponent, and it confirms the inference that her own disproportionate loss was at least partly due to the raking fire and her simultaneous disability to reply. Upon the whole, the conclusion to the writer is clear that, while Lawrence should not have courted action, the condition of the "Chesapeake" as a fighting ship was far better than has commonly been supposed. It may be added that an irresponsible contemporary statement, that his "orders were peremptory," is disproved by the Department's letter, which forms part of the Court's record. He was to "proceed to sea as soon as weather, and the force and position of the enemy, will admit." Even a successful action must be expected to compel return to port, preventing his proceeding; and there is an obvious difference between fighting an enemy when met, and going out especially to fight him. The orders were discretional.

Whether, by paying attention to favoring conditions, Captain Lawrence could have repeated the success of Commodore Rodgers in gaining the sea a month before, must remain uncertain. The "Constitution," under Captain Stewart, a seaman of very excellent reputation, was unable to do so, until the winter gales made it impossible for the blockaders to maintain an uninterrupted watch off Boston. The sailing of the "President" and "Congress" was the last successful effort for many months; and the capture of the "Chesapeake" was the first of several incidents illustrating how complete was the iron-barring of the coast, against all but small vessels.

Commodore Decatur, having found it impossible to get out from New York by the Sandy Hook route, undertook that by Long Island Sound. Passing through Hell Gate, May 24, with his little squadron,—the "United States," the "Macedonian," her late prize, and the sloop of war "Hornet,"— he was on the 26th off Fisher's Island, abreast of New London. Here he remained until June 1, obtaining various information concerning the enemy, but only certain that there was at least a ship of the line and a frigate in the neighborhood. On the last named day, that of the fight between the "Chesapeake" and the "Shannon," the wind serving, and the two enemy's vessels being far to the southwest of Montauk Point, at the east end of Long Island, the squadron put to sea together; but on approaching Block Island, which was close to their course, two more enemy's cruisers loomed up to the eastward. The hostile groups manœuvred severally to get between the Americans and their ports of refuge, New London in the one quarter, Newport in the other. In plain sight of this overwhelming force Decatur feared the results of trying to slip out to sea, and therefore beat back to New London.[141] The enemy followed, and, having now this division securely housed, instituted a close blockade. It was apprehended even that they might endeavor to take it by main force, the defences of the place being weak; but, as is commonly the case, the dangers of an attack upon land batteries were sufficient to deter the ships from an attempt, the object of which could be attained with equal certainty by means less hazardous, if less immediate.

The upshot was that the two frigates remained there blockaded to the end of the war; dependent for their safety, in Decatur's opinion, rather upon the difficulty of the channel than upon the strength of the fortifications. "Fort Trumbull, the only work here mounted or garrisoned, was in the most unprepared state, and only one or two cannon were to be had in the neighborhood for any temporary work which should be erected. I immediately directed all my exertions to strengthening the defences. Groton Heights has been hastily prepared for the reception of a few large guns, and they will be mounted immediately.... I think the place might be made impregnable; but the hostile force on our coast is so great that, were the enemy to exert a large portion of his means in an attack here, I do not feel certain he could be resisted successfully with the present defences."[142] On December 6 he reported that the squadron was moored across the channel and under Groton Heights, which had been fortified; while in the mouth of the harbor, three gunshots distant, was anchored a British division, consisting of one ship of the line, a frigate, and two smaller vessels. Two other ships of the line and several frigates were cruising in the open, between the east end of Long Island and Gay Head. This state of affairs lasted throughout the winter, during which the ships were kept in a state of expectancy, awaiting a possible opportunity; but, when the return of spring found the hope unfulfilled, it was plainly idle to look to the summer to afford what winter had denied. The frigates were lightened over a three-fathom bar, and thence, in April, 1814, removed up the Thames fourteen miles, as far as the depth of water would permit. Being there wholly out of reach of the enemy's heavy vessels, they were dismantled, and left to the protection of the shore batteries and the "Hornet," retained for that purpose. Decatur was transferred to the "President," then at New York, taking with him his ship's company; while the crew of the "Macedonian" was sent to the lakes. The enemy's vessels then off New London were three seventy-fours, four frigates, and three sloops.

This accumulation of force, to watch Decatur's two frigates and the "President," which during October and November was lying at Bristol,

Rhode Island, testified to the anxiety of the British Government to restrain or capture the larger American cruisers. Their individual power was such that it was unwilling to expose to attack by them the vessels, nominally of the same class, but actually much inferior, which were ranging all seas to protect British commerce. That this should suffer, and in some considerable degree, from the operations of well-developed privateering enterprise, pursued by a maritime people debarred from every other form of maritime activity, was to be expected, and must be endured; but the frigates carried with them the further menace, not indeed of serious injury to the colossal naval power of Great Britain, but of mortification for defeats, which, however reasonably to be accounted for by preponderance of force, are not patiently accepted by a nation accustomed to regard itself as invincible. There are few things more wearing than explaining adverse results; and the moral effect of so satisfactory a reply as the victory of the "Shannon" might well have weighed with an American captain, not to risk prestige already gained, by seeking action when conscious of deficient preparation. The clamor aroused in Great Britain by the three rapidly succeeding captures of the "Guerrière," "Macedonian," and "Java," was ample justification of the American policy of securing superior force in single cruisers, throughout their several classes; a policy entirely consistent with all sound military principle. It should be remembered, however, that a cruiser is intended generally to act singly, and depends upon herself alone for that preponderance of strength which military effort usually seeks by concentration of numbers. The advantage of great individual power, therefore, does not apply so unqualifiedly to the components of fleets, the superiority of which depends upon the mutual support of its members, by efficient combination of movement, as well as upon their separate power.

Both the Government and people of Great Britain expected with some confidence, from the large fleet placed under Sir John Warren, the utter destruction of the frigates and of the American navy generally. "We were in hopes, ere this," said a naval periodical in June, 1813, "to have announced the capture of the American navy; and, as our commander-in-chief on that station has sufficient force to effect so desirable an object, we trust, before another month elapses, to lay before our readers what we conceive ought long since to have happened."[143] The words of the Admiralty were more measured, as responsible utterances are prone to be; but their tenor was the same. Expressing to Warren disappointment with the results so far obtained, they added: "It is of the highest importance to the character and interests of the country that the naval force of the enemy should be quickly and completely disposed of. Their Lordships therefore have thought themselves justified at this moment in withdrawing ships from other important services, for the purpose of placing under your command a force with which you cannot fail to bring the naval war to a termination, either by the capture of the American national vessels, or by strictly blockading them in their own waters."[144] This expectancy doubtless weighed with Broke; and probably also prompted a challenge sent to Decatur's squadron to meet two British frigates, under pledge of fair play, and of safe return if victorious. In the latter case they at least would be badly injured; so in either event the blockaders would be relieved of much of their burden.

The presence of several American frigates, blockaded close to the point where Narragansett Bay and Long Island Sound meet, constituted a great inconvenience to all that region, by attracting thither so many enemy's cruisers. To a coasting trade—then so singularly important—projecting headlands, or capes, are the places of greatest exposure; in this resembling the danger entailed by salients in all military lines, in fortification or in the field. Traffic between New England and New York, general and local, had derived a further impetus from the fact that Newport, not being included in the commercial blockade, could still receive external supplies by neutral vessels. Intercourse depended largely on these waters; and it was to them a grave misfortune that there were no United States frigates left in New York to divert the enemy's attention. The vexations entailed were forcibly presented by the Governor of Connecticut.[145] "The British force stationed in our waters having occasioned great inquietude along the whole of our maritime frontier, every precaution consistent with due regard to the general safety has been adopted for its protection.... In our present state of preparedness, it is believed a descent upon our coast will not be attempted; a well-grounded hope is entertained that it will be attended with little success. Unfortunately, we have not the means of rendering our navigation equally secure. Serious depredations have been committed even in our harbors, and to such an extent that the usual communication through the Sound is almost wholly interrupted. Thus, while anxiously engaged in protecting our public ships [Decatur's], we are doomed to witness the unrestrained capture of our private vessels, and the consequent suspension of commercial pursuits." As "the disapprobation of the war by the people of Connecticut had been publicly declared through the proper organs shortly after hostilities commenced,"[146] it may be supposed the conditions described, accompanied by continual alarms withdrawing the militiaman from his shop or his harvest, to repel petty invasion, did not tend to conciliate opinion. An officer of the Connecticut militia wrote in December, "Our engagements with the enemy have become so frequent that it would be in vain to attempt a particular statement of each."[147]

Similar conditions prevailed along the entire seaboard, from Maine to Georgia; being of course greatest where inland navigation with wide entrances, like Long Island Sound, had given particular development to the coasting trade, and at the same time afforded to pursuers particular immunity from ordinary dangers of the sea. Incidental confirmation of the closeness of the hostile pressure is afforded by Bainbridge's report of the brig "Siren's" arrival at Boston, June 11, 1813, from New Orleans. "Although at sea between thirty and forty days, and great time along our blockaded coast, she did not see one enemy's cruiser."[148] The cause is evident. The Chesapeake and Delaware were blockaded from within. Ships watching New York and Long Island Sound would be far inside the course of one destined to Boston from the southward. From Hatteras to the Florida line the enemy's vessels, mostly of small class, kept in summer well inside the line from cape to cape, harassing even the water traffic behind the sea-islands; while at Boston, her port of arrival, the "Siren" was favored by Broke's procedure. In his eagerness to secure action with the "Chesapeake," he had detached his consort, the "Tenedos," with orders not to rejoin until June 14. Under cover of her absence, and the "Shannon's" return to Halifax with her prize, the "Siren" slipped into a harbor wholly relieved of the enemy's presence. With such conditions, a voyage along the coast could well be outside the British line of cruising.

Owing to the difficulty of the New York entrance, except with good pilotage, and to the absence thence of ships of war after Decatur's departure, that port ceased to present any features of naval activity; except as connected with the lake squadrons, which depended upon it for supplies of all kinds. The blockade of the Sound affected its domestic trade; and after May its external commerce shared the inconveniences of the commercial blockade, then applied to it, and made at least technically effective. What this pressure in the end became is shown by a casual mention a year later, under the heading "progress of luxury. A private sk of wine brought the average 'extraordinary' price of twenty-five dollars the gallon; while at the same period one auction lot of prize goods, comprising three decanters and twelve tumblers, sold for one hundred and twelve dollars."[149] The arrival in August, 1813, of a vessel in distress, which, like the "Siren," had passed along the whole Southern coast without seeing a hostile cruiser, would seem to show some lapse of watchfulness; but, although there were the occasional evasions which attend all blockades, the general fact of neutrals turned away was established. A flotilla of a dozen gunboats was kept in commission in the bay, but under an officer not of the regular navy. As might readily have been foreseen from conditions, and from experience elsewhere, the national gunboat experiment had abundantly shown that vessels of that class were not only excessively costly in expenditure, and lamentably inefficient in results, as compared with seagoing cruisers, but were also deleterious to the professional character of officers and seamen. Two years before the war Captain Campbell, then in command both at Charleston and Savannah, had commented on the unofficer-like neglect noticeable in the gunboats, and Gordon now reported the same effect upon the crew of the "Constellation," while thus detached for harbor defence.[150] The Secretary of the Navy, affirming the general observation, remarked that officers having knowledge of their business were averse to gunboat duty, while those who had it yet to acquire were unwilling, because there it could not be learned. "It is a service in which those who are to form the officers for the ships of war ought not to be employed."[151] He therefore had recommended the commissioning of volunteer officers for this work. This local New York harbor guard at times convoyed coasters in the Sound, and at times interfered, both in that quarter and off Sandy Hook, to prevent small cruisers or boats of the enemy from effecting seizures of vessels, close in shore or run on the beach. Such military action possesses a certain minor value, diminishing in some measure the grand total of loss; but it is not capable of modifying seriously the broad results of a strong commercial blockade.

The Delaware and the Chesapeake—the latter particularly—became the principal scenes of active operations by the British navy. Here in the early part of the summer there seems to have been a formed determination on the part of Sir John Warren to satisfy his Government and people by evidence of military exertion in various quarters. Rear Admiral George Cockburn, an officer of distinction and energy, had been ordered at the end of 1812 from the Cadiz station, with four ships of the line and several smaller cruisers, to re-enforce Warren. This strong detachment, a token at once of the relaxing demand upon the British navy in Europe, and of the increasing purpose of the British Government towards the United States, joined the commander-in-chief at Bermuda, and accompanied him to the Chesapeake in March. Cockburn became second in command. Early in April the fleet began moving up the bay; an opening incident, already mentioned,[152] being the successful attack by its boats upon several letters-of-marque and privateers in the Rappahannock upon the 3d of the month. Some of the schooners there captured were converted into tenders, useful for penetrating the numerous waterways which intersected the country in every direction.

The fleet, comprising several ships of the line, besides numerous smaller vessels, continued slowly upwards, taking time to land parties in many quarters, keeping the country in perpetual alarm. The multiplicity and diverseness of its operations, the particular object of which could at no moment be foreseen, made it impossible to combine resistance. The harassment was necessarily extreme, and the sustained suspense wearing; for, with reports continually arriving, now from one shore and now from the other, each neighborhood thought itself the next to be attacked. Defence depended wholly upon militia, hastily assembled, with whom local considerations are necessarily predominant. But while thus spreading consternation on either side, diverting attention from his main objective, the purpose of the British admiral was clear to his own mind. It was "to cut off the enemy's supplies, and destroy their foundries, stores, and public works, by penetrating the rivers at the head of the Chesapeake."

On April 16 an advanced division arrived off the mouth of the Patapsco, a dozen miles from Baltimore. There others successively joined, until the whole force was reported on the 22d to be three seventy-fours, with several frigates and smaller vessels, making a total of fifteen. The body of the fleet remained stationary, causing the city a strong anticipation of attack; an impression conducing to retain there troops which, under a reasonable reliance upon adequate fortifications, might have been transferred to the probable scene of operations, sufficiently indicated by its intrinsic importance. Warren now constituted a light squadron of two frigates, with a half-dozen smaller vessels, including some of those recently captured. These he placed in charge of Cockburn and despatched to the head of the bay. In addition to the usual crews there went about four hundred of the naval brigade, consisting of marines and seamen in nearly equal numbers. This, with a handful of army artillerists, was the entire force. With these Cockburn went first up the Elk River, where Washington thirty years before had taken shipping on his way to the siege of Yorktown. At Frenchtown, notwithstanding a six-gun battery lately erected, a landing was effected on April 29, and a quantity of flour and army equipments were destroyed, together with five bay schooners. Many cattle were likewise seized; Cockburn, in this and other instances, offering to pay in British government bills, provided no resistance was attempted in the neighborhood. From Frenchtown he went round to the Susquehanna, to obtain more cattle from an island, just below Havre de Grace; but being there confronted on May 2 by an American flag, hoisted over a battery at the town, he proceeded to attack the following day. A nominal resistance was made; but as the British loss, here and at Frenchtown, was one wounded on each occasion, no great cause for pride was left with the defenders. Holding the inhabitants responsible for the opposition in their neighborhood, he determined to punish the town. Some houses were burned. The guns of the battery were then embarked; and during this process Cockburn himself, with a small party, marched three or four miles north of the place to a cannon foundry, where he destroyed the guns and material found, together with the buildings and machinery.

"Our small division," he reported to Warren, "has been during the whole of this day on shore, in the centre of the enemy's country, and on his high road between Baltimore and Philadelphia." The feat testified rather to the military imbecility of the United States Government during the last decade than to any signal valor or enterprise on the part of the invaders. Enough and to spare of both there doubtless was among them; for the expedition was of a kind continuously familiar to the British navy during the past twenty years, under far greater difficulty, in many parts of the world. Seeing the trifling force engaged, the mortification to Americans must be that no greater demand was made upon it for the display of its military virtues. Besides the destruction already mentioned, a division of boats went up the Susquehanna, destroyed five vessels and more flour; after which, "everything being completed to my utmost wishes, the division embarked and returned to the ships, after being twenty-two hours in constant exertion." From thence Cockburn went round to the Sassafras River, where a similar series of small injuries was inflicted, and two villages, Georgetown and Frederickstown, were destroyed, in consequence of local resistance offered, by which five British were wounded. Assurance coming from several quarters that no further armed opposition would be made, and as there was "now neither public property, vessels, nor warlike stores remaining in the neighborhood," the expedition returned down the bay, May 7, and regained the fleet.[153]

The history of the Delaware and its waters during this period was very much the same as that of the Chesapeake; except that, the water system of the lower bay being less extensive and practicable, and the river above narrower, there was not the scope for general marauding, nor the facility for systematic destruction, which constituted the peculiar exposure of the Chesapeake and gave Cockburn his opportunity. Neither was there the same shelter from the sweep of the ocean, nor any naval establishment to draw attention. For these reasons, the Chesapeake naturally attracted much more active operations; and Virginia, which formed so large a part of its coast-line, was the home of the President. She was also the leading member of the group of states which, in the internal contests of American politics, was generally thought to represent hatred to Great Britain and attachment to France. In both bays the American Government maintained flotillas of gunboats and small schooners, together with—in the Delaware at least—a certain number of great rowing barges, or galleys; but, although creditable energy was displayed, it is impossible to detect that, even in waters which might be thought suited to their particular qualities, these small craft exerted any substantial influence upon the movements of the enemy. Their principal effect appears to have been to excite among the inhabitants a certain amount of unreasonable expectation, followed inevitably by similar unreasoning complaint.

It is probable, however, that they to some extent restricted the movements of small foraging parties beyond the near range of their ships; and they served also the purpose of watching and reporting the dispositions of the British fleet. When it returned downwards from Cockburn's expedition, it was followed by a division of these schooners and gunboats, under Captain Charles Gordon of the navy, who remained cruising for nearly a month below the Potomac, constantly sighting the enemy, but without an opportunity offering for a blow to be struck under conditions favorable to either party. "The position taken by the enemy's ships," reported Gordon, "together with the constant protection given their small cruisers, particularly in the night, rendered any offensive operations on our part impracticable."[154] In the Delaware, a British corvette, running upon a shoal with a falling tide, was attacked in this situation by a division of ten gunboats which was at hand. Such conditions were unusually favorable to them, and, though a frigate was within plain sight, she could not get within range on account of the shoalness of water; yet the two hours' action which followed did no serious injury to the grounded ship. Meantime one of the gunboats drifted from its position, and was swept by the tide out of supporting distance from its fellows. The frigate and sloop then manned boats, seven in number, pulled towards her, and despite a plucky resistance carried her; their largely superior numbers easily climbing on board her low-lying deck. Although the record of gunboats in all parts of the world is mostly unfruitful, some surprise cannot but be felt at the immunity experienced by a vessel aground under such circumstances.[155]

On May 13 Captain Stewart of the "Constellation" reported from Norfolk that the enemy's fleet had returned down the bay; fifteen sail being at anchor in a line stretching from Cape Henry to near Hampton Roads. Little had yet been done by the authorities to remedy the defenceless condition of the port, which he had deplored in his letter of March 17; and he apprehended a speedy attack either upon Hampton, on the north shore of the James River, important as commanding communications between Norfolk and the country above, or upon Craney Island, covering the entrance to the Elizabeth River, through the narrow channel of which the navy yard must be approached. There was a party now at work throwing up a battery on the island, on which five hundred troops were stationed, but he feared these preparations were begun too late. He had assigned seven gunboats to assist the defence. It was clear to his mind that, if Norfolk was their object, active operations would begin at one of these approaches, and not immediately about the place itself. Meanwhile, he would await developments, and postpone his departure to Boston, whither he had been ordered to command the "Constitution."

Much to Stewart's surprise, considering the force of the enemy, which he, as a seaman, could estimate accurately and compare with what he knew to be the conditions confronting them, most of the British fleet soon after put to sea with the commander-in-chief, leaving Cockburn with one seventy-four and four frigates to hold the bay. This apparent abandonment, or at best concession of further time to Craney Island, aroused in him contempt as well as wonder. He had commented a month before on their extremely circumspect management; "they act cautiously, and never separate so far from one another that they cannot in the course of a few hours give to each other support, by dropping down or running up, as the wind or tide serve."[156] Such precaution, however, was not out of place when confronted with the presence of gunboats capable of utilizing calms and local conditions. To avoid exposure to useless injury is not to pass the bounds of military prudence. It was another matter to have brought so large a force, and to depart with no greater results than those of Frenchtown and Havre de Grace. "They do not appear disposed to put anything to risk, or to make an attack where they are likely to meet with opposition. Their conduct while in these waters has been highly disgraceful to their arms, and evinces the respect and dread they have for their opponents."[157] He added a circumstance which throws further light upon the well-known discontent of the British crews and their deterioration in quality, under a prolonged war and the confinement attending the impressment system. "Their loss in prisoners and deserters has been very considerable; the latter are coming up to Norfolk almost daily, and their naked bodies are frequently fished up on the bay shore, where they must have been drowned in attempting to swim. They all give the same account of the dissatisfaction of their crews, and their detestation of the service they are engaged in."[158] Deserters, however, usually have tales acceptable to those to whom they come.

Whether Warren was judicious in postponing attack may be doubted, but he had not lost sight of the Admiralty's hint about American frigates. There were just two in the waters of the Chesapeake; the "Constellation," 36, at Norfolk, and the "Adams," 24, Captain Charles Morris, in the Potomac. The British admiral had been notified that a division of troops would be sent to Bermuda, to be under his command for operations on shore, and he was now gone to fetch them. Early in June he returned, bringing these soldiers, two thousand six hundred and fifty in number.[159] From his Gazette letters he evidently had in view the capture of Norfolk with the "Constellation"; for when he designates Hampton and Craney Island as points of attack, it is because of their relations to Norfolk.[160] This justified the forecast of Stewart, who had now departed; the command of the "Constellation" devolving soon after upon Captain Gordon. In connection with the military detachment intrusted to Warren, the Admiralty, while declining to give particular directions as to its employment, wrote him: "Against a maritime country like America, the chief towns and establishments of which are situated upon navigable rivers, a force of the kind under your orders must necessarily be peculiarly formidable.... In the choice of objects of attack, it will naturally occur to you that on every account any attempt which should have the effect of crippling the enemy's naval force should have a preference."[161] Except for the accidental presence of Decatur's frigates in New London, as yet scarcely known to the British commander-in-chief, Norfolk, more than any other place, met this prescription of his Government. His next movements, therefore, may be considered as resulting directly from his instructions.

The first occurrence was a somewhat prolonged engagement between a division of fifteen gunboats and the frigate "Junon," which, having been sent to destroy vessels at the mouth of the James River, was caught becalmed and alone in the upper part of Hampton Roads; no other British vessel being nearer than three miles. The cannonade continued for three quarters of an hour, when a breeze springing up brought two of her consorts to the "Junon's" aid. The gunboats, incapable of close action with a single frigate in a working breeze, necessarily now retreated. They had suffered but slightly, one killed and two wounded; but retired with the confidence, always found in the accounts of such affairs, that they had inflicted great damage upon the enemy. The commander of a United States revenue cutter, lately captured, who was on board the frigate at the time, brought back word subsequently that she had lost one man killed and two or three wounded.[162] The British official reports do not allude to the affair. As regards positive results, however, it may be affirmed with considerable assurance that the military value of gunboats in their day, as a measure of coast defence, was not what they effected, but the caution imposed upon the enemy by the apprehension of what they might effect, did this or that combination of circumstances occur. That the circumstances actually almost never arose detracted little from this moral influence. The making to one's self a picture of possible consequences is a powerful factor in most military operations; and the gunboat is not without its representative to-day in the sphere of imaginative warfare.

The "Junon" business was a casual episode. Warren was already preparing for his attack on Craney Island. This little strip of ground, a half-mile long by two hundred yards across, lies within easy gunshot to the west of the Elizabeth River, a narrow channel-way, three hundred yards from edge to edge, which from Hampton Roads leads due south, through extensive flats, to Norfolk and Portsmouth. The navy yard is four miles above the island, on the west side of the river, the banks of which there have risen above the water. Up to and beyond Craney Island the river-bed proper, though fairly clear, is submerged and hidden amid the surrounding expanse of shoal water. Good pilotage, therefore, is necessary, and incidental thereto the reduction beforehand of an enemy's positions commanding the approach. Of these Craney Island was the first. From it the flats which constitute the under-water banks of the Elizabeth extend north towards Hampton Roads, for a distance of two miles, and are not traversable by vessels powerful enough to act against batteries. For nearly half a mile the depth is less than four feet, while the sand immediately round the island was bare when the tide was out.[163] Attack here was possible only by boats armed with light cannon and carrying troops. On the west the island was separated from the mainland by a narrow strip of water, fordable by infantry at low tide. It was therefore determined to make a double assault,—one on the north, by fifteen boats, carrying, besides their crews, five hundred soldiers; the other on the west, by a division eight hundred strong,[164] to be landed four miles away, at the mouth of the Nansemond River. The garrison of the island numbered five hundred and eighty, and one hundred and fifty seamen were landed from the "Constellation" to man one of the principal batteries.

The British plan labored under the difficulty that opposite conditions of tide were desirable for the two parties which were to act in concert. The front attack demanded high water, in order that under the impulse of the oars the boats might get as near as possible before they took the ground, whence the advance to the assault must be by wading. The flanking movement required low water, to facilitate passing the ford. Between the two, the hour was fixed for an ebbing tide, probably to allow for delays, and to assure the arrival of the infantry so as to profit by the least depth. At 11 A.M. of June 22 the boat division arrived off the northwest point of the island, opposite the battery manned by the seamen, in that day notoriously among the best of artillerists. A difference of opinion as to the propriety of advancing at all here showed itself among the senior naval officers; for there will always be among seamen a dislike to operating over unknown ground with a falling tide. The captain in command, however, overruled hesitations; doubtless feeling that in a combined movement the particular interest of one division must yield to the requirements of mutual support. A spirited forward dash was therefore made; but the guiding boat, sixty yards ahead of the others, grounded a hundred yards from the battery. One or two others, disregarding her signal, shared her mishap; and two were sunk by the American fire. Under these circumstances a seaman, sounding with a boat hook, declared that he found along side three or four feet of slimy mud. This was considered decisive, and the attack was abandoned.

The shore division had already retreated, having encountered obstacles, the precise character of which is not stated. Warren's report simply said, "In consequence of the representation of the officer commanding the troops, of the difficulty of their passing over from the land, I considered that the persevering in the attempt would cost more men than the number with us would permit, as the other forts must have been stormed before the frigate and dockyard could be destroyed." The enterprise was therefore abandoned at the threshold, because of probable ulterior difficulties, the degree of which it would require to-day unprofitable labor even to conjecture; but reduced as the affair in its upshot was to an abortive demonstration, followed by no serious effort, it probably was not reckoned at home to have fulfilled the Admiralty's injunctions, that the character as well as the interest of the country required certain results. The loss was trifling,—three killed, sixteen wounded, sixty-two missing.[165]

Having relinquished his purpose against Craney Island, and with it, apparently, all serious thought of the navy yard and the "Constellation", Warren next turned his attention to Hampton. On the early morning of June 26 two thousand troops were landed to take possession of the place, which they did with slight resistance. Three stand of colors were captured and seven field guns, with their equipment and ammunition. The defences of the town were destroyed; but as no further use was made of the advantage gained, the affair amounted to nothing more than an illustration on a larger scale of the guerilla depredation carried on on all sides of the Chesapeake. With it ended Warren's attempts against Norfolk. His force may have been really inadequate to more; certainly it was far smaller than was despatched to the same quarter the following year; but the Admiralty probably was satisfied by this time that he had not the enterprise necessary for his position, and a successor was appointed during the following winter. For two months longer the British fleet as a whole remained in the bay, engaged in desultory operations, which had at least the effect of greatly increasing their local knowledge, and in so far facilitating the more serious undertakings of the next season. The Chesapeake was not so much blockaded as occupied. On June 29 Captain Cassin of the navy yard reported that six sail of the line, with four frigates, were at the mouth of the Elizabeth, and that the day before a squadron of thirteen—frigates, brigs, and schooners—had gone ten miles up the James, causing the inhabitants of Smithfield and the surroundings to fly from their homes, terrified by the transactions at Hampton. The lighter vessels continued some distance farther towards Richmond. A renewal of the attack was naturally expected; but on July 11 the fleet quitted Hampton Roads, and again ascended the Chesapeake, leaving a division of ten sail in Lynnhaven Bay, under Cape Henry. Two days later the main body entered the Potomac, in which, as has before been mentioned, was the frigate "Adams"; but she lay above the Narrows, out of reach of such efforts as Warren was willing to risk. He went as high as Blakiston Island, twenty-five to thirty miles from the river's mouth, and from there Cockburn, with a couple of frigates and two smaller vessels, tried to get beyond the Kettle Bottom Shoals, an intricate bit of navigation ten miles higher up, but still below the Narrows.[166] Two of his detachment, however, took the ground; and the enterprise of approaching Washington by this route was for that time abandoned. A year afterwards it was accomplished by Captain Gordon, of the British Navy, who carried two frigates and a division of bomb vessels as far as Alexandria.

Two United States gunboats, "The Scorpion" and "Asp", lying in Yeocomico River, a shallow tributary of the Potomac ten miles from the Chesapeake, were surprised there July 14 by the entrance of the enemy. Getting under way hastily, the "Scorpion" succeeded in reaching the main stream and retreating up it; but the "Asp", being a bad sailer, and the wind contrary, had to go back. She was pursued by boats; and although an attack by three was beaten off, she was subsequently carried when they were re-enforced to five. Her commander, Midshipman Sigourney, was killed, and of the twenty-one in her crew nine were either killed or wounded. The assailants were considerably superior in numbers, as they need to be in such undertakings. They lost eight. This was the second United States vessel thus captured in the Chesapeake this year; the revenue cutter "Surveyor" having been taken in York River, by the boats of the frigate "Narcissus", on the night of June 12. In the latter instance, the sword of the commander, who survived, was returned to him the next day by the captor, with a letter testifying "an admiration on the part of your opponents, such as I have seldom witnessed, for your gallant and desperate attempt to defend your vessel against more than double your numbers."[167] Trivial in themselves as these affairs were, it is satisfactory to notice that in both the honor of the flag was upheld with a spirit which is worth even more than victory. Sigourney had before received the commendation of Captain Morris, no mean judge of an officer's merits.

The British fleet left the Potomac July 21, and went on up the bay, spreading alarm on every side. Morris, with a body of seamen and marines, was ordered from the "Adams" to Annapolis, the capital of Maryland, on the River Severn, to command the defences. These he reported, on August 13, to be in the "miserable condition" characteristic of all the national preparations to meet hostilities. With a view to entering, the enemy was sounding the bar, an operation which frequently must be carried on beyond protection by ships' guns; "but we have no floating force to molest them." The bulk of the fleet was above the Severn, as were both admirals, and Morris found their movements "contradictory, as usual."[168] As many as twenty sail had at one time been visible from the state-house dome in the city. On August 8, fifteen, three of which were seventy-fours, were counted from North Point, at the mouth of the Patapsco, on which Baltimore lies. Kent Island, on the eastern shore of the bay abreast Annapolis, was taken possession of, and occupied for some days. At the same period attacks were reported in other quarters on that side of the Chesapeake, as elsewhere in the extensive basin penetrated by its tributaries. The prosecution of these various enterprises was attended with the usual amount of scuffling encounter, which associates itself naturally with coastwise warfare of a guerilla character. The fortune of war inclined now to one side, now to the other, in the particular cases; but in the general there could be no doubt as to which party was getting the worst, undergoing besides almost all the suffering and quite all the harassment. This is the necessary penalty of the defensive, when inadequate.

Throughout most of this summer of conflict there went on, singularly enough, a certain amount of trade by licensed vessels, neutral and

American, which passed down Chesapeake Bay and went to sea. Doubtless the aggregate amount of traffic thus maintained was inconsiderable, as compared with normal conditions, but its allowance by either party to the war is noticeable,—by the British, because of the blockade declared by them; by the Americans, because of the evident inexpediency of permitting to depart vessels having full knowledge of conditions, and almost certain to be boarded by the enemy. Sailing from blockaded ports is of course promoted in most instances by the nation blockaded, for it is in support of trade; and with the sea close at hand, although there is risk, there is also chance of safe passage through a belt of danger, relatively narrow and entered at will. The case is quite different where a hazardous navigation of sixty to a hundred miles, increasing in intricacy at its further end, and lined throughout with enemy's cruisers, interposes before the sea is reached. The difficulty here is demonstrated by the fact that the "Adams," a ship by no means large or exceptionally fettered by navigational difficulties, under a young captain burning to exercise his first command in war, waited four months, even after the bulk of the enemy's fleet had gone, before she was able to get through; and finally did so only under such conditions of weather as caused her to miss her way and strike bottom.

The motive of the British for collusion is clear. The Chesapeake was the heart of the wheat and flour production of the United States, and while some provision had been made for meeting the wants of the West Indies, and of the armies in Canada and Spain, by refraining from commercial blockade of Boston and other eastern ports, these necessary food supplies reached those places only after an expensive transport which materially increased their price; the more as they were carried by land to the point of exportation, it not suiting the British policy to connive at coasting trade even for that purpose. A neutral or licensed vessel, sailing from the Chesapeake with flour for a port friendly to the United States, could be seized under cover of the commercial blockade, which she was violating, sent to Halifax, and condemned for her technical offence. The cargo then was available for transport whither required, the whole transaction being covered by a veil of legality; but it is plain that the risks to a merchant, in attempting bonâ fide to run a blockade like that of Chesapeake Bay, exceeded too far any probable gain to have been undertaken without some assurance of compensation, which did not appear on the surface.

Taken in connection with intelligence obtained by this means, the British motive is apparent; but why did the United States administration tolerate procedures which betrayed its counsels, and directly helped to sustain the enemy's war? Something perhaps is due to executive weakness in a government constituted by popular vote; more, probably, at least during the period when immediate military danger did not threaten, to a wish to frustrate the particular advantage reaped by New England, through its exemption from the restrictions of the commercial blockade. When breadstuffs were pouring out of the country through the coast-line of a section which gloried in its opposition to the war,[169] and lost no opportunity to renew the declaration of its disapproval and its criticism of the Government, it was at least natural, perhaps even expedient, to wink at proceedings which transferred elsewhere some of the profits, and did not materially increase the advantage of the enemy. But circumstances became very different when a fleet appeared in the bay, the numbers and action of which showed a determination to carry hostile operations wherever conditions permitted. Then, betrayal of such conditions by passing vessels became an unbearable evil; and at the same time the Administration had forced upon its attention the unpleasant but notorious fact that, by the active complicity of many of its own citizens, not only the flour trade continued, but the wants of the blockading squadrons along the coast were being supplied. Neutrals, real or pretended, and coasting vessels, assuming a lawful destination, took on board cattle, fresh vegetables, and other stores acceptable to ships confined to salt provisions, and either went direct to enemy's ports or were captured by collusion. News was received of contracts made by the British admiral at Bermuda for fresh beef to be supplied from American ports, by American dealers, in American vessels; while Halifax teemed with similar transactions, without serious attempt at concealment.

Such aid and comfort to an enemy is by no means unexampled in the history of war, particularly where one of the belligerents is shrewdly commercial; but it is scarcely too much to say that it attained unusual proportions at this time in the United States, and was countenanced by a public opinion which was more than tolerant, particularly in New England, where the attitude of the majority towards the Government approached hostility. As a manifestation of contemporary national character, of unwillingness to subordinate personal gain to public welfare, to loyalty to country, it was pitiable and shameful, particularly as it affected large communities; but its instructive significance at this time is the evidence it gives that forty years of confederation, nearly twenty-five being of the closer union under the present Constitution, had not yet welded the people into a whole, or created a consciousness truly national. The capacity for patriotism was there, and readiness to suffer for patriotic cause had been demonstrated by the War of Independence; but the mass of Americans had not yet risen sufficiently above local traditions and interests to discern clearly the noble ideal of national unity, and vagueness of apprehension resulted inevitably in lukewarmness of sentiment. This condition goes far to palliate actions which it cannot excuse; the reproach of helping the enemies of one's country is somewhat less when the nation itself has scarcely emerged to recognition, as it afterwards did under the inspiring watchword,

"The Union."

The necessity to control these conditions of clandestine intercourse found official expression in a message of the President to Congress, July 20, 1813,[170] recommending "an immediate and effectual prohibition of all exports" for a limited time; subject to removal by executive order, in case the commercial blockade were raised. A summary of the conditions above related was given, as a cause for action. The President's further comment revealed the continuity of thought and policy which dictated his recommendation, and connected the proposed measure with the old series of commercial restrictions, associated with his occupancy of the State Department under Jefferson's administration. "The system of the enemy, combining with the blockade of our ports special licenses to neutral vessels, and insidious discrimination between different ports of the United States, if not counteracted, will have the effect of diminishing very materially the pressure of the war on the enemy, and encourage perseverance in it, and at the same time will leave the general commerce of the United States under all the pressure the enemy can impose, thus subjecting the whole to British regulation, in subserviency to British monopoly."

The House passed a bill meeting the President's suggestions, but it was rejected by the Senate on July 28. The Executive then fell back on its own war powers; and on July 29 the Secretary of the Navy, by direction of the President, issued a general order to all naval officers in command, calling attention to "the palpable and criminal intercourse held with the enemy's forces blockading and invading the waters of the United States." "This intercourse," he explicitly added, "is not only carried on by foreigners, under the specious garb of friendly flags, who convey provisions, water, and succors of all kinds (ostensibly destined for friendly ports, in the face, too, of a declared and rigorous blockade),[171] direct to the fleets and stations of the enemy, with constant intelligence of our naval and military force and preparation, ... but the same traffic, intercourse, and intelligence is carried on with great subtlety and treachery by profligate citizens, who, in vessels ostensibly navigating our own waters, from port to port [coasters], find means to convey succors or intelligence to the enemy, and elude the penalty of law."[172] Officers were therefore instructed to arrest all vessels, the movements or situation of which indicated an intention to effect any of the purposes indicated.

A similar order was issued, August 5, by the War Department to army officers.[173] In accordance with his instructions, Captain Morris of the "Adams," on July 29 or 30, stopped the ship "Monsoon," from Alexandria. Her agent wrote a correspondent in Boston that, when the bill failed in the Senate, he had had no doubt of her being allowed to proceed, "but the Secretary and Mr. Madison have made a sort of embargo, or directed the stoppage of vessels."[174] He added that another brig was lying in the river ready loaded, but held by the same order. Morris's indorsement on the ship's papers shows the barefacedness of the transaction. "Whereas the within-mentioned ship 'Monsoon' is laden with flour, and must pass within the control of the enemy's squadron now within, and blockading Chesapeake Bay, if she be allowed to proceed on her intended voyage, and as the enemy might derive from her such intelligence and succor as would be serviceable to themselves and injurious to the United States, I forbid her proceeding while the enemy shall be so disposed as to prevent a reasonable possibility of her getting to sea without falling into their possession."[175] At this writing the British had left the Potomac itself, and the most of them were above. A week later, at Charleston, a ship called the "Caroline" was visited by a United States naval officer, and found with a license from Cockburn to carry a cargo, free from molestation by British cruisers.[176] "With flour at Lisbon $13 per barrel, no sale, and at Halifax $20, in demand," queries a Baltimore paper of the day, "where would all the vessels that would in a few days have been off from Alexandria have gone, if the 'Monsoon' had not been stopped? They would have been captured and sent to Halifax."[177]

Morris's action was in accordance with the Secretary's order, and went no further than to stop a voyage which, in view of the existing proclaimed blockade, and of the great British force at hand, bore collusion on its face. The President's request for legislation, which Congress had denied, went much further. It was a recurrence, and the last, to the policy of commercial retaliation, fostered by himself and Jefferson in preference to armed resistance. By such measures in peace, and as far as commercial prosperity was concerned, they had opened the nation's veins without vindicating its self-respect. The military value of food supplies to the enemy in Canada and on the coast, however, could not be contested; and during the recess of Congress it received emphasis by a Canadian embargo upon the export of grain. Hence, at the next session the President's recommendation of July was given attention, and there was passed almost immediately—December 17, 1813,—a sweeping embargo law, applicable not only to external commerce but to coasters. As this ended the long series of commercial restrictions, so was it also of limited duration as compared with them, being withdrawn the following April.

By the Act of December 17, as interpreted by the Treasury, foreign merchant vessels might depart with cargoes already laden, except provisions and military stores, which must be relanded; but nothing could be shipped that was not already on board when the Act was received. Coasters, even for accustomed voyages, could obtain clearances only by permission from the President; and the rules for such permission, given through the collectors, were extremely stringent. In no case were the vessels permitted to leave interior waters, proceeding from one sound or bay to another, and be "at sea" for even a short distance; nor were they to be permitted to carry any provisions, or supplies useful to an enemy, if there was the slightest chance of their falling into his power. It would appear that the orders of July 29 had been allowed to lapse after the great body of the British left the Chesapeake; for Morris, still in the Potomac, acknowledging the receipt of this Act on December 20, writes: "There are several vessels below us in the river with flour. I have issued orders to the gunboats to detain them, and as soon as the wind will permit, shall proceed with this ship, to give all possible effect to the Act." Six days afterwards, having gone down as he intended, he found the British anchored off the mouth of the stream, at a point where the bay is little more than five miles wide. "Two American brigs passed down before us, and I have every reason to believe threw themselves into the enemy's hands last Wednesday."[178]

On September 6 the principal part of the British fleet quitted Chesapeake Bay for the season; leaving behind a ship of the line with some smaller vessels, to enforce the blockade. Viewed as a military campaign, to sustain the character as well as the interests of the country, its operations cannot be regarded as successful. With overwhelming numbers, and signally favored by the quiet inland waters with extensive ramifications which characterized the scene of war, the results, though on a more extensive scale, differed nothing in kind from the harassment inflicted all along the coast from Maine to Georgia, by the squadrons cruising outside. Ample demonstration was indeed afforded, there as elsewhere, of the steady, remorseless, far-reaching effect of a predominant sea power; and is confirmed explicitly by an incidental remark of the Russian minister at Washington writing to Warren, April 4, 1813, concerning an armistice, in connection with the abortive Russian proffer of mediation.[179] Even at this early period, "It would be almost impossible to establish an armistice, without raising the blockade, since the latter does them more harm than all the hostilities."[180] But in direct military execution the expedition had undoubtedly fallen far short of its opportunity, afforded by the wretchedly unprepared state of the region against which it had been sent. Whether the fault lay with the commander-in-chief, or with the Admiralty for insufficient means given him, is needless here to inquire. The squadron remaining through the winter perpetuated the isolation of Norfolk from the upper bay, and barred the "Constellation" and "Adams" from the sea. Ammunition and stores had to be brought by slow and unwieldly transportation from the Potomac across country, and it was not till January 18, 1814, that the "Adams" got away. Two attempts of the "Constellation" a month later were frustrated.

The principal two British divisions, the action of which has so far been considered, the one blockading the Chesapeake, the other watching Decatur's squadron in New London, marked the extremities of what may be considered the central section of the enemy's coastwise operations upon the Atlantic. Although the commercial shipping of the United States belonged largely to New England, much the greater part of the exports came from the district thus closed to the world; and within it also, after the sailing of the "President" and "Congress" from Boston, and the capture of the "Chesapeake", lay in 1813 all the bigger vessels of the navy, save the "Constitution".

In the conditions presented to the enemy, the sections of the coast-line south of Virginia, and north of Cape Cod, differed in some important respects from the central division, and from each other. There was in them no extensive estuary wide open to the sea, resembling Chesapeake and Delaware bays, and Long Island Sound, accessible to vessels of all sizes; features which naturally determined upon these points the chief effort of a maritime enemy, enabling him readily to paralyze the whole system of intercourse depending upon them, domestic as well as foreign. The southern waters abounded indeed in internal coastwise communications; not consecutive throughout, but continuous for long reaches along the shores of North and South Carolina and Georgia. These, however, were narrow, and not easily approached. Behind the sea islands, which inclose this navigation, small craft can make their voyages sheltered from the perils of the sea, and protected in great measure from attack other than by boats or very light cruisers; to which, moreover, some local knowledge was necessary, for crossing the bars, or threading the channels connecting sound with sound. Into these inside basins empty numerous navigable rivers, which promoted intercourse, and also furnished lines of retreat from danger coming from the sea. Coupled with these conditions was the fact that the United States had in these quarters no naval establishment, and no naval vessels of force. Defence was intrusted wholly to gunboats, with three or four armed schooners of somewhat larger tonnage. American offensive operation, confined here as elsewhere to commerce destroying, depended entirely on privateers. Into these ports, where there were no public facilities for repair, not even a national sloop of war entered until 1814 was well advanced.

Prior to the war, one third of the domestic export of the United States had issued from this southern section; and in the harassed year 1813 this ratio increased. The aggregate for the whole country was reduced by one half from that of 1811, and amounted to little more than one fourth of the prosperous times preceding Jefferson's embargo of 1808, with its vexatious progeny of restrictive measures; but the proportion of the South increased. The same was observable in the Middle states, containing the great centres of New York, Philadelphia, and Baltimore. There a ratio to the total, of a little under fifty per cent, rose to something above that figure. The relative diminution, corresponding to the increases just noted, fell upon New England, and is interesting because of what it indicates. Before the war the export of domestic produce from the eastern ports was twenty per cent of the national total; in 1813 it fell to ten per cent. When the domestic export is taken in conjunction with the re-exportation of foreign products, the loss of New England is still more striking. From twenty-five per cent of the whole national export, domestic and foreign, she now fell to ten per cent of the diminished total. When it is remembered that throughout 1813 the Eastern ports alone were open to neutral ships, no commercial blockade of them having yet been instituted, these results are the more noticeable.

The general explanation is that the industries of the United States at that time divided into two principal classes,—agricultural and maritime; the former of which supplied the material for commerce, while the latter furnished transportation for whatever surplus of production remained for export. Manufactures sufficed only for home demands, being yet in a state of infancy; forced, in fact, upon an unwilling New England by the policy of commercial restriction which drove her ships off the sea. Domestic products for export therefore meant almost wholly the yield of the fields, the forests, and the fisheries. The latter belonged to New England, but they fell with the war. Her soil did not supply grain enough to feed her people; and her domestic exports, therefore, were reduced to shipments of wheat and flour conveyed to her by inland transportation from the more fertile, but blockaded, regions to the southward. Despite the great demand for provisions in Halifax and the St. Lawrence region, and the facility for egress by sea, through the absence of blockade, the slowness and cost of land carriage brought forward an insufficient supply, and laid a heavy charge upon the transaction; while the license system of the British, modifying this condition of things to their own advantage, by facilitating exports from the Chesapeake, certainly did operate, as the President's message said, to regulate American commerce in conformity with British interests.

The re-exportation of foreign produce had once played a very large part in the foreign trade of New England. This item consisted chiefly in West India commodities; and although, owing to several causes, it fell off very much in the years between 1805 and 1811, it had remained still considerable. It was, however, particularly obnoxious to British interests, as then understood by British statesmen and people; and since it depended entirely upon American ships,—for it was not to the interest of a neutral to bring sugar and coffee to an American port merely to carry it away again,—it disappeared entirely when the outbreak of war rendered all American merchant vessels liable to capture. In fact, as far as the United States was concerned, although this re-exportation appeared among commercial returns, it was not an interest of commerce, accurately so called, but of navigation, of carrying trade. It had to do with ships, not with cargoes; its gain was that of the wagoner. Still, the loss by the idleness of the ships, due to the war, may be measured in terms of the cargoes. In 1805 New England re-exported foreign products to the amount of $15,621,484; in 1811, $5,944,121; in 1813, no more than $302,781. It remains to add that, as can be readily understood, all export, whether of foreign or domestic produce, was chiefly by neutrals, which were not liable to capture so long as there was no blockade proclaimed. From December 1 to 24, 1813, forty-four vessels cleared from Boston for abroad, of which five only were Americans.[181]

Under the very reduced amount of their commercial movement, the tonnage of the Middle and Southern states was more than adequate to their local necessities; and they now had no need of the aid which in conditions of normal prosperity they received from the Eastern shipping. The latter, therefore, having lost its usual local occupation, and also the office it had filled towards the other sections of the Union, was either left idle or turned perforce to privateering. September 7, 1813, there were in Boston harbor ninety-one ships, two barks, one hundred and nine brigs, and forty-three schooners; total, two hundred and forty-five, besides coasters. The accumulation shows the lack of employment. December 15, two hundred square-rigged vessels were laid up in Boston alone.[182] Insurance on American vessels was stated to be fifty per cent.[183]

Whether tonnage to any large amount was transferred to a neutral flag, as afterwards so much American shipping was during the Civil War, I have not ascertained. It was roundly intimated that neutral flags were used to cover the illicit intercourse with the enemy before mentioned; but whether by regular transfer or by fraudulent papers does not appear. An officer of the frigate "Congress," in her unprofitable voyage just mentioned, says that after parting with the "President," she fell in with a few licensed Americans and a great number of Spaniards and Portuguese.[184] The flags of these two nations, and of Sweden, certainly abounded to an abnormal extent, and did much of the traffic from America; but it seems unlikely that there was at that particular epoch any national commerce, other than British, at once large enough, and sufficiently deficient in shipping of its own, to absorb any great number of Americans. In truth, the commerce of the world had lost pretty much all its American component, because this, through a variety of causes, had come to consist chiefly of domestic agricultural products, which were thrown back upon the nation's hands, and required no carriers; the enemy having closed the gates against them, except so far as suited his own purposes. The disappearance of American merchant ships from the high seas corresponded to the void occasioned by the blockade of American staples of commerce. The only serious abatement from this generalization arises from the British system of licenses, permitting the egress of certain articles useful to themselves.

The results from the conditions above analyzed are reflected in the returns of commerce, in the movements of American coasters, and in the consequent dispositions of the enemy. In the Treasury year ending

September 30, 1813, the value of the total exports from the Eastern states was $3,049,022; from the Middle section, $17,513,930; from the South, $7,293,043. Virginia is here reckoned with the Middle, because her exports found their way out by the Chesapeake; and this appreciation is commercial and military in character, not political or social. While this was the state of foreign trade under war conditions, the effect of local circumstances upon coasting is also to be noticed. The Middle section, characterized by the great estuaries, and by the description of its products,—grain primarily, and secondly tobacco,—was relatively self-sufficing and compact. Its growth of food, as has been seen, was far in excess of its wants, and the distance by land between the extreme centres of distribution, from tide-water to tide-water, was comparatively short. From New York to Baltimore by road is but four fifths as far as from New York to Boston; and at New York and Baltimore, as at Boston, water communication was again reached for the great lines of distribution from either centre. In fact, traffic from New York southward needed to go no farther than Elk River, forty miles short of Baltimore, to be in touch with the whole Chesapeake system. Philadelphia lies half-way between New York and Baltimore, approximately a hundred miles from each.

The extremes of the Middle section of the country were thus comparatively independent of coastwise traffic for mutual intercourse, and the character of their coasts co-operated to reduce the disposition to employ coasters in war. From the Chesapeake to Sandy Hook the shore-line sweeps out to sea, is safely approachable by hostile navigators, and has for refuge no harbors of consequence, except the Delaware. The local needs of the little communities along the beaches might foster a creeping stream of very small craft, for local supply; but as a highway, for intercourse on a large scale, the sea here was too exposed for use, when taken in connection with the facility for transport by land, which was not only short but with comparatively good roads.

In war, as in other troublous times, prices are subject to complicated causes of fluctuation, not always separable. Two great staples, flour and sugar, however, may be taken to indicate with some certainty the effects of impeded water transport. From a table of prices current, of August, 1813, it appears that at Baltimore, in the centre of the wheat export, flour was $6.00 per barrel; in Philadelphia, $7.50; in New York, $8.50; in Boston, $11.87. At Richmond, equally well placed with Baltimore as regarded supplies, but with inferior communications for disposing of its surplus, the price was $4.00. Removing from the grain centre in the other direction, flour at Charleston is reported at $8.00—about the same as New York; at Wilmington, North Carolina, $10.25. Not impossibly, river transportation had in these last some cheapening effect, not readily ascertainable now. In sugar, the scale is seen to ascend in an inverse direction. At Boston, unblockaded, it is quoted at $18.75 the hundredweight, itself not a low rate; at New York, blockaded, $21.50; at Philadelphia, with a longer journey, $22.50; at Baltimore, $26.50; at Savannah, $20. In the last named place, nearness to the Florida line, with the inland navigation, favored smuggling and safe transportation. The price at New Orleans, a sugar-producing district, $9.00, affords a standard by which to measure the cost of carriage at that time. Flour in the same city, on February 1, 1813, was $25 the barrel.

In both articles the jump between Boston and New York suggests forcibly the harassment of the coasting trade. It manifests either diminution of supply, or the effect of more expensive conveyance by land; possibly both. The case of the southern seaboard cities was similar to that of Boston; for it will not be overlooked that, as the more important food products came from the middle of the country, they would be equally available for each extreme. The South was the more remote, but this was compensated in some degree by better internal water communications; and its demand also was less, for the white population was smaller and less wealthy than that of New England. The local product, rice, also went far to supply deficiencies in other grains. In the matter of manufactured goods, however, the disadvantage of the South was greater. These had to find their way there from the farther extreme of the land; for the development of manufactures had been much the most marked in the east. It has before been quoted that some wagons loaded with dry goods were forty-six days in accomplishing the journey from Philadelphia to Georgetown, South Carolina, in May of this year. Some relief in these articles reached the South by smuggling across the Florida line, and the Spanish waters opposite St. Mary's were at this time thronged with merchant shipping to an unprecedented extent; for although smuggling was continual, in peace as in war, across a river frontier of a hundred miles, the stringent demand consequent upon the interruption of coastwise traffic provoked an increased supply. "The trade to Amelia,"— the northernmost of the Spanish sea-islands,—reported the United States naval officer at St. Mary's towards the end of the war, "is immense. Upwards of fifty square-rigged vessels are now in that port under Swedish, Russian, and Spanish colors, two thirds of which are considered British property."[185] It was the old story of the Continental and License systems of the Napoleonic struggle, re-enacted in America; and, as always, the inhabitants on both sides the line co-operated heartily in beating the law.

The two great food staples chosen sufficiently indicate general conditions as regards communications from centre to centre. Upon this supervened the more extensive and intricate problem of distribution from the centres. This more especially imparted to the Eastern and Southern coasts the particular characteristics of coasting trade and coast warfare, in which they differ from the Middle states. These form the burden of the letters from the naval captains commanding the stations at Charleston, Savannah, and

Portsmouth, New Hampshire; nor is it without significance that Bainbridge at Boston, not a way port, but a centre, displayed noticeably less anxiety than the others about this question, which less touched his own command. Captain Hull, now commanding the Portsmouth Yard, writes, June 14, 1813, that light cruisers like the "Siren," lately arrived at Boston, and the "Enterprise," then with him, can be very useful by driving away the enemy's small vessels and privateers which have been molesting the coasting trade. He purposes to order them eastward, along the Maine coast, to collect coasters in convoy and protect their long-shore voyages, after the British fashion on the high seas. "The coasting trade here," he adds, "is immense. Not less than fifty sail last night anchored in this harbor, bound to Boston and other points south. The 'Nautilus' [a captured United States brig] has been seen from this harbor every week for some time past, and several other enemy's vessels are on the coast every few days." An American privateer has just come in, bringing with her as a prize one of her own class, called the "Liverpool Packet," which "within six months has taken from us property to an immense amount."[186]

Ten days later Hull's prospects have darkened. There has appeared off Portsmouth a blockading division; a frigate, a sloop, and two brigs. "When our two vessels were first ordered to this station, I believed they would be very useful in protecting the coasting trade; but the enemy's cruisers are now so much stronger that we can hardly promise security to the trade, if we undertake to convoy it." On the contrary, the brigs themselves would be greatly hazarded, and resistance to attack, if supported by the neighborhood, may entail destruction upon ports where they have taken refuge; a thought possibly suggested by Cockburn's action at Havre de Grace and Frenchtown. He therefore now proposes that they should run the blockade and cruise at sea. This course was eventually adopted; but for the moment the Secretary wrote that, while he perceived the propriety of Hull's remarks, "the call for protection on that coast has been very loud, and having sent those vessels for that special purpose, I do not now incline immediately to remove them."[187] It was necessary to bend to a popular clamor, which in this case did not, as it very frequently does, make unreasonable demands and contravene all considerations of military wisdom. A month later Hull reports the blockade so strict that it is impossible to get out by day. The commander of the "Enterprise," Johnston Blakely, expresses astonishment that the enemy should employ so large a force to blockade so small a vessel.[188] It was, however, no matter for surprise, but purely a question of business. The possibilities of injury by the "Enterprise" must be blasted at any cost, and Blakely himself a year later, in the "Wasp," was to illustrate forcibly what one smart ship can effect in the destruction of hostile commerce and hostile cruisers.

Blakely's letter was dated July 31. The "Enterprise" had not long to wait for her opportunity, but it did not fall to his lot to utilize it. Being promoted the following month, he was relieved in command by Lieutenant William Burrows. This officer had been absent in China, in mercantile employment, when the war broke out, and, returning, was captured at sea. Exchanged in June, 1813, he was ordered to the "Enterprise," in which he saw his only service in the war,—a brief month. She left Portsmouth September 1, on a coasting cruise, and on the morning of the 5th, being then off Monhegan Island, on the coast of Maine, sighted a vessel of war, which proved to be the British brig "Boxer," Commander Samuel Blyth.

The antagonists in the approaching combat were nearly of equal force, the respective armaments being, "Enterprise," fourteen 18-pounder carronades, and two long 9-pounders, the "Boxer," twelve 18-pounder carronades and two long sixes. The action began side by side, at half pistol-shot, the "Enterprise" to the right and to windward (position 1). After fifteen minutes the latter ranged ahead (2). As she did so, one of her 9-pounders, which by the forethought of Captain Burrows had been shifted from its place in the bow to the stern,[189] was used with effect to rake her opponent. She then rounded-to on the starboard tack, on the port-bow of the enemy,—ahead but well to the left (3),—in position to rake with her carronades; and, setting the foresail, sailed slowly across from left to right. In five minutes the "Boxer's" maintopmast and foretopsailyard fell. This left the "Enterprise" the mastery of the situation, which she continued to hold until ten minutes later, when the enemy's fire ceased. Her colors could not be hauled down, Blyth having nailed them to the mast. He himself had been killed at the first broadside, and almost at the same instant Burrows too fell, mortally wounded.

The "Boxer" belonged to a class of vessel, the gun brigs, which Marryat through one of his characters styled "bathing machines," only not built, as the legitimate article, to go up, but to go down. Another,—the immortal Boatswain Chucks,—proclaimed that they would "certainly d—n their inventor to all eternity;" adding characteristically, that "their low common names, 'Pincher,' 'Thrasher,' 'Boxer,' 'Badger,' and all that sort, are quite good enough for them." In the United States service the "Enterprise," which had been altered from a schooner to a brig, was considered a singularly dull sailer. As determined by American measurements, taken four days after the action, the size of the two was the same within twenty tons; the "Boxer" a little the larger. The superiority of the "Enterprise" in broadside force, was eight guns to seven; or, stated in weight of projectiles, one hundred and thirty-five pounds to one hundred and fourteen. This disparity, though real, was in no sense decisive, and the execution done by each bore no comparison to the respective armaments. The hull of the "Boxer" was pierced on the starboard side by twelve 18-pound shot, nearly two for each of the "Enterprise's" carronades. The 9-pounder had done even better, scoring five hits. On her port side had entered six of 18 pounds, and four of 9 pounds. By the official report of an inspection, made upon her arrival in Portland, it appears that her upper works and sides forward were torn to pieces.[190] In her mainmast alone were three 18-pound shot.[191] As a set-off to this principal damage received, she had to show only one 18-pound shot in the hull of the "Enterprise," one in the foremast, and one in the mainmast.[192]

From these returns, the American loss in killed and wounded, twelve, must have been largely by grapeshot or musketry. The British had twenty-one men hurt. It has been said that this difference in loss is nearly proportionate to the difference in force. This is obviously inexact; for the "Enterprise" was superior in gun power by twelve per cent, while the "Boxer's" loss was greater by seventy-five per cent. Moreover, if the statement of crews be accurate, that the "Enterprise" had one hundred and twenty and the "Boxer" only sixty-six,[193] it is clear that the latter had double the human target, and scored little more than half the hits. The contest, in brief, was first an artillery duel, side to side, followed by a raking position obtained by the American. It therefore reproduced in leading features, although on a minute scale, the affair between the "Chesapeake" and "Shannon"; and the exultation of the American populace at this rehabilitation of the credit of their navy, though exaggerated in impression, was in principle sound. The British Court Martial found that the defeat was "to be attributed to a superiority of the enemy's force, principally in the number of men, as well as to a greater degree of skill in the direction of her fire, and the destructive effects of her first broadside."[194] This admission as to the enemy's gunnery is substantially identical with the claim made for that of the "Shannon,"—notably as to the first broadside. As to the greater numbers, one hundred and twenty is certainly almost twice sixty-six, and the circumstance should be weighed; but in an engagement confined to the guns, and between 18-pounder carronade batteries, it is of less consequence than at first glance appears. A cruiser of those days expected to be ready to fight with many men away in prizes. Had it come to boarding, or had the "Boxer's" gunnery been good, disabling her opponent's men, the numbers would have become of consideration. As it was, they told for something, but not for very much.

If national credit were at issue in every single-ship action, the balance of the "Chesapeake" and "Shannon," "Enterprise" and "Boxer," would incline rather to the American side; for the "Boxer" was not just out of port with new commander, officers, and crew, but had been in commission six months, had in that time crossed the ocean, and been employed along the coast. The credit and discredit in both cases is personal, not national. It was the sadder in Blyth's case because he was an officer of distinguished courage and activity, who had begun his fighting career at the age of eleven, when he was on board a heavily battered ship in Lord Howe's battle of June 1, 1794. At thirty, with little influence, and at a period when promotion had become comparatively sluggish, he had fairly fought his way to the modest preferment in which he died. Under the restricted opportunities of the United States Navy, Burrows had seen service, and his qualities received recognition, in the hostilities with Tripoli. The unusual circumstance of both captains falling, and so young,—Burrows was but twenty-eight,— imparted to this tiny combat an unusual pathos, which was somewhat heightened by the fact that Blyth himself had acted as pall-bearer when Lawrence, three months before, was buried with military honors at Halifax. In Portland, Maine, the two young commanders were borne to their graves together, in a common funeral, with all the observance possible in a small coast town; business being everywhere suspended, and the customary tokens of mourning displayed upon buildings and shipping.

After this engagement, as the season progressed, coastwise operations in this quarter became increasingly hazardous for both parties. On October 22, Hull wrote that neither the "Enterprise" nor the "Rattlesnake" could cruise much longer. The enemy still maintained his grip, in virtue of greater size and numbers. Ten days later comes the report of a convoy, with one of the brigs, driven into port by a frigate; that the enemy appear almost every day, and never without a force superior to that of both his brigs, which he fears to trust out overnight, lest they find themselves at morning under the guns of an opponent of weightier battery. The long nights and stormy seas of winter, however, soon afforded to coasters a more secure protection than friendly guns, and Hull's letters intermit until April 6, 1814, when he announces that the enemy has made his appearance in great force; he presumes for the summer. Besides the danger and interruption of the coasting trade, Hull was increasingly anxious as to the safety of Portsmouth itself. By a recent act of Congress four seventy-fours had been ordered to be built, and one of them was now in construction there under his supervision. Despite the navigational difficulties of entering the port, which none was more capable of appreciating than he, he regarded the defences as so inadequate that it would be perfectly possible to destroy her on the sks. "There is nothing," he said, "to prevent a very small force from entering the harbor." At the same moment Decatur was similarly concerned for the squadron at New London, and we have seen the fears of Stewart for Norfolk. So marked was Hull's apprehension in this respect, that he sent the frigate "Congress" four miles up the river, where she remained to the end of the war; her crew being transferred to Lake Ontario. New York, the greater wealth of which increased both her danger and her capacity for self-protection, was looking to her own fortifications, as well as manning, provisioning, and paying the crews of the gunboats that patrolled her waters, on the side of the sea and of the Sound.

The exposure of the coasting trade from Boston Bay eastward was increased by the absence of interior coastwise channels, until the chain of islands about and beyond the Penobscot was reached. On the other hand, the character of the shore, bold, with off-lying rocks and many small harbors, conferred a distinct advantage upon those having local knowledge, as the coasting seamen had. On such a route the points of danger are capes and headlands, particularly if their projection is great, such as the promontory between Portsmouth and Boston, of which Cape Ann is a conspicuous landmark. There the coaster has to go farthest from his refuge, and the deep-sea cruiser can approach with least risk. In a proper scheme of coast defence batteries are mounted on such positions. This, it is needless to say, in view of the condition of the port fortifications, had not been done in the United States. Barring this, the whole situation of the coast, of trade, and of blockade, was one with which British naval officers had then been familiar for twenty years, through their employment upon the French and Spanish coasts, as well Mediterranean as Atlantic, and in many other parts of the world. To hover near the land, intercepting and fighting by day, manning boats and cutting out by night, harassing, driving on shore, destroying the sinews of war by breaking down communications, was to them simply an old experience to be applied under new and rather easier circumstances.

Of these operations frequent instances are given in contemporary journals and letters; but less account has been taken of the effects, as running through household and social economics, touching purse and comfort. These are traceable in commercial statistics. At the time they must have been severely felt, bringing the sense of the war vividly home to the community. The stringency of the British action is betrayed, however, by casual notices. The captain of a schooner burned by the British frigate "Nymphe" is told by her commander that he had orders to destroy every vessel large enough to carry two men. "A brisk business is now carrying on all along our coast between British cruisers and our coasting vessels, in ready money. Friday last, three masters went into Gloucester to procure money to carry to a British frigate to ransom their vessels. Thursday, a Marblehead schooner was ransomed by the "Nymphe" for $400. Saturday, she took off Cape Ann three coasters and six fishing boats, and the masters were sent on shore for money to ransom them at $200 each." There was room for the wail of a federalist paper: "Our coasts unnavigable to ourselves, though free to the enemy and the money-making neutral; our harbors blockaded; our shipping destroyed or rotting at the docks; silence and stillness in our cities; the grass growing upon the public wharves." In the district of Maine, "the long stagnation of foreign, and embarrassment of domestic trade, have extended the sad effects from the seaboard through the interior, where the scarcity of money is severely felt. There is not enough to pay the taxes."[196]

South of Chesapeake Bay the coast is not bold and [195]rocky, like that north of Cape Cod, but in its low elevation and gradual soundings resembles rather those of New Jersey and Delaware. It has certain more pronounced features in the extensive navigable sounds and channels, which lie behind the islands and sandbars skirting the shores. The North Carolina system of internal water communications, Pamlico Sound and its extensions, stood by itself. To reach that to the southward, it was necessary to make a considerable sea run, round the far projecting Cape Fear, exposed to capture outside; but from Charleston to the St. Mary's River, which then formed the Florida boundary for a hundred miles of its length, the inside passages of South Carolina and Georgia were continuous, though in many places difficult, and in others open to attack from the sea. Between St. Mary's and Savannah, for example, there were seven inlets, and Captain Campbell, the naval officer in charge of that district, reported that three of these were practicable for frigates;[197] but this statement, while literally accurate, conveys an exaggerated impression, for no sailing frigate would be likely to cross a difficult bar for a single offensive operation, merely to find herself confronted with conditions forbidding further movement.

The great menace to the inside traffic consisted in the facility with which cruisers outside could pass from entrance to entrance, contrasted with the intricacies within impeding similar action by the defence. If a bevy of unprotected coasters were discerned by an enemy's lookouts, the ship could run down abreast, send in her boats, capture or destroy, before the gunboats, if equidistant at the beginning, could overcome the obstacles due to rise and fall of tide, or narrowness of passage, and arrive to the rescue.[198] A suggested remedy was to replace the gunboats by rowing barges, similar to, but more powerful than, those used by the enemy in his attacks. The insuperable trouble here proved to be that men fit for such work, fit to contend with the seamen of the enemy, were unwilling to abandon the sea, with its hopes of prize money, or to submit to the exposure and discomfort of the life. "The crews of the gunboats," wrote Captain Campbell, "consist of all nations except Turks, Greeks, and Jews." On one occasion the ship's company of an American privateer, which had been destroyed after a desperate and celebrated resistance to attack by British armed boats, arrived at St. Mary's. Of one hundred and nineteen American seamen, only four could be prevailed upon to enter the district naval force.[199] This was partly due to the embarrassment of the national finances. "The want of funds to pay off discharged men," wrote the naval captain at Charleston, "has given such a character to the navy as to stop recruiting."[200] "Men could be had," reported his colleague at St. Mary's, now transferred to Savannah, "were it not for the Treasury notes, which cannot be passed at less than five per cent discount. Men will not ship

without cash. There are upwards of a hundred seamen in port, but they refuse to enter, even though we offer to ship for a month only."[201]
During the American Civil War, fifty years after the time of which we are speaking, this internal communication was effectually intercepted by stationing inside steamers of adequate force; but that recourse, while not absolutely impracticable for small sailing cruisers, involved a risk disproportionate to the gain. Through traffic could have been broken up by keeping a frigate in any one of the three sounds, entrance to which was practicable for vessels of that class. In view of the amount of trade passing back and forth, which Campbell stated to be in one period of four months as much as eight million dollars, it is surprising that this obvious expedient was not adopted by the enemy. That they appreciated the situation is shown by the intention, announced in 1813, of seizing one of the islands; which was effected in January, 1815, by the occupation of Cumberland and St. Simons'. As it was, up to that late period the routine methods of their European experience prevailed, with the result that their coastwise operations in the south differed little from those in the extreme north. Smaller vessels occasionally, armed boats frequently, pushed inside the inlets, seizing coasters, and at times even attacking the gunboats. While the positive loss thus inflicted was considerable, it will readily be understood that it was much exceeded by the negative effect, in deterring from movement, and reducing navigation to the limits of barest necessity.
In these operations the ships of war were seconded by privateers from the West Indies, which hovered round this coast, as the Halifax vessels did round that of New England, seeking such scraps of prize money as might be left over from the ruin of American commerce and the immunities of the licensed traders. The United States officers at Charleston and Savannah were at their wits' ends to provide security with their scanty means,—more scanty even in men than in vessels; and when there came upon them the additional duty of enforcing the embargo of December, 1813, in the many quarters, and against the various subterfuges, by which evasion would be attempted, the task was manifestly impossible. "This is the most convenient part of the world for illicit trade that I have ever seen," wrote Campbell. From a return made this summer by the Secretary of the Navy to Congress,[202] it is shown that one brig of eighteen guns, which was not a cruiser, but a station ship at Savannah, eleven gunboats, three other schooners, and four barges, were apportioned to the stretch of coast from Georgetown to St. Mary's,—over two hundred miles. With the fettered movement of the gunboats before mentioned, contrasted with the outside cruisers, it was impossible to meet conditions by distributing this force, "for the protection of the several inlets," as had at first been directed by the Navy Department. The only defensive recourse approximately satisfactory was that of the deep-sea merchant service of Great Britain, proposed also

by Hull at the northward, to assemble vessels in convoys, and to accompany them throughout a voyage. "I have deemed it expedient," wrote Campbell from St. Mary's, "to order the gun vessels to sail in company, not less than four in number, and have ordered convoy to the inland trade at stated periods, by which means vessels may be protected, and am sorry to say this is all that can be effected in our present situation."[203] In this way a fair degree of immunity was attained. Rubs were met with occasionally, and heavy losses were reported from time to time. There was a certain amount of fighting and scuffling, in which advantage was now on one side, now on the other; but upon the whole it would appear that the novelty of the conditions and ignorance of the ground rather imposed upon the imagination of the enemy, and that their operations against this inside trade were at once less active and less successful than under the more familiar features presented by the coasts of Maine and Massachusetts.

Whatever more or less of success or injury attended the coastwise trade in the several localities, the point to be observed is that the enemy's operations effectually separated the different sections of the country from one another, so far as this means of intercourse was concerned; thereby striking a deadly blow at the mutual support which might be given by communities differing so markedly in resources, aptitudes, and industries. The remark before made upon the effect of headlands, on the minor scale of a particular shore-line, applied with special force to one so extensive as that of the United States Atlantic coast in 1813. Cape Cod to the north and Cape Fear to the south were conspicuous examples of such projection. Combined with the relatively shelterless and harborless central stretch, intervening between them, from the Chesapeake to Sandy Hook, they constituted insuperable obstacles to sustained intercommunication by water. The presence of the enemy in great numbers before, around, and within the central section, emphasized the military weakness of position which nature herself had there imposed. To get by sea from one end of the country to the other it was necessary to break the blockade in starting, to take a wide sweep out to sea, and again to break it at the desired point of entrance. This, however, is not coasting.

The effect which this coast pressure produced upon the welfare of the several sections is indicated here and there by official utterances. The war party naturally inclined to minimize unfavorable results, and their opponents in some measure to exaggerate them; but of the general tendency there can be no serious doubt. Mr. Pearson, an opposition member of the House from North Carolina, speaking February 16, 1814, when the record of 1813 was made up, and the short-lived embargo of December was yet in force, said: "Blocked up as we are by the enemy's squadron upon our coast, corked up by our still more unmerciful embargo and non-importation laws, calculated as it were to fill up the little chasm in the ills which the enemy alone could not inflict; the entire coasting trade destroyed, and even the little pittance of intercourse from one port to the other in the same state destroyed [by the embargo], the planters of the Southern and Middle states, finding no market at home for their products, are driven to the alternative of wagoning them hundreds of miles, in search of a precarious market in the Northern and Eastern states, or permitting them to rot on their hands. Many articles which are, or by habit have become, necessary for comfort, are obtained at extravagant prices from other parts of the Union. The balance of trade, if trade it may be called, from these and other causes being so entirely against the Southern and Middle states, the whole of our specie is rapidly travelling to the North and East. Our bank paper is thrown back upon the institutions from which it issued; and as the war expenditures in the Southern and Middle states, where the loans have been principally obtained, are proportionately inconsiderable, the bills of these banks are daily returning, and their vaults drained of specie, to be locked up in Eastern and Western states, never to return but with the return of peace and prosperity."[204]

The isolation of North Carolina was extreme, with Cape Fear to the south and the occupied Chesapeake north of her. The Governor of the central state of Pennsylvania, evidently in entire political sympathy with the national Administration, in his message to the legislature at the same period,[205] is able to congratulate the people on the gratifying state of the commonwealth; a full treasury, abundant yield of agriculture, and the progress of manufacturing development, which, "however we may deprecate and deplore the calamities of protracted war, console us with the prospect of permanent and extensive establishments equal to our wants, and such as will insure the real and practical independence of our country." But he adds: "At no period of our history has the immense importance of internal navigation been so strikingly exemplified as since the commencement of hostilities. The transportation of produce, and the intercourse between citizens of the different states, which knit more strongly the bonds of social and political union, are greatly retarded, and, through many of their accustomed channels, entirely interrupted by the water craft of the enemy, sinking, burning, and otherwise destroying, the property which it cannot appropriate to its own use." He looks forward to a renewal of similar misfortune in the following year, an anticipation more than fulfilled. The officials of other states, according to their political complexion, either lamented the sufferings of the war and its supposed injustice, or comforted themselves and their hearers by reflecting upon the internal fruitfulness of the country, and its increasing self-sufficingness. The people were being equipped for independence of the foreigner by the progress of manufactures, and by habits of economy and self-denial, enforced by deprivation arising from the suppression of the coasting trade and the rigors of the commercial blockade.

The effect of the latter, which by the spring of 1814 had been in force nearly a twelvemonth over the entire coast south of Narragansett Bay, can be more directly estimated and concisely stated, in terms of money, than can the interruption of the coasting trade; for the statistics of export and import, contrasted with those of years of peace, convey it directly. It has already been stated that the exports for the year ending September 30, 1814, during which the operation of the blockade was most universal and continuous, fell to $7,000,000, as compared with $25,000,000 in 1813, and $45,000,000 in 1811, a year of peace though of restricted intercourse. Such figures speak distinctly as well as forcibly; it being necessary, however, to full appreciation of the difference between 1813 and 1814, to remember that during the first half of the former official period—from October 1, 1812, to April 1, 1813,—there had been no commercial blockade beyond the Chesapeake and Delaware; and that, even after it had been instituted, the British license system operated to the end of September to qualify its effects.

Here and there interesting particulars may be gleaned, which serve to illustrate these effects, and to give to the picture that precision of outline which heightens impression. "I believe," wrote a painstaking Baltimore editor in December, 1814, "that there has not been an arrival in Baltimore from a foreign port for a twelvemonth";[206] yet the city in 1811 had had a registered tonnage of 88,398, and now boasted that of the scanty national commerce still maintained, through less secluded ports, at least one half was carried on by its celebrated schooners,[207] the speed and handiness of which, combined with a size that intrusted not too many eggs to one basket, imparted special facilities for escaping pursuit and minimizing loss. A representative from Maryland at about this time presented in the House a memorial from Baltimore merchants, stating that "in consequence of the strict blockade of our bays and rivers the private-armed service is much discouraged," and submitting the expediency "of offering a bounty for the destruction of enemy's vessels;" a suggestion the very extravagance of which indicates more than words the extent of the depression felt. The price of salt in Baltimore, in November, 1814, was five dollars the bushel. In Charleston it was the same, while just across the Spanish border, at Amelia Island, thronged with foreign merchant ships, it was selling at seventy cents.[208]

Such a contrast, which must necessarily be reproduced in other articles not indigenous, accounts at once for the smuggling deplored by Captain Campbell, and at the same time testifies both to the efficacy of the blockade and to the pressure exercised upon the inland navigation by the outside British national cruisers and privateers. This one instance, affecting one of the prime necessaries of life, certifies to the stringent exclusion from the sea of the coast on which Charleston was the chief seaport. Captain Dent, commanding this naval district, alludes to the constant presence of blockaders, and occasionally to vessels taken outside by them, chased ashore, or intercepted in various inlets; narrating particularly the singular incident that, despite his remonstrances, a flag of truce was sent on board the enemy by local authorities to negotiate a purchase of goods thus captured.[209] This unmilitary proceeding, which evinces the necessities of the neighborhood, was of course immediately stopped by the Government.

A somewhat singular incidental circumstance, supporting the other inferences, is found in the spasmodic elevation of the North Carolina coast into momentary commercial consequence as a place of entry and deposit; not indeed to a very great extent, but ameliorating to a slight degree the deprivation of the regions lying north and south,—the neighborhood of Charleston on the one hand, of Richmond and Baltimore on the other. "The waters of North Carolina, from Wilmington to Ocracoke, though not favorable to commerce in time of peace, by reason of their shallowness and the danger of the coast, became important and useful in time of war, and a very considerable trade was prosecuted from and into those waters during the late war, and a coasting trade as far as Charleston, attended with less risk than many would imagine. A vessel may prosecute a voyage from Elizabeth City [near the Virginia line] to Charleston without being at sea more than a few hours at any one time."[210] Some tables of arrivals show a comparative immunity for vessels entering here from abroad; due doubtless to the unquestioned dangers of the coast, which conspired with the necessarily limited extent of the traffic to keep the enemy at a distance. It was not by them wholly overlooked. In July, 1813, Admiral Cockburn anchored with a division off Ocracoke bar, sent in his boats, and captured a privateer and letter-of-marque which had there sought a refuge denied to them by the blockade elsewhere. The towns of Beaufort and Portsmouth were occupied for some hours. The United States naval officer at Charleston found it necessary also to extend the alongshore cruises of his schooners as far as Cape Fear, for the protection of this trade on its way to his district.

The attention aroused to the development of internal navigation also bears witness to the pressure of the blockade. "It is my opinion," said the Governor of Pennsylvania, "that less than one half the treasure expended by the United States for the protection of foreign commerce, if combined with state and individual wealth, would have perfected an inland water communication from Maine to Georgia." It was argued by others that the extra money spent for land transportation of goods, while the coasting trade was suspended, would have effected a complete tide-water inland navigation such as here suggested; and there was cited a declaration of Robert Fulton, who died during the war, that within twenty-one months as great a sum had been laid out in wagon hire as would have effected this object. Whatever the accuracy of these estimates, their silent witness to the influence of the blockade upon commerce, external and coastwise, quite overbears President Madison's perfunctory denials of its effectiveness, based upon the successful evasions which more or less attend all such operations.

Perhaps, however, the most signal proof of the pressure exerted is to be seen in the rebound, the instant it was removed; in the effect upon prices, and upon the movements of shipping. Taken in connection with the other evidence, direct and circumstantial, so far cited, what can testify more forcibly to the strangulation of the coasting trade than the fact that in the month of March, 1815,—news of the peace having been received February 11,—there sailed from Boston one hundred and forty-four vessels, more than half of them square-rigged; and that of the whole all but twenty-six were for United States ports. Within three weeks of April there arrived at Charleston, exclusive of coasters, one hundred and fifty-eight vessels; at Savannah, in the quarter ending June 30, two hundred and three. Something of this outburst of activity, in which neutrals of many nations shared, was due, as Mr. Clay said, to the suddenness with which commerce revived after momentary suspension. "The bow had been unstrung that it might acquire fresh vigor and new elasticity"; and the stored-up products of the country, so long barred within, imparted a peculiar nervous haste to the renewal of intercourse. The absolute numbers quoted do not give as vivid impression of conditions at differing times as do some comparisons, easily made. In the year 1813, as shown by the returns of the United States Treasury, out of 674,853 tons of registered—sea-going—shipping, only 233,439—one third—paid the duties exacted upon each several voyage, and of these many doubtless sailed under British license.[211] In 1814 the total tonnage, 674,632, shows that ship-building had practically ceased; and of this amount one twelfth only, 58,756 tons, paid dues for going out.[212] In 1816, when peace conditions were fully established, though less than two years had passed, the total tonnage had increased to 800,760; duties, being paid each voyage, were collected on 865,219.[213] Thus the foreign voyages that year exceeded the total shipping of the country, and by an amount greater than all the American tonnage that put to sea in 1814.

The movement of coasting vessels, technically called "enrolled," is not so clearly indicated by the returns, because all the trips of each were covered by one license annually renewed. A licensed coaster might make several voyages, or she might make none. In 1813 the figures show that, of 471,109 enrolled tonnage, 252,440 obtained licenses. In 1814 there is, as in the registered shipping, a diminution of the total to 466,159, of which a still smaller proportion, 189,662, took out the annual license. In 1816 the enrolment was 522,165, the licensing 414,594. In the fishing craft, a class by themselves, the employment rose from 16,453 in 1814 to 48,147 in 1816;[214] the difference doubtless being attributable chiefly to the reopening of the cod fishing on the banks of Newfoundland, necessarily closed to the American flag by the maritime hostilities.

The influence of the peace upon prices is likewise a matter too interesting to a correct appreciation of effects to be wholly passed over. In considering it, the quotations before the receipt of the news doubtless represent conditions more correctly than do the immediate changes. The official tidings of peace reached New York, February 11, 1815. The Evening Post, in its number of February 14, says, "We give to-day one of the effects of the prospect of peace, even before ratification. Our markets of every kind experienced a sudden, and to many a shocking, change. Sugar, for instance, fell from $26 per hundredweight to $12.50. Tea, which sold on Saturday at $2.25, on Monday was purchased at a $1.00. Specie, which had got up to the enormous rate of 22 per cent premium, dropped down to 2. The article of tin, in particular, fell from the height of $80 the box to $25. Six per cents rose from 76 to 88; ten per cents and Treasury notes from 92 to 98. Bank sk generally rose from five to ten per cent." In Philadelphia, flour which sold at $7.50 the barrel on Saturday had risen to $10 on Monday; a testimony that not only foreign export but home supply to the eastward was to be renewed. The fall in foreign products, due to freedom of import, was naturally accompanied by a rise in domestic produce, to which an open outlet with proportionate increase of demand was now afforded. In Philadelphia the exchange on Boston reflected these conditions; falling from twenty-five per cent to thirteen.

It may then be concluded that there is little exaggeration in the words used by "a distinguished naval officer" of the day, in a letter contributed to Niles' Register, in its issue of June 17, 1815. "No sooner had the enemy blockaded our harbors, and extended his line of cruisers from Maine to Georgia, than both foreign and domestic commerce came at once to be reduced to a deplorable state of stagnation; producing in its consequences the utter ruin of many respectable merchants, as well as of a great multitude besides, connected with them in their mercantile pursuits. But these were not the only consequences. The regular supply of foreign commodities being thereby cut off, many articles, now become necessaries of life, were raised to an exorbitant price, and bore much upon the finances of the citizen, whose family could not comfortably exist without them. Add to this, as most of the money loaned to the Government for the purposes of the war came from the pockets of merchants, they were rendered incapable of continuing these disbursements in consequence of this interruption to their trade; whence the cause of that impending bankruptcy with which the Government was at one time threatened.... At a critical period of the war [April, 1814] Congress found it necessary to remove all restrictions upon commerce, both foreign and domestic. It is a lamentable fact, however, that the adventurous merchant found no alleviation from these indulgences, his vessels being uniformly prevented by a strong blockading force, not only from going out, but from coming into port, at the most imminent risk of capture. The risk did not stop here; for the islands and ports most frequented by American vessels being known to the enemy, he was enabled from his abundance of means to intercept them there also. The coasting trade, that most valuable appendage to an extensive mercantile establishment in the United States, was entirely annihilated. The southern and northern sections of the Union were unable to exchange their commodities, except upon a contracted scale through the medium of land carriage, and then only at a great loss; so that, upon the whole, nothing in a national point of view appeared to be more loudly called for by men of all parties than a naval force adequate to the protection of our commerce, and the raising of the blockade of our coast."

Such was the experience which sums up the forgotten bitter truth, concerning a war which has left in the United States a prevalent impression of distinguished success, because of a few brilliant naval actions and the closing battle of New Orleans. The lesson to be deduced is not that the country at that time should have sought to maintain a navy approaching equality to the British. In the state of national population and revenue, it was no more possible to attempt this than that it would be expedient to do it now, under the present immense development of resources and available wealth. What had been possible during the decade preceding the war,—had the nation so willed,—was to place the navy on such a footing, in numbers and constitution, as would have made persistence in the course Great Britain was following impolitic to the verge of madness, because it would add to her war embarrassments the activity of an imposing maritime enemy, at the threshold of her most valuable markets,—the West Indies,—three thousand miles away from her own shores and from the seat of her principal and necessary warfare. The United States could not have encountered Great Britain single-handed—true; but there was not then the slightest prospect of her having to do so. The injuries of which she complained were incidental to a state of European war; inconceivable and impossible apart from it. She was therefore assured of the support of most powerful allies, occupying the attention of the British navy and draining the resources of the British empire. This condition of things was notorious, as was the fact that, despite the disappointment of Trafalgar, Napoleon was sedulously restoring the numbers of a navy, to the restraining of which his enemy was barely competent.

The anxiety caused to the British Admiralty by the operations of the small American squadrons in the autumn of 1812 has already been depicted in quotations from its despatches to Warren.[215] Three or four divisions, each containing one to two ships of the line, were kept on the go, following a general round in successive relief, but together amounting to five or six battle ships—to use the modern term—with proportionate cruisers. It was not possible to diminish this total by concentrating them, for the essence of the scheme, and the necessity which dictated it, was to cover a wide sweep of ocean, and to protect several maritime strategic points through which the streams of commerce, controlled by well-known conditions, passed, intersected, or converged. So also the Admiralty signified its wish that one ship of the line should form the backbone of the blockade before each of the American harbors. For this purpose Warren's fleet was raised to a number stated by the Admiralty's letter to him of January 9, 1813, to be "upwards of ten of the line, exclusive of the six sail of the line appropriated to the protection of the West India convoys." These numbers were additional to detachments which, outside of his command, were patrolling the eastern Atlantic, about the equator, and from the Cape Verde Islands to the Azores, as mentioned in another letter of February 10. "In all, therefore, about twenty sail of the line were employed on account of American hostilities; and this, it will be noticed, was after Napoleon's Russian disaster was fully known in England. It has not been without interfering for the moment with other very important services that my Lords have been able to send you this re-enforcement, and they most anxiously hope that the vigorous and successful use you will make of it will enable you shortly to return some of the line of battle ships to England, which, if the heavy American frigates should be taken or destroyed, you will immediately do, retaining four line of battle ships." Attention should fasten upon the importance here attached by the British Admiralty to the bigger ships; for it is well to learn of the enemy, and to appreciate that it was not solely light cruisers and privateers, but chiefly the heavy vessels, that counted in the estimate of experienced British naval officers. The facts are little understood in the United States, and consequently are almost always misrepresented.

The reasons for this abundance of force are evident. As regards commerce Great Britain was on the defensive; and the defensive cannot tell upon which of many exposed points a blow may fall. Dissemination of effort, however modified by strategic ingenuity, is thus to a certain extent imposed. If an American division might strike British trade on the equator between 20° and 30° west longitude, and also in the neighborhood of the Cape Verdes and of the Azores, preparation in some form to protect all those points was necessary, and they are too wide apart for this to be effected by mere concentration. So the blockade of the United States harbors. There might be in New York no American frigates, but if a division escaped from Boston it was possible it might come upon the New York blockade in superior force, if adequate numbers were not constantly kept there. The

British commercial blockade, though offensive in essence, had also its defensive side, which compelled a certain dispersion of force, in order to be in local sufficiency in several quarters.

These several dispersed assemblages of British ships of war constituted the totality of naval effort imposed upon Great Britain by "the fourteen sail of vessels of all descriptions"[216] which composed the United States navy. It would not in the least have been necessary had these been sloops of war— were they fourteen or forty. The weight of the burden was the heavy frigates, two of which together were more than a match for three of the same nominal class—the 38-gun frigate—which was the most numerous and efficient element in the British cruising force. The American forty-four was unknown to British experience, and could be met only by ships of the line. Add to this consideration the remoteness of the American shore, and its dangerous proximity to very vital British interests, and there are found the elements of the difficult problem presented to the Admiralty by the combination of American force—such as it was—with American advantage of position for dealing a severe blow to British welfare at the period, 1805-1812, when the empire was in the height of its unsupported and almost desperate struggle with Napoleon; when Prussia was chained, Austria paralyzed, and Russia in strict bonds of alliance—personal and political— with France.

If conditions were thus menacing, as we know them to to have been in 1812, when war was declared, and the invasion of Russia just beginning, when the United States navy was "fourteen pendants," what would they not have been in 1807, had the nation possessed even one half of the twenty ships of the line which Gouverneur Morris, a shrewd financier, estimated fifteen years before were within her competency? While entirely convinced of the illegality of the British measures, and feeling keenly—as what American even now cannot but feel?—the humiliation and outrage to which his country was at that period subjected, the writer has always recognized the stringent compulsion under which Great Britain lay, and the military wisdom, in his opinion, of the belligerent measures adopted by her to sustain her strength through that unparalleled struggle; while in the matter of impressment, it is impossible to deny—as was urged by Representative Gaston of North Carolina and Gouverneur Morris—that her claim to the service of her native seamen was consonant to the ideas of the time, as well as of utmost importance to her in that hour of dire need. Nevertheless, submission by America should have been impossible; and would have been avoidable if for the fourteen pendants there had been a dozen sail of the line, and frigates to match. To an adequate weighing of conditions there will be indeed resentment for impressment and the other mortifications; but it is drowned in wrath over the humiliating impotence of an administration which, owing to preconceived notions as to peace, made such endurance necessary. It is not always ignominious to suffer ignominy; but it always is so to deserve it.

President Washington, in his last annual message, December 7, 1796, defined the situation then confronting the United States, and indicated its appropriate remedy, in the calm and forcible terms which characterized all his perceptions. "It is in our own experience, that the most sincere neutrality is not a sufficient guard against the depredations of nations at war. To secure respect for a neutral flag requires a naval force, organized and ready, to vindicate it from insult or aggression. This may even prevent the necessity of going to war, by discouraging belligerent powers from committing such violations of the rights of the neutral party as may, first or last, leave no other option" [than war]. The last sentence is that of the statesman and soldier, who accurately appreciates the true office and sphere of arms in international relations. His successor, John Adams, yearly renewed his recommendation for the development of the navy; although, not being a military man, he seems to have looked rather exclusively on the defensive aspect, and not to have realized that possible enemies are more deterred by the fear of offensive action against themselves than by recognition of a defensive force which awaits attack at an enemy's pleasure. Moreover, in his administration, it was not Great Britain, but France, that was most actively engaged in violating the neutral rights of American shipping, and French commercial interests then presented nothing upon which retaliation could take effect. The American problem then was purely defensive,—to destroy the armed ships engaged in molesting the national commerce.

President Jefferson, whose influence was paramount with the dominant party which remained in power from his inauguration in 1801 to the war, based his policy upon the conviction, expressed in his inaugural, that this "was the only government where every man would meet invasions of the public order as his own personal concern;" and that "a well-disciplined militia is our best reliance for the first moments of war, till regulars may relieve them." In pursuance of these fundamental principles, it was doubtless logical to recommend in his first annual message that, "beyond the small force which will probably be wanted for actual service in the Mediterranean [against the Barbary pirates], whatever annual sum you may think proper to appropriate to naval preparations would perhaps be better employed in providing those articles which may be kept without waste or consumption, and be in readiness when any exigence calls them into use. Progress has been made in providing materials for seventy-four gun ships;" but this commended readiness issued in not laying their keels till after the war began.

Upon this first recommendation followed the discontinuance of building ships for ocean service, and the initiation of the gunboat policy;

culminating, when war began, in the decision of the administration to lay up the ships built for war, to keep them out of British hands. The urgent remonstrances of two or three naval captains obtained the reversal of this resolve, and thereby procured for the country those few successes which, by a common trick of memory, have remained the characteristic feature of the War of 1812.

Note.—After writing the engagement between the "Boxer" and the "Enterprise," the author found among his memoranda, overlooked, the following statement from the report of her surviving lieutenant, David McCreery: "I feel it my duty to mention that the bulwarks of the 'Enterprise' were proof against our grape, when her musket balls penetrated through our bulwarks." (Canadian Archives, M. 389, 3. p. 87.) It will be noted that this does not apply to the cannon balls, and does not qualify the contrast in gunnery.

FOOTNOTES:

[128] Broke's Letter to Lawrence, June, 1813. Naval Chronicle, vol. xxx. p. 413.
[129] Rodgers' Report of this cruise is in Captains' Letters, Sept. 27, 1813.
[130] Captains' Letters, Dec. 14, 1813.
[131] Captains' Letters, June 3, 1812.
[132] The Department's orders to Evans and the letter transferring them to Lawrence, captured in the ship, can be found published in the Report on Canadian Archives, 1896, p. 74. A copy is attached to the Record of the subsequent Court of Inquiry, Navy Department MSS.
[133] James' Naval History, vol. vi., edition of 1837. The account of the action between the "Chesapeake" and "Shannon" will be found on pp. 196-206.
[134] Secretary to the Admiralty, In-Letters, May, 1814, vol. 505, p. 777.
[135] Naval Chronicle, vol. xxx, p. 413.
[136] Broke, in his letter of challenge, "was disappointed that, after various verbal messages sent into Boston, Commodore Rodgers, with the 'President' and 'Congress,' had eluded the 'Shannon' and 'Tenedos,' by sailing the first chance, after the prevailing easterly winds had obliged us to keep an offing from the coast."
[137] For the reason here assigned, and others mentioned in the narrative, the author has preferred to follow in the main James' account, analyzed, and compared with Broke's report (Naval Chronicle, vol. xxx. p. 83), and with the testimony in the Court of Inquiry held in Boston on the surrender of the "Chesapeake," and in the resultant courts martial upon Lieutenant Cox and other persons connected with the ship, which are in the Navy Department MSS. The official report of Lieutenant Budd, the senior

surviving officer of the "Chesapeake", is published in Niles' Register (vol. iv, p. 290), which gives also several unofficial statements of onlookers, and others.

[138] Not "across"; the distinction is important, being decisive of general raking direction.

[139] Actually, a contemporary account, borrowed by the British "Naval Chronicle" (vol. xxx. p. 161) from a Halifax paper, but avouched as trustworthy, says the "Chesapeake" was terribly battered on the larboard bow as well as quarter. The details in the text indicate merely the local preponderance of injury, and the time and manner of its occurrence.

[140] A slight qualification is here needed, in that of the injured of the "Shannon" some were hurt in the boarding, not by the cannonade; but the general statement is substantially accurate.

[141] Decatur to Navy Department. Captains' Letters, June, 1813.

[142] Decatur to Navy Department. Captains' Letters, June, 1813.

[143] Naval Chronicle, vol. xxix. p. 497.

[144] Croker to Warren, Jan. 9, 1813. Admiralty Out-Letters, British Records Office. My italics.

[145] Message of the Governor of Connecticut, October, 1813. Niles' Register, vol. v. p. 121.

[146] Message of the Governor of Connecticut, October, 1813. Niles' Register, vol. v. p. 121.

[147] Niles' Register, vol. v. p. 302.

[148] Captains' Letters.

[149] Niles' Register, vol. vi. p. 136.

[150] Captains' Letters, Nov. 3 and Dec. 31, 1809; March 26, 1810; and Oct. 12, 1813.

[151] American State Papers, Naval Affairs, vol. i. p. 307.

[152] Ante, page 16.

[153] The official reports of Warren and Cockburn concerning these operations are published in the Naval Chronicle, vol. xxx. pp. 162-168.

[154] Captains' Letters, June 21, 1813.

[155] The American official account of this affair is given in Niles' Register, vol. iv. pp. 375, 422. James' Naval History, vol. vi. pp. 236-238, gives the British story.

[156] Captains' Letters, April, 1813.

[157] Captains' Letters, May 21, 1813.

[158] Ibid.

[159] James, Naval History (edition 1837), vol. vi. p. 231.

[160] Warren's Gazette Letters, here referred to, can be found in Naval Chronicle, vol. xxx. pp. 243, 245.

[161] Croker to Warren, March 20, 1813. Admiralty Out-Letters, Records Office.

[162] Niles' Register, vol. iv. p. 404.

[163] The rise of the tide is about two and a half feet.

[164] This is the number stated by James, the British naval historian, and is somewhat difficult to reconcile with Warren's expression, "the troops and a re-enforcement of seamen and marines from the ships." To be effective, the attack should have been in greater numbers.

[165] The British story of this failure, outside the official despatches, is given in James' Naval History, vol. vi. pp. 232-234.

[166] Report of the commander of the "Scorpion" to Captain Morris, July 21, 1813. Captains' Letters.

[167] This letter, from the commanding officer of the "Narcissus", is in Niles' Register, vol. iv. p. 279.

[168] Morris to Navy Department, August 13, 23, and 27. Captains' Letters.

[169] Captain Hayes, of the "Majestic," in charge of the blockade of Boston, wrote to Warren, October 25, 1813: "Almost every vessel I meet has a license, or is under a neutral flag. Spanish, Portuguese, and Swedes are passing in and out by hundreds, and licensed vessels out of number from the West Indies. I find the licenses are sent blank to be filled up in Boston. This is of course very convenient, and the Portuguese consul is said to be making quite a trade of that flag, covering the property and furnishing the necessary papers for any person at a thousand dollars a ship." Canadian Archives, M. 389. 3. p. 189.

[170] Annals of Congress, 1813-1814, vol. i. p. 500.

[171] This parenthesis shows that the censures were not directed against New England only, for the blockade so far declared did not extend thither.

[172] Niles' Register, vol. iv. pp. 370, 386.

[173] Ibid., p. 387.

[174] Niles' Register, vol. iv. p. 387.

[175] Ibid., p. 402.

[176] Ibid.

[177] Ibid. Author's italics.

[178] Morris to Navy Department, Dec. 20 and 26, 1813. Captains' Letters.

[179] Post, chapter xviii.

[180] British Records Office, Secret Papers MSS.

[181] Niles' Register, vol. v. p. 311.

[182] The Columbian Centinel, Boston, Sept. 7 and Dec. 15, 1813.

[183] Ibid., Dec. 18.

[184] Ibid.

[185] Campbell to the Navy Department, Nov. 11, 1814. Captains' Letters.

[186] Captains' Letters.

[187] Ibid., June 24, 1813.

[188] Hull to Navy Department, July 31, 1813. Ibid.

[189] Cooper tells the story that when this gun was transported, and

preparations being made to use it as a stern instead of a bow chaser, the crew—to whom Burrows was as yet a stranger, known chiefly by his reputation for great eccentricity—came to the mast to express a hope that the brig was not going to retreat.

[190] Report of Lieutenant Tillinghast to Captain Hull. Captains' Letters, Sept. 9, 1813.

[191] Hull to Bainbridge, Sept. 10. Niles' Register, vol. v. p. 58.

[192] Report of the carpenter of the "Enterprise." Captains' Letters.

[193] There is a discrepancy in the statements concerning the "Boxer's" crew. Hull reported officially, "We have sixty-seven, exclusive of those killed and thrown overboard." (Sept. 25. Captains' Letters.) Lieutenant McCall, who succeeded to the command after Burrows fell, reported that "from information received from officers of the 'Boxer' it appears that there were between twenty and thirty-five killed, and fourteen wounded." (U.S. State Papers, Naval Affairs, vol. i. p. 297.) The number killed is evidently an exaggerated impression received, resembling some statements made concerning the "Chesapeake;" but it is quite likely that the "Boxer's" loss should be increased by several bodies thrown overboard.

[194] Naval Chronicle, vol. xxxii. p. 473.

[195] Columbian Centinel, July 28, Sept. 1, and Nov. 13, 1813.

[196] Ibid., Sept. 25.

[197] Campbell to Navy Department, Jan. 4, 1814. Captains' Letters.

[198] For full particulars see Captains' Letters (Campbell), June 12, 1813; Jan. 2 and 4, Aug. 20, Sept. 3, Oct. 8, Oct. 15, Dec. 4, 1814.

[199] Campbell, Dec. 2, 1814. Captains' Letters.

[200] Dent to Navy Department, Jan. 28, 1815. Ibid.

[201] Campbell, Feb. 3, 1815. Ibid.

[202] June 7, 1813. Navy Department MSS.

[203] Captains' Letters, Sept. 3, 1814.

[204] Benton's Abridgment of the Debates of Congress, vol. v. p. 202.

[205] Dec. 10, 1813. Niles' Register, vol. v. pp. 257-260.

[206] Niles' Register, vol. vii. p. 194.

[207] Ibid., vol. viii. p. 234.

[208] Ibid., vol. vii. p. 168. Quoted from a Charleston, S.C., paper.

[209] Captains' Letters, May 3, 23, 24; June 27, 29; August 7, 17; Nov. 9, 13, 23, 1813.

[210] Niles' Register, vol. viii. p. 311. Quoted from a Norfolk paper.

[211] American State Papers, Commerce and Navigation, vol. i. p. 1017.

[212] Ibid., vol. ii. p. 12.

[213] American State Papers, Commerce and Navigation, vol. ii. p. 87.

[214] Ibid., vol. i. p. 1017; vol. ii. pp. 12, 87.

[215] Ante, vol. i. pp. 402-404.

[216] Admiralty's Letter to Warren. Feb. 10, 1813.

MARITIME OPERATIONS

External To The Waters Of The United States, 1813-1814

In broad generalization, based upon analysis of conditions, it has been said that the seacoast of the United States was in 1812 a defensive frontier, from which, as from all defensive lines, there should be, and was, opportunity for offensive returns; for action planned to relieve the shore-line, and the general military situation, by inflicting elsewhere upon the opponent injury, harassment, and perplexity. The last chapter dealt with the warfare depending upon the seaboard chiefly from the defensive point of view; to illustrate the difficulties, the blows, and the sufferings, to which the country was exposed, owing to inability to force the enemy away from any large portion of the coast. The pressure was as universal as it was inexorable and irresistible.

It remains still to consider the employment and effects of the one offensive maritime measure left open by the exigencies of the war; the cruises directed against the enemy's commerce, and the characteristic incidents to which they gave rise. In this pursuit were engaged both the national ships of war and those equipped by the enterprise of the mercantile community; but, as the operations were in their nature more consonant to the proper purpose of privateers, so the far greater number of these caused them to play a part much more considerable in effect, though proportionately less fruitful in conspicuous action. Fighting, when avoidable, is to the privateer a misdirection of energy. Profit is his object, by depredation upon the enemy's commerce; not the preservation of that of his own people. To the ship of war, on the other hand, protection of the national shipping is the primary concern; and for that reason it becomes her to shun no encounter by which she may hope to remove from the seas a hostile cruiser.

The limited success of the frigates in their attempts against British trade has been noted, and attributed to the general fact that their cruises were confined to the more open sea, upon the highways of commerce. These were now travelled by British ships under strict laws of convoy, the effect of which was not merely to protect the several flocks concentrated under their particular watchdogs, but to strip the sea of those isolated vessels, that in time of peace rise in irregular but frequent succession above the horizon, covering the face of the deep with a network of tracks. These solitary wayfarers were now to be found only as rare exceptions to the general rule, until the port of destination was approached. There the homing impulse overbore the bonds of regulation; and the convoys tended to the conduct noted by Nelson as a captain, "behaving as all convoys that ever I saw did, shamefully ill, parting company every day." Commodore John Rodgers has before been quoted, as observing that the British practice was to rely upon pressure on the enemy over sea, for security near home; and that the waters surrounding the British Islands themselves were the field where commerce destruction could be most decisively effected.

The first United States vessel to emphasize this fact was the brig "Argus," Captain William H. Allen, which sailed from New York June 18, 1813, having on board a newly appointed minister to France, Mr. William H. Crawford, recently a senator from Georgia. On July 11 she reached L'Orient, having in the twenty-three days of passage made but one prize.[217] Three days later she proceeded to cruise in the chops of the English Channel, and against the local trade between Ireland and England; continuing thus until August 14, thirty-one days, during which she captured nineteen sail, extending her depredations well up into St. George's Channel. The contrast of results mentioned, between her voyage across and her occupancy of British waters, illustrates the comparative advantages of the two scenes of operations, regarded in their relation to British commerce.

On August 12 the British brig of war "Pelican," Captain Maples, anchored at Cork from the West Indies. Before her sails were furled she received orders to go out in search of the American ship of war whose depredations had been reported. Two hours later she was again at sea. The following evening, at half-past seven, a burning vessel to the eastward gave direction to her course, and at daybreak, August 14, she sighted a brig of war in the northeast, just quitting another prize, which had also been fired. The wind, being south, gave the windward position to the "Pelican," which stood in pursuit; the "Argus" steering east, near the wind, but under moderate sail to enable her opponent to close (positions 1). The advantage in size and armament was on this occasion on the British side; the "Pelican" being twenty per cent larger, and her broadside seventeen per cent heavier.

At 5.55 A.M., St. David's Head on the coast of Wales bearing east, distant about fifteen miles, the "Argus" wore, standing now to the westward, with the wind on the port side (2). The "Pelican" did the same, and the battle opened at six; the vessels running side by side, within the range of grapeshot and musketry,—probably under two hundred yards apart (2). Within five minutes Captain Allen received a wound which cost him his leg, and in the end his life. He at first refused to be taken below, but loss of blood soon so reduced him that he could no longer exercise command. Ten minutes later the first lieutenant was stunned by the graze of a grapeshot along his head, and the charge of the ship devolved on the second. By this time the rigging of the "Argus" had been a good deal cut, and the "Pelican" bore up (3) to pass under her stern; but the American brig, luffing close to the wind and backing her maintopsail (3), balked the attempt, throwing herself across the enemy's path, and giving a raking broadside, the poor aim of which seems to have lost her the effect that should have resulted from this ready and neat manœuvre. The main braces of the "Argus" had already been shot away, as well as much of the other gear upon which the after sails depended; and at 6.18 the preventer (duplicate) braces, which formed part of the preparation for battle, were also severed. The vessel thus became unmanageable, falling off before the wind (4), and the "Pelican" was enabled to work round her at will. This she did, placing herself first under the stern (4), and then on the bow (5) of her antagonist, where the only reply to her broadside was with musketry.

In this helpless situation the "Argus" surrendered, after an engagement of a little over three quarters of an hour. The British loss was two killed and five wounded; the American, six killed and seventeen wounded, of whom five afterwards died. Among these was Captain Allen, who survived only four days, and was buried with military honors at Plymouth, whither Captain Maples sent his prize.[218] After every allowance for disparity of force, the injury done by the American fire cannot be deemed satisfactory, and suggests the consideration whether the voyage to France under pressure of a diplomatic mission, and the busy preoccupation of making, manning, and firing prizes, during the brief month of Channel cruising, may not have interfered unduly with the more important requirements of fighting efficiency. The surviving officer in command mentions in explanation, "the superior size and metal of our opponent, and the fatigue which the crew of the 'Argus' underwent from a very rapid succession of prizes."

From the broad outlook of the universal maritime situation, this rapid succession of captures is a matter of more significance than the loss of a single brig of war. It showed the vulnerable point of British trade and local intercommunication; and the career of the "Argus," prematurely cut short though it was, tended to fix attention upon facts sufficiently well known, but perhaps not fully appreciated. From this time the opportunities offered by the English Channel and adjacent waters, long familiar to French corsairs, were better understood by Americans; as was also the difficulty of adequately policing them against a number of swift and handy cruisers, preying upon merchant vessels comparatively slow, lumbering, and undermanned. The subsequent career of the United States ship "Wasp," and the audacious exploits of several privateers, recall the impunity of Paul Jones a generation before, and form a sequel to the brief prelude, in which the leading part, though ultimately disastrous, was played by the "Argus."

While the cruise of the "Argus" stood by no means alone at this time, the attending incidents made it conspicuous among several others of a like nature, on the same scene or close by; and it therefore may be taken as indicative of the changing character of the war, which soon began to be manifest, owing to the change of conditions in Europe. In general summary, the result was to transfer an additional weight of British naval operations to the American side of the Atlantic, which in turn compelled American cruisers, national and private, in pursuit of commerce destruction, to get away from their own shores, and to seek comparative security as well as richer prey in distant waters. To this contributed also the increasing stringency of British convoy regulation, enforced with special rigor in the Caribbean Sea and over the Western Atlantic. It was impossible to impose the same strict prescription upon the coastwise trade, by which chiefly the indispensable continuous intercourse between the several parts of the United Kingdom was maintained. Before the introduction of steam this had a consequence quite disproportionate to the interior traffic by land; and its development, combined with the feeling of greater security as the British Islands were approached, occasioned in the narrow seas, and on the coasts of Europe, a dispersion of vessels not to be seen elsewhere. This favored the depredations of the light, swift, and handy cruisers that alone are capable of profiting by such an opportunity, through their power to evade the numerous, but necessarily scattered, ships of war, which under these circumstances must patrol the sea, like a watchman on beat, as the best substitute for the more formal and regularized convoy protection, when that ceases to apply.

From the end of the summer of 1813, when this tendency to distant enterprise became predominant, to the corresponding season a year later, there were captured by American cruisers some six hundred and fifty British vessels, chiefly merchantmen; a number which had increased to between four and five hundred more, when the war ended in the following winter.[219] An intelligible account of such multitudinous activities can be framed only by selecting amid the mass some illustrative particulars, accompanied by a general estimate of the conditions they indicate and the results they exemplify. Thus it may be stated, with fair approach to precision, that from September 30, 1813, to September 30, 1814, there were taken six hundred and thirty-nine British vessels, of which four hundred and twenty-four were in seas that may be called remote from the United

States. From that time to the end of the war, about six months, the total captures were four hundred and fourteen, of which those distant were two hundred and ninety-three. These figures, larger actually and in impression than they are relatively to the total of British shipping, represent the offensive maritime action of the United States during the period in question; but, in considering them, it must be remembered that such results were possible only because the sea was kept open to British commerce by the paramount power of the British navy. This could not prevent all mishaps; but it reduced them, by the annihilation of hostile navies, to such a small percentage of the whole shipping movement, that the British mercantile community found steady profit both in foreign and coasting trade, of which the United States at the same time was almost totally deprived.

The numerous but beggarly array of American bay-craft and oyster boats, which were paraded to swell British prize lists, till there seemed to be a numerical set-off to their own losses, show indeed that in point of size and value of vessels taken there was no real comparison; but this was due to the fact, not at once suggested by the figures themselves, that there were but few American merchant vessels to be taken, because they did not dare to go to sea, with the exception of the few to whom exceptional speed gave a chance of immunity, not always realized. In the period under consideration, September, 1813, to September, 1814, despite the great falling off of trade noted in the returns, over thirty American merchant ships and letters of marque were captured at sea;[220] at the head of the list being the "Ned," whose hair-breadth escapes in seeking to reach a United States port have been mentioned already.[221] She met her fate near the French coast, September 6, 1813, on the outward voyage from New York to Bordeaux. Privateering, risky though it was, offered a more profitable employment, with less chance of capture; because, besides being better armed and manned, the ship was not impeded in her sailing by the carriage of a heavy cargo. While the enemy was losing a certain small proportion of vessels, the United States suffered practically an entire deprivation of external commerce; and her coasting trade was almost wholly suppressed, at the time that her cruisers, national and private, were causing exaggerated anxiety concerning the intercourse between Great Britain and Ireland, which, though certainly molested, was not seriously interrupted.

Further evidence of the control exerted by the British Navy, and of the consequent difficulty under which offensive action was maintained by the United States, is to be found in the practice, from this time largely followed, of destroying prizes, after removing from them packages of little weight compared to their price. The prospect of a captured vessel reaching an American port was very doubtful, for the same reason that prevented the movement of American commerce; and while the risk was sometimes run, it usually was with cargoes which were at once costly and bulky, such as West India goods, sugars and coffees. Even then specie, and light costly articles, were first removed to the cruiser, where the chances for escape were decidedly better. Recourse to burning to prevent recapture was permissible only with enemy's vessels. If a neutral were found carrying enemy's goods, a frequent incident of maritime war, she must be sent in for adjudication; which, if adverse, affected the cargo only. Summary processes, therefore, could not be applied in such cases, and the close blockade of the United States coast seriously restricted the operations of her cruisers in this particular field.

Examination of the records goes to show that, although individual American vessels sometimes made numerous seizures in rapid succession, they seldom, if ever, effected the capture or destruction of a large convoy at a single blow. This was the object with which Rodgers started on his first cruise, but failed to accomplish. A stroke of this kind is always possible, and he had combined conditions unusually favorable to his hopes; but, while history certainly presents a few instances of such achievement on the large scale, they are comparatively rare, and opportunity, when it offers, can be utilized only by a more numerous force than at any subsequent time gathered under the American flag. In 1813 two privateers, the "Scourge" of New York and "Rattlesnake" of Philadelphia, passed the summer in the North Sea, and there made a number of prizes,—twenty-two,—which being reported together gave the impression of a single lucky encounter; were supposed in fact to be the convoy for which Rodgers in the "President" had looked unsuccessfully the same season.[222] The logs, however, showed that these captures were spread over a period of two months, and almost all made severally. Norway being then politically attached to Denmark, and hostile to Great Britain, such prizes as were not burned were sent into her ports. The "Scourge" appears to have been singularly fortunate, for on her homeward trip she took, sent in, or destroyed, ten more enemy's vessels; and in an absence extending a little over a year had taken four hundred and twenty prisoners,—more than the crew of a 38-gun frigate.[223]

At the same time the privateer schooner "Leo," of Baltimore, was similarly successful on the coast of Spain and Portugal. By an odd coincidence, another of the same class, bearing the nearly identical name, "Lion," was operating at the same time in the same waters, and with like results; which may possibly account for a contemporary report in a London paper, that an American off the Tagus had taken thirty-two British vessels. The "Leo" destroyed thirteen, and took four others; while the "Lion" destroyed fifteen, having first removed from them cargo to the amount of $400,000, which she carried safely into France. A curious circumstance, incidental to the presence of the privateers off Cape Finisterre, is that Wellington's troops, which had now passed the Pyrenees and were operating in southern France, had for a long time to wait for their great-coats, which had been stored in Lisbon for the summer, and now could not be returned by sea to Bayonne and Bordeaux before convoy was furnished to protect the transports against capture. Money to pay the troops, and for the commissariat, was similarly detained. Niles' Register, which followed carefully the news of maritime capture, announced in November, 1813, that eighty British vessels had been taken within a few months in European seas by the "President," "Argus," and five privateers. Compared with the continuous harassment and loss to which the enemy had become hardened during twenty years of war with France, allied often with other maritime states, this result, viewed singly, was not remarkable; but coming in addition to the other sufferings of British trade, and associated with similar injuries in the West Indies, and disquiet about the British seas themselves, the cumulative effect was undeniable, and found voice in public meetings, resolutions, and addresses to the Government.

Although the United States was not in formal alliance with France, the common hostility made the ports of either nation a base of operations to the other, and much facilitated the activities of American cruisers in British seas. One of the most successful of the privateers, the "True Blooded Yankee," was originally equipped at Brest, under American ownership, though it does not appear whether she was American built. On her first cruise her prizes are reported at twenty-seven. She remained out thirty-seven days, chiefly off the coast of Ireland, where she is said to have held an island for six days. Afterwards she burned several vessels in a Scotch harbor. Her procedure illustrates the methods of privateering in more respects than one. Thus, two large ships, one from Smyrna and one from Buenos Ayres, were thought sufficiently valuable to attempt sending into a French port, although the enemy watched the French coast as rigorously as the American. The recapture of a third, ordered to Morlaix, received specific mention, because one of the prize crew, being found to be an Englishman, was sentenced to death by an English court.[224] Eight others were destroyed; and, when the privateer returned to port, she carried in her own hold a miscellaneous cargo of light goods, too costly to risk in a less nimble bottom. Among these are named eighteen bales of Turkey carpets, forty-three bales of raw silk, seventy packs of skins, etc.[225] The "True Blooded Yankee" apparently continued to prefer European waters; for towards the end of 1814 she was taken there and sent into Gibraltar.

While there were certain well-known districts, such as these just mentioned, and others before specified, in which from causes constant in operation there was always to be found abundant material for the hazardous occupation of the commerce-destroyer, it was not to them alone that American cruisers went. There were other smaller but lucrative fields, into which an occasional irruption proved profitable. Such were the gold-coast on the west shore of Africa, and the island groups of Madeira, the Canaries, and Cape Verde, which geographically appertain to that continent. Thither Captain Morris directed the frigate "Adams," in January, 1814, after first escaping from his long blockade in the Potomac. This voyage, whence he returned to Savannah in April, was not remunerative; his most valuable prize, an East India ship, being snatched out of his hands, when in the act of taking possession, by an enemy's division in charge of a convoy of twenty-five sail, to which probably she had belonged, and had been separated by the thick weather that permitted her capture.[226] A year before this the privateer "Yankee," of Bristol, Rhode Island, had had better success. When she returned to Narragansett Bay in the spring of 1813, after a five months' absence, she reported having scoured the whole west coast of Africa, taking eight vessels, which carried in the aggregate sixty-two guns, one hundred and ninety-six men, and property to the amount of $296,000. In accordance with the practice already noticed, of distributing the spoil in order better to insure its arrival, she brought back in her own hold the light but costly items of six tons of ivory, thirty-two bales of fine goods, and $40,000 in gold-dust. This vessel was out again several times; and when the war closed was said to have been the most successful of all American cruisers. Her prizes numbered forty, of which thirty-four were ships or brigs; that is, of the larger classes of merchantmen then used. The estimated value of themselves and cargoes, $3,000,000, is to be received with reserve.[228]

It was in this neighborhood that the privateer schooner "Globe," Captain Moon, of Baltimore, mounting eight 9-pounder carronades and one long gun, met with an [227]adventure illustrative of the fighting incidental to the business. To this the privateersmen as a class were in no wise loath, where there was a fair prospect of the gain for which they were sent to look. Being off Funchal, in the island of Madeira, November 1, 1813, two brigs, which proved to be English packets, the "Montague" and "Pelham," were seen "backing and filling;" that is, keeping position in the open roadstead which constitutes the harbor, under sail, but not anchored. Packets, being in government service, were well armed for their size, and as mail carriers were necessarily chosen for speed; they therefore frequently carried specie. In one taken by the "Essex," Captain Porter found $55,000, which as ready cash helped him much to pay his frigate's way in a long and adventurous career. It does not appear that the "Globe" at first recognized the character of these particular vessels; but she lay-by during the night, watching for their quitting the shelter of neutral waters. This they did at 9 P.M., when the privateer pursued, but lost sight of them in a squall. The next morning they were seen in the southwest, and again chased. At 10.15 A.M. the "Montague" began firing her stern guns. The schooner replied, but kept on to board, knowing her superiority in men, and at 12.30 ran alongside (1). The attack being smartly met, and the vessels separating almost immediately, the attempt failed disastrously; there being left on board the packet the two lieutenants of the "Globe" and three or four seamen. Immediately upon this repulse, the "Pelham" crossed the privateer's bow and raked her (P 2), dealing such destruction to sails and rigging as to leave her unmanageable. The "Montague" and "Globe" now lay broadside to broadside (2), engaging; and ten minutes later the "Montague" by her own report was completely disabled (M 3). Captain Moon claimed that she struck; and this was probably the case, if his further incidental mention, that the mailbags were seen to be thrown overboard, is not a mistake. The action then continued with the "Pelham," within pistol-shot (3), for an hour or so, when the schooner, being found in a sinking condition, was compelled to haul off; "having seven shot between wind and water, the greater part of our standing and running rigging shot away, and not a sail but was perfectly riddled and almost useless." After separating, the several combatants all steered with the tradewinds for the Canaries; the British going to Teneriffe, and the American to the Grand Canary.[229]

From the injuries received, it is apparent that, for the armaments of the vessels, this was a very severe as well as determined engagement. The British had six killed and twelve wounded; the American five killed and thirteen wounded, besides the prisoners lost in boarding. All three captains were severely hurt, that of the "Montague" being killed. The figures given are those reported by each side; how exaggerated the rumors current about such encounters, and the consequent difficulty to the historian, is shown by what each heard about the other's casualties. A Spanish brig from Teneriffe told Moon that the enemy had twenty-seven men killed; while the British were equally credibly informed that the "Globe" lost thirty-three killed and nineteen wounded.

Near about this time, in the same neighborhood of Madeira, the privateer schooner "Governor Tompkins," of New York, captured in rapid succession three British merchant vessels which had belonged to a convoy from England to Buenos Ayres, but after its dispersal in a gale were pursuing their route singly. Two of these reached an American port, their bulky and heavy ladings of dry goods and hardware not permitting transfer or distribution. The sale of one cargo realized $270,000.[230] At about the same moment came in a brig of like value, not improbably another wanderer from the same group, captured near Madeira by the ship "America," of Salem. This vicinity, from the islands to the equator, between 20° and 30° west longitude, belongs essentially to the thronged highway and cross-roads of commerce, which has been noted as a favorite cruising ground of American ships of war. Hereabouts passed vessels both to and from the East Indies and South America. The bad luck of several frigates, and the rough handling of the "Globe" by the packets, illustrate one side of the fortune of war, as the good hap of the "America" and "Governor Tompkins" shows the other.

It is, however, the beginnings and endings of commercial routes, rather than the intermediate stretch, which most favor enterprises against an enemy's trade. In the thronging of vessels, the Caribbean Sea, with its teeming archipelago, was second only, if second, to the waters surrounding the United Kingdom. England was one extremity, and the several West India Islands the other, of a traffic then one of the richest in the world; while the tropical articles of this exchange, if not absolute necessaries of life, had become by long indulgence indispensable to the great part of civilized mankind. Here, therefore, the numbers, the efforts, and the successes of American privateers most nearly rivalled the daring achievements of their fellows in the Narrow Seas and the approaches to Great Britain and Ireland. The two regions resembled each other in another respect. Not only was there for both an external trade, mainly with one another, but in each there was also a local traffic of distribution and collection of goods, from and to central ports, in which was concentrated the movement of import and export. As has been remarked concerning the coastwise carriage of the United Kingdom, this local intercourse, to be efficient, could not be regulated and hampered to the same extent as the long voyage, over-sea, transportation. A certain amount of freedom and independence was essential, and the risk attendant upon such separate action must be compensated, as far as might be, by diminishing the size of the vessels engaged; a resource particularly applicable to the moderate weather and quiet seas prevalent in the tropics.

Both the exposure of trade under such relaxed conditions, and the relative security obtained by the convoy system, rigidly applied, are shown by a few facts. From September 1, 1813, to March 1, 1814, six months, the number of prizes taken by Americans, exclusive of those on the Lakes, was reported as two hundred and seventy. Of these, nearly one third—eighty-six—were to, from, or within the West Indies. Since in many reports the place of capture is not given, nor any data sufficient to fix it, it is probable that quite one third belonged to this trade. This evidences the scale, both of the commerce itself and of its pursuers, justifying a contemporary statement that "the West Indies swarm with American privateers;" and it suggests also that many of the seizures were local traders between the islands, or at least vessels taking their chance on short runs. On the other hand, the stringency with which the local officials enforced the Convoy Act was shown, generally, by the experience at this time of the United States naval vessels, the records of which, unlike those of most privateers, have been preserved by filing or publication; and, specifically, by a number of papers found in a prize by the United States frigate "Constitution," Captain Charles Stewart, while making a round of these waters in the first three months of 1814. Among other documents was a petition, signed by many merchants of Demerara, praying convoy for fifty-one vessels which were collected and waiting for many weary weeks, as often had to be done. In one letter occurs the following: "With respect to procuring a license for the "Fanny" to run it, in case any other ships should be about to do so, we do not believe that, out of forty vessels ready to sail, any application has been made for such license, though out of the number are several out-port vessels well armed and manned. Indeed, we are aware application would be perfectly useless, as the present Governor, when at Berbice, would not permit a vessel from that colony to this [adjoining] without convoy. If we could obtain a license, we could not justify ourselves to shippers, who have ordered insurance with convoy."[231]

The expense and embarrassment incident to such detentions are far-reaching, and the effects are as properly chargeable as are captures themselves to the credit of the cruisers, by the activity of which they are occasioned. The "Constitution" could report only four prizes as the result of a three months' cruise, necessarily shortened by the approach of spring. This made it imperative for a vessel, denied admission to most home ports by her draught of water, to recover the shelter of one of them before the blockade again began, and the exhaustion of her provisions should compel her to attempt entrance under risk of an engagement with superior force. As it was, she was chased into Salem, and had to lighten ship to escape. But Stewart had driven an enemy's brig of war into Surinam, chased a packet off Barbados, and a frigate in the Mona Passage; and the report of these occurrences, wherever received, imposed additional precaution, delay, and expense.

At the same time that the "Constitution" was passing through the southern Caribbean, the naval brigs "Rattlesnake" and "Enterprise" were searching its northern limits. These had put out from Portsmouth, New Hampshire, when the winter weather drove the blockaders from there, as from Boston, whence the "Constitution" had sailed. Starting early in January, 1814, these two light cruisers kept company, passing east of Bermuda to the island of St. Thomas, at the northeast corner of the Caribbean. Thence they turned west, skirting the north shores of Porto Rico and Santo Domingo as far as the Windward Passage. Through this they entered the Caribbean, followed the south coast of Cuba, between it and Jamaica, rounded Cape San Antonio, at its western extremity, and thence, traversing the Straits of Florida, returned along the coast of the United States. Having already been chased twice in this cruise, they were compelled by a third pursuer to separate, February 25. The stranger chose to keep after the "Enterprise," which being a very dull sailer was obliged in a flight of seventy hours to throw overboard most of her battery to escape. The two put into

Wilmington, North Carolina, a port impracticable to a frigate.[232]
In this long round the brigs overhauled eleven vessels, two only of which
were under the British flag. Two were Americans; the rest neutrals, either
Swedes or Spaniards. Of the two enemies, only one was a merchant ship.
The other was a privateer, the chase of which gave rise to a curious and
significant incident. Being near the Florida coast, and thinking the brigs to
be British, twenty or thirty of the crew took to the boats and fled ashore to
escape anticipated impressment. As Marryat remarks, a British private
vessel of that day feared a British ship of war more than it did an enemy of
equal force. Of the neutrals stopped, one was in possession of a British
prize crew, and another had on board enemy's goods. For these reasons
they were sent in for adjudication, and arrived safely. Judged by these small
results from the several cruises of the "Enterprise," "Rattlesnake," and
"Constitution," the large aggregate of captures before quoted, two hundred
and seventy, would indicate that to effect them required a great number of
cruisers, national and private. That this inference is correct will be shown
later, by some interesting and instructive figures.

While the making of prizes was the primary concern of the American
privateers, their cruises in the West Indies, as elsewhere, gave rise to a
certain amount of hard fighting. One of the most noted of these
encounters, that of the schooner "Decatur," of Charleston, with the man-
of-war schooner "Dominica," can hardly be claimed for the United States;
for, though fought under the flag, her captain, Diron, was French, as were
most of the crew. The "Dominica" was in company with a King's packet,
which she was to convoy part of the way to England from St. Thomas. On
August 5, 1813, the "Decatur" met the two about three hundred miles
north of the island. The British vessel was superior in armament, having
fifteen guns; all carronades, except two long sixes. The "Decatur's" battery
was six carronades, and one long 18-pounder. For long distances the latter
was superior in carrying power and penetration to anything on board the
"Dominica;" but the American captain, knowing himself to have most men,
sought to board, and the artillery combat was therefore mainly at close
quarters, within carronade range. It began at 2 P.M. At 2.30 the schooners
were within half-gunshot of one another; the "Dominica" in the position of
being chased, because of the necessity of avoiding the evident intention of
the "Decatur" to come hand to hand. Twice the latter tried to run
alongside, and twice was foiled by watchful steering, accompanied in each
case by a broadside which damaged her rigging and sails, besides killing two
of her crew. The third attempt was successful, the "Decatur's" bow coming
against the quarter of the "Dominica," the jib-boom passing through her
mainsail. The crew of the privateer clambered on board, and there followed
a hand-to-hand fight equally honorable to both parties. The British captain,
Lieutenant Barretté, a young man of twenty-five, who had already proved

his coolness and skill in the management of the action, fell at the head of his men, of whom sixty out of a total of eighty-eight were killed or wounded before their colors were struck. The assailants, who numbered one hundred and three, lost nineteen. The packet, though armed, took no part in the fight, and when it was over effected her escape.[233] The "Decatur" with her prize reached Charleston safely, August 20; bringing also a captured merchantman. The moment of arrival was most opportune; two enemy's brigs, which for some time had been blockading the harbor, having left only the day before.

In March, 1814, the privateer schooner "Comet," of Baltimore, not being able to make her home port, put into Wilmington, North Carolina. She had been cruising in the West Indies, and had there taken twenty vessels, most of which were destroyed after removing valuables. In the course of her operations she encountered near St. Thomas the British ship "Hibernia;" the size of which, and her height above the water, by preventing boarding, enabled her successfully to repel attack, and the privateer was obliged to haul off, having lost three men killed and thirteen wounded. The American account of this affair ascribes twenty-two guns to the "Hibernia." The British story says that she had but six, with a crew of twenty-two men; of whom one was killed and eleven wounded. The importance of the matter in itself scarcely demands a serious attempt to reconcile this discrepancy; and it is safer to accept each party's statement of his own force. The two agree that the action lasted eight or nine hours, and that both were much cut up. It is evident also from each narrative that they lay alongside most of the time, which makes it probable that the ship's height saved her from being overborne by superior numbers.

The "Saucy Jack," of Charleston, passed through several severe combats, in one of which she was even worse mauled than the "Comet" in the instance just cited. On April 30, 1814, off St. Nicolas Mole, in the Windward Passage between Cuba and Santo Domingo, she met the British ship "Pelham," a vessel of five hundred and forty tons, and mounting ten guns, bound from London to Port au Prince. The "Pelham" fought well, and the action lasted two hours, at the end of which she was carried by boarding. Her forty men were overpowered by numbers, but nevertheless still resisted with a resolution which commanded the admiration of the victors. She lost four killed and eleven wounded; among the latter her captain, dangerously. The privateer had two killed and nine wounded. Both vessels reached Charleston safely, and the "Saucy Jack" at once fitted out again. It is told that, between daylight and dark of the day she began to enlist, one hundred and thirty able-bodied seamen had shipped; and this at a time when the navy with difficulty found crews.[234]

The "Saucy Jack" returned to the West Indies for another cruise, in which she encountered one of those rude deceptions which privateers often experienced. She had made already eight prizes, for one of which, the ship "Amelia," she had had to fight vigorously, killing four and wounding five of the enemy, while herself sustaining a loss of one killed and one wounded, when on October 31, 1814, about 1 A.M., being then off Cape Tiburon at the west end of Haïti, she sighted two vessels standing to the westward. Chase was made, and an hour later the privateer opened fire. The strangers replied, at the same time shortening sail, which looked ominous; but the "Saucy Jack," willing to justify her name, kept on to close. At 6 A.M., having arrived within a few hundred yards, the enemy were seen to be well armed, but appeared not to be well manned. At seven, by which time it was daylight, the "Saucy Jack" began an engagement with the nearer, and ten minutes later ran her alongside, when she was found to be full of soldiers. The privateer sheered off at once, and took to her heels, followed by an incessant fire of grape and musketry from those whom she had recently pursued. This awkward position, which carried the chance of a disabling shot and consequent capture, lasted till eight, when the speed of the schooner took her out of range, having had in all eight men killed and fifteen wounded; two round shot in the hull, and spars and rigging much cut up. It was afterwards ascertained that her opponent was the "Volcano" bombship, convoying the transport "Golden Fleece," on board which were two hundred and fifty troops from Chesapeake Bay for Jamaica. The "Volcano" lost an officer and two men killed, and two wounded; proving that under somewhat awkward circumstances the "Saucy Jack" could give as well as take.[235]

A little later in this season a group of nine sail, from the West Indies for Europe, was encountered by the privateer "Kemp," of Baltimore, broad off the coast of North Carolina. Excluded, like the "Comet" and others, from return to the port where she belonged, the "Kemp" had been in Wilmington, which she left November 29, 1814; the strangers being sighted at 8 A.M. December 1. One was a convoying frigate, which, when the "Kemp" pursued, gave chase and drove her off that afternoon. The privateer outran her pursuer, and during the night by devious courses gave her the slip; thereupon steering for the position where she judged she would again fall in with the merchant vessels. In this she was successful, at daylight discovering them,—three ships, three brigs, and two schooners. At 11 A.M. one ship was overtaken, but proving to be Spanish, from Havana to Hamburg, was allowed to proceed, while the "Kemp" again followed the others. At noon they were five miles to windward, drawn up in a line to fight; for in those days of war and piracy most merchant ships carried at least a few guns for defence, and in this case their numbers, combined in mutual support, might effect a successful resistance. At two they took the initiative, bearing down together and attacking. The "Kemp" engaged them all, and in half an hour the untrained squadron was naturally in confusion.

One after the other, six of the seven were boarded, or without waiting to be attacked struck their colors as the schooner drew up; but while four were being taken into possession, the two others seized the opportunity and made off. Two ships and two brigs remained in the hands of the captor. All were laden with sugar and coffee, valuable at any time, but especially so in the then destitute condition of the United States. After this unusual, if not wholly unique, experience, the "Kemp" returned to port, having been absent only six days. Her prisoners amounted to seventy-one, her own crew being fifty-three. The separation of the escort from the convoy, the subsequent judicious search for the latter, and the completeness of the result, constitute this a very remarkable instance of good management accompanied by good fortune; success deserved and achieved.[236]

The privateer brig "Chasseur," of Baltimore, Captain Thomas Boyle, was one of the typically successful and renowned cruisers of the time. She carried a battery of sixteen 12-pounder carronades, and in the course of the war thirty prizes are credited to her. In the late summer of 1814 she cruised off the coast of Great Britain and Ireland, returning at the end of October; having made eighteen captures during an absence of three months. From these she paroled and sent in by cartels one hundred and fifty prisoners, bringing back with her forty-three, of whom she had not been able thus to rid herself.[237] After refitting she went to the West Indies for a winter cruise, which extended from the Windward Islands to the neighborhood of Havana. Here she signalized the approaching end of her career by an action, fought after peace not only had been concluded at Ghent, but already was known in the United States. On February 26, 1815, at 11 A.M., being then twenty miles east of Havana, and six miles from the Cuban coast, a schooner was seen in the northeast (1), running down before the northeast trade-wind. Sail was made to intercept her (2), there being at the time visible from the "Chasseur's" masthead a convoy lying-to off Havana, information concerning which probably accounts for her presence at this spot. The chase steered more to the northward (2), bringing the wind on her starboard side, apparently wishing to avoid a meeting. The "Chasseur" followed her motions, and when within about three miles the stranger's foretopmast went over the side, showing the press of sail she was carrying. After clearing the wreck she hauled close on the wind, heading northerly. At 1 P.M., she began to fire her stern gun and showed British colors; but only three port-holes were visible on her port side,—towards the "Chasseur." Believing from appearances that he had before him a weakly armed vessel making a passage, and seeing but few men on her deck, Captain Boyle pressed forward without much preparation and under all sail. At 1.26 P.M. the "Chasseur" had come within pistol-shot (3), on the port side, when the enemy disclosed a tier of ten ports and opened his broadside, with round shot, grape, and musket balls. The American schooner, having much way on, shot ahead, and as she was to leeward in doing so, the British vessel kept off quickly (4) to run under her stern and rake. This was successfully avoided by imitating the movement (4), and the two were again side by side, but with the "Chasseur" now to the right (5). The action continued thus for about ten minutes, when Boyle found his opponent's battery too heavy for him. He therefore ran alongside (6), and in the act of boarding the enemy struck. She proved to be the British schooner "St. Lawrence," belonging to the royal navy; formerly a renowned Philadelphia privateer, the "Atlas." Her battery, one long 9-pounder and fourteen 12-pounder carronades, would have been no very unequal match for the sixteen of her antagonist; but the "Chasseur" had been obliged recently to throw overboard ten of these, while hard chased by the Barrosa frigate, and had replaced them with some 9-pounders from a prize, for which she had no proper projectiles. The complement allowed the "St. Lawrence" was seventy-five, though it does not seem certain that all were on board; and she was carrying also some soldiers, marines, and naval officers, bound to New Orleans, in ignorance probably of the disastrous end of that expedition. The "Chasseur" had eighty-nine men, besides several boys. The British loss reported by her captain was six killed and seventeen wounded; the American, five killed and eight wounded.[238]

This action was very creditably fought on both sides, but to the American captain belongs the meed of having not only won success, but deserved it. His sole mistake was the over-confidence in what he could see, which made him a victim to the very proper ruse practised by his antagonist in concealing his force. His manœuvring was prompt, ready, and accurate; that of the British vessel was likewise good, but a greater disproportion of injury should have resulted from her superior battery. In reporting the affair to his owners, Captain Boyle said, apologetically: "I should not willingly, perhaps, have sought a contest with a King's vessel, knowing that is not our object; but my expectations at first were a valuable vessel, and a valuable cargo also. When I found myself deceived, the honor of the flag intrusted to my care was not to be disgraced by flight." The feeling expressed was modest as well as spirited, and Captain Boyle's handsome conduct merits the mention that the day after the action, when the captured schooner was released as a cartel to Havana, in compassion to her wounded, the commander of the "St. Lawrence" gave him a letter, in the event of his being taken by a British cruiser, testifying to his "obliging attention and watchful solicitude to preserve our effects, and render us comfortable during the short time we were in his possession;" in which, he added, the captain "was carefully seconded by all his officers."[239]

These instances, occurring either in the West Indies, or, in the case of the "Kemp," affecting vessels which had just loaded there, are sufficient, when taken in connection with those before cited from other quarters of the globe, to illustrate the varied activities and fortunes of privateering. The general subject, therefore, need not further be pursued. It will be observed that in each case the cruiser acts on the offensive; being careful, however, in choosing the object of attack, to avoid armed ships, the capture of which seems unlikely to yield pecuniary profit adequate to the risk. The gallantry and skill of Captain Boyle of the "Chasseur" made particularly permissible to him the avowal, that only mistake of judgment excused his committing himself to an encounter which held out no such promise; and it may be believed that the equally capable Captain Diron, if free to do as he pleased, would have chosen the packet, and not her escort the "Dominica," as the object of his pursuit. This the naval schooner of course could not permit. It was necessary, therefore, first to fight her; and, although she was beaten, the result of the action was to insure the escape of the ship under her charge. These examples define exactly the spirit and aim of privateering, and distinguish them from the motives inspiring the ship of war. The object of the privateer is profit by capture; to which fighting is only incidental, and where avoidable is blamable. The mission of a navy on the other hand is primarily military; and while custom permitted the immediate captor a share in the proceeds of his prizes, the taking of them was in conception not for direct gain, personal or national, but for injury to the enemy.

It may seem that, even though the ostensible motive was not the same, the two courses of operation followed identical methods, and in outcome were indistinguishable. This is not so. However subtle the working of the desire for gain upon the individual naval officer, leading at times to acts of doubtful propriety, the tone and spirit of a profession, even when not clearly formulated in phrase and definition, will assert itself in the determination of personal conduct. The dominating sense of advantage to the state, which is the military motive, and the dominating desire for gain in a mercantile enterprise, are very different incentives; and the result showed itself in a fact which has never been appreciated, and perhaps never noted, that the national ships of war were far more effective as prize takers than were the privateers. A contrary impression has certainly obtained, and was shared by the present writer until he resorted to the commonplace test of adding up figures.

Amid much brilliant achievement, privateering, like all other business pursuits, had also a large and preponderant record of unsuccess. The very small number of naval cruisers necessarily yielded a much smaller aggregate of prizes; but when the respective totals are considered with reference to the numbers of vessels engaged in making them, the returns from the individual vessels of the United States navy far exceed those from the privateers. Among conspicuously successful cruisers, also, the United States ships "Argus," "Essex," "Peacock," and "Wasp" compare favorably in general results with the most celebrated privateers, even without allowing for the evident fact that a few instances of very extraordinary qualities and record are more likely to be found among five hundred vessels than among twenty-two; this being the entire number of naval pendants actually engaged in open-sea cruising, from first to last. These twenty-two captured one hundred and sixty-five prizes, an average of 7.5 each, in which are included the enemy's ships of war taken. Of privateers of all classes there were five hundred and twenty-six; or, excluding a few small nondescripts, four hundred and ninety-two. By these were captured thirteen hundred and forty-four vessels, an average of less than three; to be exact, 2.7. The proportion, therefore, of prizes taken by ships of war to those by private armed vessels was nearly three to one.

Comparison may be instituted in other ways. Of the twenty-two national cruisers, four only, or one in five, took no prize; leaving to the remaining eighteen an average of nine. Out of the grand total of five hundred and twenty-six privateers only two hundred and seven caught anything; three hundred and nineteen, three out of five, returned to port empty-handed, or were themselves taken. Dividing the thirteen hundred and forty-four prizes among the two hundred and seven more or less successful privateers, there results an average of 6.5; so that, regard being had only to successful cruisers, the achievement of the naval vessels was to that of the private armed nearly as three to two. These results may be accepted as disposing entirely of the extravagant claims made for privateering as a system, when compared with a regular naval service, especially when it is remembered with what difficulty the American frigates could get to sea at all, on account of their heavy draft and the close blockade; whereas the smaller vessels, national or private, had not only many harbors open, but also comparatively numerous opportunities to escape. The frigate "United States" never got out after her capture of the "Macedonian," in 1812; the "Congress" was shut up after her return in December, 1813; and the "Chesapeake" had been captured in the previous June. All these nevertheless count in the twenty-two pendants reckoned above.

The figures here cited are from a compilation by Lieutenant George F. Emmons,[240] of the United States Navy, published in 1853 under the title, "The United States Navy from 1775 to 1853." Mr. Emmons made no analyses, confining himself to giving lists and particulars; his work is purely statistical. Counting captures upon the lakes, and a few along the coast difficult of classification, his grand total of floating craft taken from the enemy reaches fifteen hundred and ninety-nine; which agrees nearly with the sixteen hundred and thirty-four of Niles, whom he names among his sources of information. From an examination of the tables some other details of interest may be drawn. Of the five hundred and twenty-six privateers and letters-of-marque given by name, twenty-six were ships, sixty-seven brigs, three hundred and sixty-four schooners, thirty-five sloops, thirty-four miscellaneous; down to, and including, a few boats putting out from the beach. The number captured by the enemy was one hundred and forty-eight, or twenty-eight per cent. The navy suffered more severely. Of the twenty-two vessels reckoned above, twelve were taken, or destroyed to keep them out of an enemy's hands; over fifty per cent. Of the twelve, six were small brigs, corresponding in size and nautical powers to the privateer. Three were frigates—the "President," "Essex," and "Chesapeake." One, the "Adams," was not at sea when destroyed by her own captain to escape capture. Only two sloops of war, the first "Wasp" and the "Frolic,"[241] were taken; and of these the former, as already known, was caught when partially dismasted, at the end of a successful engagement.

Contemporary with the career of the "Argus," the advantage of a sudden and unexpected inroad, like hers, upon a region deemed safe by the enemy, was receiving confirmation in the remote Pacific by the cruise of the frigate "Essex." This vessel, which had formed part of Commodore Bainbridge's squadron at the close of 1812, was last mentioned as keeping her Christmas off Cape Frio,[242] on the coast of Brazil, awaiting there the coming of the consorts whom she never succeeded in joining. Captain Porter maintained this station, hearing frequently about Bainbridge by vessels from Bahia, until January 12, 1813. Then a threatened shortness of provisions, and rumors of enemy's ships in the neighborhood, especially of the seventy-four "Montagu" combined to send him to St. Catherine's Island, another appointed rendezvous, and the last upon the coast of Brazil. In this remote and sequestered anchorage hostile cruisers would scarcely look for him, at least until more likely positions had been carefully examined.

At St. Catherine's Porter heard of the action between the "Constitution" and "Java" off Bahia, a thousand miles distant, and received also a rumor, which seemed probable enough, that the third ship of the division, the "Hornet," had been captured by the "Montagu." He consequently left port January 26, for the southward, still with the expectation of ultimately joining the Commodore off St. Helena, the last indicated point of assembly; but having been unable to renew his stores in St. Catherine's, and ascertaining that there was no hope of better success at Buenos Ayres, or the other Spanish settlements within the River La Plata, he after reflection decided to cut loose from the squadron and go alone to the Pacific. There he could reasonably hope to support himself by the whalers of the enemy; that class of vessel being always well provided for long absences. This alternative course he knew would be acceptable to the Government, as well as to his immediate commander.[243] The next six weeks were spent in the tempestuous passage round Cape Horn, the ship's company living on half-allowance of provisions; but on March 14, 1813, the "Essex" anchored in Valparaiso, being the first United States ship of war to show the national flag in the Pacific. By a noteworthy coincidence she had already been the first to carry it beyond the Cape of Good Hope.

Chile received the frigate hospitably, being at the time in revolt against Spain; but the authority of the mother country was still maintained in Peru, where a Spanish viceroy resided, and it was learned that in the capacity of ally of Great Britain he intended to fit out privateers against American whalers, of which there were many in these seas. As several of the British whalers carried letters-of-marque, empowering them to make prizes, the arrival of the "Essex" not only menaced the hostile interests, but promised to protect her own countrymen from a double danger. Her departure therefore was hastened; and having secured abundant provision, such as the port supplied, she sailed for the northward a week after anchoring. A privateer from Peru was met, which had seized two Americans. Porter threw overboard her guns and ammunition, and then released her with a note for the viceroy, which served both as a respectful explanation and a warning. One of the prizes taken by this marauder was recaptured March 27, when entering Callao, the port of Lima.

The "Essex" then went to the Galapagos Islands, a group just south of the equator, five hundred miles from the South American mainland. These belong now to Ecuador, and at that day were a noted rendezvous for whalers. In this neighborhood the frigate remained from April 17 to October 3, during which period she captured twelve British whalers out of some twenty-odd reported in the Pacific; with the necessary consequence of driving all others to cover for the time being. The prizes were valuable, some more, some less; not only from the character of their cargoes, but because they themselves were larger than the average merchant ship, and exceptionally well found. Three were sent to Valparaiso in convoy of a fourth, which had been converted into a consort of the "Essex," under the name of the "Essex Junior," mounting twenty very light guns. September 30 she returned, bringing word that a British squadron, consisting of the 36-gun frigate "Phœbe," Captain James Hillyar, and the sloops of war "Cherub" and "Raccoon," had sailed for the Pacific. The rumor was correct, though long antedating the arrival of the vessels. In consequence of it, Porter, considering that his work at the Galapagos was now complete, and that the "Essex" would need overhauling before a possible encounter with a division, the largest unit of which was superior to her in class and force, decided to move to a position then even more remote from disturbance than St. Catherine's had been. On October 25 the "Essex" and "Essex Junior" anchored at the island of Nukahiva, of the Marquesas group, having with them three of the prizes. Of the others, besides those now at Valparaiso, two had been given up to prisoners to convey them to England, and three had been sent to the United States. That all the last were captured on the way detracts nothing from Porter's merit, but testifies vividly to the British command of the sea.

At the Marquesas, by aid of the resources of the prizes, the frigate was thoroughly overhauled, refitted, and provisioned for six months. Porter had not only maintained his ship, but in part paid his officers and crew from the proceeds of his captures. On December 12 he sailed for Chile, satisfied with the material outcome of his venturous cruise, but wishing to add to it something of further distinction by an encounter with Hillyar, if obtainable on terms approaching equality. With this object the ship's company were diligently exercised at the guns and small arms during the passage, which lasted nearly eight weeks; the Chilean coast being sighted on January 12, far to the southward, and the "Essex" running slowly along it until February 3, when she reached Valparaiso. On the 8th the "Phœbe" and "Cherub" came in and anchored; the "Raccoon" having gone on to the North Pacific.

The antagonists now lay near one another, under the restraint of a neutral port, for several days, during which some social intercourse took place between the officers; the two captains renewing an acquaintance made years before in the Mediterranean. After a period of refit, and of repose for the crews, the British left the bay, and cruised off the port. The "Essex" and "Essex Junior" remained at anchor, imprisoned by a force too superior to be encountered without some modifying circumstances of advantage. Porter found opportunities for contrasting the speed of the two frigates, and convinced himself that the "Essex" was on that score superior; but the respective armaments introduced very important tactical considerations, which might, and in the result did, prove decisive. The "Essex" originally had been a 12-pounder frigate, classed as of thirty-two guns; but her battery now was forty 32-pounder carronades and six long twelves. Captain Porter in his report of the battle stated the armament of the "Phœbe" to be thirty long 18-pounders and sixteen 32-pounder carronades. The British naval historian James gives her twenty-six long eighteens, fourteen 32-pounder carronades, and four long nines; while to the "Cherub" he attributes a carronade battery of eighteen thirty-twos and six eighteens, with two long sixes. Whichever enumeration be accepted, the broadside of the "Essex" within carronade range considerably outweighed that of the "Phœbe" alone, but was much less than that of the two British ships combined; the light built and light-armed "Essex Junior" not being of account to either side. There remained always the serious chance that, even if the "Phœbe" accepted single combat, some accident of wind might prevent the "Essex" reaching her before being disabled by her long guns. Hillyar, moreover, was an old disciple of Nelson, fully imbued with the teaching that achievement of success, not personal glory, must dictate action; and, having a well established reputation for courage and conduct, he did not intend to leave anything to the chances of fortune incident to engagement between equals. He would accept no provocation to fight apart from the "Cherub."

Forced to accept this condition, Porter now turned his attention to escape.

Valparaiso Bay is an open roadstead, facing north. The high ground above the anchorage provides shelter from the south-southwest wind, which prevails along this coast throughout the year with very rare intermissions. At times, as is common under high land, it blows furiously in gusts. The British vessels underway kept their station close to the extreme western point of the bay, to prevent the "Essex" from passing to southward of them, and so gaining the advantage of the wind, which might entail a prolonged chase and enable her, if not to distance pursuit, at least to draw the "Phœbe" out of support of the "Cherub." Porter's aim of course was to seize an opportunity when by neglect, or unavoidably, they had left a practicable opening between them and the point. In the end, his hand was forced by an accident.

On March 28 the south wind blew with unusual violence, and the "Essex" parted one of her cables. The other anchor failed to hold when the strain came upon it, and the ship began to drift to sea. The cable was cut and sail made at once; for though the enemy were too nearly in their station to have warranted the attempt to leave under ordinary conditions, Porter, in the emergency thus suddenly thrust upon him, thought he saw a prospect of passing to windward. The "Essex" therefore was hauled close to the wind under single-reefed topsails, heading to the westward; but just as she came under the point of the bay a heavy squall carried away the maintopmast. The loss of this spar hopelessly crippled her, and made it impossible even to regain the anchorage left. She therefore put about, and ran eastward until within pistol-shot of the coast, about three miles north of the city. Here she anchored, well within neutral waters; Hillyar's report stating that she was "so near shore as to preclude the possibility of passing ahead of her without risk to his Majesty's ships." Three miles, then the range of a cannon-shot, estimated liberally, was commonly accepted as the width of water adjacent to neutral territory, which was under the neutral protection. The British captain decided nevertheless to attack.

The wind remaining southerly, the "Essex" rode head to it; the two hostile vessels approaching with the intention of running north of her, close under her stern. The wind, however, forced them off as they drew near; and their first attack, beginning about 4 P.M. and lasting ten minutes, produced no visible effect, according to Hillyar's report. Porter states, on the contrary, that considerable injury was done to the "Essex"; and in particular the spring which he was trying to get on the cable was thrice shot away, thus preventing the bringing of her broadside to bear as required. The "Phœbe" and her consort then wore, which increased their distance, and stood out again to sea. While doing this they threw a few "random shots;" fired, that is, at an elevation so great as to be incompatible with certainty of aim. During this cannonade the "Essex," with three 12-pounders run out of her stern ports, had deprived the "Phœbe" of "the use of her mainsail, jib and mainstay." On standing in again Hillyar prepared to anchor, but ordered the "Cherub" to keep underway, choosing a position whence she could most annoy their opponent.

At 5.35 P.M., by Hillyar's report,—Porter is silent as to the hour,—the attack was renewed; the British ships both placing themselves on the starboard—seaward—quarter of the "Essex." Before the "Phœbe" reached the position in which she intended to anchor, the "Essex" was seen to be underway. Hillyar could only suppose that her cable had been severed by a shot; but Porter states that under the galling fire to which she was subjected, without power to reply, he cut the cable, hoping, as the enemy were to leeward, he might bring the ship into close action, and perhaps even board the "Phœbe." The decision was right, but under the conditions a counsel of desperation; for sheets, tacks, and halliards being shot away, movement depended upon sails hanging loose,—spread, but not set. Nevertheless, he was able for a short time to near the enemy, and both accounts agree that hereupon ensued the heat of the combat; "a serious conflict," to use Hillyar's words, to which corresponds Porter's statement that "the firing on both sides was now tremendous." The "Phœbe," however, was handled, very properly, to utilize to the full the tactical advantages she possessed in the greater range of her guns, and in power of manœuvring. In the circumstances under which she was acting, the sail power left her was amply sufficient; having simply to keep drawing to leeward, maintaining from her opponent a distance at which his guns were useless and her own effective.

Under these conditions, seeing success to be out of the question, and suffering great loss of men, Porter turned to the last resort of the vanquished, to destroy the vessel and to save the crew from captivity. The "Essex" was pointed for the shore; but when within a couple of hundred yards the wind, which had so far favored her approach, shifted ahead. Still clinging to every chance, a kedge with a hawser was let go, to hold her where she was; perhaps the enemy might drift unwittingly out of range. But the hawser parted, and with it the frigate's last hold upon the country which she had honored by an heroic defence. Porter then authorized any who might wish to swim ashore to do so; the flag being kept flying to warrant a proceeding which after formal surrender would be a breach of faith. At 6.20 the "Essex" at last lowered her colors.[244] Out of a ship's company of two hundred and fifty-five, with which she sailed in the morning, fifty-eight were killed, or died of their wounds, and sixty-five were wounded. The missing were reported at thirty-one. By agreement between Hillyar and Porter, the "Essex Junior" was disarmed, and neutralized, to convey to the United States, as paroled prisoners of war, the survivors who remained on board at the moment of surrender. These numbered one hundred and thirty-two. It is an interesting particular, linking those early days of the

United States navy to a long subsequent period of renown, and worthy therefore to be recalled, that among the combatants of the "Essex" was Midshipman David G. Farragut, then thirteen years old. His name figures among the wounded, as well as in the list of passengers on board the "Essex Junior."

The disaster to the "Essex" is connected by a singular and tragical link with the fate of an American cruiser of like adventurous enterprise in seas far distant from the Pacific. After the defeat at Valparaiso, Lieutenant Stephen Decatur McKnight and Midshipman James Lyman of the United States frigate were exchanged as prisoners of war against a certain number of officers and seamen belonging to one of the "Essex's" prizes; which, having continued under protection of the neutral port, had undergone no change of belligerent relation by the capture of her captor. When the "Essex Junior" sailed, these two officers remained behind, by amicable arrangement, to go in the "Phœbe" to Rio Janeiro, there to give certain evidence needed in connection with the prize claims of the British frigate; which done, it was understood they would be at liberty to return to their own country by such conveyance as suited them. After arrival in Rio, the first convenient opportunity offering was by a Swedish brig sailing for Falmouth, England. In her they took passage, leaving Rio August 23, 1814. On October 9 the brig fell in with the United States sloop of war "Wasp," in mid-ocean, about three hundred miles west of the Cape Verde Islands, homeward bound. The two passengers transferred themselves to her. Since this occurrence nothing further has ever been heard of the American ship; nor would the incident itself have escaped oblivion but for the anxiety of friends, which after the lapse, of time prompted systematic inquiry to ascertain what had become of the missing officers.

The captain of the "Wasp" was Master-Commandant, or, as he would now be styled, Commander Johnstone Blakely; the same who had commanded the "Enterprise" up to a month before her engagement with the "Boxer," when was demonstrated the efficiency to which he had brought her ship's company. He sailed from Portsmouth, New Hampshire, May 1, 1814. Of his instructions,[245] the most decisive was to remain for thirty days in a position on the approaches to the English Channel, about one hundred and fifty miles south of Ireland, in which neighborhood occurred the most striking incidents of the cruise. On the outward passage was taken only one prize, June 2. She was from Cork to Halifax, twelve days out; therefore probably from six to eight hundred miles west of Ireland. The second, from Limerick for Bordeaux, June 13, would show the "Wasp" on her station; on which, Blakely reported, it was impossible to keep her, even approximately, being continually drawn away in pursuit, and often much further up the English Channel than desired, on account of the numerous sails passing.[246] When overhauled, most of these were found to be neutrals.

Nevertheless, seven British merchant vessels were taken; all of which were destroyed, except one given up to carry prisoners to England.

While thus engaged, the "Wasp" on June 28 sighted a sail, which proved to be the British brig of war "Reindeer," Captain Manners, that had left Plymouth six days before. The place of this meeting was latitude 48-½° North, longitude 11° East; therefore nearly in the cruising ground assigned to Blakely by his instructions. The antagonists were unequally matched; the American carrying twenty 32-pounder carronades and two long guns, the British sixteen 24-pounders and two long; a difference against her of over fifty per cent. The "Reindeer" was to windward, and some manœuvring took place in the respective efforts to keep or to gain this advantage. In the end the "Reindeer" retained it, and the action began with both on the starboard tack, closehauled, the British sloop on the weather quarter of the "Wasp,"—behind, but on the weather side, which in this case was to the right (1). Approaching slowly, the "Reindeer" with great deliberation fired five times, at two-minute intervals, a light gun mounted on her forecastle, loaded with round and grape shot. Finding her to maintain this position, upon which his guns would not train, Blakely put the helm down, and the "Wasp" turned swiftly to the right (2), bringing her starboard battery to bear. This was at 3.26 P.M. The action immediately became very hot, at very close range (3), and the "Reindeer" was speedily disabled. The vessels then came together (4), and Captain Manners, who by this time had received two severe wounds, with great gallantry endeavored to board with his crew, reduced by the severe punishment already inflicted to half its originally inferior numbers. As he climbed into the rigging, two balls from the "Wasp's" tops passed through his head, and he fell back dead on his own deck. No further resistance was offered, and the "Wasp" took possession. She had lost five killed and twenty-one wounded, of whom six afterwards died. The British casualties were twenty-three killed and forty-two wounded. The brig herself, being fairly torn to pieces, was burned the next day.[247]

The results of this engagement testify to the efficiency and resolution of both combatants; but a special meed of praise is assuredly due to Captain Manners, whose tenacity was as marked as his daring, and who, by the injury done to his stronger antagonist, demonstrated both the thoroughness of his previous general preparation and the skill of his management in the particular instance. Under his command the "Reindeer" had become a notable vessel in the fleet to which she belonged; but as equality in force is at a disadvantage where there is serious inferiority in training and discipline, so the best of drilling must yield before decisive superiority of armament, when there has been equal care on both sides to insure efficiency in the use of the battery. To Blakely's diligence in this respect his whole career bears witness.

After the action Blakely wished to remain cruising, which neither the condition of his ship nor her losses in men forbade; but the number of prisoners and wounded compelled him to make a harbor. He accordingly went into L'Orient, France, on July 8. Despite the change of government, and the peace with Great Britain which attended the restoration of the Bourbons, the "Wasp" was here hospitably received and remained for seven weeks refitting, sailing again August 27. By September 1 she had taken and destroyed three more enemy's vessels; one of which was cut out from a convoy, and burnt under the eyes of the convoying 74-gun ship. At 6.30 P.M. of September 1 four sails were sighted, from which Blakely selected to pursue the one most to windward; for, should this prove a ship of war, the others, if consorts, would be to leeward of the fight, less able to assist. The chase lasted till 9.26, when the "Wasp" was near enough to see that the stranger was a brig of war, and to open with a light carronade on the forecastle, as the "Reindeer" had done upon her in the same situation. Confident in his vessel, however, Blakely abandoned this advantage of position, ran under his antagonist's lee to prevent her standing down to join the vessels to leeward, and at 9.29 began the engagement, being then on her lee bow. At ten the "Wasp" ceased firing and hailed, believing the enemy to be silenced; but receiving no reply, and the British guns opening again, the combat was renewed. At 10.12, seeing the opponent to be suffering greatly, Blakely hailed again and was answered that the brig had surrendered. The "Wasp's" battery was secured, and a boat was in the act of being lowered to take possession, when a second brig was discovered close astern. Preparation was made to receive her and her coming up awaited; but at 10.36 the two others were also visible, astern and approaching. The "Wasp" then made sail, hoping to decoy the second vessel from her supports; but the sinking condition of the one first engaged detained the new-comer, who, having come within pistol-shot, fired a broadside which took effect only aloft, and then gave all her attention to saving the crew of her comrade. As the "Wasp" drew away she heard the repeated signal guns of distress discharged by her late adversary, the name of which never became known to the captain and crew of the victorious ship.[248]

The vessel thus engaged was the British brig "Avon," of sixteen 32-pounder carronades, and two long 9-pounders; her force being to that of the "Wasp" as four to five. Her loss in men was ten killed and thirty-two wounded; that of the "Wasp" two killed and one wounded. The "Avon" being much superior to the "Reindeer," this comparatively slight injury inflicted by her testifies to inferior efficiency. The broadside of her rescuer, the "Castilian," of the same weight as her own, wholly missed the "Wasp's" hull, though delivered from so near; a circumstance which drew from the British historian, James, the caustic remark that she probably would have done no better than the "Avon," had the action continued. The "Wasp" was much damaged in sails and rigging; the "Avon" sank two hours and a half after the "Wasp" left her and one hour after being rejoined by the "Castilian." The course of the "Wasp" after this event is traced by her captures. The meeting with the "Avon" was within a hundred miles of that with the "Reindeer." On September 12 and 14, having run south three hundred and sixty miles, she took two vessels; being then about two hundred and fifty miles west from Lisbon. On the 21st, having made four degrees more southing, she seized the British brig "Atalanta," a hundred miles east of Madeira. This prize being of exceptional value, Blakely decided to send her in, and she arrived safely at Savannah on November 4, in charge of Midshipman David Geisinger, who lived to become a captain in the navy.[249] She brought with her Blakely's official despatches, including the report of the affair with the "Avon." This was the last tidings received from the "Wasp" until the inquiries of friends elicited the fact that the two officers of the "Essex" had joined her three weeks after the capture of the "Atalanta," nine hundred miles farther south. Besides these, there were among the lost two lieutenants who had been in the "Constitution" when she took the "Guerrière" and the "Java," and one who had been in the "Enterprise" in her action with the "Boxer."

Coincident in time with the cruise of the "Wasp" was that of her sister ship, the "Peacock"; like her also newly built, and named after the British brig sunk by Captain Lawrence in the "Hornet." The finest achievement of the "Wasp," however, was near the end of her career, while it fell to the "Peacock" to begin with a successful action. Having left New York early in March, she went first to St. Mary's, Georgia, carrying a quantity of warlike stores. In making this passage she was repeatedly chased by enemies. Having landed her cargo, she sailed immediately and ran south as far as one of the Bahama Islands, called the Great Isaac, near to which vessels from Jamaica and Cuba bound to Europe must pass, because of the narrowness of the channel separating the islands from the Florida coast. In this neighborhood she remained from April 18 to 24, seeing only one neutral and two privateers, which were pursued unsuccessfully. This absence of unguarded merchant ships, coupled with the frequency of hostile cruisers met before, illustrates exactly the conditions to which attention has been repeatedly drawn, as characterizing the British plan of action in the Western Atlantic. Learning that the expected Jamaica convoy would be under charge of a seventy-four, two frigates, and two sloops, and that the merchant ships in Havana, fearing to sail alone, would await its passing to join, Captain Warrington next stood slowly to the northward, and on April 29, off Cape Canaveral, sighted four sail, which proved to be the British brig "Epervier" of eighteen 32-pounder carronades,[250] also northward bound, with three merchant vessels under her convoy; one of these being Russian, and one Spanish, belonging therefore to nations still at war with France, though neutral towards the United States. The third, a merchant brig, was the first British commercial vessel seen since leaving Savannah.

As usual and proper, the "Epervier," seeing that the "Peacock" would overtake her and her convoy, directed the latter to separate while she stood down to engage the hostile cruiser. The two vessels soon came to blows. The accounts of the action on both sides are extremely meagre, and preclude any certain statement as to manœuvres; which indeed cannot have been material to the issue reached. The "Epervier," for reasons that will appear later, fought first one broadside and then the other; but substantially the contest appears to have been maintained side to side. From the first discharge of the "Epervier" two round shot struck the "Peacock's" foreyard nearly in the same place, which so weakened the spar as to deprive the ship of the use of her foresail and foretopsail; that is, practically, of all sail on the foremast. Having thenceforth only the jibs for headsail, she had to be kept a little off the wind. The action lasted forty-five minutes, when the "Epervier" struck. Her loss in men was eight killed, and fifteen wounded; the "Peacock" had two wounded.

In extenuation of this disproportion in result, James states that in the first broadside three of the "Epervier's" carronades were unshipped; and that, when those on the other side were brought into action by tacking, similar mishaps occurred. Further, the moment the guns got warm they drew out the breeching bolts. Allowing full force to these facts, they certainly have some bearing on the general outcome; but viewed with regard to the particular question of efficiency, which is the issue of credit in every fight,[251] there remains the first broadside, and such other discharges as the carronades could endure before getting warm. The light metal of those guns indisputably caused them to heat rapidly, and to kick nastily; but it can scarcely be considered probable that the "Epervier" was not able to get in half a dozen broadsides. The result, two wounded, establishes inefficiency, and a practical certainty of defeat had all her ironwork held; for the "Peacock," though only three months commissioned, was a good ship under a thoroughly capable and attentive captain. A comical remark of James in connection with this engagement illustrates the weakness of prepossession, in all matters relating to Americans, which in him was joined to a painstaking accuracy in ascertaining and stating external facts. "Two well-directed shot," he says, disabled the "Peacock's" foreyard. It was certainly a capital piece of luck for the "Epervier" that her opponent at the outset lost the use of one of her most important spars; but the implication that the shot were directed for the point hit is not only preposterous but, in a combat between vessels nearly equal, depreciatory. The shot of a first broadside had no business to be so high in the air.

James alleges also poor quality and a mutinous spirit in the crew, and that at the end, when their captain called upon them to board, they refused, saying,

"She is too heavy for us." To this the adequate reply is that the brig had been in commission since the end of 1812,—sixteen months; time sufficient to bring even an indifferent crew to a very reasonable degree of efficiency, yet not enough to cause serious deterioration of material. That after the punishment received the men refused to board, if discreditable to them under the conditions, is discreditable also to the captain; not to his courage, but to his hold upon the men whom he had commanded so long. The establishment of the "Epervier's" inefficiency certainly detracts from the distinction of the "Peacock's" victory; but it was scarcely her fault that her adversary was not worthier, and it does not detract from her credit for management and gunnery, considering that the combat began with the loss of her own foresails, and ended with forty-five shot in the hull, and five feet of water in the hold, of her antagonist.

By dark of the day of action the prize was in condition to make sail, and the "Peacock's" yard had been fished and again sent aloft. The two vessels then steered north for Savannah. The next evening two British frigates appeared. Captain Warrington directed the "Epervier" to keep on close along shore, while he stood southward to draw away the enemy. This proved effective; the "Epervier" arriving safely May 2 at the anchorage at the mouth of the Savannah River, where the "Peacock" rejoined her on the 4th. The "Adams," Captain Morris, was also there; having arrived from the coast of Africa on the day of the fight, and sailing again a week after it, May 5, for another cruise.

On June 4 the "Peacock" also started upon a protracted cruise, from which she returned to New York October 30, after an absence of one hundred and forty-seven days.[252] She followed the Gulf Stream, outside the line of British blockaders, to the Banks of Newfoundland, thence to the Azores, and so on to Ireland; off the south of which, between Waterford and Cape Clear, she remained for four days. After this she passed round the west coast, and to the northward as far as Shetland and the Faroe Islands. She then retraced her course, crossed the Bay of Biscay, and ran along the Portuguese coast; pursuing in general outline the same path as that in which the "Wasp" very soon afterwards followed. Fourteen prizes were taken; of which twelve were destroyed, and two utilized as cartels to carry prisoners to England. Of the whole number, one only was seized from September 2, when the ship was off the Canaries, to October 12, off Barbuda in the West Indies; and none from there to the United States. "Not a single vessel was seen from the Cape Verde to Surinam," reported Warrington; while in seven days spent between the Rock of Lisbon and Cape Ortegal, at the northwest extremity of the Spanish peninsula, of twelve sail seen, nine of which were spoken, only two were British.

In these conditions were seen, exemplified and emphasized, the alarm felt and precautions taken, by both the mercantile classes and the Admiralty, in consequence of the invasion of European waters by American armed vessels, of a class and an energy unusually fitted to harass commerce. The lists of American prizes teem with evidence of extraordinary activity, by cruisers singularly adapted for their work, and audacious in proportion to their confidence of immunity, based upon knowledge of their particular nautical qualities. The impression produced by their operations is reflected in the representations of the mercantile community, in the rise of insurance, and in the stricter measures instituted by the Admiralty. The Naval Chronicle, a service journal which since 1798 had been recording the successes and supremacy of the British Navy, confessed now that "the depredations committed on our commerce by American ships of war and privateers have attained an extent beyond all former precedent.... We refer our readers to the letters in our correspondence. The insurance between Bristol and Waterford or Cork is now three times higher than it was when we were at war with all Europe. The Admiralty have been overwhelmed with letters of complaint or remonstrance."[253] In the exertions of the cruisers the pace seems to grow more and more furious, as the year 1814 draws to its close amid a scene of exasperated coast warfare, desolation, and humiliation, in America; as though they were determined, amid all their pursuit of gain, to make the enemy also feel the excess of mortification which he was inflicting upon their own country. The discouragement testified by British shippers and underwriters was doubtless enhanced and embittered by disappointment, in finding the movement of trade thus embarrassed and intercepted at the very moment when the restoration of peace in Europe had given high hopes of healing the wounds, and repairing the breaches, made by over twenty years of maritime warfare, almost unbroken.

In London, on August 17, 1814, directors of two insurance companies presented to the Admiralty remonstrances on the want of protection in the Channel; to which the usual official reply was made that an adequate force was stationed both in St. George's Channel and in the North Sea. The London paper from which this intelligence was taken stated that premiums on vessels trading between England and Ireland had risen from an ordinary rate of less than one pound sterling to five guineas per cent. The Admiralty, taxed with neglect, attributed blame to the merchant captains, and announced additional severity to those who should part convoy. Proceedings were instituted against two masters guilty of this offence.[254] September 9, the merchants and shipowners of Liverpool remonstrated direct to the Prince Regent, going over the heads of the Admiralty, whom they censured. Again the Admiralty alleged sufficient precautions, specifying three frigates and fourteen sloops actually at sea for the immediate protection of St. George's Channel and the western Irish coast against depredations, which they nevertheless did not succeed in suppressing.[255]

At the same time the same classes in Glasgow were taking action, and passing resolutions, the biting phrases of which were probably prompted as much by a desire to sting the Admiralty as by a personal sense of national abasement. "At a time when we are at peace with all the rest of the world, when the maintenance of our marine costs so large a sum to the country, when the mercantile and shipping interests pay a tax for protection under the form of convoy duty, and when, in the plenitude of our power, we have declared the whole American coast under blockade, it is equally distressing and mortifying that our ships cannot with safety traverse our own channels, that insurance cannot be effected but at an excessive premium, and that a horde of American cruisers should be allowed, unheeded, unmolested, unresisted, to take, burn, or sink our own vessels in our own inlets, and almost in sight of our own harbours."[256] In the same month the merchants of Bristol, the position of which was comparatively favorable to intercourse with Ireland, also presented a memorial, stating that the rate of insurance had risen to more than twofold the amount at which it was usually effected during the continental war, when the British Navy could not, as it now might, direct its operations solely against American cruisers. Shipments consequently had been in a considerable degree suspended. The Admiralty replied that the only certain protection was by convoy. This they were ready to supply but could not compel, for the Convoy Act did not apply to trade between ports of the United Kingdom.

This was the offensive return made by America's right arm of national safety; the retort to the harrying of the Chesapeake, and of Long Island Sound, and to the capture and destruction of Washington. But, despite the demonstrated superiority of a national navy, on the whole, for the infliction of such retaliation, even in the mere matter of commerce destroying,—not to speak of confidence in national prowess, sustained chiefly by the fighting successes at sea,—this weighty blow to the pride and commerce of Great Britain was not dealt by the national Government; for the national Government had gone to war culpably unprepared. It was the work of the people almost wholly, guided and governed by their own shrewdness and capacity; seeking, indeed, less a military than a pecuniary result, an indemnity at the expense of the enemy for the loss to which they had been subjected by protracted inefficiency in administration and in statesmanship on the part of their rulers. The Government sat wringing its hands, amid the ruins of its capital and the crash of its resources; reaping the reward of those wasted years during which, amid abounding warning, it had neglected preparation to meet the wrath to come. Monroe, the Secretary of State, writing from Washington to a private friend, July 3, 1814, said, "Even in this state, the Government shakes to the foundation. Let a strong force land anywhere, and what will be the effect?" A few months later, December 21, he tells Jefferson, "Our finances are in a deplorable state. The means of the country have scarcely yet been touched, yet we have neither money in the Treasury nor credit."[257] This statement was abundantly confirmed by a contemporary official report of the Secretary of the Treasury. At the end of the year, Bainbridge, commanding the Boston navy yard, wrote the Department, "The officers and men of this station are really suffering for want of pay due them, and articles now purchased for the use of the navy are, in consequence of payment in treasury notes, enhanced about thirty per cent. Yesterday we had to discharge one hundred seamen, and could not pay them a cent of their wages. The officers and men have neither money, clothes, nor credit, and are embarrassed with debts."[258] No wonder the privateers got the seamen.

The decision to abandon the leading contention of the war had been reached long before.[259] In an official letter, dated June 27, 1814, to the commissioners appointed to treat for peace, after enumerating the threatening conditions confronting the country, now that the European conflict was at an end, Monroe wrote, "On mature consideration it has been decided that, under all the circumstances above alluded to, incident to a prosecution of the war, you may omit any stipulation on the subject of impressment, if found indispensably necessary to terminate it. You will of course not recur to this expedient until all your efforts to adjust the controversy in a more satisfactory manner have failed."[260] The phraseology of this instruction disposes completely of the specious plea, advanced by partisans of the Administration, that the subject was dropped because impressment was no longer a live issue; the maritime war of Europe being over. It was dropped because it had to be dropped; because the favorable opportunities presented in 1812 and 1813 had been lost by the incompetency of the national Government, distributed over a period of nearly a dozen years of idle verbal argumentation; because in 1814 there stood between it and disastrous reverse, and loss of territory in the north, only the resolution and professional skill of a yet unrecognized seaman on the neglected waters of Lake Champlain.

Before concluding finally the subject of the offensive maritime operations against the enemy's commerce, it may be mentioned that in the last six months of the war, that is within one fifth of its duration, were made one third of the total captures. Duly to weigh this result, regard must be had to the fact that, when the navy is adequate, the most numerous seizures of commercial shipping are usually effected at the beginning, because the scattered merchantmen are taken unawares. The success of the last few months of this war indicates the stimulus given to privateering, partly by the conditions of the country, imperiously demanding some relief from the necessity, and stagnancy of occupation, caused by the blockade; partly by the growing appreciation of the fact that a richer harvest was to be reaped by seeking the most suitable fields with the most suitable vessels. In an energetic and businesslike people it will be expected that the experience of the two preceding twelvemonths would have produced decided opinions and practical results in the construction of privateers, as well as in the direction given them. It is one thing to take what is at hand and make the most of it in an emergency; it is another to design thoughtfully a new instrument, best qualified for the end in view. The cruiser needed speed and handiness,—that is the first and obvious requirement; but, to escape the numerous enemies gradually let loose to shorten her career, it became increasingly requisite that she should have also weight of armament, to fight, and weight of hull—tonnage—to hold her way in rough and head seas. These qualities were not irreconcilable; but, to effect the necessary combination, additional size was inevitable.

Accordingly, recognition of these facts is found in the laying down of privateers for the particular business. Niles' Register, a Baltimore weekly, notes with local pride that, although the port itself is bolted and barred by the blockade of the Chesapeake, the Baltimore model for schooners is in demand from Maine to Georgia; that they are being built, often with Baltimore capital, in many places from which escape is always possible. In Boston, there are in construction three stout hulls, pierced for twenty-two guns; clearly much heavier in tonnage, as in armament, than the schooner rate, and bearing the linked names of "Blakely," "Reindeer," and "Avon." Mention is made of one vessel of twenty-two long, heavy guns, which has already sailed, and of two others, to carry as many as thirty to thirty-six, nearly ready.[261]

Between the divergent requirements of size and numbers, there is always a middle term; a mean, not capable of exact definition, but still existent within certain not very widely separated extremes. For commerce destroying by individual cruisers, acting separately, which was the measure that commended itself to the men of 1812, vessels approaching the tonnage of the national sloops of war seemed, by their successes and their immunity from capture, to realize very nearly the best conditions of advantage. The national brigs which put to sea were all captured, save one; and she was so notoriously dull of sailing that her escape was attributed to mere good luck, experienced on several critical occasions. Nearly all the sloops escaped; while the three frigates lost, the "Chesapeake," "Essex," and "President," were taken under circumstances that offered no parallel to the exigencies to which the privateer was liable. They were not run down, uninjured, in a fair race. The only sloop so lost was the "Frolic," of the class of the "Wasp" and "Peacock;" and the circumstances under which she was caught by a frigate are not sufficiently known to pronounce whether she might have been saved, as her sister ship, the "Hornet," was, from the hot pursuit of a seventy-four. Under some conditions of wind and sea, inferiority of bulk inflicts irredeemable disadvantage of speed; but, taking one thing with another, in a system of commerce destroying which rejected squadron action, and was based avowedly upon dissemination of vessels, the gain of the frigate over the sloop due to size did not counterbalance the loss in distribution of effort which results from having only one ship, instead of two, for a first outlay.

That some such convictions, the fruit of rude experience in actual cruising, were gradually forming in men's understanding, is probable from the particulars cited; and they would receive additional force from the consideration that, to make a profit out of privateering under existing conditions, it would be necessary, not only to capture vessels of weak force, but to return safely to port with at least some notable salvage from their cargoes. In other words, there must be power to fight small cruisers, and to escape large ones under all probable disadvantage of weather. Whatever the conclusions of practical seamen and shipowners in this respect, they found no reflection in the dominant power in the Administration and Congress. The exploits of the "Comet," the "Chasseur," and a few other fortunate privateer schooners or brigs of small size, among them being cited specifically the "Mammoth," which in the autumn of 1814 made twenty-one prizes in three months, produced a strong popular impression; and this was diligently but somewhat thoughtlessly deepened by the press, as such popular movements are apt to be, without thorough mastery of all facts, contra as well as pro. It was undeniable, also, that in the threatening aspect of affairs, when Great Britain's whole strength was freed to be exerted against the country, want of time to prepare new means was a weighty element in decision, and recourse must be had to resources immediately at hand for the retaliatory depredation upon the enemy's commerce, from the effect of which so much was expected then, as it is now. For this reason the scheme had naval backing, prominent in which was Captain Porter, who had reached home in the July after the capture of the "Essex."

Under these circumstances, the Secretary of the Navy addressed a letter, October 22, 1814,[262] to the naval committees of both houses of Congress, enlarging on the greater attention of the enemy drawn to the heavy frigates, and the increased difficulty of their getting to sea. He recommended an appropriation of $600,000 for the purchase of fast-sailing schooners for preying on the hostile commerce. In consequence, a bill was introduced to build or purchase for the navy twenty vessels, to carry not less than eight nor more than fourteen guns; in short, of privateer class, but to be under naval control, not only as regarded discipline and organization but direction of effort. It was intended that a squadron of them should be intrusted to Captain Porter, another to Captain Perry;[263] and Porter drew up a plan of operations, which he submitted to the Department, providing for the departure of the vessels, their keeping together for support in one quarter, scattering in another, and again reuniting at a fixed rendezvous.[264] Both officers reported great difficulty in procuring suitable vessels, owing to the extent of privateering, the lack of necessary funds, and the depreciation of Government credit, which caused its drafts to be refused.

When introducing the bill into the lower House, the Chairman of the Naval Committee, after paying some compliments to the military achievements of the naval vessels, said that in regard to depredation on the commerce of the enemy, he believed their efficiency could not be compared to that of vessels of a smaller class. This note dominated the brief discussion; the speakers in favor being significantly enough from Maryland, prepossessed doubtless by local pride in their justly celebrated schooners. Mr. Ingersoll, of Pennsylvania, moved an amendment to allow vessels of twenty-two guns; an increase of fifty per cent. The limitation to fourteen guns, he remarked, was inserted in the Senate by a gentleman from Maryland; but it was not the fact that the best privateers were limited to fourteen guns. One or two which had arrived lately, after reaping a rich harvest, carried sixteen. Mr. Lowndes, of South Carolina, seconded this amendment, hoping that the Senate limitation would be rejected. He quoted Captain Perry, who had "never known an instance in which a brig of the United States had failed to overtake a schooner." One member only, Mr. Reed, of Massachusetts, spoke against the whole scheme. Though opposed to the war, he said, he wished it conducted on correct principles. He "was warranted by facts in saying that no force would be half as efficient, in proportion to its expense; none would be of so much service to the country; none certainly would touch the enemy half so much as a naval force of a proper character;" which, he affirmed, this was not. Ingersoll's amendment was rejected, obtaining only twenty-five votes. The bill went again to conference, and on November 11, 1814, was reported and passed, fixing the limits of armament at from eight to sixteen guns; a paltry addition of two. Forty years later the editor of the "Debates of Congress," Senator Benton, wrote, "This was a movement in the right direction. Private armed vessels, and the success of small ships of war cruising as privateers, had taught Congress that small vessels, not large ships, were the effective means of attacking and annoying the enemy's commerce."[265]

The final test was not permitted, to determine what success would have attended the operations of several Baltimore schooners, united under the single control of a man like Porter or Perry, and limited strictly to the injury of the enemy's commerce by the destruction of prizes, without thought of profit by sending them in. The advent of peace put a stop to an experiment which would have been most instructive as well as novel. Looking to other experiences of the past, it may be said with confidence little short of certainty that, despite the disadvantage of size, several schooners thus working in concert, and with pure military purpose, would effect vastly more than the same number acting separately, with a double eye to gain and glory. The French privateer squadrons of Jean Bart and Duguay Trouin, in the early eighteenth century, the example of the celebrated "Western" squadrons of British frigates in the war of the French Revolution, as protectors and destroyers of commerce, demonstrated beyond peradventure the advantage of combined action in this, as in all military enterprise; while the greater success of the individual United States cruiser over the average privateer, so singularly overlooked by the national legislators, gives assurance that Porter's and Perry's schooners would collectively have done incomparable work. This, however, is far from indicating that divisions of larger vessels,—sloops or frigates,—under officers of their known energy, could not have pushed home into the English Channel, or elsewhere where British commerce congregated, an enterprise the results of which would have caused the ears of those that heard them to tingle.

FOOTNOTES:

[217] Captain Allen to Navy Department. Niles' Register, vol. v. p. 46.

[218] The American official report of this action can be found in Niles' Register, vol. viii. p. 43. The British is in the Naval Chronicle, vol. xxx. p. 247. Niles also gives it, vol. v. p. 118.

[219] The prize data have been taken from the successive volumes of Niles' Register.

[220] Data concerning American vessels captured by British ships have been drawn chiefly from prize lists, or official reports, in the Naval Chronicle.

[221] Ante, p. 19.

[222] Niles' Register, vol. v. p. 175.

[223] Niles gives an abstract of the log of the "Scourge," vol. vi. p. 269.

[224] Niles' Register, vol. v. p. 90.

[225] Ibid., vol. vi. p. 69.

[226] For Morris' letter see Niles' Register, vol. vi. p. 180.

[227] Ibid., vol. iv. p. 86.

[228] Ibid., vol. vii. p. 366.

[229] Niles' Register, vol. v. p. 413. Naval Chronicle, vol. xxxi. p. 25.

[230] Niles' Register, vol. v. p. 414; vol. vi. p. 151.

[231] Stewart's Letter is dated April 4, 1814, and, with the enclosures mentioned, will be found among the Captains' Letters, Navy Department MSS.

[232] For the official reports of this cruise, and list of prizes, see Niles, vol. vi. pp. 69-71.

[233] Niles' Register, vol. v. pp. 14, 15. Naval Chronicle, vol. xxx. p. 348.
[234] Niles' Register, vol. vi. pp. 225, 371.
[235] Niles' Register, vol. vii. p. 293, gives both the American and British accounts.
[236] Niles' Register, vol. vii. p. 293.
[237] Niles' Register, vol. vii. pp. 128, 290.
[238] Niles' Register, vol. viii. p. 61.
[239] It may not be amiss here to quote an incident similarly creditable to privateersmen, a class usually much abused, and too often with good cause. It was told by a British colonel to Colonel Winfield Scott, while a prisoner in Canada. This gentleman with his wife had been passengers from England in a transport captured near Halifax by an American privateer. Although there was no fighting, the wife, who was in a critical state of health, was dangerously affected by the attendant alarm. As soon as the circumstances were mentioned to the captain of the cruiser, he placed at the husband's disposition all that part of the vessel where their quarters were, posting a sentry to prevent intrusion and to secure all their personal effects from molestation. Scott's Autobiography, vol. i. p. 70.
[240] Afterwards Rear-Admiral Emmons.
[241] The new United States sloop of war "Frolic," named after the vessel taken by the "Wasp," was captured by the frigate "Orpheus," April 20, 1814.
[242] Ante, p. 3.
[243] Porter to the Secretary of the Navy, July 3, 1814. Niles' Register, vol. vi. p. 338.
[244] Porter's Report of this action is to be found in Niles' Register, vol. vi. pp. 338-341. Hillyar's in Naval Chronicle, vol. xxxii. pp. 168-170.
[245] The Secretary of the Navy to Blakely, March 3, 1814. Navy Department MSS.
[246] Blakely to the Navy Department, Niles' Register, vol. vii. p. 115.
[247] The particulars of this action are taken from the minutes of the "Wasp," enclosed in Blakely's Report, Niles' Register, vol. vii. p. 115.
[248] Blakely's Report, Niles' Register, vol. vii. p. 192.
[249] Niles' Register, vol. vii. p. 173.
[250] James says that two of these guns were 18-pounders; but the first lieutenant of the "Peacock," who brought the prize into port, and from there wrote independently of Warrington, agrees with him in saying eighteen thirty-twos. Niles' Register, vol. vi. pp. 180, 196.
[251] In a "Synopsis of Naval Actions," between British and American vessels, contributed to the Naval Chronicle by a "British naval officer on the American station," occurs the remark relative to the defeat of the "Avon": "Miserable gunnery on our side, attributable ... above all to not drilling the men at firing at the guns; a practice the Americans never

neglect." Naval Chronicle, vol. xxxiv. p. 469.

[252] For Captain Warrington's report of this cruise, see Niles' Register, vol. vii. p. 155.

[253] Naval Chronicle, vol. xxxii. p. 244. See also, Ibid., pp. 211, 218.

[254] London paper, quoted in Niles' Register, vol. vii. p. 175.

[255] Niles' Register, vol. vii. p. 190. Naval Chronicle, vol. xxxii. p. 244.

[256] Niles' Register, vol. vii. p. 190.

[257] Writings of James Monroe.

[258] Captains' Letters, Dec. 11, 1814. Bainbridge's italics.

[259] It will be remembered that after the repeal of the Orders in Council, June 23, 1812, impressment remained the only sine quâ non of the United States.

[260] American State Papers, Foreign Relations, vol. iii. p. 704. Author's italics. This was the result of a Cabinet meeting held the same day. "June 27, 1814. In consequence of letters from Bayard and Gallatin of May 6-7, and other accounts from Europe of the ascendancy and views of Great Britain, and the dispositions of the great Continental Powers, the question was put to the Cabinet: 'Shall a treaty of peace, silent on the subject of impressment, be authorized?' Agreed to by Monroe, Campbell, Armstrong, and Jones. Rush absent. Our minister to be instructed, besides trying other conditions, to make a previous trial to insert or annex some declaration, or protest, against any inference, from the silence of the Treaty on the subject of impressment, that the British claim was admitted or that of the United States abandoned." (Works of Madison, vol. iii. p. 408.)

[261] Niles' Register, vol. vii. p. 190.

[262] Navy Department MSS.

[263] For Porter's and Perry's correspondence on this subject see Captains' Letters, Navy Department MSS., Oct. 14 and 25, Nov. 29, Dec. 2, 9, and 25, 1814; Jan. 9, 1815.

[264] Porter to Secretary, Feb. 8, 1815. Captains' Letters.

[265] Benton's Abridgment of Debates in Congress, vol. v. p. 359, note.

THE NIAGARA CAMPAIGN, AND EVENTS ON THE GREAT LAKES, IN 1814

Active operations in the field for the winter of 1813-14 came to an end with the successful incursion of the British army upon the territory of the State of New York, before narrated.[266] This had resulted in the capture of Fort Niagara and in the wasting of the frontier, with the destruction of the villages of Lewiston, Manchester, Buffalo, and others, in retaliation for the American burning of Newark. Holding now the forts on both banks of the Niagara, at its entrance into Lake Ontario, the British controlled the harbor of refuge which its mouth afforded; and to this important accession of strength for naval operations was added an increased security for passing troops, at will and secretly, from side to side of the river. From a military standpoint each work was a bridge-head, assuring freedom of movement across in either direction; that such transit was by boats, instead of by a permanent structure, was merely an inconvenient detail, not a disability. The command of the two forts, and of a third called Mississaga, on the Canadian side, immediately overlooking the lake, appears to have been vested in a single officer, to whom, as to a common superior, were issued orders involving the action of the three.

This disposition recognized implicitly the fact that the forts, taken together, constituted a distinct element in the general British scheme of operations. Fort Niagara by position threatened the line of communications of any American army seeking to act on the Canadian side. An effective garrison there, unless checked by an adequate force stationed for the particular purpose, could move at any unexpected moment against the magazines or trains on the American side; and it was impossible to anticipate what number might be thus employed at a given time, because intercourse between Niagara and George was open. If by original or acquired superiority of numbers, as had been the case in 1813, the American general should push his opponent back towards the head of the lake, Fort George would in turn become an additional menace to his communications. Therefore, properly to initiate a campaign for the command of the Niagara peninsula, in 1814, it would be necessary either to reduce both these works, which, if they were properly garrisoned, meant an expenditure of time; or else to blockade them by a large detachment of troops, which meant a constant expenditure of force, diminishing that available for operations in the field. The British military situation thus comprised two factors, distinct but complementary; the active army in the field, and the stationary fortifications which contributed to its support by sheltering its supplies and menacing those of the enemy. The British commander of the district, Lieutenant-General Drummond, estimated that the blockaders before either fort, being ever on the defensive against a sortie which they could not foresee, must in numbers considerably exceed the besieged, covered as these were by their works, and able to receive re-enforcement from the opposite shore. Consequently, when the officer in immediate local control, Major-General Riall, embarrassed by the smallness of his field force, suggested the destruction of Fort Niagara, except a citadel of restricted extent, needing a less numerous garrison, his superior replied that not only would such smaller work be much more easily taken, but that in every event the loss through holding the place was more than compensated by the danger and the precautions entailed upon the enemy.[267]

The inactivity, substantially unbroken, which prevailed throughout the winter of 1813-14, was due principally to the unusual mildness of the weather. This impeded movement in all quarters, by preventing the formation of ice and of the usual hard snow surface, which made winter the most favorable season for land transportation. Chauncey at Sackett's Harbor chafed and fretted over the detention of the stores and guns for his new ships then building, upon which he was reckoning for control of the lake. "The roads are dreadful," he wrote on February 24, "and if the present mild weather continues we shall experience difficulty." A week later, "I have the mortification to inform you that all our heavy guns are stopped at and below Poughkeepsie in consequence of the badness of the roads, and that the teamsters have abandoned them there." He has given up hopes of a frost, and counts now only upon water communication; but the delay and change of route were the cause of two smart affairs with which the lake operations opened, for on March 29 he announces that the guns are still below Albany, and now must come by way of Oswego and the lake,[268] instead of securely inland by sleds. Yeo reported a like delay on his side in the equipment of his new ships, owing to the unusual scarcity of snow.

The same conditions imposed similar, if less decisive, limitations upon the movements of bodies of men. The most important instance of purpose frustrated was in an enterprise projected by Drummond against Put-in Bay, where were still lying the "Detroit" and "Queen Charlotte", the most powerful of the prizes taken by Perry the previous September, the injuries to which had prevented their removal to the safer position of Erie. On January 21 he communicated to Governor-General Prevost the details of an expedition of seventeen hundred and sixty men,[269] two hundred of them seamen, who were to start from the Niagara frontier by land against Detroit, and from there to cross on the ice to the Bass Islands, where it was hoped they could seize and burn the vessels. The occupation of Fort Niagara, and other dispositions made of his division on the peninsula, had so narrowed his front of defence, and thereby strengthened it, as to warrant this large detachment.

This project was one of several looking to regaining control of Lake Erie, which during the remainder of the war occupied unceasingly the attention of British officers. Although the particular destination was successfully concealed, the general fact of preparations for some offensive undertaking did not escape the observation of the Americans, who noted that in the recent raid and destruction care had been taken to spare a great number of sleighs, and to collect them within the British lines. From this it was inferred that, when Lake Erie froze over, a dash would be made against the naval station and ships at Erie.[270] This would be undoubtedly a more valuable achievement, but the enemy knew that the place was in some measure defended, with ample re-enforcements at call; whereas a descent upon Put-in Bay could encounter no other resistance than that of the small permanent garrison of seamen. The mildness of the weather, leaving the lake open on January 17, relieved the apprehension of the United States authorities, and on February 3 Drummond had to report that his scheme must be abandoned, as after that late period of the winter better conditions could not be expected.[271]

In default of the control of Lake Erie, measures were taken by the British to supply the remote and isolated posts of Mackinac and St. Joseph's by land carriage from Toronto to Lake Simcoe, a distance of only forty miles, and thence across the ice to Matchedash Bay, on Lake Huron; where also were being built batteaux and gunboats, to transport the stores to their destination when navigation opened. As far as Huron this land route was out of reach of probable molestation, but from there it was necessary to proceed at the earliest moment; for, although there was no American naval force then on that lake, one might be expected to arrive from Erie early in the season. To this cross-country line there was an alternative one still more remote, from Montreal up the Ottawa River, and thence by other water communication, striking Lake Huron much higher up. It was practicable only for canoes with light lading, and in other respects not satisfactory. The maintenance of Mackinac therefore must depend upon armed control of the upper lakes; and to this the destruction of the prizes at the islands would doubtless have contributed, morally and materially.

On the American side as little was accomplished during the winter. Wilkinson's army, which at the end of 1813 was cantoned at French Mills, on the Salmon River, just within the New York boundary, was withdrawn from that position February 13. The greater part marched to Lake Champlain, where they again took winter quarters in two divisions; one at Burlington, Vermont, the other at Plattsburg. The third contingent, under the command of General Brown, was sent to Sackett's Harbor, where it arrived February 24.

The Secretary of War, General Armstrong, despite his vacillating course the previous year, had never lost sight of his perfectly accurate conviction that Kingston, if not Montreal, was the true objective for the northern army. Convinced that he had been misled in the spring of 1813 by the opinions of the commanders on the spot, Chauncey and Dearborn, he was again anxious, as he had been in the intervening autumn, to retrieve the error. On February 28 he issued to Brown two sets of instructions;[272] the one designed to transpire, in order to mislead the enemy, the other, most secret, conveying the real intention of the Department. In the former, stress was laid upon the exposure of western New York, and the public humiliation at seeing Fort Niagara in the hands of the British. Brigadier-General Scott accordingly had been sent there to organize a force for the capture of the fort and the protection of the frontier; but, as his numbers were probably insufficient, Brown was directed to march to Batavia, and thence to Buffalo, with the two thousand troops he had just brought from French Mills. This letter was meant to reach the enemy's ears. The other, embodying the true object aimed at, read thus: "It is obviously Prevost's policy, and probably his intention, to re-establish himself on Lake Erie during the ensuing month. But to effect this other points of his line must be weakened, and these will be either Kingston or Montreal. If the detachment from the former be great, a moment may occur in which you may do, with the aid of Commodore Chauncey, what I last year intended Pike should have done without aid, and what we now all know was very practicable, viz.: to cross the river, or head of the lake, on the ice, and carry Kingston by a coup de main." The letter ended by making the enterprise depend upon a concurrence of favorable conditions; in brief, upon the discretion of the general, with whom remained all the responsibility of final decision and action.

These instructions were elicited, immediately, by recent information that the effective garrison in Kingston was reduced to twelve hundred, with no prospect of increase before June, when re-enforcements from Europe were expected. Certainly, Drummond at this time thought the force there no stronger than it should be, and early in April was apprehensive on that account for the safety of the place.[273] Brown and Chauncey, however, agreed that less than four thousand men was insufficient for the undertaking. Singularly enough, this number was precisely that fixed upon by Yeo and Drummond, in consultation, as necessary for the reduction of Sackett's Harbor; which they concurred with Prevost in considering the quickest and surest solution of the difficulty attending their situation about Niagara, owing to the exhaustion of local resources upon the peninsula.[274] The scarcity thus experienced was aggravated by the number of dependent Indian warriors, who with their families had followed the British retreat from Malden and Detroit, and now hung like lead upon the movements and supplies of the army. "Nearly twelve hundred barrels of flour monthly to Indians alone," complained the commanding officer, who had long since learned that for this expenditure there was no return in military usefulness. In the felt necessity to retain the good-will of the savages, no escape from the dilemma was open, except in the maintenance of a stream of supplies from Lower Canada by keeping command of the Lake;[275] to secure which nothing was so certain as to capture Sackett's and destroy the shipping and plant.

Having decided that the enterprise against Kingston was not feasible, Brown fell into the not unnatural mistake of construing the Secretary's other letter to present not merely a ruse, but an alternative line of action, more consonant to his active martial temper than remaining idle in garrison. Accordingly, he left Sackett's with his two thousand, an event duly chronicled in a letter of Drummond's, that on Sunday, March 13, three thousand five hundred left Sackett's for Niagara; a statement sufficiently characteristic of the common tendency of an enemy's force to swell, as it passes from mouth to mouth. The division had progressed as far as the present city of Syracuse, sixty miles from Sackett's, and Brown himself was some forty miles in advance of it, at Geneva, when one of his principal subordinates persuaded him that he had misconstrued the Department's purpose. In considerable distress he turned about, passing through Auburn on the 23d at the rate of thirty miles a day, so said a contemporary newspaper,[276] and hurried back to Sackett's. There further consultation with Chauncey convinced him again that he was intended to go to Niagara, and he resumed his march. Before April 1 he reached Batavia, where his instructions read he would receive further orders. General Scott was already at Buffalo, and there the troops were placed under his immediate charge for organization and drill; Brigadier-General Gaines being sent back to command at Sackett's, where he arrived April 10.

At this moment Chauncey was undergoing his turn of qualms. "The enemy," he wrote the following day, "have prepared a force of three thousand troops, with gunboats and a number of small craft, to attack the harbor the moment the fleet leaves it. They may, however, be determined to make the attack at all hazards, and I am sorry to say our force is but little adapted to the defence of the place. There are not a thousand effective men besides the sailors and marines."[277] His information was substantially correct. Drummond had arranged to concentrate three thousand men from the north shore of the lake; but he wanted besides eight hundred from the peninsula, and for lack of these the project was abandoned.

The movement of Brown's small contingent to Buffalo, though contrary to the intention of the Government, may be considered to have opened the campaign of 1814; destined to prove as abortive in substantial results as that of the year before, but not so futile and inglorious to the American arms. The troops engaged had been formed under the skilful organization and training of Scott. Led by Brown, who, though not an educated soldier nor a master of the technicalities of the profession, was essentially an aggressive fighting man of masculine qualities, they failed indeed to achieve success, for which their numbers were inadequate; but there was no further disgrace. Wilkinson, indeed, in his district, contrived to give to the beginning of operations the air of absurdity that ever hung round his path. Although he was the senior officer on the whole frontier, the Department had not notified him of Brown's orders. This vicious practice of managing the campaign from a point as distant as Washington then was, ignoring any local centre of control, drew subsequently the animadversion of the President, who in a minute to the Secretary remarked that "it does not appear that Izard,"—Wilkinson's successor,—"though the senior officer of the district, has been made acquainted with the plan of operations under Brown."[278] On the present occasion Wilkinson explained that, hearing of Brown's march by common report, and having ascertained that the enemy was sending re-enforcements up the St. Lawrence, he undertook an incursion into Lower Canada as a diversion against such increase of the force with which Brown must contend.[279] His enterprise was directed against La Colle, a few miles from Plattsburg, within the Canada boundary; but upon arriving before the position it was found that the garrison were established in a stone mill, upon which the guns brought along could make no impression. After this somewhat ludicrous experience, the division, more than three thousand strong, retreated, having lost over seventy men. The result was scarcely likely to afford Brown much relief by its deterrent influence upon the enemy.

This affair happened March 30, and in the course of the following month Wilkinson was finally superseded. He was succeeded by General Izard, who assumed command May 4, and remained in the neighborhood of Champlain, while Brown continued immediately responsible for Sackett's Harbor and for the force at Buffalo. On April 14 Yeo launched two new ships, the "Prince Regent" of fifty-eight guns and the "Princess Charlotte" of forty; and he at the same time had under construction one destined to carry one hundred and two heavy guns, superior therefore in size and armament to most of the British ocean navy, and far more formidable than any in which Nelson ever served. Fortunately for the Americans, this vessel, which Yeo undertook without authority from home, was not ready until October; but the former two, added to his last year's fleet, gave him for the moment a decided preponderance over Chauncey, who also was building but had not yet completed.

Under these circumstances the project of attacking Sackett's in force was again most seriously agitated among the British officials, military and naval, upon whom the destitution of the Niagara peninsula pressed with increasing urgency. Such an intention rarely fails to transpire, especially across a border line where the inhabitants on either side speak the same tongue and are often intimately acquainted. Desertion, moreover, was frequent from both parties. The rumor brought Brown back hastily to the place, where he arrived April 24. The enemy, however, again abandoned their purpose, and after embarking a considerable body of troops turned their arms instead against Oswego.

It will be remembered that the mildness of the winter had prevented the transport of guns and stores by land, and made necessary to accumulate them by water carriage at Oswego, whence there remained the lake voyage to Sackett's Harbor. This, though a coasting operation, involved much danger while the enemy possessed naval control. Meanwhile Oswego became a somewhat congested and much exposed intermediate station, inviting attack. Chauncey therefore had taken the precaution of retaining the most important articles, guns and their equipment, at the falls of the Oswego River, some twelve miles inland. The enemy's change of plan becoming suspected, Brown detached a small party—two hundred and ninety effectives—to defend the place, in conjunction with the few seamen already there. The British fleet appeared on May 5, but the attack was not made until the following day, weather conditions being unfavorable. Despite the unprepared state of the defences characteristic of the universal American situation, on both lakes and seaboard, in this singular war, the officer in command offered a spirited resistance, inflicting considerable loss; but the urgency to preserve his force, for the superior necessity of protecting under more favorable circumstances the valuable property in the rear, compelled him to retreat, to escape the risk of being surrounded and captured. He accordingly drew off in good order, having lost six killed and thirty-eight wounded; besides twenty-five missing, probably prisoners. The casualties of the British, by their official reports, were eighteen killed and seventy-three wounded. They kept possession of the town during the night, retiring next day with two small schooners, over two thousand barrels of provisions, and a quantity of cordage.[280] The most serious loss to the

Americans was that of nine heavy cannon; but the bulk of the armament for the fleet remained safe at the falls.

After this Yeo took position with his squadron off Sackett's Harbor, where the Americans on May 1 had launched a new big ship, the "Superior", to carry sixty-two guns, thirty-two long 32-pounders, and thirty carronades of the same calibre. Besides her there was building still another, of somewhat smaller force, without which Chauncey would not consider himself able to contend with the enemy.[281] On the 20th of the month he reported that "five sail were now anchored between Point Peninsula and Stoney Island, about ten miles from the harbor, and two brigs between Stoney Island and Stoney Point, completely blocking both passes." He added, "This is the first time that I have experienced the mortification of being blockaded on the lakes."[282] The line thus occupied by the enemy covered the entire entrance to Black River Bay, within which Sackett's Harbor lies. This situation was the more intolerable under the existing necessity of bringing the guns by water. Drummond, whose information was probably good, wrote at this period that not more than fifteen of the heavy cannon needed for the new ships had arrived, and that they could come from Oswego only by the lake, as the roads were impassable except for horsemen. Carronades, cordage, and other stores were going on by wagon from Utica, but the long guns which were imperatively required could not do so.[283]

American contrivance proved equal to the dilemma, and led to a marked British misadventure. A few miles south of Black River Bay, and therefore outside the line of the British blockade, there was an inlet called Stoney Creek, from the head of which a short land carriage of three miles would strike Henderson's Bay. This, like Sackett's, is an indentation of Black River Bay, and was well within the hostile ships. The transit from Oswego to Stoney Creek, however, remained open to an enemy's attack, and to be effected without loss required address, enterprise, and rapidity of movement. The danger was lessened by the number of streams which enter Mexico Bay, the deep bight formed by the southern and eastern shores of Lake Ontario, between Oswego and Sackett's. These, being navigable for batteaux, constituted a series of harbors of refuge.

Chauncey directed all the lighter equipment to be turned back from Oswego River to North Bay, on Lake Oneida, and the long guns to be placed in batteaux, ready to move instantly, either up or down, as the movements of the enemy or a favorable opportunity might determine. Discretionary power to act according to circumstances was then given to Captain Woolsey, in local command on the Oswego. Woolsey made great parade of his preparations to send everything, guns included, back across the portage from the river, to North Bay. The reports reached Yeo, as intended, but did not throw him wholly off his guard. On May 27 Woolsey despatched an officer in a fast pulling boat to reconnoitre the coast, while he himself went with the requisite force to the falls. On the 28th the batteaux, nineteen in number, carrying twenty-one long 32-pounders, and thirteen lighter pieces, besides ten heavy cables, were run over the rapids, reaching Oswego at sunset. The lookout boat had returned, reporting all clear, and after dark the convoy started. Besides the regular crews, there were embarked one hundred and fifty riflemen from the army. The next morning at sunrise one batteau was missing, but the other eighteen entered the Salmon River, over twenty miles from Oswego. The nights were short at that season, and the boats heavy; moreover there had been drenching rain.

At Salmon River, a party of one hundred and twenty Oneida Indians joined, who were to move along the coast on the flank of the convoy through the next stage of the journey, by day, to support the defence should the approach of an enemy compel refuge to be sought in one of the creeks. As soon as they had taken up their march the batteaux also started, and at noon, May 29, reached Big Sandy Creek, ten miles further on, but eight miles short of the final destination at Stoney Creek. Here greater care became necessary, on account of the nearness of the enemy's fleet; and while awaiting information the division moved two miles up the Big Sandy, where it anchored.

The missing batteau, carrying two long 24's and a cable, had been captured; having wandered away from the rest of the detachment, despite the watchful care exerted to keep them together. Her crew betrayed the extent of the operation of which they formed part, and a division of boats was sent in quest, in charge of two captains of the blockading vessels; the senior officer of the whole being Commander Popham. On his way Popham fell in with another group of armed boats, which he took under his command, raising his total to three gun-vessels and four smaller boats, with near two hundred seamen and marines. Certain intelligence being received that the convoy had entered the Big Sandy, he steered thither, arriving off its mouth soon after daylight of May 30. A reconnaissance on shore discovering the masts of the batteaux plainly visible over a marsh, with apparently no intervening forest, an immediate attack was decided. Having landed a party of flankers on either bank, the expedition proceeded up stream with due caution, firing an occasional round into the brush to dislodge any possible ambush. It was not known that an escort, beyond the usual crews, had accompanied the movement. Such a precaution might indeed have been inferred from the importance of the object; but the same reason naturally, and not improperly, decided Popham that considerable risk was justifiable in order to frustrate his enemy's purpose.

Woolsey was already forewarned of his coming. At 2 A.M. of the same day, May 30, he had received from Chauncey an express, in accordance with which an officer was sent out upon the lake, to reconnoitre towards the entrance of Black River Bay. At six o'clock he returned, having been seen and pursued by some of Popham's division. The riflemen and Indians were now advanced half a mile below the batteaux, where they found cover and concealment in the woods. At eight the British guns were heard. At nine a re-enforcement of cavalry and light artillery arrived from Sackett's Harbor, but it was decided that they should remain by the batteaux, the force already below being best adapted for bush fighting. Towards ten o'clock the riflemen and Indians attacked; a circumstance attributed by Captain Popham to an accident befalling the 68-pounder carronade in the bow of the leading gunboat, which compelled her to turn round, to bring into action her stern gun, a 24-pounder. "The enemy thought we were commencing a retreat, when they advanced their whole force, one hundred and fifty riflemen, near two hundred Indians, and a numerous body of militia and cavalry, who soon overpowered the few men I had.... The winding of the creek, which gave the enemy a great advantage in advancing to intercept our retreat, rendered further resistance unavailing." The entire detachment surrendered, having had fourteen killed and twenty-eight wounded; besides whom two captains, six lieutenants, and one hundred and thirty-three seamen and marines remained prisoners. The American loss was but two wounded; a result showing clearly enough the disadvantage under which the British labored.

This affair has been related in detail,[284] because, although on a small scale, it was actually one of great consequence; but yet more because it illustrates aptly one kind of those minor operations of war, upon the success of which so much greater matters turn. The American management throughout was admirable in its detailed foresight and circumspection. To this was due the trivial loss attending its final success; a loss therefore attesting far greater credit than would the attaining of the same result by lavish expenditure of blood. To Captain Popham must be attributed both enterprise and due carefulness in undertaking an advance he knew to be hazardous, but from which, if successful, he was entitled to expect nothing less than the capture of almost the entire armament of a very large ship. In such circumstances censure because of failure is unjust, unless the risk is shown to be taken reckless of due precautions, which was not the case in this instance. Yeo, whose deficiency in seamen was reported at two hundred and seventy-nine,[285] three days after this affair, appears to have been more exasperated by the loss of the men than sensible of the merit of his subordinate. He had charged him not to enter any creek in the endeavor to capture the stores, and apparently laid the disaster to disregard of this order. The subsequent customary court martial decided that Popham, having greatly re-enforced himself by junction with a division of vessels, in a manner which Yeo could not have contemplated, was fully justified by the importance of preventing the convoy from reaching Sackett's Harbor. The court regretted that Sir James Yeo should have used such reproachful expressions in his letter to the Admiralty communicating Captain Popham's capture. Popham, and his second, Spilsbury, were included in the promotions of a year later.

Soon after this mishap Yeo abandoned the immediate blockade of Sackett's Harbor, returning to Kingston June 6. The recent experience demonstrated that it would be impossible to prevent the forwarding of supplies by the mere presence of the fleet at the mouth of the port. The armament of the "Superior" had arrived despite his efforts, and her speedy readiness to take the lake was assured. An exchange of letters between himself and Drummond as to his proper course[286] led to the conclusion that the blockade had not had all the effect expected; and that, in view of the large re-enforcements of men coming forward from England, the true policy was to avoid battle until the third new ship, the "St. Lawrence" of one hundred and two guns, should be ready. "The enemy," wrote Yeo, "are not in sufficient force to undertake any expedition in the face of our present squadron, but any disaster on our side might give them a serious ascendancy." Drummond, who had rejoiced that the blockade "assures us a free intercourse throughout the lake," concurred in this view. "I have no hesitation in saying that there exists at present no motive or object, connected with the security of Upper Canada, which can make it necessary for you to act otherwise than cautiously on the defensive," until the large ship is ready or other circumstances arise.

On June 7 the Cabinet of the United States held a meeting, in which was settled the plan of campaign on the northern frontier;[287] where alone, and for a brief period only, an expected superiority of numbers would permit offensive operations. As in the year before, the decision, in general terms, was to direct the main effort against the enemy's right and centre, Mackinac and the Niagara peninsula, instead of against his left, at Montreal or Kingston. The principal movement was to be by a concentration near Buffalo of forces from New York and the western territory, which the Secretary of War estimated might place under Brown's command five thousand regular troops and three thousand volunteers. He had proposed that these, with the assistance of the Erie navy, should be landed on the coast between Fort Erie, at the entrance of the Niagara River, and Point Abino, ten miles to the westward. Thence they were to act against Burlington Heights, at the head of Lake Ontario, the tenure of which by Vincent in 1813, had baffled, on two occasions, the advance of the Americans, and maintained the land communications of the British with York (Toronto) despite their enemy's control of the water. The Secretary's anticipation was that, after gaining this position, the force could proceed along the north shore of the lake towards York, receiving its supplies by the fleet, which was expected to be ready by June 15. Chauncey himself stated

June 8 that he would be ready by July 1, if men were sent him.[288] On the 11th was launched a second new ship, the "Mohawk," to carry forty-two guns. The crew of the "Congress" was ordered up from Portsmouth, and part of them, with other re-enforcements, were reported to have arrived before June 20. June 24 Chauncey wrote, "I shall sail the first week in July to offer the enemy battle."[289] He did not, however, take the Lake until August 1.

The Cabinet had approved the Secretary's suggestion, but extended the place of debarkation to be between Fort Erie and Long Point, eighty miles from the Niagara River, and well west of Burlington Heights. Subsidiary to this main attack, General Izard at Plattsburg was to make a diversion towards Montreal. Coincidently with these movements an expedition of four or five of the Erie fleet, with eight hundred to one thousand troops, should go against Mackinac; their first object, however, being Matchedash Bay, on Lake Huron, which was the seat of an incipient naval establishment, and the point of deposit for supplies proceeding to Mackinac from York by way of Lake Simcoe. This attempt to choke the communications of Mackinac, by holding a vital point upon their line, was to have its counterpart in the east by the provision of fifteen armed boats on the St. Lawrence, supported by posts on the river garrisoned by detachments from Izard's army, so as to intercept the water transport between Montreal and Kingston. It may be mentioned that this particular method had specially commended itself to both Yeo and Chauncey, as most suited to embarrass the British situation throughout the upper province. In a subsequent report to the Admiralty, Yeo characterized the failure of the Americans to do this as an extreme stupidity, which had lost them the war, but upon a repetition of which in future hostilities Great Britain should not rely.[290] The importance of this intercourse is indicated by a mention of Chauncey's, that in the week before June 15 more than two hundred boats passed Ogdensburg for Kingston.[291]

All this, however, simply emphasizes the fact that the decisive point of attack was Montreal or Kingston; not the line between them, which would become useless if either fell. Still less could the Niagara peninsula, though a valuable link in a chain of communication from the lower to the upper lakes, compare in importance with either of the places named. It matters not that a chain is complete in itself, if it is severed from one of the extremities which it is designed to connect. As regards any attempt on the part of the Americans to interrupt the traffic, Drummond appears to have been satisfied with Yeo's promise that "every brigade of batteaux should have a suitable convoy of gunboats."

The Secretary of War, in his communication to the President before the Cabinet met, had indicated plainly his preference for leaving Mackinac alone and concentrating upon the central point of effort, Niagara or

Burlington. "Burlington and York carried, a barrier is interposed which completely protects Detroit and Malden, makes doubtful and hazardous the enemy's intercourse with the western Indians, reduces Mackinac to a possession perfectly useless, renders probable the evacuation of Fort Niagara, and takes from the enemy half his motive for continuing the naval conflict on Lake Ontario. On the other hand, take Mackinac, and what is gained but Mackinac itself?"[292] The reasoning was indisputable, although Armstrong acquiesced in the decision of the Cabinet. The main feature of the plan adopted, the reduction of Burlington Heights and a successful advance on York, was of doubtful issue; but, if successful, the vital end of the chain upon which Mackinac depended for existence dropped useless to the ground. All side enterprise that did not directly contribute to this decisive movement should have been discarded in favor of concentration upon Brown's army, to which its execution was committed, and the actual strength of which was insufficient for the task. At the opening of the campaign its total strength was four thousand seven hundred and eighty, of whom eight hundred and thirty were militia.[293] On July 1 there were present for duty three thousand five hundred. There were also six hundred Indians of the Six Nations. In this impotent conclusion resulted the Secretary's estimate of five thousand regulars and three thousand volunteers.

On July 2 Brown announced to his troops that he was authorized by the Government to put them in motion against the enemy.[294] He had decided to leave Fort Niagara, with its menace to his communications, in his rear, unguarded, and to throw his command directly upon the enemy on the west bank of the river. The crossing was made that night in two divisions; one landing opposite Black Rock, below Fort Erie, the other above that post, which surrendered July 3, at 5 P.M. The garrison numbered one hundred and thirty-seven. From there Brown proposed to turn north and advance towards Ontario, where he hoped to join hands with the navy, which was expected by him, and by the Government, to be on hand to co-operate. This expectation was based on Chauncey's own assurance that he would take the lake on July 1, if supplied with men, who were known since to have arrived. It does not appear, however, that he had received specific instructions as to the course he was intended to follow; and, in assuming that he would go to the head of the lake, for direct co-operation, the Government and the general were reckoning without their host, and in ignorance of his views. He was as loath to leave Kingston and Sackett's in his rear, unwatched, as Brown was willing to take the same risk with regard to Niagara. It was a profound difference of temperament in two capable men, to whom the Government failed to impart the unifying element of orders.

On July 4 Scott's brigade, which had crossed below the fort, advanced from

Fort Erie fifteen miles, to Street's Creek, a small stream, bridged near its mouth, entering the Niagara two miles south of the Chippewa River, the defensive line selected by the British, who now fell back upon it. The Chippewa is of respectable size, one hundred and fifty yards wide, and from twelve to twenty feet deep, running from west to east. In general direction it is parallel to Street's Creek; both entering the Niagara at right angles to its course. In the belt separating the two the ground is flat, and was in great part open; but midway between them there was a strip of thick wood extending down to within a few hundred feet of the Niagara. This formed a dense curtain, hiding movements on either side from the other. The British forces under Riall were now north of the Chippewa, Scott's brigade south of Street's; each having a bridge by which to advance into the space between. The other American brigade, Ripley's, was in rear of Scott—to the south.

In this relative situation, Scott's pickets on the left being disquieted by the British and Indians in the intervening woods, Brown ordered up the militia and American Indians under General Porter to expel them. This was done; but upon reaching the clearing on the further side, the Indians, who were in the lead, encountered a heavy fire, which drove them back upon the militia, and the whole body retreated in a confusion which ended in a rout.[295] Riall had crossed the Chippewa, and was advancing in force, although he believed Brown's army much to outnumber his own now on the field, which in fact it did. Gordon Drummond, in his instructions to him some months before, (March 23), had remarked that with the Americans liberties might be taken which would seem hazardous "to a military man unacquainted with the character of the enemy he had to contend with, or with the events of the last two campaigns on that frontier."[296] This unflattering, but not unreasonable, deduction from the performances of Dearborn and others in 1813, as of Smyth and Van Rensselaer in 1812, was misplaced in the present instance; but it doubtless governed Riall's action, and justified it to himself and his superiors. He had not been engaged since he drove the militia of New York before him like sheep, in the preceding December; and he would have attacked on the very night after the crossing, but that a regiment from York, which he had reason to expect twenty-four hours before, did not arrive until the morning of the 5th. The instant it came he made his dispositions to move at 4 P.M. of the same day.

It was this advance which met Porter and threw his division back, uncovering the wood on the west. Scott at the same moment was marching his brigade into the open space between Street's Creek and the Chippewa; not to meet the enemy, whom he did not expect, but for some drill in the cool of a hot summer's afternoon. As he went forward, the Commander-in-Chief, who had been reconnoitring in front, rode by, galloping to the rear to bring up his remaining force; for, while the army in the aggregate was superior to Riall, the one brigade was inferior. In passing, he called to Scott, "You will have a battle"; and the head of the latter's column, as it crossed the bridge, came at once under the enemy's guns.

Although inferior, exposed, and in a sense surprised, both commander and men were equal to the occasion. The division deployed steadily under fire, and its leader, sending hastily one battalion to check the enemy in the wood, formed front with the remainder of his force to meet those in the plain. These, being yet unopposed, advanced beyond the line of the wood, passing their own detachment within it, which was held in check by the Americans charged with that duty. Losing thus their support on that side, the British presented a new right flank, to use Scott's expression. Thereupon he extended his two wings as far as he dared, leaving between them a considerable interval, so as to overlap his opponent at either extremity; which done, he threw his left forward. His brigade thus formed an obtuse angle, the apex to the rear, the bullets therefore converging and crossing upon the space in front, into which it and the enemy were moving. In the approach both parties halted several times to fire, and Scott says that the superiority of aim in his own men was evident. When within sixty paces a mutual rush, or charge, ensued; but the overlapping of the Americans crowded the flanks of the enemy in upon his centre and produced confusion, to which the preceding fire doubtless had contributed. Scott's own description is that "the wings of the enemy being outflanked, and in some measure doubled upon, were mouldered away like a rope of sand."[297] In this brief and brilliant struggle only the one brigade was engaged.

Riall's account agrees substantially with that of Scott, mentioning particularly "the greatest regularity" with which his opponents "deployed and opened fire."[298] He directed a charge by the three regiments in line, "but I am sorry to say that they suffered so severely that I was obliged to withdraw them, finding their further efforts against the superior numbers of the enemy would be unavailing." He was right in believing that the aggregate of Brown's army, although much short of the six thousand he estimated, was superior to that which he could bring together without abandoning posts he had to hold; but he was mistaken in thinking that in the actual collision his opponents were more numerous than the fifteen hundred regulars at which he states his own force, besides three hundred militia. Scott's brigade, with its supporting artillery, when it crossed four days before, was less than fifteen hundred; and the militia and Indians were routed before he began to fight. His artillery also was of lighter weight. The superiority of the American fire was shown by the respective losses. They were: British, one hundred and forty-eight killed, two hundred and twenty-one wounded, forty-six missing; American, fifty-six killed, two hundred and thirty-nine wounded, thirty-six missing. Of this total, there fell to Scott's command forty-four killed, and two hundred and twenty-four wounded; demonstrating conclusively that it alone was seriously engaged. Not a man was reported missing. The other brigade lost only three killed and three wounded. At the end of the action it was coming up on Scott's left, where he was most exposed, but it did not arrive until he had wrought his own deliverance. The remaining casualties were among the militia and Indians.

After the battle of Chippewa, Riall fell back towards Fort George, and subsequently to the creek called Twenty Mile, west of Niagara, on Lake Ontario. Brown followed as far as Queenston, where he arrived July 10. On the 13th he wrote to Chauncey, begging for the fleet to meet him on the lake shore, west of Fort George, to arrange a plan of operations; in which case he had no doubt of breaking the power of the enemy in Upper Canada in a short time. "All accounts," he said, "represent the force of the enemy at Kingston as very light. Sir James Yeo will not fight,"—which was certain. "For God's sake, let me see you. I have looked for your fleet with the greatest anxiety since the 10th."[299]

Chauncey had not left Sackett's Harbor, nor did he do so; to the utter consternation, not of Brown only, but of the Government. On July 7 he chronicled the burning of an enemy's schooner on the north shore of the lake,[300] an exploit creditable enough in itself, but utterly trivial in relation to pending issues; and on the 8th he wrote that some changes of officers and crews, incidental to the absence of a particular captain, would detain him a few days longer. These were flimsy reasons for inactivity at a moment of great national interest, and when the operations in progress had been begun absolutely upon ' the presupposition of naval control and co-operation, for which he had undertaken to provide the means, even if not pledged as to the manner. Then followed a silence of over two weeks; after which, on July 25, he wrote again by his second to say that "the squadron had been prevented being earlier fitted for sea, in consequence of the delay in obtaining blocks and ironwork." He himself was too unwell to write, and had been so for some days. It is probable that lapse of energy consequent upon illness had something to do with this remarkable paralysis of action, in a man usually bustling and efficient; and there may naturally have been unwillingness to relinquish command,—which would have been his proper course,—after the mortifications of the previous year, when he was just flattering himself with the prospect of a new opportunity.

This inaction, at the critical moment of Brown's advance, caused the Government extreme perplexity and distress. In Chauncey was reposed a confidence expressed by the Secretary of the Navy to Congress the year before, when the resolution of thanks to Perry was pending. He then "intimated the propriety of noticing in an appropriate manner the commander-in-chief of the naval force upon the lakes, under whose immediate command Captain Perry acted;" and spoke of the "zeal, talent, constancy, courage, and prudence of the highest order, which appears to me to merit particular distinction." Such preconceived opinion was hard to shake; but as day succeeded day of expectation and suspense, the patience of the Administration gave way. Letters bearing those elaborated phrases of assurance which most clearly testify uneasiness were sent him, but did not arrive till after Brown had retreated and he himself taken the lake. On July 24 the Secretary writes, "I have expressed the solicitude which has produced this letter, but my confidence in your patriotism, skill, judgment, and energy is entire." On August 3, however, he says the explanation about blocks and ironwork—apparently just received—is so extraordinary at such a moment that "I cannot withhold from you the extreme anxiety and astonishment which the protracted and fatal delay of the squadron has excited in the mind of the President;" and on the 5th, "the known detention of the squadron at Sackett's Harbor until the 27th ultimo, the very feeble and precarious state of your health, the evils which have already resulted from delay," etc., "have induced the President, though with extreme reluctance, and undiminished confidence in your zeal and capacity, to order Commodore Decatur to proceed to Sackett's Harbor and take upon himself the naval command on Lake Ontario."

The proposed change did not take place, the squadron having already resumed active cruising. The Secretary repeated his expressions of confidence, but does not appear to have renewed his recommendations to Congress. Chauncey, stung by the reflections, open and implied, upon his conduct, retorted with a defence and definition of his course, as proposed and realized, which raises the whole question of the method of naval co-operation under the circumstances, and of its probable effectiveness. Replying to Brown's letter of July 13, quoted above, he said positively that he had never given the general ground to expect him at the head of the lake.[304] This assertion he repeated to the Secretary, whose letters to him demonstrate that the Government had left him entire discretion as to his particular method of procedure. Acting therefore upon his own judgment, he justified his course by alleging that direct co-operation at the Niagara end of the lake was impossible, because the heavy ships could not get within two miles of the forts, and Brown's army had never advanced to the lake shore; consequently, the fleet could neither have acted directly by itself, nor yet in support of a land force, with which it could not communicate. So much for the negative side of the argument. Positively, he said, the mission of the navy was to seek and fight the enemy's squadron; and this duty was emphasized by the fact that to go westward to Niagara, while the enemy was at Kingston, would expose to capture Sackett's Harbor, the safety of which had remained a dominant anxiety with Chauncey since its narrow escape the previous year.

The protection of his own base, and the controlling or beating the organized force of the enemy, are unquestionably two leading considerations which should govern the general conduct of a general officer, land or sea. In these particulars Chauncey's statement was unassailable; but, whether well or ill, he seems to have been incapable of rising to the larger estimate of naval control, to which the rules enunciated, conduce simply as a formulation of principles, giving to action preciseness and steadiness of direction. The destruction of the enemy's fleet is the means to obtain naval control; but naval control in itself is only a means, not an object. The object of the campaign, set by the Government, was the acquirement of mastery upon the Niagara peninsula, to the accomplishment of which Brown's army was destined. Naval control would minister thereto, partly by facilitating the re-enforcement and supply of the American army, and, conversely, by impeding that of the British. Of these two means, the latter was the more efficacious, because, owing to the thoroughly denuded condition of the Canadian territory, from the Niagara to Detroit, local resources were exhausted, and dependence was wholly upon the water; whereas the United States forces, near a fruitful friendly region, and in possession of Lake Erie, had other independent and sufficient streams of maintenance.

To weaken the British was by so much to strengthen Brown, even though direct communication with him were impossible. It was of this that the British stood in continual anxious terror, as shown by their letters; and this it was that Chauncey gives no sign of recognizing. Of support to his own colleague he spoke with ill-timed scorn: "That you might find the fleet somewhat of a convenience in the transportation of provisions and stores for the use of the army, and an agreeable appendage to attend its marches and countermarches, I am ready to believe; but, Sir, the Secretary of the Navy has honored us with a higher destiny—we are intended to seek and to fight the enemy's fleet. This is the great purpose of the Government in creating this fleet; and I shall not be diverted in my efforts to effectuate it by any sinister attempt to render us subordinate to, or an appendage of, the army." It would be difficult to cite an apter instance of wresting sound principles to one's own destruction. Whatever the antecedent provocation, this is no temper in which to effect military objects. It is indeed hard to believe that an army so little numerous as that of Brown could have accomplished the ambitious designs confided to it; but that does not affect the clear duty of affording it the utmost assistance that ingenuity could devise and energy effect. The words quoted were written August 10, but ignore entirely an alternative suggested in a letter received that day from the Secretary, dated July 24, itself the repetition of one made July 20: "To destroy the enemy's fleet, or to blockade his force and cut off his entire communication with the head of the lake." The civilian here indicated clearly what the naval officer should have known from the very first moment.

As before said, the contemporary correspondence of British officers abundantly shows their anxiety lest Chauncey, in these important weeks, should do what he did not do. Sir James Yeo had deliberately formulated the policy of remaining inactive in Kingston until the completion of the 102-gun ship, which would give him command of the lake beyond chance of dispute. To occupy the American fleet meanwhile with a local blockade, which he intended not to contest, was precisely what he wanted. To distress the army at Niagara to the point of evacuating the peninsula was the one only thing that might impel—or compel—him to come out and fight, despite his deliberate intention. "Several small vessels," wrote the Commissary-General a month later[305] to Sir George Prevost, "were despatched while the enemy's squadron were unable to leave Sackett's Harbor; but since the enemy commands the lake, that resource for the moment is cut off, and only batteaux can be employed. These are [306] a very useful conveyance, not only from the danger of the enemy's small vessels, which can approach the shore without difficulty, but also from want of proper steersmen, pilots, and middlemen.... This feeble means of transport will never effect the forming of a sufficient depot at York, Burlington Heights, and Niagara; and, unless the commissariat can be aided to a great extent by the Royal Navy, the most disastrous consequences must ensue."

At the date this was written, August 27, Chauncey's force was that which he had promised should be ready July 1, but with which he did not sail until August 1,—too late. The very efficiency of his action in August condemns therefore his inaction in July. Besides his two new big ships, which matched Yeo's two, he had added to the fleet of the previous year, then superior to the British, two brigs of the armament and tonnage of the ocean sloops of war,—the "Peacock" and class. Against these Yeo had nothing to show. It was therefore open to Chauncey to blockade Kingston with an equal force, thus covering Sackett's, and to despatch to the head of the lake vessels adequate to embarrass Riall and Drummond most seriously. From York to Niagara by land was eighty miles of road impassable to laden wagons; by lake thirty miles of water facility. From Kingston to York, an additional distance of a hundred and fifty miles, the same relative difficulty of transportation obtained. Yet as late as July 13, Drummond could write from Kingston, "As troops cannot be forwarded without provisions, I have requested Sir James Yeo to send his two brigs immediately, with as much flour and pork as they can carry to York and Burlington." On the 16th, "The 'Charwell' sailed yesterday for the head of the lake with provisions and ammunition. I have strong hopes she will arrive safe, as the enemy's whole squadron are lying in Sackett's with their sails bent, and apparently ready for sea, though no guns forward of the foremast could be perceived on board

the 'Mohawk.'"[307]
Yeo, holding both York and the mouth of the Niagara, ventured thither two brigs and two schooners, under Captain Dobbs, one of his officers. "Without their valuable aid in the transport of troops and stores," wrote Drummond, August 12, "I certainly should not have been able to attempt offensive operations so soon after my arrival." By that time, when Brown had of necessity abandoned the offensive, "Commodore Chauncey has left three of his brigs to watch our vessels in the Niagara. They continue cruising off that place."[308] Chauncey, in his letter of vindication to the Secretary, had maintained that "if our whole fleet were at the head of the lake, it would not detain a regiment from [York to] Fort George more than twenty-four hours.... Any one who knows anything of the navigation of this lake knows that boats may cross the head of the lake, from York to the opposite shore, unobserved by any fleet during the night."[309] Admitting that there is no literal exaggeration in this statement, it takes no account of the enemy's apprehensions, nor of the decisive difficulty of running vessels of a size to transport the heavy stores, without which the army could not remain. No one familiar with maritime affairs will deny the impossibility of wholly suppressing all furtive movement of small coasters, but it is equally certain much can be done to impede that full course of supplies which constitutes security of communication. To Chauncey's affirmation, Drummond gives an incidental reply, September 2: "The enemy's blockading squadron not having been seen for some days, I sent the 'Vincent' across to York, where she has arrived in safety, and Captain Dobbs has directed the 'Charwell' to push across the first morning the wind is fair. By their aid I got rid of many encumbrances (prisoners and sick), and shall receive the supplies that are waiting at York for this division."[310]
It is needless to multiply quotations from the utterances, and frequent outcries, that run throughout this correspondence. Chauncey, from early July, had it in his hand seriously to molest the British communications, and at the same time to contain the British squadron in Kingston. Such action would subject Yeo to the just and humiliating imputation of suffering the harassment of the army without an attempt at relief, or else would compel him to come out and fight under conditions which, "whatever the result," to use Nelson's words, "would leave his squadron in a state to do no further harm," till the big ship was ready. Thus also Chauncey would cover his base; for, as Prevost wrote, "while Kingston is blockaded, no movement against Sackett's Harbor can take place." It was Chauncey's misfortune himself to demonstrate his own shortcoming by the profound distress he inflicted, when sounder measures were instituted after the censure of the Government,—too late.
One of the most conspicuous instances of the effect of this neglect was realized in the desperate and sanguinary engagement of Lundy's Lane, the

occurrence of which, at the time and in the manner it did, as stated by one of the chief actors, Winfield Scott, was due directly to the freedom of the lake to the British. Brown had remained at Queenston for some days after July 10, in painful suspense. A reconnaissance in force was made on the 15th by the militia brigade under General Porter, accompanied by two pieces of artillery, which moved round Fort George as far as Lake Ontario, whence the general reported "we had an opportunity to examine the northern face of Forts Riall and Niagara, about two miles distant."[311] Beyond a few random shots, no opposition was experienced. On the 20th the army as a whole advanced to the neighborhood of Fort George, and made a demonstration of throwing up siege works; not without serious intention, for Brown had not yet abandoned hope of receiving the cannon of necessary weight, 24-pounders, from Sackett's Harbor. He had with him only eighteens. Riall was greatly alarmed, exaggerating the force before him, and receiving reports of re-enforcements expected by the lake. On July 22 he sent hasty and pressing word of the impending emergency to Drummond, who arrived the same evening at York from Kingston; but in the afternoon of the day he was able to give better tidings. The Americans were falling back again upon Queenston, abandoning the positions recently assumed.[312]

Brown had hoped that by his advance, blowing up the works at Queenston, and leaving his rear evidently much exposed, Riall might be induced to attack. The British general was much disposed to do so; but refrained, fearing for his own communications. On the morning of the 23d an express from General Gaines, commanding at Sackett's Harbor, reached Brown at Queenston, informing him that Chauncey was sick, that no one knew when the fleet would sail, and that an endeavor had been made to send forward by batteaux, coasting the south shore, the 24-pounder guns needed for besieging Fort George; but the officer in command had stopped at the mouth of Black River Bay, thinking himself in danger from the British squadron.[313] A contemporary account reads: "July 20, Morgan with the riflemen and cannon prevented from sailing by Yeo's blockade of the harbor."[314] Apparently, Yeo had even come out of port, in order by menace of attack to arrest the forwarding of this essential succor. Chauncey's incidental mention is positive that he approached no nearer than the Ducks, some large islands thirty miles south of Kingston, and forty west of Sackett's;[315] but it is obvious that in the quiescence of the American squadron such a position was prohibitive of movement by batteaux. It may readily be conceived that had Brown's demonstration against the fort been coupled with an attempt to land the guns from a naval division, Riall might have felt compelled to come out of his lines.

Neither guns nor naval division appeared, and Drummond, able to move troops freely across the lake, concerted now a plan for striking a dangerous blow from Fort Niagara, against Brown's communications on the New York side; the exposed condition of which was known to him. This was the immediate offensive of which he had spoken; his ability to undertake which he attributed to naval aid. He had as adjutant-general Lieutenant-Colonel Harvey, the same who suggested and executed the brilliant stroke that disconcerted Dearborn's campaign in 1813; and who on the present occasion drew up the instructions to Riall, and to Lieutenant-Colonel Tucker, the officer in charge of the forts, with a delightful lucidity which characterizes all papers signed by him.[316] The brigs "Star" and "Charwell" left York July 23, with a re-enforcement of four hundred men for Fort Niagara, in which post the officer commanding was directed to concentrate so many more as would enable him to carry a full regiment of regulars against batteries that were being put up at Youngstown. This movement was to be made at daylight of Monday, July 25, and General Riall was instructed to support it by a threatening demonstration on his side of the river. On the evening of the 24th, Drummond himself sailed from York in one of Yeo's schooners, and by daybreak reached Niagara.

Upon his arrival,—or possibly before,—he learned that the Americans had retired further, to the Chippewa. The motive for this backward step was to draw necessary supplies across the river, from the magazines at Fort Schlosser, and to leave there all superfluous baggage, prior to a rush upon Burlington Heights, which Brown had now substituted as the point of attack, in consequence of his disappointment about the siege guns.[317] It had been his intention to rest over the 25th, in order to start forward fresh on the 26th. This retrograde movement, inducing Riall to advance, changed the situation found by Drummond. He decided therefore to apply his re-enforcements to the support of Riall directly, and to have the enterprise from Niagara proceed with somewhat smaller numbers towards Lewiston,—opposite Queenston,—where a body of Americans were posted. This advance appears to have been detected very soon, for Drummond writes, "Some unavoidable delay having occurred in the march of the troops up the right bank, the enemy had moved off previous to Colonel Tucker's arrival." Brown, in his report of this circumstance, wrote, "As it appeared that the enemy with his increased force was about to avail himself of the hazard under which our baggage and stores were on our [American] side of Niagara, I conceived the most effectual method of recalling him from the object was to put myself in motion towards Queenston. General Scott with his brigade were accordingly put in march on the road leading thither." The result was the battle of Lundy's Lane.

Scott in his autobiography attributes the report of an advance towards Schlosser to a mistake on the part of the officer making it. It was not so. There was an actual movement, modified in detail from the original elaborate plan, the execution of which was based by the British general upon the local control of the lake, enabling him to send re-enforcements. The employment of Dobbs' four vessels, permitted by Chauncey's inaction, thus had direct effect upon the occurrence and the result of the desperately contested engagement which ensued, upon the heights overlooking the lower torrent of the Niagara. From the Chippewa to the Falls is about two miles, through which the main road from Lake Erie to Ontario follows the curving west bank of the stream. A half mile further on it was joined at right angles by the crossroad, known as Lundy's Lane. As Scott's column turned the bend above the Falls there were evidences of the enemy's presence, which at first were thought to indicate only a detachment for observation; but a few more paces disclosed the Lane held by a line of troops, superior in number to those encountered with equal unexpectedness on the Chippewa, three weeks before.

Scott hesitated whether to fall back; but apprehensive of the effect of such a step upon the other divisions, he sent word to Brown that he would hold his ground, and prepared for battle, making dispositions to turn the enemy's left,—towards the Niagara. It was then near sundown. A hot engagement followed, in the course of which the pressure on the British left caused it to give ground. In consequence, the American right advancing and the British left receding, the two lines swung round perpendicular to the Lane, the Americans standing with their backs to the precipices, beneath which roar the lower rapids of Niagara. At this period General Riall, who had received a severe wound, was captured while being carried to the rear.

As this change of front was taking place Brown arrived, with Ripley's brigade and Porter's militia, which were brought into line with Scott; the latter occupying the extreme right, Ripley the centre, and Porter the left. When this arrangement had been completed the attack was resumed, and a hill top, which was the key of the British position, was carried; the artillery there falling into the hands of the Americans. "In so determined a manner were these attacks directed against our guns," reported Drummond, "that our artillery men were bayoneted by the enemy in the act of loading, and the muzzles of the enemy's guns were advanced within a few yards of ours.... Our troops having for a moment been pushed back, some of our guns remained for a few minutes in the enemy's hands."[318] Upon this central fact both accounts agree, but on the upshot of the matter they differ. "Not only were the guns quickly recovered," continued Drummond, "but the two pieces which the enemy had brought up were captured by us." He admits, however, the loss as well as gain of one 6-pounder. Brown, on the contrary, claimed that the ground was held and that the enemy retired, leaving his guns. "He attempted to drive us from our position and to regain his artillery; our line was unshaken and the enemy repulsed. Two other attempts having the same object had the same issue."[319] By this time both Brown and Scott had been severely wounded and carried off the field.

In this situation the Commander-in-Chief directed the officer now in command to withdraw the troops to the camp, three miles behind, for refreshment, and then to re-occupy the field of battle. Whether this was feasible or not would require an inquiry more elaborate than the matter at stake demands. It is certain that the next day the British resumed the position without resistance, and continued to hold it.

To Americans the real interest and value of this action, combined with its predecessor at Chippewa, and with the subsequent equally desperate fighting about Fort Erie, were that the contest did not close without this conspicuous demonstration that in capable hands the raw material of the American armies could be worked up into fighting quality equal to the best. Regarded as an international conflict, the war was now staggering to its end, which was but a few months distant; and in every direction little but shame and mortification had befallen the American arms on land. It would have been a calamity, indeed, had the record closed for that generation with the showing of 1812 and 1813. Nothing is gained by explaining or excusing such results; the only expiation for them is by the demonstration of repentance, in works worthy of men and soldiers. This was abundantly afforded by Brown's brief campaign of 1814, otherwise fruitless. Not only the regular troops, fashioned by Scott in a few brief months from raw recruits to disciplined fighters, proved their mettle; the irregulars associated with them, though without the same advantage of training and concert of movement, caught their enthusiasm, gained confidence from their example, and emulated their deeds. The rabble which scarcely waited for a shot before scattering at the approach of Riall's columns in December, 1813, abandoning their homes to destruction, had earned the discriminating eulogium of General Brown before the year 1814 closed. In August, after Lundy's Lane, he, a New Yorker himself, wrote to the Governor of New York:[320] "This state has suffered in reputation in this war; its militia have done nothing, or but little, and that, too, after the state had been for a long time invaded." On September 20, after the sanguinary and successful sortie from Fort Erie, he wrote again: "The militia of New York have redeemed their character—they behaved gallantly. Of those called out by the last requisition, fifteen hundred have crossed the state border to our support. This re-enforcement has been of immense importance to us; it doubled our effective strength, and their good conduct cannot but have the happiest effect upon the nation."[321]

The American losses at Lundy's Lane were, killed one hundred and seventy-one, wounded five hundred and seventy-two, missing one hundred and seventeen; total, eight hundred and sixty. Those of the British were, killed eighty-four, wounded five hundred and fifty-nine, missing one hundred and ninety-three, prisoners forty-two; total, eight hundred and seventy-eight. Of the British missing and prisoners, one hundred and sixty-nine were reported by the Americans as in their hands; among them nineteen officers. This substantial equality in casualties corresponds to a similar equality in the numbers engaged. The Americans had present for duty two thousand six hundred and forty-four, including over four hundred militia; Drummond in his report states that first and last he had upon the field not more than two thousand eight hundred. That he estimates the force opposed to him to have been at least five thousand, may be coupled with his mention of "the reiterated and determined attacks which the enemy made upon our centre," as showing the impression produced upon his mind during the progress of the struggle. The comparison of numbers engaged with injuries sustained justifies the inference that, in result, the actual contest upon the ground was at least a drawn battle, if not the positive success claimed by Brown and Scott. Colonel Hercules Scott, of the British 103d Regiment, who to be sure shows somewhat of the malcontent ever present in camps, but who afterwards fell well at the front in the assault upon Fort Erie, was in this action; and in a private letter uses an expression which practically corroborates the American assertion that they held the ground at the end, and withdrew afterwards. "In the last attack they gained possession of five out of seven of our guns, but the fire kept upon them was so severe that it afterwards appeared they had not been able to carry them off; for we found them next morning on the spot they had been taken. No [We?] boast of a 'Great Victory,' but in my opinion it was nearly equal on both sides."[322] Equality of loss, or even a technical victory, does not imply equality of subsequent conditions. Brown had at the front all his available force; he had no reserves or depots upon which to draw. He had expended the last shot in the locker. Drummond not only had been receiving re-enforcements, absolutely small, yet considerable in proportion to the contending numbers, but he was continuing to receive them. Lundy's Lane was July 25; Chauncey did not take the lake until August 1, and it was the 5th when he came off Niagara, where he at once intercepted and drove ashore one of the British brigs, which was fired by her captain. He thus had immediate ocular demonstration of what had been going on in his absence; but it was already too late for the American squadron to turn the scales of war. If this could have been accomplished at all, it would have been by such intervention as in this instance; by injuring the enemy rather than by helping the friend. But this would have been possible only in the beginning. Brown felt himself unable longer to keep the field; and the army, now under General Ripley, withdrew the following day, July 26, to Fort Erie, where it proceeded to strengthen the work itself, and to develop a fortified line depending upon it, covering the angle of ground made by the shores of the Niagara River and Lake Erie. Brown was carried to Buffalo to recover of his wounds, which were not dangerous, though severe. He subsequently resumed chief command, but Scott was unable to serve again during the campaign.

General Gaines was summoned from Sackett's Harbor, and on August 5 took charge at Fort Erie.

From this time the operations on either side were limited to the effort to take or to hold this position. Drummond's experience at Lundy's Lane, and the extent of his loss, made him cautious in pursuit; and time was yielded to the enemy to make good their entrenchment. On the early morning of August 15 the British assaulted, and were repelled with fifty-seven killed, three hundred and nine wounded, and five hundred and thirty-nine missing.[323] The Americans, covered by their works, reported a loss of less than one hundred. "I am now reduced to a most unpleasant predicament with regard to force," wrote Drummond to Prevost.[324] "I have ordered the 6th and 82d from York to this frontier. I had intended to order another regiment from Kingston, but from the badness of the roads since the recent rains I could not calculate upon their arrival here before our squadron will be able to take the lake, and as even at present the diminution of stores and provisions is beginning to be felt, I intreat your excellency will impress upon the Commodore the necessity of conveying to this division, the very moment the squadron can leave harbor, a full supply of each, as well as a re-enforcement of troops."

After this sharp reverse Drummond settled down to a siege, in the course of which he complained frequently and grievously of the annoyance caused him by Chauncey's blockade, established August 6, with three vessels competent seriously to interrupt transportation of supplies, or of men in large detachments. The season was still propitious for marching; but as early as August 21 Drummond was afraid "that relief by control of the lake may not reach us in time." September 11, "Our batteries have almost been silent for several days from the reduced state of the ammunition." September 14, "The sudden and most unlooked for return to the head of Lake Ontario of the two brigs, by which the Niagara has been so long blockaded, and my communication with York cut off, has had the effect of preventing the junction of the 97th regiment, which arrived at York the 10th, and probably would have been here the following day but for this unlucky circumstance."[325] September 24, "The deficiency of provisions and transport is the difficulty attending every operation in this country, as it prevents the collection at any one point of an adequate force for any object. These difficulties we must continue to experience, until our squadron appears superior on the lake." It would be impossible to depict more strongly the course incumbent upon Chauncey in July, or to condemn more severely, by implication, his failure then to do what he could, taking the chance of that chapter of accidents, "to be in the way of good luck," which it is the duty of every military leader to consider as among the clear possibilities of war. "The blockade of Kingston," wrote Prevost on October 11 to Lord Bathurst,[326] "has been vigorously maintained for the last six weeks by the enemy's squadron. The vigilance of the American cruisers on Lake Ontario was felt even by our batteaux creeping along the shore with provisions for Drummond's division. In consequence, I found that the wants of that army had grown to an alarming extent."[327]

In pushing his siege works, Drummond by September 15 had erected three batteries, the last of which, then just completed, "would rake obliquely the whole American encampment."[328] Brown determined then upon a sortie in force, which was made on the afternoon of September 17, with entire success. It was in this attack that the New York militia, of whom fifteen hundred had crossed to the fort, bore an honorable and distinguished part. Brown states the actual force engaged in the fighting at one thousand regulars and one thousand militia, to whose energy and stubbornness Drummond again pays the compliment of estimating them at five thousand. The weight of the onslaught was thrown on the British right flank, and there doubtless the assailants were, and should have been, greatly superior. Two of the three batteries were carried, one of them being that which had directly incited the attack. "The enemy," reported Drummond, "was everywhere driven back; not however before he had disabled the guns in No. 3 battery, and exploded its magazine;"[329] that is, not before he had accomplished his purpose.

Nor was this all. The stroke ended the campaign. Drummond had nearly lost hope of a successful issue, and this blow destroyed what little remained. The American navy still held the lake; the big ship in Kingston still tarried; rains torrential and almost incessant were undermining the ramparts of Forts George and Niagara, causing serious alarm for the defence, and spreading sickness among his troops, re-enforcements to which could with difficulty be sent. The British returns of loss in repelling the sortie gave one hundred and fifteen killed, one hundred and forty-eight wounded, three hundred and sixteen missing; total, five hundred and seventy-nine. The Americans, whose casualties were five hundred and eleven, reported that they brought back three hundred and eighty-five prisoners; among whom the roll of officers tallies with the British list. Four days afterwards, September 21, Drummond abandoned his works, leaving his fires burning and huts standing, and fell back secretly by night to the Chippewa.

Brown was in no condition to follow. In a brief ten weeks, over which his adventurous enterprise spread, he had fought four engagements, which might properly be called general actions, if regard were had to the total force at his disposal, and not merely to the tiny scale of the campaign. Barring the single episode of the battle of New Orleans, his career on the Niagara peninsula is the one operation of the land war of 1812 upon which thoughtful and understanding Americans of the following generation could look back with satisfaction. Of how great consequence this evidence of national military character was, to the men who had no other experience, is difficult to be appreciated by us, in whose memories are the successes of the Mexican contest and the fierce titanic strife of the Civil War. In truth, Chippewa, Lundy's Lane, and New Orleans, are the only names of 1812 preserved to popular memory,[330] ever impatient of disagreeable reminiscence. Hull's surrender was indeed an exception; the iron there burned too deep to leave no lasting scar. To Brown and his distinguished subordinates we owe the demonstration of what the War of 1812 might have accomplished, had the Government of the United States since the beginning of the century possessed even a rudimentary conception of what military preparation means to practical statesmanship.

Shortly after the sortie which decided Drummond to retire, the defenders of Fort Erie were brought into immediate relation with the major part of the forces upon Lake Champlain, under General Izard. Both belonged to the same district, the ninth, which in Dearborn's time had formed one general command; but which it now pleased the Secretary of War, General Armstrong, to manage as two distinct divisions, under his own controlling directions from Washington. The Secretary undoubtedly had a creditable amount of acquired military knowledge, but by this time he had manifested that he did not possess the steadying military qualities necessary to play the role of a distant commander-in-chief. Izard, at the time of his appointment, reported everything connected with his command, the numbers and discipline of the troops, their clothing and equipment, in a deplorable state of inefficiency.[331] The summer months were spent in building up anew the army on Champlain, and in erecting fortifications; at Plattsburg, where the main station was fixed, and at Cumberland Head, the promontory which defines the eastern side of Plattsburg Bay. Upon the maintenance of these positions depended the tenure of the place itself, as the most suitable advanced base for the army and for the fleet, mutually indispensable for the protection of that great line of operations.

On July 27, before the Secretary could know of Lundy's Lane, but when he did anticipate that Brown must fall back on Fort Erie, he wrote to Izard that it would be expedient for him to advance against Montreal, or against Prescott,—on the St. Lawrence opposite Ogdensburg,—in case large re-enforcements had been sent from Montreal to check Brown's advance, as was reported. His own inclination pointed to Prescott, with a view to the contingent chance of an attack upon Kingston, in co-operation with Chauncey and the garrison at Sackett's.[332] This letter did not reach Izard till August 10. He construed its somewhat tentative and vacillating terms as an order. "I will make the movement you direct, if possible; but I shall do it with the apprehension of risking the force under my command, and with the certainty that everything in this vicinity, save the lately erected works at Plattsburg and Cumberland Head, will, in less than three days after my departure, be in possession of the enemy."[333] Izard, himself, on July 19, had favored a step like this proposed; but, as he correctly observed, the time for it was when Brown was advancing and might be helped. Now, when Brown had been brought to a stand, and was retiring, the movement would not aid him, but would weaken the Champlain frontier; and that at the very moment when the divisions from Wellington's army, which had embarked at Bordeaux, were arriving at Quebec and Montreal.

On August 12, Armstrong wrote again, saying that his first order had been based upon the supposition that Chauncey would meet and beat Yeo, or at least confine him in port. This last had in fact been done; but, if the enemy should have carried his force from Montreal to Kingston, and be prepared there, "a safer movement was to march two thousand men to Sackett's, embark there, and go to Brown's assistance."[334] Izard obediently undertook this new disposition, which he received August 20; but upon consultation with his officers concluded that to march by the northern route, near the Canada border, would expose his necessarily long column to dangerous flank attack. He therefore determined to go by way of Utica.[335] On August 29 the division, about four thousand effectives, set out from the camp at Chazy, eight miles north of Plattsburg, and on September 16 reached Sackett's. Bad weather prevented immediate embarkation, but on the 21st about two thousand five hundred infantry sailed, and having a fair wind reached next day the Genesee, where they were instantly put ashore. A regiment of light artillery and a number of dragoons, beyond the capacity of the fleet to carry, went by land and arrived a week later.

In this manner the defence of Lake Champlain was deprived of four thousand fairly trained troops at the moment that the British attack in vast superiority of force was maturing. Their advance brigade, in fact, crossed the frontier two days after Izard's departure. At the critical moment, and during the last weeks of weather favorable for operations, the men thus taken were employed in making an unprofitable march of great length, to a quarter where there was now little prospect of successful action, and where they could not arrive before the season should be practically closed. Brown, of course, hailed an accession of strength which he sorely needed, and did not narrowly scrutinize a measure for which he was not responsible. On September 27, ten days after the successful sortie from Fort Erie, he was at Batavia, in New York, where he had an interview with Izard, who was the senior. In consequence of their consultation Izard determined that his first movement should be the siege of Fort Niagara.[336] In pursuance of this resolve his army marched to Lewiston, where it arrived October 5. There he had a second meeting with Brown, accompanied on this occasion by Porter, and under their representations decided that it would be more proper to concentrate all the forces at hand on the Canadian bank of the Niagara, south of the Chippewa, and not to undertake a siege while Drummond kept the field.[337]

Despite many embarrassments, and anxieties on the score of supplies and provisions while deprived of the free use of the lake, the British general was now master of the situation. His position rested upon the Chippewa on one flank, and upon Fort Niagara on the other. From end to end he had secure communication, for he possessed the river and the boats, below the falls. By these interior lines, despite his momentary inferiority in total numbers, he was able to concentrate his forces upon a threatened extremity with a rapidity which the assailants could not hope to rival. Fort Niagara was not in a satisfactory condition to resist battery by heavy cannon; but Izard had none immediately at hand. Drummond was therefore justified in his hope that "the enemy will find the recapture of the place not to be easily effected."[338] His line of the Chippewa rested on the left upon the Niagara. On its right flank the ground was impassable to everything save infantry, and any effort to turn his position there would have to be made in the face of artillery, to oppose which no guns could be brought forward. Accordingly when Izard, after crossing in accordance with his last decision, advanced on October 15 against the British works upon the Chippewa, he found they were too strong for a frontal attack, the opinion which Drummond himself entertained,[339] while the topographical difficulties of the country baffled every attempt to turn them. Drummond's one serious fear was that the Americans, finding him impregnable here, might carry a force by Lake Erie, and try to gain his rear from Long Point, or by the Grand River.[340] Though they would meet many obstacles in such a circuit, yet the extent to which he would have to detach in order to meet them, and the smallness of his numbers, might prove very embarrassing.

Izard entertained no such project. After his demonstration of October 15, which amounted to little more than a reconnaisance in force, he lapsed into hopelessness. The following day he learned by express that the American squadron had retired to Sackett's Harbor and was throwing up defensive works. With his own eyes he saw, too, that the British water service was not impeded. "Notwithstanding our supremacy on Lake Ontario, at the time I was in Lewiston [October 5-8] the communication between York and the mouth of the Niagara was uninterrupted. I saw a large square-rigged vessel arriving, and another, a brig, lying close to the Canada shore. Not a vessel of ours was in sight."[341] The British big ship, launched September 10, was on October 14 reported by Yeo completely equipped. The next day he would proceed up the lake to Drummond's relief. Chauncey had not waited for the enemy to come out. Convinced that the first use of naval superiority would be to reduce his naval base, he took his ships into port October 8; writing to Washington that the "St. Lawrence" had her sails bent, apparently all ready for sea, and that he expected an attack in ten days.[342] "I confess I am greatly embarrassed," wrote Izard to Monroe, who had now superseded Armstrong as Secretary of War. "At the head of the most efficient army the United States have possessed during this war, much must be expected from me; and yet I can discern no object which can be achieved at this point worthy of the risk which will attend its attempt." The enemy perfectly understood his perplexity, and despite his provocations refused to play into his hands by leaving the shelter of their works to fight. On October 21, he broke up his camp, and began to prepare winter quarters for his own command opposite Black Rock, sending Brown with his division to Sackett's Harbor. Two weeks later, on November 5, having already transported all but a small garrison to the American shore, he blew up Fort Erie and abandoned his last foothold on the peninsula.

During the operations along the Niagara which ended thus fruitlessly, the United States Navy upon Lake Erie met with some severe mishaps. The Cabinet purpose, of carrying an expedition into the upper lakes against Michilimackinac, was persisted in despite the reluctance of Armstrong. Commander Arthur Sinclair, who after an interval had succeeded Perry, was instructed to undertake this enterprise with such force as might be necessary; but to leave within Lake Erie all that he could spare, to co-operate with Brown. Accordingly he sailed from Erie early in June, arriving on the 21st off Detroit, where he was to embark the troops under Colonel Croghan for the land operations. After various delays St. Joseph's was reached July 20, and found abandoned. Its defences were destroyed. On the 26th the vessels were before Mackinac, but after a reconnaisance Croghan decided that the position was too strong for the force he had. Sinclair therefore started to return, having so far accomplished little except the destruction of two schooners, one on Lake Huron, and one on Lake Superior, both essential to the garrison at Mackinac; there being at the time but one other vessel on the lakes competent to the maintenance of their communications.

This remaining schooner, called the "Nancy," was known to be in Nottawasaga Bay, at the south end of Georgian Bay, near the position selected by the British as a depot for stores coming from York by way of Lake Simcoe. After much dangerous search in uncharted waters, Sinclair found her lying two miles up a river of the same name as the bay, where she was watching a chance to slip through to Mackinac. Her lading had been completed July 31, and the next day she had already started, when a messenger brought word that approach to the island was blocked by the American expedition. The winding of the river placed her present anchorage within gunshot of the lake; but as she could not be seen through the brush, Sinclair borrowed from the army a howitzer, with which, mounted in the open beyond, he succeeded in firing both the "Nancy" and the blockhouse defending the position. The British were thus deprived of their last resource for transportation in bulk upon the lake. What this meant to Mackinac may be inferred from the fact that flour there was sixty dollars the barrel, even before Sinclair's coming.

Having inflicted this small, yet decisive, embarrassment on the enemy, Sinclair on August 16 started back with the "Niagara" and "Hunter" for Erie, whither he had already despatched the "Lawrence"—Perry's old flagship—and the "Caledonia." He left in Nottawasaga Bay the schooners "Scorpion" and "Tigress," "to maintain a rigid blockade until driven from the lake by the inclemency of the weather," in order "to cut the line of communications from Michilimackinac to York." Lieutenant Daniel Turner of the "Scorpion," who had commanded the "Caledonia" in Perry's action, was the senior officer of this detachment.

After Sinclair's departure the gales became frequent and violent. Finding no good anchorage in Nottawasaga Bay, Turner thought he could better fulfil the purpose of his instructions by taking the schooners to St. Joseph's, and cruising thence to French River, which enters Georgian Bay at its northern end. On the night of September 3, the "Scorpion" being then absent at the river, the late commander of the "Nancy," Lieutenant Miller Worsley, got together a boat's crew of eighteen seamen, and obtained the co-operation of a detachment of seventy soldiers. With these, followed by a number of Indians in canoes, he attacked the "Tigress" at her anchors and carried her by boarding. The night being very dark, the British were close alongside when first seen; and the vessel was not provided with boarding nettings, which her commander at his trial proved he had not the cordage to make. Deprived of this essential defence, which in such an exposed situation corresponds to a line of intrenched works on shore, her crew of thirty men were readily overpowered by the superior numbers, who could come upon them from four quarters at once, and had but an easy step to her low-lying rail. The officer commanding the British troops made a separate report of the affair, in which he said that her resistance did credit to her officers, who were all severely wounded.[343] Transferring his men to the prize, Worsley waited for the return of the "Scorpion," which on the 5th anchored about five miles off, ignorant of what had happened. The now British schooner weighed and ran down to her, showing American colors; and, getting thus alongside without being suspected, mastered her also. Besides the officers hurt, there were of the "Tigress'" crew three killed and three wounded; the British having two killed and eight wounded. No loss seems to have been incurred on either side in the capture of the "Scorpion." In reporting this affair Sir James Yeo wrote: "The importance of this service is very great. Had not the naval force of the enemy been taken, the commanding officer at Mackinac must have surrendered."[344] He valued it further for its influence upon the Indians, and upon the future of the naval establishment which he had in contemplation for the upper lakes.

When Sinclair reached Detroit from Nottawasaga he received news of other disasters. According to his instructions, before starting for the upper lakes he had left a division of his smaller vessels, under Lieutenant Kennedy, to support the army at Niagara. When Brown fell back upon Fort Erie, after Lundy's Lane, three of these, the "Ohio," "Somers," and "Porcupine," anchored close by the shore, in such a position as to flank the approaches to the fort, and to molest the breaching battery which the British were erecting. As this interfered with the besiegers' plans for an assault, Captain Dobbs, commanding the naval detachment on Ontario which Yeo had assigned to co-operate with Drummond, transported over land from below the falls six boats or batteaux, and on the night of August 12 attacked the American schooners, as Worsley afterwards did the "Tigress" and "Scorpion." The "Ohio" and "Somers," each with a crew of thirty-five men, were carried and brought successfully down the river within the British lines. Dobbs attributed the escape of the "Porcupine" to the cables of the two others being cut, in consequence of which they with the victorious assailants on board drifted beyond possibility of return.[345] To these four captures by the enemy must be added the loss by accident of the "Caledonia"[346] and "Ariel," reported by Sinclair about this time. Perry's fleet was thus disappearing by driblets; but the command of the lake was not yet endangered, for there still remained, besides several of the prizes, the two principal vessels, "Lawrence" and "Niagara."[347]

With these Sinclair returned to the east of the lake, and endeavored to give support to the army at Fort Erie; but the violence of the weather and the insecurity of the anchorage on both shores, as the autumn drew on, not only prevented effectual co-operation, but seriously threatened the very existence of the fleet, upon which control of the water depended. In an attempt to go to Detroit for re-enforcements for Brown, a gale of wind was encountered which drifted the vessels back to Buffalo, where they had to anchor and lie close to a lee shore for two days, September 18 to 20, with topmasts and lower yards down, the sea breaking over them, and their cables chafing asunder on a rocky bottom. After this, Drummond having raised the siege of Fort Erie, the fleet retired to Erie and was laid up for the winter.

FOOTNOTES:

[266] Ante, pp. 118-121.
[267] Documentary History of the Campaign on the Niagara Frontier in 1814, by Ernest Cruikshank, Part I. p. 5.
[268] Captains' Letters, Feb. 24, March 4 and 29, 1814.
[269] Canadian Archives, C. 682, p. 32.
[270] Niles' Register, Feb. 5, 1814, vol. v. pp. 381, 383.
[271] Canadian Archives. C. 682, p. 90.

[272] Armstrong, Notices of the War of 1812, vol. ii. p. 213.
[273] Canadian Archives, C. 683, p. 10.
[274] Ibid., pp. 53, 61-64.
[275] Ibid., C. 682, p. 194.
[276] Niles' Register, April 9, 1814, vol. vi. p. 102.
[277] Captains' Letters, April 11, 1814.
[278] Writings of Madison, Edition of 1865, vol. ii. p. 413.
[279] Wilkinson's letter to a friend, April 9, 1814. Niles' Register, vol. vi. p. 166. His official report of the affair is given, p. 131.
[280] Yeo's Report, Canadian Archives, M. 389.6, p. 116.
[281] The armaments of the corresponding two British vessels were: "Prince Regent", thirty long 24-pounders, eight 68-pounder carronades, twenty 32-pounder carronades; "Princess Charlotte", twenty-four long 24-pounders, sixteen 32-pounder carronades. Canadian Archives, M. 389.6, p. 109.
[282] Captains' Letters.
[283] Canadian Archives, C. 683, p. 157.
[284] Woolsey's Report, forwarded by Chauncey June 2, is in Captains' Letters. It is given, together with several other papers bearing on the affair, in Niles' Register, vol. vi. pp. 242, 265-267. For Popham's Report, see Naval Chronicle, vol. xxxii. p. 167.
[285] Canadian Archives, C. 683, p. 225.
[286] Cruikshank's Documentary History, 1814, pp. 18-20.
[287] Writings of Madison (Edition of 1865), vol. iii. p. 403.
[288] Captains' Letters.
[289] Ibid.
[290] Yeo to Admiralty, May 30, 1815. Canadian Archives, M. 389.6, p. 310. For Chauncey's opinion to the same effect, see Captains' Letters, Nov. 5, 1814.
[291] Captains' Letters, June 15, 1814.
[292] Armstrong to Madison, April 31 (sic), 1814. Armstrong's Notices of War of 1812, vol. ii. p. 413.
[293] These official returns are taken by the present writer from Mr. Henry Adams' History of the United States.
[294] Cruikshank's Documentary History of the Niagara Campaign of 1814, p. 37.
[295] Cruikshank, Documentary History.
[296] Ibid., p. 4.
[297] Scott's Autobiography, vol. i. pp. 130-132.
[298] Cruikshank's Documentary History, p. 31.
[299] Niles' Register, vol. vii. p. 38.
[300] Captains' Letters.
[301] Secretary of the Navy to Chauncey, July 24, 1814, Secretary's Letters.

[302] Secretary to Chauncey, Aug. 3, 1814. Ibid.
[303] Ibid., Dec. 29, 1813.
[304] Chauncey to Brown, Aug. 10, 1814. Niles' Register, vol. vii. p. 38.
[305] August 27. Cruikshank's Documentary History, pp. 180-182. The whole letter has interest as conveying an adequate idea of the communications difficulty.
[306] This word is wanting; but the context evidently requires it.
[307] Cruikshank's Documentary History, 1814, pp. 58, 60.
[308] Cruikshank's Documentary History, 1814, p. 134.
[309] Captains' Letters. Aug. 19, 1814.
[310] Cruikshank's Documentary History, 1814, p. 191.
[311] Cruikshank's Documentary History, 1814, p. 68.
[312] Cruikshank's Documentary History, 1814. Riall to Drummond, July 20, 21, 22, pp. 75-81.
[313] Ibid., p. 87.
[314] Ibid., p. 78.
[315] "Sir James Yeo has not been nearer Sackett's Harbor than the Ducks since June 5." Captains' Letters, Aug. 19, 1814.
[316] Cruikshank's Documentary History, 1814, pp. 82, 84.
[317] Brown's Report of Lundy's Lane to Secretary of War, Aug. 7, 1814. Ibid., p. 97.
[318] Drummond's Report of the Engagement, July 27. Cruikshank, pp. 87-92.
[319] Brown's Report. Ibid., p. 99.
[320] Brown to Governor Tompkins, Aug. 1, 1814. Cruikshank, p. 103.
[321] Ibid., p. 207.
[322] Cruikshank's Documentary History, 1814, p. 131. Author's italics.
[323] The American account of this total is: killed, left on the field, 222; wounded, left on the field, 174; prisoners, 186. Total, 582. Two hundred supposed to be killed on the left flank (in the water) and permitted to float down the Niagara.
[324] Aug. 16. Cruikshank, pp. 146-147.
[325] Cruikshank's Documentary History, 1814, pp. 199, 200. Author's italics.
[326] Bathurst was Secretary of State for War and the Colonies.
[327] Cruikshank's Documentary History, 1814, pp. 229, 245.
[328] Ibid., p. 207. Brown to Tompkins, Sept. 20, 1814.
[329] Cruikshank's Documentary History, p. 205.
[330] An interesting indication of popular appreciation is found in the fact that two ships of the line laid down by Chauncey in or near Sackett's Harbor, in the winter of 1814-15, were named the "New Orleans" and the "Chippewa." Yeo after the peace returned to England by way of Sackett's and New York, and was then greatly surprised at the rapidity with which

these two vessels, which he took to be of one hundred and twenty guns each, (Canadian Archives, M. 389.6, p. 310), had been run up, to meet his "St. Lawrence" in the spring, had the war continued. The "New Orleans" remained on the Navy List, as a seventy-four, "on the sks," until 1882, when she was sold. For years she was the exception to a rule that ships of her class should bear the name of a state of the Union. The other square-rigged vessels on Ontario were sold, in May, 1825. (Records of the Bureau of Construction and Repair, Navy Department.)

[331] Izard to Secretary of War, May 7, 1814. Official Correspondence of the Department of War with Major-General Izard, 1814 and 1815.

[332] Izard Correspondence, p. 64.

[333] Izard Correspondence, p. 65.

[334] Ibid., p. 69.

[335] Ibid., p. 63.

[336] Izard Correspondence, p. 93.

[337] Ibid., p. 98.

[338] Oct. 6, 1814. Cruikshank's Documentary History, 1814, p. 240.

[339] Izard Correspondence, p. 102; Cruikshank, p. 242.

[340] Cruikshank, p. 240.

[341] Izard Correspondence, p. 103.

[342] Captains' Letters.

[343] Canadian Archives, C. 685, pp. 172-174.

[344] Ibid., M. 389.6, p. 222.

[345] The Reports of Captain Dobbs and the American lieutenant, Conkling, are in Cruikshank's Documentary History, p. 135.

[346] Captains' Letters, Sept. 12, 1814.

[347] This account of naval events on the upper lakes in 1814 has been summarized from Sinclair's despatches, Captains' Letters, May 2 to Nov. 11, 1814, and from certain captured British letters, which, with several of Sinclair's, were published in Niles' Register, vol. vii. and Supplement.

SEABOARD OPERATIONS IN 1814

Washington, Baltimore, And Maine

The British command of the water on Lake Ontario was obtained too late in the year 1814 to have any decisive effect upon their operations. Combined with their continued powerlessness on Lake Erie, this caused their campaign upon the northern frontier to be throughout defensive in character, as that of the Americans had been offensive. Drummond made no attempt in the winter to repeat the foray into New York of the previous December, although he and Prevost both considered that they had received provocation to retaliate, similar to that given at Newark the year before. The infliction of such vindictive punishment was by them thrown upon Warren's successor in the North Atlantic command, who responded in word and will even more heartily than in deed. The Champlain expedition, in September of this year, had indeed offensive purpose, but even there the object specified was the protection of Canada, by the destruction of the American naval establishments on the lake, as well as at Sackett's Harbor;[348] while the rapidity with which Prevost retreated, as soon as the British squadron was destroyed, demonstrated how profoundly otherwise the spirit of a simple defensive had possession of him, as it had also of the more positive and aggressive temperaments of Drummond and Yeo, and how essential naval control was in his eyes. In this general view he had the endorsement of the Duke of Wellington, when his attention was called to the subject, after the event.

Upon the seaboard it was otherwise. There the British campaign of 1814 much exceeded that of 1813 in offensive purpose and vigor, and in effect. This was due in part to the change in the naval commander-in-chief; in part also to the re-enforcements of troops which the end of the European war enabled the British Government to send to America. Early in the year 1813, Warren had represented to the Admiralty the impossibility of his giving personal supervision to the management of the West India stations, and had suggested devolving the responsibility upon the local admirals, leaving him simply the power to interfere when circumstances demanded.[349] The Admiralty then declined, alleging that the character of the war required unity of direction over the whole.[350] Later they changed their views. The North Atlantic, Jamaica, and Leeward Islands stations were made again severally independent, and Warren was notified that as the American command, thus reduced, was beneath the claims of an officer of his rank,— a full admiral,—a successor would be appointed.[351] Vice-Admiral Sir Alexander Cochrane accordingly relieved him, April 1, 1814; his charge embracing both the Atlantic and Gulf coasts. At the same period the Lakes Station, from Champlain to Superior inclusive, was constituted a separate command; Yeo's orders to this effect being dated the same day as Cochrane's, January 25, 1814.

Cochrane brought to his duties a certain acrimony of feeling, amounting almost to virulence. "I have it much at heart," he wrote Bathurst, "to give them a complete drubbing before peace is made, when I trust their northern limits will be circumscribed and the command of the Mississippi wrested from them." He expects thousands of slaves to join with their masters' horses, and looks forward to enlisting them. They are good horsemen; and, while agreeing with his lordship in deprecating a negro insurrection, he thinks such bodies will "be as good Cossacks as any in the Russian army, and more terrific to the Americans than any troops that can be brought forward." Washington and Baltimore are equally accessible, and may be either destroyed or laid under contribution.[352] These remarks, addressed to a prominent member of the Cabinet, are somewhat illuminative as to the formal purposes, as well as to the subsequent action, of British officials. The sea coast from Maine to Georgia, according to the season of the year, was made to feel the increasing activity and closeness of the British attacks; and these, though discursive and without apparent correlation of action, were evidently animated throughout by a common intention of bringing the war home to the experience of the people.

As a whole, the principal movements were meant to serve as a diversion, detaining on the Chesapeake and seaboard troops which might otherwise be sent to oppose the advance Prevost was ordered to make against Sackett's Harbor and Lake Champlain; for which purpose much the larger part of the re-enforcements from Europe had been sent to Canada. The instructions to the general detailed to command on the Atlantic specified as his object "a diversion on the coast of the United States in favor of the army employed in the defence of Upper and Lower Canada."[353] During the operations, "if in any descent you shall be enabled to take such a position as to threaten the inhabitants with the destruction of their property, you are hereby authorized to levy upon them contributions in return for your forbearance." Negroes might be enlisted, or carried away, though in no case as slaves. Taken in connection with the course subsequently pursued at Washington, such directions show an aim to inflict in many quarters suffering and deprivation, in order to impress popular consciousness with the sense of an irresistible and ubiquitous power incessantly at hand. Such moral impression, inclining those subject to it to desire peace, conduced also to the retention of local forces in the neighborhood where they belonged, and so furthered the intended diversion.

The general purpose of the British Government is further shown by some incidental mention. Gallatin, who at the time of Napoleon's abdication was in London, in connection with his duties on the Peace Commission, wrote two months afterwards: "To use their own language, they mean to inflict on America a chastisement which will teach her that war is not to be declared against Great Britain with impunity. This is a very general sentiment of the nation; and that such are the opinions of the ministry was strongly impressed on the mind of ―― by a late conversation he had with Lord Castlereagh. Admiral Warren also told Levett Harris, with whom he was intimate at St. Petersburg, that he was sorry to say the instructions given to his successor on the American station were very different from those under which he acted, and that he feared very serious injury would be done to America."[354]

Thus inspired, the coast warfare, although more active and efficient than the year before, and on a larger scale, continued in spirit and in execution essentially desultory and wasting. As it progressed, a peculiar bitterness was imparted by the liberal construction given by British officers to the word "retaliation." By strict derivation, and in wise application, the term summarizes the ancient retribution of like for like,—an eye for an eye, a tooth for a tooth; and to destroy three villages for one, as was done in retort for the burning of Newark, the inhabitants in each case being innocent of offence, was an excessive recourse to a punitive measure admittedly lawful. Two further instances of improper destruction by Americans had occurred during the campaign of 1814. Just before Sinclair sailed for Mackinac, he suggested to a Colonel Campbell, commanding the troops at Erie, that it would be a useful step to visit Long Point, on the opposite Canada shore, and destroy there a quantity of flour, and some mills which contributed materially to the support of the British forces on the Niagara peninsula.[355] This was effectively done, and did add seriously to Drummond's embarrassment; but Campbell went further and fired some private houses also, on the ground that the owners were British partisans and had had a share in the burning of Buffalo. A Court of Inquiry, of which

General Scott was president, justified the destruction of the mills, but condemned unreservedly that of the private houses.[356] Again, in Brown's advance upon Chippewa, some American "volunteers," despatched to the village of St. David's, burned there a number of dwellings. The commanding officer, Colonel Stone, was ordered summarily and immediately by Brown to retire from the expedition, as responsible for an act "contrary to the orders of the Government, and to those of the commanding general published to the army."[357]

In both these cases disavowal had been immediate; and it had been decisive also in that of Newark. The intent of the American Government was clear, and reasonable ultimate compensation might have been awaited; at least for a time. Prevost, however, being confined to the defensive all along his lines, communicated the fact of the destruction to Cochrane, calling upon him for the punishment which it was not in his own power then to inflict. Cochrane accordingly issued an order[358] to the ships under his command, to use measures of retaliation "against the cities of the United States, from the Saint Croix River to the southern boundary, near the St. Mary's River;" "to destroy and lay waste," so he notified the United States Government, "such towns and districts upon the coast as may be found assailable."[359] In the first heat of his wrath, he used in his order an expression, "and you will spare merely the lives of the unarmed inhabitants of the United States," which he afterwards asked Prevost to expunge, as it might be construed in a sense he never meant;[360] and he reported to his Government that he had sent private instructions to exercise forbearance toward the inhabitants.[361] It can easily be believed that, like many words spoken in passion, the phrase far outran his purposes; but it has significance and value as indicating the manner in which Americans had come to be regarded in Great Britain, through the experience of the period of peace and the recent years of war.

However the British Government might justify in terms the impressment of seamen from American ships, or the delay of atonement for such an insult as that of the Chesapeake, the nation which endured the same, content with reams of argument instead of blow for blow, had sunk beneath contempt as an inferior race, to be cowed and handled without gloves by those who felt themselves the masters. Nor was the matter bettered by the notorious fact that the interference with the freedom of American trade, which Great Britain herself admitted to be outside the law, had been borne unresisted because of the pecuniary stake involved. The impression thus produced was deepened by the confident boasts of immediate successes in Canada, made by leading members of the party which brought on the war; followed as these were by a display of inefficiency so ludicrous that opponents, as well native as foreign, did not hesitate to apply to it the word "imbecility." The American for a dozen years had been clubbed without giving evidence of rebellion, beyond words; now that he showed signs of restiveness, without corresponding evidence of power, he should feel the lash, and there need be no nicety in measuring punishment. Codrington, an officer of mark and character, who joined Cochrane at this time as chief of staff, used expressions which doubtless convey the average point of view of the British officer of that day: President Madison, "by letting his generals burn villages in Canada again, has been trying to excite terror; but as you may shortly see by the public exposition of the Admiral's orders, the terror and the suffering will probably be brought home to the doors of his own fellow citizens. I am fully convinced that this is the true way to end this Yankee war, whatever may be said in Parliament against it."[362]

It is the grievous fault of all retaliation, especially in the heat of war, that it rarely stays its hand at an equal measure, but almost invariably proceeds to an excess which provokes the other party to seek in turn to even the scale. The process tends to be unending; and it is to the honor of the United States Government that, though technically responsible for the acts of agents which it was too inefficient to control, it did not seriously entertain the purpose of resorting to this means, to vindicate the wrongs of its citizens at the expense of the subjects of its opponent. Happily, the external brutality of attitude which Cochrane's expression so aptly conveyed yielded for the most part to nobler instincts in the British officers. There was indeed much to condemn, much done that ought not to have been done; but even in the contemporary accounts it is quite possible to trace a certain rough humanity, a wish to deal equitably with individuals, for whom, regarded nationally, they professed no respect. Even in the marauding of the Chesapeake, the idea of compensation for value taken was not lost to view; and in general the usages of war, as to property exempt from destruction or appropriation, were respected, although not without the rude incidents certain to occur where atonement for acts of resistance, or the price paid for property taken, is fixed by the victor.

If retaliation upon any but the immediate culprit is ever permissible, which in national matters will scarcely be contested, it is logically just that it should fall first of all upon the capital, where the interests and honor of the nation are centred. There, if anywhere, the responsibility for the war and all its incidents is concrete in the representatives of the nation, executive and legislative, and in the public offices from which all overt acts are presumed to emanate. So it befell the United States. In the first six months of 1814, the warfare in the Chesapeake continued on the same general lines as in 1813; there having been the usual remission of activity during the winter, to resume again as milder weather drew on. The blockade of the bay was sustained, with force adequate to make it technically effective, although Baltimore boasted that several of her clipper schooners got to sea. On the part of the United States, Captain Gordon of the navy had been relieved in charge of the bay flotilla by Commodore Barney, of revolutionary and privateering renown. This local command, in conformity with the precedent at New York, and as was due to so distinguished an officer, was made independent of other branches of the naval service; the commodore being in immediate communication with the Navy Department. On April 17, he left Baltimore and proceeded down the bay with thirteen vessels; ten of them being large barges or galleys, propelled chiefly by oars, the others gunboats of the ordinary type. The headquarters of this little force became the Patuxent River, to which in the sequel it was in great measure confined; the superiority of the enemy precluding any enlarged sphere of activity. Its presence, however, was a provocation to the British, as being the only floating force in the bay capable of annoying them; the very existence of which was a challenge to their supremacy. To destroy it became therefore a dominant motive, which was utilized also to conceal to the last their purpose, tentative indeed throughout, to make a dash at Washington.

The Patuxent enters Chesapeake Bay from the north and west, sixty miles below Baltimore, and twenty above the mouth of the Potomac, to the general direction of which its own course in its lower part is parallel. For boats drawing no more than did Barney's it is navigable for forty miles from its mouth, to Pig Point; whence to Washington by land is but fifteen miles. A pursuit of the flotilla so far therefore brought pursuers within easy striking distance of the capital, provided that between them and it stood no obstacle adequate to impose delay until resistance could gather. It was impossible for such a pursuit to be made by the navy alone; for, inadequate as the militia was to the protection of the bay shore from raiding, it was quite competent to act in conjunction with Barney, when battling only against boats, which alone could follow him into lairs accessible to him, but not to even the smaller vessels of the enemy. Ships of the largest size could enter the river, but could ascend it only a little way. Up the Patuxent itself, or in its tributaries, the Americans therefore had always against the British Navy a refuge, in which they might be blockaded indeed, but could not be reached. For all these reasons, in order to destroy the flotilla, a body of troops must be used; a necessity which served to mask any ulterior design.

In the course of these operations, and in support of them, the British Navy had created a post at Tangier Island, ten miles across the bay, opposite the mouth of the Potomac.[363] Here they threw up fortifications, and established an advanced rendezvous. Between the island and the eastern shore, Tangier Sound gave sheltered anchorage. The position was in every way convenient, and strategically central. Being the junction of the water routes to Baltimore and Washington, it threatened both; while the narrowness of the Chesapeake at this point constituted the force there assembled an inner blockading line, well situated to move rapidly at short notice in any direction, up or down, to one side or the other. At such short distance from the Patuxent, Barney's movements were of course well under observation, as he at once experienced. On June 1, he left the river, apparently with a view to reaching the Potomac. Two schooners becalmed were then visible, and pursuit was made with the oars; but soon a large ship was seen under sail, despatching a number of barges to their assistance. A breeze springing up from southwest put the ship to windward, between the Potomac and the flotilla, which was obliged to return to the Patuxent, closely followed by the enemy. Some distant shots were exchanged, but Barney escaped, and for the time was suffered to remain undisturbed three miles from the bay; a 74-gun ship lying at the river's mouth, with barges plying continually about her. The departure of the British schooners, however, was construed to indicate a return with re-enforcements for an attack; an anticipation not disappointed. Two more vessels soon joined the seventy-four; one of them a brig. On their appearance Barney shifted his berth two miles further up, abreast St. Leonard's Creek. At daylight of June 9, one of the ships, the brig, two schooners, and fifteen rowing barges, were seen coming up with a fair wind. The flotilla then retreated two miles up the creek, formed there across it in line abreast, and awaited attack. The enemy's vessels could not follow; but their boats did, and a skirmish ensued which ended in the British retiring. Later in the day the attempt was renewed with no better success; and Barney claimed that, having followed the boats in their retreat, he had seriously disabled one of the large schooners anchored off the mouth of the creek to support the movement.

There is no doubt that the American gunboats were manfully and skilfully handled, and that the crews in this and subsequent encounters gained confidence and skill, the evidences of which were shown afterwards at Bladensburg, remaining the only alleviating remembrance from that day of disgrace. From Barney would be expected no less than the most that man can do, or example effect; but his pursuit was stopped by the ship and the brig, which stayed within the Patuxent. The flotilla continued inside the creek, two frigates lying off its mouth, until June 26, when an attack by the boats, in concert with a body of militia,—infantry and light artillery,—decided the enemy to move down the Patuxent. Barney took advantage of this to leave the creek and go up the river. We are informed by a journal of the day that the Government was by these affairs well satisfied with the ability of the flotilla to restrain the operations of the enemy within the waters of the Chesapeake, and had determined on a considerable increase to it. Nothing seems improbable of that Government; but, if this be true, it must have been easily satisfied. Barney had secured a longer line of retreat, up the river; but the situation was not materially changed. In either case, creek or river, there was but one way out, and that was closed. He could only abide the time when the enemy should see fit to come against him by land and by water, which would seal his fate.[364]

On June 2 there had sailed from Bordeaux for America a detachment from Wellington's army, twenty-five hundred strong, under Major-General Ross. It reached Bermuda July 25, and there was re-enforced by another battalion, increasing its strength to thirty-four hundred. On August 3 it left Bermuda, accompanied by several ships of war, and on the 15th passed in by the capes of the Chesapeake. Admiral Cochrane had preceded it by a few days, and was already lying there with his own ship and the division under Rear-Admiral Cockburn, who hitherto had been in immediate charge of operations in the bay. There were now assembled over twenty vessels of war, four of them of the line, with a large train of transports and store-ships. A battalion of seven hundred marines were next detailed for duty with the troops, the landing force being thus raised to over four thousand. The rendezvous at Tangier Island gave the Americans no certain clue to the ultimate object, for the reason already cited; and Cochrane designedly contributed to their distraction, by sending one squadron of frigates up the Potomac, and another up the Chesapeake above Baltimore.[365] On August 18 the main body of the expedition moved abreast the mouth of the Patuxent, and at noon of that day entered the river with a fair wind.

The purposes at this moment of the commanders of the army and navy, acting jointly, are succinctly stated by Cochrane in his report to the Admiralty: "Information from Rear-Admiral Cockburn that Commodore Barney, with the Potomac flotilla, had taken shelter at the head of the Patuxent, afforded a pretext for ascending that river to attack him near its source, above Pig Point, while the ultimate destination of the combined force was Washington, should it be found that the attempt might be made with any prospect of success."[366] August 19, the troops were landed at Benedict, twenty-five miles from the mouth of the river, and the following day began their upward march, flanked by a naval division of light vessels; the immediate objective being Barney's flotilla.

For the defence of the capital of the United States, throughout the region by which it might be approached, the Government had selected Brigadier-General Winder; the same who the year before had been captured at Stoney Creek, on the Niagara frontier, in Vincent's bold night attack. He was appointed July 2 to the command of a new military district, the tenth, which comprised "the state of Maryland, the District of Columbia, and that part of Virginia lying between the Potomac and the Rappahannock;"[367] in brief, Washington and Baltimore, with the ways converging upon them from the sea. This was just seven weeks before the enemy landed in the Patuxent; time enough, with reasonable antecedent preparation, or trained troops, to concert adequate resistance, as was shown by the British subsequent failure before Baltimore.

The conditions with which Winder had to contend are best stated in the terms of the Court of Inquiry[368] called to investigate his conduct, at the head of which sat General Winfield Scott. After fixing the date of his appointment, and ascertaining that he at once took every means in his power to put his district in a proper state of defence, the court found that on August 24, the day of the battle of Bladensburg, he "was enabled by great and unremitting exertions to bring into the field about five or six thousand men, all of whom except four hundred were militia; that he could not collect more than half his men until a day or two previously to the engagement, and six or seven hundred of them did not arrive until fifteen minutes before its commencement; ... that the officers commanding the troops were generally unknown to him, and but a very small number of them had enjoyed the benefit of military instruction or experience." So far from attributing censure, the Court found that, "taking into consideration the complicated difficulties and embarrassments under which he labored, he is entitled to no little commendation, notwithstanding the result; before the action he exhibited industry, zeal, and talent, and during its continuance a coolness, a promptitude, and a personal valor, highly honorable to himself." The finding of a court composed of competent experts, convened shortly after the events, must be received with respect. It is clear, however, that they here do not specify the particular professional merits of Winder's conduct of operations, but only the general hopelessness of success, owing to the antecedent conditions, not of his making, under which he was called to act, and which he strenuously exerted himself to meet. The blame for a mishap evidently and easily preventible still remains, and, though of course not expressed by the Court, is necessarily thrown back upon the Administration, and upon the party represented by it, which had held power for over twelve years past. A hostile corps of less than five thousand men had penetrated to the capital, through a well populated country, which was, to quote the Secretary of War, "covered with wood, and offering at every step strong positions for defence;"[369] but there were neither defences nor defenders.

The sequence of events which terminated in this humiliating manner is instructive. The Cabinet, which on June 7 had planned offensive operations in Canada, met on July 1 in another frame of mind, alarmed by the news from Europe, to plan for the defence of Washington and Baltimore. It will be remembered that it was now two years since war had been declared. In counting the force on which reliance might be placed for meeting a possible enemy, the Secretary of War thought he could assemble one thousand regulars, independent of artillerists in the forts.[2] The Secretary of the Navy could furnish one hundred and twenty marines, and the crews of Barney's flotilla, estimated at five hundred.[2] For the rest, dependence must be upon militia, a call for which was issued to the number of ninety-three thousand, five hundred.[370] Of these, fifteen thousand were assigned to Winder, as follows: From Virginia, two thousand; from Maryland, six thousand; from Pennsylvania, five thousand; from the District of Columbia, two thousand.[371] So ineffective were the administrative measures for bringing out this paper force of citizen soldiery, the efficiency of which the leaders of the party in power had been accustomed to vaunt, that Winder, after falling back from point to point before the enemy's advance, because only so might time be gained to get together the lagging contingents, could muster in the open ground at Bladensburg, five miles from the capital, where at last he made his stand, only the paltry five or six thousand stated by the court. On the morning of the battle the Secretary of War rode out to the field, with his colleagues in the Administration, and in reply to a question from the President said he had no suggestions to offer; "as it was between regulars and militia, the latter would be beaten."[372] The phrase was Winder's absolution; pronounced for the future, as for the past. The responsibility for there being no regulars did not rest with him, nor yet with the Secretary, but with the men who for a dozen years had sapped the military preparation of the nation.

Under the relative conditions of the opposing forces which have been stated, the progress of events was rapid. Probably few now realize that only a little over four days elapsed from the landing of the British to the burning of the Capitol. Their army advanced along the west bank of the Patuxent to Upper Marlborough, forty miles from the river's mouth. To this place, which was reached August 22, Ross continued in direct touch with the navy; and here at Pig Point, nearly abreast on the river, the American flotilla was cornered at last. Seeing the inevitable event, and to preserve his small but invaluable force of men, Barney had abandoned the boats on the 21st, leaving with each a half-dozen of her crew to destroy her at the last moment. This was done when the British next day approached; one only escaping the flames.

The city of Washington, now the goal of the enemy's effort, lies on the Potomac, between it and a tributary called the Eastern Branch. Upon the east bank of the latter, five or six miles from the junction of the two streams, is the village of Bladensburg. From Upper Marlborough, where the British had arrived, two roads led to Washington. One of these, the left going from Marlborough, crossed the Eastern Branch near its mouth; the other, less direct, passed through Bladensburg. Winder expected the British to advance by the former; and upon it Barney with the four hundred seamen remaining to him joined the army, at a place called Oldfields, seven miles from the capital. This route was militarily the more important, because from it branches were thrown off to the Potomac, up which the frigate squadron under Captain Gordon was proceeding, and had already passed the Kettle-bottoms, the most difficult bit of navigation in its path. The side roads would enable the invaders to reach and co-operate with this naval division; unless indeed Winder could make head against them. This he was not able to do; but he remained almost to the last moment in perplexing uncertainty whether they would strike for the capital, or for its principal defence on the Potomac, Fort Washington, ten miles lower down.[373]

For the obvious reasons named, because the doubts of their opponent facilitated their own movements by harassing his mind, as well as for the strategic advantage of a central line permitting movement in two directions at choice, the British advanced, as anticipated, by the left-hand road, and at nightfall of August 23 were encamped about three miles from the Americans. Here Winder covered a junction; for at Oldfields the road by which the British were advancing forked. One division led to Washington direct, crossing the Eastern Branch of the Potomac where it is broadest and deepest, near its mouth; the other passed it at Bladensburg. Winder feared to await the enemy, because of the disorder to which his inexperienced troops would be exposed by a night attack, causing possibly the loss of his artillery; the one arm in which he felt himself superior. He retired therefore during the night by the direct road, burning its bridge. This left open the way to Bladensburg, which the British next day followed, arriving at the village towards noon of the 24th. Contrary to Winder's instruction, the officer stationed there had withdrawn his troops across the stream, abandoning the place, and forming his line on the crest of some hills on the west bank. The impression which this position made upon the enemy was described by General Ross, as follows: "They were strongly posted on very commanding heights, formed in two lines, the advance occupying a fortified house, which with artillery covered the bridge over the Eastern Branch, across which the British troops had to pass. A broad and straight road, leading from the bridge to Washington, ran through the enemy's position, which was carefully defended by artillerymen and riflemen."[374] Allowing for the tendency to magnify difficulties overcome, the British would have had before them a difficult task, if opposed by men accustomed to mutual support and mutual reliance, with the thousand-fold increase of strength which comes with such habit and with the moral confidence it gives.

The American line had been formed before Winder came on the ground. It extended across the Washington road as described by Ross. A battery on the hill-top commanded the bridge, and was supported by a line of infantry on either side, with a second line in the rear. Fearing, however, that the enemy might cross the stream higher up, where it was fordable in many places, a regiment from the second line was reluctantly ordered forward to extend the left; and Winder, when he arrived, while approving this disposition, carried thither also some of the artillery which he had brought with him.[375] The anxiety of the Americans was therefore for their left. The British commander was eager to be done with his job, and to get back to his ships from a position militarily insecure. He had long been fighting

Napoleon's troops in the Spanish peninsula, and was not yet fully imbued with Drummond's conviction that with American militia liberties might be taken beyond the limit of ordinary military precaution. No time was spent looking for a ford, but the troops dashed straight for the bridge. The fire of the American artillery was excellent, and mowed down the head of the column; but the seasoned men persisted and forced their way across. At this moment Barney was coming up with his seamen, and at Winder's request brought his guns into line across the Washington road, facing the bridge. Soon after this, a few rockets passing close over the heads of the battalions supporting the batteries on the left started them running, much as a mule train may be stampeded by a night alarm. It was impossible to rally them. A part held for a short time; but when Winder attempted to retire them a little way, from a fire which had begun to annoy them, they also broke and fled.[376]

The American left was thus routed, but Barney's battery and its supporting infantry still held their ground. "During this period," reported the Commodore,—that is, while his guns were being brought into battery, and the remainder of his seamen and marines posted to support them,—"the engagement continued, the enemy advancing, and our own army retreating before them, apparently in much disorder. At length the enemy made his appearance on the main road, in force, in front of my battery, and on seeing us made a halt. I reserved our fire. In a few minutes the enemy again advanced, when I ordered an 18-pounder to be fired, which completely cleared the road; shortly after, a second and a third attempt was made by the enemy to come forward, but all were destroyed. They then crossed into an open field and attempted to flank our right; he was met there by three 12-pounders, the marines under Captain Miller, and my men, acting as infantry, and again was totally cut up. By this time not a vestige of the American army remained, except a body of five or six hundred, posted on a height on my right, from whom I expected much support from their fine situation."[377]

In this expectation Barney was disappointed. The enemy desisted from direct attack and worked gradually round towards his right flank and rear. As they thus moved, the guns of course were turned towards them; but a charge being made up the hill by a force not exceeding half that of its defenders, they also "to my great mortification made no resistance, giving a fire or two, and retired. Our ammunition was expended, and unfortunately the drivers of my ammunition wagons had gone off in the general panic." Barney himself, being wounded and unable to escape from loss of blood, was left a prisoner. Two of his officers were killed, and two wounded. The survivors stuck to him till he ordered them off the ground. Ross and Cockburn were brought to him, and greeted him with a marked respect and politeness; and he reported that, during the stay of the British in

Bladensburg, he was treated by all "like a brother," to use his own words.[378]

The character of this affair is sufficiently shown by the above outline narrative, re-enforced by the account of the losses sustained. Of the victors sixty-four were killed, one hundred and eighty-five wounded. The defeated, by the estimate of their superintending surgeon, had ten or twelve killed and forty wounded.[379] Such a disparity of injury is usual when the defendants are behind fortifications; but in this case of an open field, and a river to be crossed by the assailants, the evident significance is that the party attacked did not wait to contest the ground, once the enemy had gained the bridge. After that, not only was the rout complete, but, save for Barney's tenacity, there was almost no attempt at resistance. Ten pieces of cannon remained in the hands of the British. "The rapid flight of the enemy," reported General Ross, "and his knowledge of the country, precluded the possibility of many prisoners being taken."[380]

That night the British entered Washington. The Capitol, White House, and several public buildings were burned by them; the navy yard and vessels by the American authorities. Ross, accustomed to European warfare, did not feel Drummond's easiness concerning his position, which technically was most insecure as regarded his communications. On the evening of June 25 he withdrew rapidly, and on that of the 26th regained touch with the fleet in the Patuxent, after a separation of only four days. Cockburn remarked in his official report that there was no molestation of their retreat; "not a single musket having been fired."[381] It was the completion of the Administration's disgrace, unrelieved by any feature of credit save the gallant stand of Barney's four hundred.

The burning of Washington was the impressive culmination of the devastation to which the coast districts were everywhere exposed by the weakness of the country, while the battle of Bladensburg crowned the humiliation entailed upon the nation by the demagogic prejudices in favor of untrained patriotism, as supplying all defects for ordinary service in the field. In the defenders of Bladensburg was realized Jefferson's ideal of a citizen soldiery,[382] unskilled, but strong in their love of home, flying to arms to oppose an invader; and they had every inspiring incentive to tenacity, for they, and they only, stood between the enemy and the centre and heart of national life. The position they occupied, though unfortified, had many natural advantages; while the enemy had to cross a river which, while in part fordable, was nevertheless an obstacle to rapid action, especially when confronted by the superior artillery the Americans had. The result has been told; but only when contrasted with the contemporary fight at Lundy's Lane is Bladensburg rightly appreciated. Occurring precisely a month apart, and with men of the same race, they illustrate exactly the difference in military value between crude material and finished product.

Coincident with the capture of Washington, a little British squadron—two frigates and five smaller vessels—ascended the Potomac. Fort Washington, a dozen miles below the capital, was abandoned August 27 by the officer in charge, removing the only obstacle due to the foresight of the Government. He was afterwards cashiered by sentence of court martial. On the 29th, Captain Gordon, the senior officer, anchored his force before Alexandria, of which he kept possession for three days. Upon withdrawing, he carried away all the merchantmen that were seaworthy, having loaded them with merchandise awaiting exportation. Energetic efforts were made by Captains Rodgers, Perry, and Porter, of the American Navy, to molest the enemy's retirement by such means as could be extemporized; but both ships and prizes escaped, the only loss being in life: seven killed and forty-five wounded.

After the burning of Washington, the British main fleet and army moved up the Chesapeake against Baltimore, which would undoubtedly have undergone the lot of Alexandria, in a contribution laid upon shipping and merchandise. The attack, however, was successfully met. The respite afforded by the expedition against Washington had been improved by the citizens to interpose earthworks on the hills before the city. This local precaution saved the place. In the field the militia behaved better than at Bladensburg, but showed, nevertheless, the unsteadiness of raw men. To harass the British advance a body of riflemen had been posted well forward, and a shot from these mortally wounded General Ross; but, "imagine my chagrin, when I perceived the whole corps falling back upon my main position, having too credulously listened to groundless information that the enemy was landing on Back River to cut them off."[383]

The British approached along the narrow strip of land between the Patapsco and Back rivers. The American general, Stricker, had judiciously selected for his line of defence a neck, where inlets from both streams narrowed the ground to half a mile. His flanks were thus protected, but the water on the left giving better indication of being fordable, the British directed there the weight of the assault. To meet this, Stricker drew up a regiment to the rear of his main line, and at right angles, the volleys from which should sweep the inlet. When the enemy's attack developed, this regiment "delivered one random fire," and then broke and fled; "totally forgetful of the honor of the brigade, and of its own reputation," to use Stricker's words.[384] This flight carried along part of the left flank proper. The remainder of the line held for a time, and then retired without awaiting the hostile bayonet. The American report gives the impression of an orderly retreat; a British participant, who admits that the ground was well chosen, and that the line held until within twenty yards, wrote that after that he never witnessed a more complete rout. The invaders then approached the city, but upon viewing the works of defence, and learning that the fleet would not be able to co-operate, owing to vessels sunk across the channel, the commanding officer decided that success would not repay the loss necessary to achieve it. Fleet and army then withdrew.

The attacks on Washington and Baltimore, the seizure of Alexandria, and the general conduct of operations in the Chesapeake, belong strictly to the punitive purpose which dictated British measures upon the seaboard. Similar action extended through Long Island Sound, and to the eastward, where alarm in all quarters was maintained by the general enterprise of the enemy, and by specific injury in various places. "The Government has declared war against the most powerful maritime nation," wrote the Governor of Massachusetts to the legislature, "and we are disappointed in our expectations of national defence. But though we may be convinced that the war was unnecessary and unjust, and has been prosecuted without any useful or practicable object with the inhabitants of Canada, while our seacoast has been left almost defenceless, yet I presume there will be no doubt of our right to defend our possessions against any hostile attack by which their destruction is menaced." "The eastern coast," reports a journal of the time, "is much vexed by the enemy. Having destroyed a great portion of the coasting craft, they seem determined to enter the little outports and villages, and burn everything that floats."[385] On April 7, six British barges ascended the Connecticut River eight miles, to Pettipaug, where they burned twenty-odd sea-going vessels.[386] On June 13, at Wareham, Massachusetts, a similar expedition entered and destroyed sixteen.[387] These were somewhat large instances of an action everywhere going on, inflicting indirectly incalculably more injury than even the direct loss suffered; the whole being with a view to bring the meaning of war close home to the consciousness of the American people. They were to be made to realize the power of the enemy and their own helplessness.

An attempt looking to more permanent results was made during the summer upon the coast of Maine. The northward projection of that state, then known as the District of Maine,[388] intervened between the British provinces of Lower Canada and New Brunswick, and imposed a long détour upon the line of communications between Quebec and Halifax, the two most important military posts in British North America. This inconvenience could not be remedied unless the land in question were brought into British possession; and when the end of the war in Europe gave prospect of a vigorous offensive from the side of Canada, the British ministry formulated the purpose of demanding there a rectification of frontier. The object in this case being acquisition, not punishment, conciliation of the inhabitants was to be practised; in place of the retaliatory action prescribed for the sea-coast elsewhere.

Moose Island, in Passamaquoddy Bay, though held by the United States, was claimed by Great Britain to have been always within the boundary line of New Brunswick. It was seized July 11, 1814; protection being promised to persons and property. In August, General Sherbrooke, the Governor of Nova Scotia, received orders "to occupy so much of the District of Maine as shall insure an uninterrupted communication between Halifax and Quebec."[389] His orders being discretional as to method, he decided that with the force available he would best comply by taking possession of Machias and the Penobscot River.[390] On September 1, a combined naval and army expedition appeared at the mouth of the Penobscot, before Castine, which was quickly abandoned. A few days before, the United States frigate "Adams," Captain Charles Morris, returning from a cruise, had run ashore upon Isle au Haut, and in consequence of the injuries received had been compelled to make a harbor in the river. She was then at Hampden, thirty miles up. A detachment of seamen and soldiers was sent against her. Her guns had been landed, and placed in battery for her defence, and militia had gathered for the support necessary to artillery so situated; but they proved unreliable, and upon their retreat nothing was left but to fire the ship.[391] This was done, the crew escaping. The British penetrated as far as Bangor, seized a number of merchant vessels, and subsequently went to Machias, where they captured the fort with twenty-five cannon. Sherbrooke then returned with the most of his force to Halifax, whence he issued a voluminous proclamation[392] to the effect that he had taken possession of all the country between the Penobscot and New Brunswick; and promised protection to the inhabitants, if they behaved themselves accordingly. Two regiments were left at Castine, with transports to remove them in case of attack by superior numbers. This burlesque of occupation, "one foot on shore, and one on sea," was advanced by the British ministry as a reason justifying the demand for cession of the desired territory to the northward. Wellington, when called into counsel concerning American affairs, said derisively that an officer might as well claim sovereignty over the ground on which he had posted his pickets. The British force remained undisturbed, however, to the end of the war. Amicable relations were established with the inhabitants, and a brisk contraband trade throve with Nova Scotia. It is even said that the news of peace was unwelcome in the place. It was not evacuated until April 27, 1815.[393]

FOOTNOTES:

[348] "Some Account of the Life of Sir George Prevost." London, 1823, pp. 136, 137. The author has not been able to find the despatch of June 3, 1814, there quoted.
[349] Warren to Croker, Feb. 26, 1813. Admiralty In-Letters MSS.
[350] Croker to Warren, March 20, 1813. Admiralty Out-Letters.
[351] Warren to Croker, Jan. 28, 1814. Canadian Archives MSS.

[352] Cochrane to Bathurst, July 14, 1814. War Office In-Letters MSS.

[353] Bathurst's Instructions to the officer in command of the troops detached from the Gironde. May 20, 1814. From copy sent to Cochrane. Admiralty In-Letters, from Secretary of State.

[354] Gallatin to Monroe, London, June 13, 1814. Adams' Writings of Gallatin, vol. i. p. 627.

[355] Sinclair, Erie, May 13, 1814. Captains' Letters.

[356] Cruikshank's Documentary History of the Campaign of 1814, p. 18.

[357] Ibid., p. 74.

[358] Cruikshank's Documentary History, pp. 414, 415.

[359] American State Papers, Foreign Relations, vol. iii. pp. 693, 694.

[360] Cochrane to Prevost, July 26, 1814. Canadian Archives MSS., C. 684, p. 231.

[361] Report on Canadian Archives, 1896, p. 54.

[362] Life of Sir Edward Codrington, vol. i. p. 313.

[363] See Map of Chesapeake Bay, ante, p. 156.

[364] This account of Barney's movements is summarized from his letters, and others, published in Niles' Register, vol. vi. pp. 244, 268, 300.

[365] Report of Admiral Cochrane, Naval Chronicle, vol. xxxii. p. 342.

[366] Report of Admiral Cochrane, Naval Chronicle, vol. xxxii. p. 342.

[367] American State Papers, Military Affairs, vol. i. p. 524.

[368] The finding of the Court of Inquiry was published in Niles' Register for Feb. 25, 1815, from the official paper, the National Intelligencer. Niles, vol. vii. p. 410.

[369] Report of Secretary Armstrong to a Committee of the House of Representatives. American State Papers, Military Affairs, vol. i. p. 526.

[370] Ibid., pp. 538, 540, 524.

[371] Ibid., p. 524.

[372] Works of Madison (Ed. 1865), vol. iii. p. 422.

[373] Winder's Narrative. American State Papers, Military Affairs, vol. i pp. 552-560.

[374] Ross's Despatch, Aug. 30, 1814. Naval Chronicle, vol. xxxii. p. 338.

[375] Narrative of Monroe, the Secretary of State. American State Papers, Military Affairs, vol. i. p. 536.

[376] Winder's Narrative.

[377] Barney's Report, Aug. 29, 1814. State Papers, Military Affairs, vol. i. p. 579.

[378] Barney's Report.

[379] American State Papers, Military Affairs, vol. i. p. 530.

[380] Ross's Despatch.

[381] Report of Rear-Admiral Cockburn, Naval Chronicle, vol. xxxii. p. 345.

[382] Ante, p. 213.

[383] Report of Brigadier-General Stricker of the Maryland militia. Niles'

Register, vol. vii. pp. 27, 28.

[384] Ibid.

[385] Niles' Register, vol. vi. p. 317.

[386] Ibid., pp. 118, 133, 222.

[387] Ibid., p. 317.

[388] Maine was then attached politically to Massachusetts.

[389] Sherbrooke to Prevost, Aug. 2, 1814. Canadian Archives MSS., C. 685, p. 28.

[390] Sherbrooke to Prevost, Aug. 24, 1814. Ibid., p. 147.

[391] Morris' reports (Captains' Letters, Navy Dept.) are published in Niles' Register, vol. vii. pp. 62, 63; and Supplement, p. 136.

[392] Sept. 21, 1814. Niles' Register, vol. vii. p. 117.

[393] Ibid., p. 347, and vol. viii. pp. 13, 214.

LAKE CHAMPLAIN AND NEW ORLEANS

General Brown's retirement within the lines of Fort Erie, July 26, 1814, may be taken as marking the definitive abandonment by the United States of the offensive on the Canada frontier. The opportunities of two years had been wasted by inefficiency of force and misdirection of effort. It was generally recognized by thoughtful men that the war had now become one of defence against a greatly superior enemy, disembarrassed of the other foe which had hitherto engaged his attention, and imbued with ideas of conquest, or at least of extorting territorial cession for specific purposes. While Brown was campaigning, the re-enforcements were rapidly arriving which were to enable the British to assume the aggressive; although, in the absence of naval preponderance on the lakes, their numbers were not sufficient to compel the rectification of frontier by surrender of territory which the British Government now desired. Lord Castlereagh, Secretary for Foreign Affairs, and the leading representative of the aims of the Cabinet, wrote in his instructions to the Peace Commissioners, August 14, 1814: "The views of the Government are strictly defensive. Territory as such is by no means their object; but, as the weaker Power in North America, Great Britain considers itself entitled to claim the use of the lakes as a military barrier."[394] The declaration of war by the United States was regarded by most Englishmen as a wanton endeavor to overthrow their immemorial right to the services of their seamen, wherever found; and consequently the invasion of Canada had been an iniquitous attempt to effect annexation under cover of an indefensible pretext. To guard against the renewal of such, the lakes must be made British waters, to which the American flag should have only commercial access. Dominion south of the lakes would not be exacted, "provided the American Government will stipulate not to preserve or construct any fortifications upon or within a limited distance of

241

their shores." "On the side of Lower Canada there should be such a line of demarcation as may establish a direct communication between Quebec and Halifax."[395]
Such were the political and military projects with which the British ministry entered upon the summer campaign of 1814 in Canada. Luckily, although Napoleon had fallen, conditions in Europe were still too unsettled and volcanic to permit Great Britain seriously to weaken her material force there. Two weeks later Castlereagh wrote to the Prime Minister: "Are we prepared to continue the war for territorial arrangements?" "Is it desirable to take the chances of the campaign, and then be governed by circumstances?"[396] The last sentence defines the policy actually followed; and the chances went definitely against it when Macdonough destroyed the British fleet on Lake Champlain. Except at Baltimore and New Orleans,—mere defensive successes,—nothing but calamity befell the American arms. To the battle of Lake Champlain it was owing that the British occupancy of United States soil at the end of the year was such that the Duke of Wellington advised that no claim for territorial cession could be considered to exist, and that the basis of uti possidetis, upon which it was proposed to treat, was untenable.[397] The earnestness of the Government, however, in seeking the changes specified, is indicated by the proposition seriously made to the Duke to take the command in America.
Owing to the military conditions hitherto existing on the American continent, the power to take the offensive throughout the lake frontier had rested with the United States Government; and the direction given by this to its efforts had left Lake Champlain practically out of consideration. Sir George Prevost, being thrown on the defensive, could only conform to the initiative of his adversary. For these reasons, whatever transactions took place in this quarter up to the summer of 1814 were in characteristic simply episodes; an epithet which applies accurately to the more formidable, but brief, operations here in 1814, as also to those in Louisiana. Whatever intention underlay either attempt, they were in matter of fact almost without any relations of antecedent or consequent. They stood by themselves, and not only may, but should, be so considered. Prior to them, contemporary reference to Lake Champlain, or to Louisiana, is both rare and casual. For this reason, mention of earlier occurrences in either of these quarters has heretofore been deferred, as irrelevant and intrusive if introduced among other events, with which they coincided in time, but had no further connection. A brief narrative of them will now be presented, as a necessary introduction to the much more important incidents of 1814.
At the beginning of hostilities the balance of naval power on Lake Champlain rested with the United States, and so continued until June, 1813. The force on each side was small to triviality, nor did either make any serious attempt to obtain a marked preponderance. The Americans had,

however, three armed sloops, the "President," "Growler," and "Eagle," to which the British could oppose only one. Both parties had also a few small gunboats and rowing galleys, in the number of which the superiority lay with the British. Under these relative conditions the Americans ranged the lake proper at will; the enemy maintaining his force in the lower narrows, at Isle aux Noix, which was made a fortified station.

On June 1, 1813, a detachment of British boats, coming up the lake, passed the boundary line and fired upon some small American craft. The "Eagle" and "Growler," being then at Plattsburg, started in pursuit on the 2d, and by dark had entered some distance within the narrows, where they anchored. The following morning they sighted three of the enemy's gunboats and chased them with a fair south wind; but, being by this means led too far, they became entangled in a place where manœuvring was difficult. The officers of the royal navy designated for service on Lake Champlain had not yet arrived, and the flotilla was at the disposition of the commanding army officer at Isle aux Noix. Only one sloop being visible at first to the garrison, he sent out against her the three gunboats; but when the second appeared he landed a number of men on each bank, who took up a position to rake the vessels. The action which followed lasted three hours. The circumstances were disadvantageous to the Americans; but the fair wind with which they had entered was ahead for return, and to beat back was impossible in so narrow a channel. The "Eagle" received a raking shot, and had to be run ashore to avoid sinking. Both then surrendered, and the "Eagle" was afterwards raised. The two prizes were taken into the British service; and as this occurrence followed immediately after the capture of the "Chesapeake" by the "Shannon," they were called "Broke" and "Shannon." These names afterwards were changed, apparently by Admiralty order, to "Chub" and "Finch," under which they took part in the battle of Lake Champlain, where they were recaptured.

Although not built for war, but simply purchased vessels of not over one hundred tons, this loss was serious; for by it superiority on the lake passed to the British, and with some fluctuation so remained for a twelvemonth,— till May, 1814. They were still too deficient in men to profit at once by their success; the difficulty of recruiting in Canada being as great as in the United States, and for very similar reasons. "It is impossible to enlist seamen in Quebec for the lakes, as merchants are giving twenty-five to thirty guineas for the run to England. Recruits desert as soon as they receive the bounty."[398] After some correspondence, Captain Everard, of the sloop of war "Wasp," then lying at Quebec, consented to leave his ship, go with a large part of her crew to Champlain, man the captured sloops, and raid the American stations on the lake. A body of troops being embarked, the flotilla left Isle aux Noix July 29. On the 30th they came to Plattsburg, destroyed there the public buildings, with the barracks at Saranac, and brought off a quantity of stores. A detachment was sent to Champlain Town, and a landing made also at Swanton in Vermont, where similar devastation was inflicted on public property. Thence they went up the lake to Burlington, where Macdonough, who was alarmingly short of seamen since the capture of the "Eagle" and "Growler," had to submit to seeing himself defied by vessels lately his own. After seizing a few more small lake craft, Everard on August 3 hastened back, anxious to regain his own ship and resume the regular duties, for abandoning which he had no authority save his own. The step he had taken was hardly to be anticipated from a junior officer, commanding a ship on sea service so remote from the scene of the proposed operation; and the rapidity of his action took the Americans quite by surprise, for there had been no previous indication of activity. As soon as Macdonough heard of his arrival at Isle aux Noix, he wrote for re-enforcements, but it was too late. His letter did not reach New York till the British had come and gone.[399]

Upon Everard's return both he and Captain Pring, of the royal navy, who had been with him during the foray and thenceforth remained attached to the fortunes of the Champlain flotilla, recommended the building of a large brig of war and two gunboats, in order to preserve upon the lake the supremacy they had just asserted in act. With the material at hand, they said, these vessels could all be afloat within eight weeks after their keels were laid.[400] This suggestion appears to have been acted upon; for in the following March it was reported that there were building at St. John's a brig to carry twenty guns, a schooner of eighteen, and twelve 2-gun galleys. However, the Americans also were by this time building, and at the crucial moment came out a very little ahead in point of readiness.

Nothing further of consequence occurred during 1813. After the British departed, Macdonough received a re-enforcement of men. He then went in person with such vessels as he had to the foot of the lake, taking station at Plattsburg, and advancing at times to the boundary line, twenty-five miles below. The enemy occasionally showed themselves, but were apparently indisposed to action in their then state of forwardness. Later the American flotilla retired up the lake to Otter Creek in Vermont, where, on April 11, 1814, was launched the ship "Saratoga," which carried Macdonough's pendant in the battle five months afterwards. On May 10, Pring, hoping to destroy the American vessels before ready for service, made another inroad with his squadron, consisting now of the new brig, called the "Linnet," five armed sloops, and thirteen galleys. On the 14th he was off Otter Creek and attacked; but batteries established on shore compelled him to retire. Macdonough in his report of this transaction mentions only eight galleys, with a bomb vessel, as the number of the enemy engaged. The new brig was probably considered too essential to naval control to be risked against shore guns; a decision scarcely to be contested, although Prevost seems to have been dissatisfied as usual with the exertions of the navy. The American force at this time completed, or approaching completion, was, besides the "Saratoga," one schooner, three sloops,[401] and ten gunboats or galleys. Of the sloops one only, the "Preble," appears to have been serviceable. The "President" and another called the "Montgomery" were not in the fight at Plattsburg; where Macdonough certainly needed every gun he could command. A brig of twenty guns, called the "Eagle," was subsequently laid down and launched in time for the action. Prevost reported at this period that a new ship was building at Isle aux Noix, which would make the British force equal to the American.

Before the end of May, 1814, Macdonough's fleet was ready, except the "Eagle"; and on the 29th he was off Plattsburg, with the "Saratoga," the schooner "Ticonderoga," the sloop "Preble," and ten galleys. The command of the lake thus established permitted the transfer of troops and stores, before locked up in Burlington. The "Saratoga" carried twenty-six guns; of which eight were long 24-pounders, the others carronades, six 42-pounders, and twelve 32's. She was so much superior to the "Linnet," which had only sixteen guns, long 12-pounders, that the incontestable supremacy remained with the Americans, and it was impossible for the British squadron to show itself at all until their new ship was completed. She was launched August 25,[402] and called the "Confiance."[403] The name excited some derision after her defeat and capture, but seems to have had no more arrogant origin than the affectionate recollection of the Commander-in-Chief on the lakes, Sir James Yeo, for the vessel which he had first and long commanded, to which he had been promoted for distinguished gallantry in winning her, and in which he finally reached post-rank. The new "Confiance," from which doubtless much was hoped, was her namesake. She was to carry twenty-seven 24-pounders. One of these, being on a pivot, fought on either side of the ship; thus giving her fourteen of these guns for each broadside. In addition, she had ten carronades, four of them 32-pounders, and six 24's.

On July 12, 1814, Prevost had reported the arrival at Montreal of the first of four brigades from Wellington's Peninsular Army. These had sailed from Bordeaux at the same period as the one destined for the Atlantic coast operations, under General Ross, already related. He acknowledged also the receipt of instructions, prescribing the character of his operations, which he had anxiously requested the year before. Among these instructions were "to give immediate protection to his Majesty's possessions in America," by "the entire destruction of Sackett's Harbor, and of the naval establishments on Lake Erie and Lake Champlain."[404] They will be obeyed, he wrote, as soon as the whole force shall have arrived; but defensive measures only will be practicable, until the complete command of Lakes Ontario and Champlain shall be obtained, which cannot be expected before September.[405] The statement was perfectly correct. The command of these lakes was absolutely essential to both parties to the war, if intending to maintain operations in their neighborhood.

On August 14, Prevost reported home that the troops from Bordeaux had all arrived, and, with the exception of a brigade destined for Kingston, would be at their points of formation by the 25th; at which date his returns show that he had under his general command, in Upper and Lower Canada, exclusive of officers, twenty-nine thousand four hundred and thirty-seven men. All these were British regulars, with the exception of four thousand seven hundred and six; of which last, two thousand two hundred belonged to "foreign" regiments, and the remainder to provincial corps. Of this total, from eleven thousand to fourteen thousand accompanied him in his march to Plattsburg. Under the same date he reported that the "Confiance" could not be ready before September 15; for which time had he patiently waited, he would at least have better deserved success. His decision as to his line of advance was determined by a singular consideration, deeply mortifying to American recollection, but which must be mentioned because of its historical interest, as an incidental indication of the slow progress of the people of the United States towards national sentiment. "Vermont has shown a disinclination to the war, and, as it is sending in specie and provisions, I will confine offensive operations to the west side of Lake Champlain."[406] Three weeks later he writes again, "Two thirds of the army are supplied with beef by American contractors, principally of Vermont and New York."[407]

That this was no slander was indignantly confirmed by a citizen of Vermont, who wrote to General Izard, June 27, "Droves of cattle are continually passing from the northern parts of this state into Canada for the British." Izard, in forwarding the letter, said: "This confirms a fact not only disgraceful to our countrymen but seriously detrimental to the public interest. From the St. Lawrence to the ocean an open disregard prevails for the laws prohibiting intercourse with the enemy. The road to St. Regis [New York] is covered with droves of cattle, and the river with rafts destined for the enemy. On the eastern side of Lake Champlain the high roads are insufficient for the cattle pouring into Canada. Like herds of buffaloes they press through the forests, making paths for themselves. Were it not for these supplies, the British forces in Canada would soon be suffering from famine."[408] The British commissary at Prescott wrote, June 19, 1814, "I have contracted with a Yankee magistrate to furnish this post with fresh beef. A major came with him to make the agreement; but, as he was foreman of the grand jury of the court in which the Government prosecutes the magistrates for high treason and smuggling, he turned his back and would not see the paper signed."[409] More vital still in its treason to the interests of the country, Commodore Macdonough reported officially, June 29, that one of his officers had seized two spars, supposed from their size to be for the fore and mizzen masts of the "Confiance," on the way to Canada, near the lines, under the management of citizens of the United States; and eight days later there were intercepted four others, which from their dimensions were fitted for her mainmast and three topmasts.[410] By this means the British ship was to be enabled to sail for the attack on the American fleet, and by this only; for to drag spars of that weight up the rapids of the Richelieu, or over the rough intervening country, meant at least unendurable delay. "The turpitude of many of our citizens in this part of the country," wrote Macdonough, "furnishes the enemy with every information he wants."[411]

On August 29, four days after Prevost's divisions were expected to be assembled at their designated rendezvous, Izard, in the face of the storm gathering before him, started with his four thousand men from Plattsburg for Sackett's Harbor, in obedience to the intimation of the War Department, which he accepted as orders. Brigadier-General Macomb was left to hold the works about Plattsburg with a force which he stated did not exceed fifteen hundred effectives.[412] His own brigade having been broken up to strengthen Izard's division, none of this force was organized, except four companies of one regiment. The remainder were convalescents, or recruits of new regiments; soldiers as yet only in name, and without the constituted regimental framework, incorporation into which so much facilitates the transition from the recruit to the veteran. On September 4 seven hundred militia from the neighborhood joined, in response to a call from Macomb; and before the final action of the 11th other militia from New York, and volunteers from Vermont, across the lake, kept pouring in from all quarters, in encouraging contrast to their fellow citizens who were making money by abetting the enemy.

Prevost's army, which had been assembled along the frontier of Lower Canada, from the Richelieu River to the St. Lawrence, began its forward march August 31; the leading brigade entering the State of New York, and encamping that night at Champlain Town, a short distance south of the boundary. By September 4 the whole body had reached to the village of Chazy, twenty-five miles from Plattsburg. Thus far, to the mouth of the Little Chazy River, where the supplies of the army were to be landed, no opposition was experienced. The American squadron waiting on the defensive at Plattsburg, the left flank of the British received constant support from their flotilla of gunboats and galleys under the command of Captain Pring, who seized also the American Island La Motte, in the narrows of the lake, abreast the Little Chazy. The following day, September 5, delays began to be met through the trees felled and bridges broken by Macomb's orders. On the 6th there was some skirmishing between the advanced guards; but the American militia "could not be prevailed on to stand, notwithstanding the exertions of their officers, although the fields were divided by strong stone walls, and they were told that the enemy could not possibly cut them off."[413] Deprived of this support, the small body of regulars could do little, and the British Peninsulars pushed on contemptuously, and almost silently. "They never deployed in their whole march," reported Macomb, "always pressing on in column." That evening they entered Plattsburg. Macomb retreated across the Saranac, which divided the town. He removed from the bridges their planking, which was used to form breastworks to dispute any attempt to force a passage, and then retired to the works previously prepared by Izard. These were on the bluffs on the south side of the Saranac, overlooking the bay, and covering the peninsula embraced between the lake and the river.

From the 7th to the 11th, the day of the battle, the British were employed in preparations for battering the forts, preliminary to an assault, and there was constant skirmishing at the bridges and fords. Macomb utilized the same time to strengthen his works, aided by the numbers of militia continually arriving, who labored night and day with great spirit. Prevost's purposes and actions were dominated by the urgency of haste, owing to the lateness of the season; and this motive co-operated with a certain captiousness of temper to precipitate him now into a grave error of judgment and of conduct. At Plattsburg he found the small American army intrenched behind a fordable river, the bridges of which had been made useless; and in the bay lay the American squadron, anchored with a view to defence. The two were not strictly in co-operation, in their present position. Tactically, they for the moment contributed little to each other's support; for the reason that the position chosen judiciously by Macdonough for the defence of the bay was too far from the works of the army to receive—or to give—assistance with the guns of that day. The squadron was a little over a mile from the army. It could not remain there, if the British got possession of the works, for it would be within range of injury at long shot; but in an engagement between the hostile fleets the bluffs could have no share, no matter which party held them, for the fire would be as dangerous to friend as to foe.

The question of probability, that the American squadron was within long gunshot of the shore batteries, is crucial, for upon it would depend the ultimate military judgment upon the management of Sir George Prevost. That he felt this is evident by letters addressed on his behalf to Macdonough; by A.W. Cochran, a lawyer of Quebec, to whom Prevost, after his recall to England for trial, left the charge of collecting testimony, and by Cadwalader Colden of New York.[414] Both inquire specifically as to this distance, Colden particularizing that "it would be all important to learn that the American squadron were during the engagement beyond the effectual range of the batteries." To Colden, Macdonough replied guardedly, "It is my opinion that our squadron was anchored one mile and a half from the batteries." The answer to Cochran has not been found; but on the back of the letter from him the Commodore sketched his recollection of the situation, which is here reproduced. Without insisting unduly on the precision of such a piece, it seems clear that he thought his squadron but little more than half way towards the other side of the bay. Cumberland Head being by survey two miles from the batteries, it would follow that the vessels were a little over a mile from them. This inference is adopted as more dependable than the estimate, "a mile and a half." Such eye reckoning is notoriously uncertain; and this seemingly was made by recollection, not contemporaneously.[415]

The 24- and 32-pounder long gun of that day ranged a sea mile and a half, with an elevation of less than fifteen degrees.[416] They could therefore annoy a squadron at or within that distance. The question is not of best fighting range. It is whether a number of light built and light draught vessels could hold their ground under such a cannonade, knowing that a hostile squadron awaited them without. Even at such random range, a disabling shot in hull or spars must be expected. At whatever risk, departure is enforced.

Tracing from pencil sketch of Battle of L. Champlain, made by Com. Macdonough on back of a letter of inquiry, addressed to him within a year of the action.

To a similar letter from Colden, General Macomb replied that he did not think the squadron within range. There is also a statement in Niles' Register[417] that several British officers visited Macomb at Plattsburg, and at their request experiments were made, presumably trial shots, to ascertain whether the guns of the forts could have annoyed the American squadron. It was found they could not. Macomb's opinion may have rested upon this, and the conclusion may be just; but it is open to remark that, as the squadron was not then there, its assumed position depended upon memory,—like Macdonough's sketch. Macomb said further, that "a fruitless attempt was made during the action to elevate the guns so as to bear on the enemy; but none were fired, all being convinced that the vessels were beyond their reach." The worth of this conviction is shown by the next remark, which he repeated under date of August 1, 1815.[418] "This opinion was strengthened by observations on the actual range of the guns of the 'Confiance'—her heaviest metal [24-pounders] falling upwards of five hundred yards short of the shore." The "Confiance" was five hundred yards further off than the American squadron, and to reach it her guns would be elevated for that distance only. Because under such condition they dropped their shot five hundred yards short of three thousand five hundred yards, it is scarcely legitimate to infer that guns elevated for three thousand could not carry so far.

The arguments having been stated, it is to be remarked that, whatever the truth, it is knowledge after the fact as far as Prevost was concerned. In his report dated September 11, 1814, the day of the action, he speaks of the difficulties which had been before him; among them "blockhouses armed with heavy ordnance." This he then believed; and whether this ordnance could reach the squadron he could only know by trying. It was urgently proper, in view of his large land force, and of the expectations of his Government, which had made such great exertions for an attainable and important object, that he should storm the works and try. After a careful estimate of the strength of the two squadrons, I think that a seaman would certainly say that in the open the British was superior; but decidedly inferior for an attack upon the American at anchor. This was the opinion of the surviving British officers, under oath, and of Downie. General Izard, who had been in command at Plattsburg up to a fortnight before the attack, wrote afterwards to the Secretary of War, "I may venture to assert that without the works, Fort Moreau and its dependencies, Captain Macdonough would not have ventured to await the enemy's attack in Plattsburg Bay, but would have retired to the upper part of Lake Champlain."[419] The whole campaign turning upon naval control, the situation was eminently one that called upon the army to drive the enemy from his anchorage. The judgment of the author endorses the words of Sir James Yeo: "There was not the least necessity for our squadron giving the enemy such decided advantages by going into their bay to engage them. Even had they been successful, it could not in the least have assisted the troops in storming the batteries; whereas, had our troops taken their batteries first, it would have obliged the enemy's squadron to quit the bay and given ours a fair chance."[420] At the Court Martial two witnesses, Lieutenant Drew of the "Linnet," and Brydone, master of the "Confiance," swore that after the action Macdonough removed his squadron to Crab Island, out of range of the batteries. Macdonough in his report does not mention this; nor was it necessary that he should.

In short, though apparently so near, the two fractions of the American force, the army and the navy, were actually in the dangerous military condition of being exposed to be beaten in detail; and the destruction of either would probably be fatal to the other. The largest two British vessels, "Confiance" and "Linnet," were slightly inferior to the American "Saratoga" and "Eagle" in aggregate weight of broadside; but, like the "General Pike" on Ontario in 1813, the superiority of the "Confiance" in long guns, and under one captain, would on the open lake have made her practically equal to cope with the whole American squadron, and still more with the "Saratoga" alone, assuming that the "Linnet" gave the "Eagle" some occupation.

It would seem clear, therefore, that the true combination for the British general would have been to use his military superiority, vast in quality as in numbers, to reduce the works and garrison at Plattsburg. That accomplished, the squadron would be driven to the open lake, where the "Confiance" could bring into play her real superiority, instead of being compelled to sacrifice it by attacking vessels in a carefully chosen position, ranged with a seaman's eye for defence, and prepared with a seaman's foresight for every contingency. Prevost, however, became possessed with the idea that a joint attack was indispensable,[421] and in communicating his purpose to the commander of the squadron, Captain Downie, he used language indefensible in itself, tending to goad a sensitive man into action contrary to his better judgment; and he clenched this injudicious proceeding with words which certainly implied an assurance of assault by the army on the works, simultaneous with that of the navy on the squadron.

Captain Downie had taken command of the Champlain fleet only on September 2. He was next in rank to Yeo on the lakes, a circumstance that warranted his orders; the immediate reason for which, however, as explained by Yeo to the Admiralty, was that his predecessor's temper had shown him unfit for chief command. He had quarrelled with Pring, and Yeo felt the change essential. Downie, upon arrival, found the "Confiance" in a very incomplete state, for which he at least was in no wise responsible. He had brought with him a first lieutenant in whom he had merited confidence, and the two worked diligently to get her into shape. The crew had been assembled hurriedly by draughts from several ships at Quebec, from the 39th regiment, and from the marine artillery. The last detachment came on board the night but one before the battle. They thus were unknown by face to their officers, and largely to one another. Launched August 25, the ship hauled from the wharf into the stream September 7, and the same day started for the front, being towed by boats against a head wind and downward current. Behind her dragged a batteau carrying her powder, while her magazine was being finished.

The next day a similar painful advance was made, and the crew then were stationed at the guns, while the mechanics labored at their fittings. That night she anchored off Chazy, where the whole squadron was now gathered. The 9th was spent at anchor, exercising the guns; the mechanics still at work. In fact, the hammering and driving continued until two hours before the ship came under fire, when the last gang shoved off, leaving her still unfinished. "This day"—the 9th—wrote the first lieutenant, Robertson, "employed setting-up rigging, scraping decks, manning and arranging the gunboats. Exercised at great guns. Artificers employed fitting beds, coins, belaying pins, etc;"[422]—essentials for fighting the guns and working the sails. It scarcely needs the habit of a naval seaman to recognize that even three or four days' grace for preparation would immensely increase efficiency. Nevertheless, such was the pressure from without that the order was given for the squadron to go into action next day; and this was prevented only by a strong head wind, against which there was not channel space to beat.

As long as Prevost was contending with the difficulties of his own advance he seems not to have worried Downie; but as soon as fairly before the works of Plattsburg he initiated a correspondence, which on his part became increasingly peremptory. It will be remembered that he not only was much the senior in rank,—as in years,—but also Governor-General of Canada. Nor should it be forgotten that he had known and written a month before that the "Confiance" could not be ready before September 15. He knew, as his subsequent action showed, that if the British fleet were disabled his own progress was hopeless; and, if he could not understand that to a ship so lately afloat a day was worth a week of ordinary conditions, he should at least have realized that the naval captain could judge better than he when she was ready for battle. On September 7 he wrote to urge Downie, who replied the same day with assurances of every exertion to hasten matters. The 8th he sent information of Macdonough's arrangements by an aid, who carried also a letter saying that "it is of the highest importance that the ships, vessels, and gunboats, under your command, should combine a co-operation with the division of the army under my command. I only wait for your arrival to proceed against General Macomb's last position on the south bank of the Saranac." On the 9th he wrote, "In consequence of your communication of yesterday I have postponed action until your squadron is prepared to co-operate. I need not dwell with you on the evils resulting to both services from delay." He inclosed reports received from deserters that the American fleet was insufficiently manned; and that when the "Eagle" arrived, a few days before, they had swept the guard houses of prisoners to complete her crew. A postscript conveyed a scarcely veiled intimation that an eye was kept on his proceedings. "Captain Watson of the provincial cavalry is directed to remain at Little Chazy until you are preparing to get underway, when he is instructed to return to this place with the intelligence."[423]

Thus pressed, Downie, as has been said, gave orders to sail at midnight, with the expectation of rounding into Plattsburg Bay about dawn, and proceeding to an immediate attack. This purpose was communicated formally to Prevost. The preventing cause, the head wind, was obvious enough, and spoke for itself; but the check drew from Prevost words which stung Downie to the quick. "In consequence of your letter the troops have been held in readiness, since six o'clock this morning, to storm the enemy's works at nearly the same moment as the naval action begins in the bay. I ascribe the disappointment I have experienced to the unfortunate change of wind, and shall rejoice to learn that my reasonable expectations have been frustrated by no other cause." The letter was sent by the aid, Major Coore, who had carried the others; and both he and Pring, who were present, testified to the effect upon Downie. Coore, in a vindication of Prevost, wrote, "After perusing it, Captain Downie said with some warmth, 'I am surprised Sir George Prevost should think necessary to urge me upon this subject. He must feel I am as desirous of proceeding to active operations as he can be; but I am responsible for the squadron, and no man shall make me lead it into action before I consider it in fit condition.'"[424] Nevertheless, the effect was produced; for he remarked afterward to Pring, "This letter does not deserve an answer, but I will convince him that the naval force will not be backward in their share of the attack."[425]

It was arranged that the approach of the squadron should be signalled by scaling the guns,—firing cartridges without shot; and Downie certainty understood, and informed his officers generally, that the army would assault in co-operation with the attack of the fleet. The precise nature of his expectation was clearly conveyed to Pring, who had represented the gravity of this undertaking. "When the batteries are stormed and taken possession of by the British land forces, which the commander of the land forces has promised to do at the moment the naval action commences, the enemy will be obliged to quit their position, whereby we shall obtain decided advantage over them during their confusion. I would otherwise prefer fighting them on the lake, and would wait until our force is in an efficient state; but I fear they would take shelter up the lake and would not meet me on equal terms."[426] The following morning, September 11, the wind being fair from northeast, the British fleet weighed before daylight and stood up the narrows for the open lake and Plattsburg Bay. About five o'clock the agreed signal was given by scaling the guns, the reports of which it was presumed must certainly be heard by the army at the then distance of six or seven miles, with the favorable air blowing. At 7.30, near Cumberland Head, the squadron hove-to, and Captain Downie went ahead in a boat to reconnoitre the American position.

For defence against the hostile squadron, Macdonough had had to rely solely on his own force, and its wise disposition by him. On shore, a defensive position is determined by the circumstances of the ground selected, improved by fortification; all which gives strength additional to the number of men. A sailing squadron anchored for defence similarly gained force by adapting its formation to the circumstances of the anchorage, and to known wind conditions, with careful preparations to turn the guns in any direction; deliberate precautions, not possible to the same extent to the assailant anchoring under fire. To this is to be added the release of the crew from working sails to manning the guns.

Plattsburg Bay, in which the United States squadron was anchored, is two miles wide, and two long. It lies north and south, open to the southward. Its eastern boundary is called Cumberland Head. The British vessels, starting from below, in a channel too narrow to beat, must come up with a north wind. To insure that this should be ahead, or bring them close on the wind, after rounding the Head,—a condition unfavorable for attack,— Macdonough fixed the head of his line as far north as was safe; having in mind that the enemy might bring guns to the shore north of the Saranac. His order thence extended southward, abreast of the American works, and somewhat nearer the Cumberland than the Plattsburg side. The wind conditions further made it expedient to put the strongest vessels to the northward,—to windward,—whence they would best be able to manœuvre as circumstances might require. The order from north to south therefore was: the brig "Eagle," twenty guns; the ship "Saratoga," twenty-six; the "Ticonderoga" schooner, seven, and the sloop "Preble," seven.

Macdonough's dispositions being perfectly under observation, Captain Downie framed his plan accordingly.[427] The "Confiance" should engage the "Saratoga;" but, before doing so, would pass along the "Eagle," from north to south, give her a broadside, and then anchor head and stern across the bows of the "Saratoga." After this, the "Linnet," supported by the "Chub," would become the opponent of the "Eagle," reduced more nearly to equality by the punishment already received. Three British vessels would thus grapple the two strongest enemies. The "Finch" was to attack the American rear, supported by all the British gunboats—eleven in number. There were American gunboats, or galleys, as well, which Macdonough distributed in groups, inshore of his order; but, as was almost invariably the case, these light vessels exerted no influence on the result.

This being the plan, when the wind came northeast on the morning of September 11, the British stood up the lake in column, as follows: "Finch," "Confiance," "Linnet," "Chub." Thus, when they rounded Cumberland Head, and simultaneously changed course towards the American line, they would be properly disposed to reach the several places assigned. As the vessels came round the Head, to Downie's dismay no co-operation by the army was visible. He was fairly committed to his movement, however, and could only persist. As the initial act was to be the attack upon the "Eagle" by the "Confiance," she led in advance of her consorts, which caused a concentration of the hostile guns upon her; the result being that she was unable to carry out her part. The wind also failed, and she eventually anchored five hundred yards from the American line. Her first broadside is said to have struck down forty, or one fifth of the "Saratoga's" crew. As in the case of the "Chesapeake," this shows men of naval training, accustomed to guns; but, as with the "Chesapeake," lack of organization, of the habit of working together, officers and men, was to tell ere the end. Fifteen minutes after the action began Captain Downie was killed, leaving in command Lieutenant Robertson.

The "Linnet" reached her berth and engaged the "Eagle" closely; but the "Chub," which was to support her, received much damage to her sails and rigging, and the lieutenant in charge was nervously prostrated by a not very severe wound. Instead of anchoring, she was permitted to drift helplessly, and so passed through the American order, where she hauled down her colors. Though thus disappointed of the assistance intended for her, the "Linnet" continued to fight manfully and successfully, her opponent finally quitting the line; a result to which the forward battery of the "Confiance" in large measure contributed.[428] The "Finch," by an error of judgment on the part of her commander, did not keep near enough to the wind. She therefore failed to reach her position, near the "Ticonderoga;" and the breeze afterwards falling, she could not retrieve her error. Ultimately, she went ashore on Crab Island, a mile to the southward. This remoteness enabled her to keep her flag flying till her consorts had surrendered; but the credit of being last to strike belongs really to the "Linnet," Captain Pring. By the failure of the "Finch," the "Ticonderoga" underwent no attack except by the British gunboats. Whatever might possibly have come of this was frustrated by the misbehavior of most of them. Four fought with great gallantry and persistence, eliciting much admiration from their opponents; but the remainder kept at distance, the commander of the whole actually running away, and absconding afterwards to avoid trial. The "Ticonderoga" maintained her position to the end; but the weak "Preble" was forced from her anchors, and ran ashore under the Plattsburg batteries.

The fight thus resolved itself into a contest between the "Saratoga" and "Eagle," on one side, the "Confiance" and "Linnet" on the other. The wind being north-northeast, the ships at their anchors headed so that the forward third of the "Confiance's" battery bore upon the "Eagle," and only the remaining two thirds upon the "Saratoga." This much equalized conditions all round. It was nine o'clock when she anchored. At 10.30 the "Eagle," having many of her guns on the engaged side disabled, cut her cable, ran down the line, and placed herself south of the "Saratoga," anchoring by the stern. This had the effect of turning towards the enemy her other side, the guns of which were still uninjured. "In this new position," wrote Lieutenant Robertson, "she kept up a destructive fire on the "Confiance," without being exposed to a shot from that ship or the "Linnet." On the other hand, Macdonough found the "Saratoga" suffer from the "Linnet," now relieved of her immediate opponent."[429]

By this time the fire of both the "Saratoga" and "Confiance" had materially slackened, owing to the havoc among guns and men. Nearly the whole battery on the starboard side of the United States ship was dismounted, or otherwise unserviceable. The only resource was to bring the uninjured side towards the enemy, as the "Eagle" had just done; but to use the same method, getting under way, would be to abandon the fight, for there was not astern another position of usefulness for the "Saratoga." There was nothing for it but to "wind"[430] the ship—turn her round where she was.

Then appeared the advantage attendant upon the defensive, if deliberately utilized. The "Confiance" standing in had had shot away, one after another, the anchors and ropes upon which she depended for such a manœuvre.[431] The "Saratoga's" resources were unimpaired. A stern anchor was let go, the bow cable cut, and the ship winded, either by force of the wind, or by the use of "springs"[432] before prepared, presenting to the "Confiance" her uninjured broadside—for fighting purposes a new vessel. The British ship, having now but four guns that could be used on the side engaged,[433] must do the like, or be hopelessly overmatched. The stern anchor prepared having been shot away, an effort was made to swing her by a new spring on the bow cable; but while this slow process was carrying on, and the ship so far turned as to be at right angles with the American line, a raking shot entered, killing and wounding several of the crew. Then, reported Lieutenant Robertson, the surviving officer in command, "the ship's company declared they would stand no longer to their quarters, nor could the officers with their utmost exertions rally them." The vessel was in a sinking condition, kept afloat by giving her a marked heel to starboard, by running in the guns on the port side, so as to bring the shot holes out of water.[434] The wounded on the deck below had to be continually moved, lest they should be drowned where they lay. She drew but eight and a half feet of water. Her colors were struck at about 11 A.M.; the "Linnet's" fifteen minutes later. By Macdonough's report, the action had lasted two hours and twenty minutes, without intermission.

Few combats have been more resolutely contested. The "Saratoga" had fifty-five round shot in her hull; the "Confiance," one hundred and five.[435] Of the American crew of two hundred and ten men, twenty-eight were killed and twenty-nine wounded. The British loss is not known exactly. Robertson reported that there were thirty-eight bodies sent ashore for interment, besides those thrown overboard in action. This points to a loss of about fifty killed, and James states the wounded at about sixty; the total was certainly more than one hundred in a ship's company of two hundred and seventy.

There was reason for obstinacy, additional to the natural resolution of the parties engaged. The battle of Lake Champlain, more nearly than any other incident of the War of 1812, merits the epithet "decisive." The moment the issue was known, Prevost retreated into Canada; entirely properly, as indicated by the Duke of Wellington's words before and after. His previous conduct was open to censure, for he had used towards Captain Downie urgency of pressure which induced that officer to engage prematurely; "goaded" into action, as Yeo wrote. Before the usual naval Court Martial, the officers sworn testified that Downie had been led to expect co-operation, which in their judgment would have reversed the issue; but that no proper assault was made. Charges were preferred, and Prevost was summoned home; but he died before trial. There remains therefore no sworn testimony on his side, nor was there any adequate cross-examination of the naval witnesses. In the judgment of the writer, it was incumbent upon Prevost to assault the works when Downie was known to be approaching, with a fair wind, in the hope of driving the American squadron from its anchors to the open lake, where the real superiority of the British could assert itself.[436]

Castlereagh's "chances of the campaign" had gone so decidedly against the British that no ground was left to claim territorial adjustments. To effect these the war must be continued; and for this Great Britain was not prepared, nor could she afford the necessary detachment of force. In the completeness of Napoleon's downfall, we now are prone to forget that remaining political conditions in Europe still required all the Great Powers to keep their arms at hand.

The war was practically ended by Prevost's retreat. What remained was purely episodical in character, and should be so regarded. Nevertheless, although without effect upon the issue, and indeed in great part transacted after peace had been actually signed, it is so directly consecutive with the war as to require united treatment.

Very soon after reaching Bermuda, Vice-Admiral Cochrane, in pursuance of the "confidential communications with which he was charged," the character of which, he intimated to Warren,[437] was a reason for expediting the transfer of the command, despatched the frigate "Orpheus" to the Appalachicola River to negotiate with the Creek and other Indians. The object was to rouse and arm "our Indian allies in the Southern States," and to arrange with them a system of training by British officers, and a general plan of action; by which, "supporting the Indian tribes situated on the confines of Florida, and in the back parts of Georgia, it would be easy to reduce New Orleans, and to distress the enemy very seriously in the neighboring provinces."[438]

The "Orpheus" arrived at the mouth of the Appalachicola May 10, 1814, and on the 20th her captain, Pigot, had an interview with the principal Creek chiefs. He found[439] that the feeling of their people was very strong against the Americans; and from the best attainable information he estimated that twenty-eight hundred warriors were ready to take up arms with the British. There were said to be as many more Choctaws thus disposed; and perhaps a thousand other Indians, then dispersed and unarmed, could be collected. The negroes of Georgia would probably also come over in crowds, once the movement started. With a suitable number of British subalterns and drill sergeants, the savages could be fitted to act in concert with British troops in eight or ten weeks; for they were already familiar with the use of fire-arms, and were moreover good horsemen. The season of the year being still so early, there was ample time for the necessary training. With these preparations, and adequate supplies of arms and military stores, Pigot thought that a handful of British troops, co-operating with the Creeks and Choctaws, could get possession of Baton Rouge, from which New Orleans and the lower Mississippi would be an easy conquest. Between Pensacola, still in the possession of Spain, and New Orleans, Mobile was the only post held by the United States. In its fort were two hundred troops, and in those up country not more than seven hundred. When transmitting this letter, which, with his own of June 20, was received at the Admiralty August 8, Cochrane endorsed most of Pigot's recommendations. He gave as his own estimate, that to drive the Americans entirely out of Louisiana and the Floridas would require not more than three thousand British troops; to be landed at Mobile, where they would be joined by all the Indians and the disaffected French and Spaniards.[440] In this calculation reappears the perennial error of relying upon disaffected inhabitants, as well as savages. Disaffection must be supported by intolerable conditions, before inhabitants will stake all; not merely the chance of life, but the certainty of losing property, if unsuccessful. Cochrane took the further practical step of sending at once such arms and ammunition as the fleet could spare, together with four officers and one hundred and eight non-commissioned officers and privates of the marine corps, to train the Indians. These were all under the command of Major Nicholls, who for this service was given the local rank of Colonel. The whole were despatched July 23, in the naval vessels "Hermes" and "Carron," for the Appalachicola. The Admiral, while contemplating evidently a progress towards Baton Rouge, looked also to coastwise operations; for he asked the Government to furnish him vessels of light draught, to carry heavy guns into Lake Ponchartrain, and to navigate the shoal water between it and Mobile, now called Mississippi Sound.

The Admiralty in reply[441] reminded Cochrane of the former purpose of the Government to direct operations against New Orleans, with a very large force under Lord Hill, Wellington's second in the Peninsular War. Circumstances had made it inexpedient to send so many troops from Europe at this moment; but, in view of the Admiral's recommendation, General Ross would be directed to co-operate in the intended movement at the proper season, and his corps would be raised to six thousand men, independent of such help in seamen and marines as the fleet might afford. The re-enforcements would be sent to Negril Bay, at the west end of Jamaica, which was made the general rendezvous; and there Cochrane and Ross were directed to join not later than November 20. The purpose of the Government in attempting the enterprise was stated to be twofold. "First, to obtain command of the embouchure of the Mississippi, so as to deprive the back settlements of America of their communication with the sea; and, secondly, to occupy some important and valuable possession, by the restoration of which the conditions of peace might be improved, or which we might be entitled to exact the cession of, as the price of peace." Entire discretion was left with the two commanders as to the method of proceeding, whether directly against New Orleans, by water, or to its rear, by land, through the country of the Creeks; and they were at liberty to abandon the undertaking in favor of some other, should that course seem more suitable. When news of the capture of Washington was received, two thousand additional troops were sent to Bermuda, under the impression that the General might desire to push his success on the Atlantic coast. These ultimately joined the expedition two days before the attack on Jackson's lines. Upon the death of General Ross, Sir Edward Pakenham was ordered to replace him; but he did not arrive until after the landing, and had therefore no voice in determining the general line of operations adopted.

These were the military instructions. To them were added certain others, political in character, dictated mainly by the disturbed state of Europe, and with an eye to appease the jealousies existing among the Powers, which extended to American conditions, colonial and commercial. While united against Napoleon, they viewed with distrust the aggrandizement of Great Britain. Ross was ordered, therefore, to discountenance any overture of the inhabitants to place themselves under British dominion; but should he find a general and decided disposition to withdraw from their recent connection with the United States, with the view of establishing themselves as an independent people, or of returning under the dominion of Spain, from which they then had been separated less than twenty years, he was to give them every support in his power. He must make them clearly understand, however, that in the peace with the United States neither independence nor restoration to Spain could be made a sine quâ non;[442] there being about that a finality, of which the Government had already been warned in the then current negotiations with the American commissioners. These instructions to Ross were communicated to Lord Castlereagh at Vienna, to use as might be expedient in the discussions of the Conference.

No serious attempt was made in the direction of Baton Rouge, through the back countries of Georgia and Florida; nor does there appear any result of consequence from the mission of Colonel Nicholls. On September 17 the "Hermes" and "Carron," supported by two brigs of war, made an attack upon Fort Bowyer, a work of logs and sand commanding the entrance to Mobile Bay. After a severe cannonade, lasting between two and three hours, they were repulsed; and the "Hermes," running aground, was set on fire by her captain to prevent her falling into the hands of the enemy. Mobile was thus preserved from becoming the starting point of the expedition, as suggested by Cochrane; and that this object underlay the attempt may be inferred from the finding of the Court Martial upon Captain Percy of the "Hermes," which decided that the attack was perfectly justified by the circumstances stated at the trial.[443]

In October, 1810, by executive proclamation of President Madison, the United States had taken possession of the region between Louisiana and the River Perdido,[444] being the greater part of what was then known as West Florida. The Spanish troops occupying Mobile, however, were not then disturbed;[445] nor was there a military occupation, except of one almost uninhabited spot near Bay St. Louis.[446] This intervention was justified on the ground of a claim to the territory, asserted to be valid; and occasion for it was found in the danger of a foreign interference, resulting from the subversion of Spanish authority by a revolutionary movement. By Great Britain it was regarded as a usurpation, to effect which advantage had been taken of the embarrassment of the Spaniards when struggling against Napoleon for national existence. On May 14, 1812, being then on the verge of war with Great Britain, the ally of Spain, an Act of Congress declared the whole country annexed, and extended over it the jurisdiction of the United States. Mobile was occupied April 15, 1813. Pensacola, east of the Perdido, but close to it, remained in the hands of Spain, and was used as a base of operations by the British fleet, both before and after the attack of the "Hermes" and her consorts upon Fort Bowyer. From there Nicholls announced that he had arrived in the Floridas for the purpose of annoying "the only enemy Great Britain has in the world"[447]; and Captain Percy thence invited the pirates of Barataria to join the British cause. Cochrane also informed the Admiralty that for quicker communication, while operating in the Gulf, he intended to establish a system of couriers through Florida, between Amelia Island and Pensacola, both under Spanish jurisdiction.[448] On the score of neutrality, therefore, fault can scarcely be found with General Jackson for assaulting the latter, which surrendered to him November 7. The British vessels departed, and the works were blown up; after which the place was restored to the Spaniards.

In acknowledging the Admiralty's letter of August 10, Cochrane said that the diminution of numbers from those intended for Lord Hill would not affect his plans; that, unless the United States had sent very great re-enforcements to Louisiana, the troops now to be employed were perfectly adequate, even without the marines. These he intended to send under Rear-Admiral Cockburn, to effect a diversion by occupying Cumberland Island, off the south coast of Georgia, about November 10, whence the operations would be extended to the mainland. It was hoped this would draw to the coast the American force employed against the Indians, and so favor the movements in Louisiana.[449] While not expressly stated, the inference seems probable that Cochrane still—October 3—expected to land at Mobile. For some reason Cockburn's attack on Cumberland Island did not occur until January 12, when the New Orleans business was already concluded; so that, although successful, and prosecuted further to the seacoast, it had no influence upon the general issues. Cochrane, with the division from the Atlantic coast, joined the re-enforcements from England in Negril Bay, and thence proceeded to Mississippi Sound; anchoring off Ship Island, December 8. On the 2d General Jackson had arrived in New Orleans, whither had been ordered a large part of the troops heretofore acting against the Creeks. The British commanders had now determined definitely to attack the city from the side of the sea. As there could be little hope for vessels dependent upon sails to pass the forts on the lower Mississippi, against the strong current, as was done by Farragut's steamers fifty years later, it was decided to reach the river far above those works, passing the army through some of the numerous bayous which intersect the swampy delta to the eastward. From Ship Island this desired approach could be made through Lake Borgne.

For the defence of these waters there were stationed five American gunboats and two or three smaller craft, the whole under command of Lieutenant Thomas ap Catesby Jones. As even the lighter British ships of war could not here navigate, on account of the shoalness, and the troops, to reach the place of debarkation, the Bayou des Pêcheurs, at the head of Lake Borgne, must go sixty miles in open boats, the hostile gun vessels had first to be disposed of. Jones, who from an advanced position had been watching the enemy's proceedings in Mississippi Sound, decided December 12 that their numbers had so increased as to make remaining hazardous. He therefore retired, both to secure his retreat and to cause the boats of the fleet a longer and more harassing pull to overtake him. The movement was none too soon, for that night the British barges and armed boats left the fleet in pursuit. Jones was not able to get as far as he wished, on account of failure of wind; but nevertheless on the 13th the enemy did not come up with him. During the night he made an attempt at further withdrawal; but calm continuing, and a strong ebb-tide running, he was compelled again to anchor at 1 A.M. of the 14th, and prepared for battle. His five gunboats, with one light schooner, were ranged in line across the channel way, taking the usual precautions of springs on their cables and boarding nettings triced up. Unluckily for the solidity of his order, the current set two of the gunboats, one being his own, some distance to the eastward,—in advance of the others.

At daylight the British flotilla was seen nine miles distant, at anchor. By Jones' count it comprised forty-two launches and three light gigs.[450] They soon after weighed and pulled towards the gunboats. At ten, being within long gunshot, they again anchored for breakfast; after which they once more took to the oars. An hour later they closed with their opponents. The British commander, Captain Lockyer, threw his own boat, together with a half-dozen others, upon Jones' vessel, "Number 156,"[451] and carried her after a sharp struggle of about twenty minutes, during which both Lockyer and Jones were severely wounded. Her guns were then turned against her late comrades, in support of the British boarders, and at the end of another half-hour, at 12.40 P.M., the last of them surrendered.

That this affair was very gallantly contested on both sides is sufficiently shown by the extent of the British loss—seventeen killed and seventy-seven wounded.[452] They were of course in much larger numbers than the Americans. No such attempt should be made except with this advantage, and the superiority should be as great as is permitted by the force at the disposal of the assailant.

This obstacle to the movement of the troops being removed, debarkation began at the mouth of the Bayou des Pêcheurs;[453] whence the British, undiscovered during their progress, succeeded in penetrating by the Bayou Bienvenu and its tributaries to a point on the Mississippi eight miles below New Orleans. The advance corps, sixteen hundred strong, arrived there at noon, December 23, accompanied by Major-General Keane, as yet in command of the whole army. The news reached Jackson two hours later.

Fresh from the experiences of Washington and Baltimore, the British troops flattered themselves with the certainty of a quiet night. The Americans, they said to each other, have never dared to attack. At 7.30, however, a vessel dropped her anchor abreast them, and a voice was heard, "Give them this for the honor of America!" The words were followed by the discharge of her battery, which swept through the camp. Without artillery to reply, having but two light field guns, while the assailant—the naval schooner "Caroline," Lieut. J.D. Henley—had anchored out of musket range, the invaders, suffering heavily, were driven to seek shelter behind the levee, where they lay for nearly an hour.[454] At the end of this, a dropping fire was heard from above and inland. Jackson, with sound judgment and characteristic energy, had decided to attack at once, although, by his own report, he could as yet muster only fifteen hundred men, of whom but six hundred were regulars. A confused and desperate night action followed, the men on both sides fighting singly or in groups, ignorant often whether those before them were friends or foes. The Americans eventually withdrew, carrying with them sixty-six prisoners. Their loss in killed and wounded was one hundred and thirty-nine; that of the British, two hundred and thirteen.

The noise of this rencounter hastened the remainder of the British army, and by the night of December 24 the whole were on the ground. Meantime, the "Caroline" had been joined by the ship "Louisiana," which anchored nearly a mile above her. In her came Commodore Patterson, in chief naval command. The presence of the two impelled the enemy to a slight retrograde movement, out of range of their artillery. The next morning, Christmas, Sir Edward Pakenham arrived from England. A personal examination satisfied him that only by a reconnaissance in force could he ascertain the American strength and preparations, and that, as a preliminary to such attempt, the vessels whose guns swept the line of advance must be driven off. On the 26th the "Caroline" tried to get up stream to Jackson's camp, but could not against a strong head wind; and on the 27th the British were able to burn her with hot shot. The "Louisiana" succeeded in shifting her place, and thenceforth lay on the west bank of the stream, abreast of and flanking the entrenchments behind which Jackson was established.

These obstacles gone, Pakenham made his reconnaissance. As described by a participant,[455] the British advanced four or five miles on December 28, quite unaware what awaited them, till a turn in the road brought them face to face with Jackson's entrenchments. These covered a front of three fourths of a mile, and neither flank could be turned, because resting either on the river or the swamp. They were not yet complete, but afforded good shelter for riflemen, and had already several cannon in position, while the "Louisiana's" broadside also swept the ground in front. A hot artillery fire opened at once from both ship and works, and when the British infantry advanced they were met equally with musketry. The day's results convinced Pakenham that he must resort to the erection of batteries before attempting an assault; an unfortunate necessity, as the delay not only encouraged the defenders, but allowed time for re-enforcement, and for further development of their preparations. While the British siege pieces were being brought forward, largely from the fleet, a distance of seventy miles, the American Navy was transferring guns from the "Louisiana" to a work on the opposite side of the river, which would flank the enemies' batteries, as well as their columns in case of an attempt to storm.

When the guns had arrived, the British on the night of December 31 threw up entrenchments, finding convenient material in the sugar hogsheads of the plantations. On the morning of January 1 they opened with thirty pieces at a distance of five hundred yards; but it was soon found that in such a duel they were hopelessly overmatched, a result to which contributed the enfilading position of the naval battery. "To the well-directed exertions from the other side of the river," wrote Jackson to Patterson, after the close of the operations, "must be ascribed in great measure that harassment of the enemy which led to his ignominious flight." The British guns were silenced, and for the moment abandoned; but during the night they were either withdrawn or destroyed. It was thus demonstrated that no adequate antecedent impression could be made on the American lines by cannonade; and, as neither flank could be turned, no resource remained, on the east shore at least, but direct frontal assault.

But while Jackson's main position was thus secure, he ran great risk that the enemy, by crossing the river, and successful advance there, might establish themselves in rear of his works; which, if effected, would put him at the same disadvantage that the naval battery now imposed upon his opponents.

His lines would be untenable if his antagonist commanded the water, or gained the naval battery on his flank, to which the crew of the "Louisiana" and her long guns had now been transferred. This the British also perceived, and began to improve a narrow canal which then led from the head of the bayou to the levee, but was passable by canoes only. They expected ultimately to pierce the levee, and launch barges upon the river; but the work was impeded by the nature of the soil, the river fell, and some of the heavier boats grounding delayed the others, so that, at the moment of final assault, only five hundred men had been transported instead of thrice that number, as intended.[456] What these few effected showed how real and great was the danger.

The canal was completed on the evening of January 6, on which day the last re-enforcements from England, sixteen hundred men under Major-General Lambert, reached the front. Daylight of January 8 was appointed for the general assault; the intervening day and night being allowed for preparations, and for dragging forward the boats into the river. It was expected that the whole crossing party of fifteen hundred, under Colonel Thornton, would be on the west bank, ready to move forward at the same moment as the principal assault, which was also to be supported by all the available artillery, playing upon the naval battery to keep down its fire. There was therefore no lack of ordinary military prevision; but after waiting until approaching daylight began to throw more light than was wished upon the advance of the columns, Pakenham gave the concerted signal. Owing to the causes mentioned, Thornton had but just landed with his first detachment of five hundred. Eager to seize the battery, from which was to be feared so much destructive effect on the storming columns on the east bank, he pushed forward at once with the men he had, his flank towards the river covered by a division of naval armed boats; "but the ensemble of the general movement," wrote the British general, Lambert, who succeeded Pakenham in command, "was thus lost, and in a point which was of the last importance to the attack on the left bank of the river."

Not only was Thornton too weak, but he was eight hours[457] late, though not by his own fault. Commodore Patterson, whose duties kept him on the west bank, reported that the naval battery was actively and effectively employed upon the flank of the storming columns, and it was not until some time after the engagement opened that he was informed of the near approach of the British detachment on that side. In prevision of such an attempt, a line of works had been thrown up at the lower end of the naval battery, at right angles to it, to cover its flank. This was weak, however, at the extremity farthest from the river, and thither the British directed their attack. The defenders there, some very newly joined Kentucky militia, broke and fled, and their flight carried with them all the other infantry. The seamen of the battery, deprived of their supports, retreated after spiking their guns, which fell into the enemy's hands; and Thornton, who was severely wounded, was able to date his report of success from the "Redoubt on the right bank of the Mississippi."[458] He advanced actually, and without serious opposition, a mile above—that is, in rear of—Jackson's lines and the "Louisiana's" anchorage. "This important rout," wrote Jackson, "had totally changed the aspect of affairs. The enemy now occupied a position from which they might annoy us without hazard, and by means of which they might have been enabled to defeat, in a great measure, the effects of our success on this side of the river. It became, therefore, an object of the first consequence to dislodge him as soon as possible."

Jackson himself attributed his success in this desirable object as much to negotiation as to the force he would be able to apply. The story of the main assault and its disastrous repulse is familiar. In itself, it was but an instance of a truth conspicuously illustrated, before and after, on many fields, of the desperate character of a frontal attack upon protected men accustomed to the use of fire-arms—even though they be irregulars. Could Thornton's movement have been made in full force assigned, and at the moment intended,—so that most of the advance on both sides the river could have been consummated before dawn,—a successful flanking operation would have been effected; and it is far from improbable that Jackson, finding the naval guns turned against him, would have been driven out of his lines. With raw troops under his command, and six thousand veterans upon his heels, no stand could have been made short of the town, nor in it.

As it was, the failure of the two parts of the British to act coincidently caused them to be beaten in detail: for the disastrous and bloody repulse of the columns on the east bank led to the withdrawal of the tiny body on the west.[459] No further attempt was made. On the 18th of January the British withdrew. In pursuance of the full discretionary power given by their orders as to any further employment upon the American coast of the forces under their command, General Lambert and the Admiral then concerted an attack upon Fort Bowyer, at the entrance to Mobile Bay. This surrendered February 11, the day that the news of the Peace reached New York.

The ocean as well as the land had its episodes of fighting after peace had been signed. The United States frigate "President," which during the first two years of the war had been commanded continuously by Commodore John Rodgers, was in May, 1814, transferred to Decatur, who took to her with him the crew of his old ship, the "United States," irretrievably shut up in New London. The "President" remained in New York throughout the year, narrowly watched by the enemy. In a letter of August 10, Decatur speaks of the unfavorable conditions of the season for sailing; that four British ships kept close to Sandy Hook, at times even anchored. He then mentions also "the great apprehension and danger" which New York was undergoing, in common with the entire seaboard, and the wish of the city government that the crew of the ship should remain for defence of the port.[460] It will be remembered that this was in the anxious period preceding the development of the British menace to the coast, which issued in the capture of Washington and Alexandria, and the attack on Baltimore. Philadelphia also trembled; and Decatur received an order to carry the "President's" crew to her protection, if threatened.[461]

On New Year Day, 1815, the "President" was still in the bay, awaiting a chance to sail. She was deeply laden for a long absence, and was to be accompanied by a merchant brig, the "Macedonian," carrying further stores. The sloops "Hornet" and "Peacock," and brig "Tom Bowline," were likewise watching to slip out. On the night of January 14, 1815, in a heavy northwester, the "President's" attempt was made; the pilots for the occasion having undertaken to mark the channel by boats suitably stationed. Despite these precautions the ship grounded, and beat heavily on the bottom for an hour and a half. By this she was seriously injured, and would have gone back had the wind permitted. As it was, she had to be forced over, and at 10 P.M. went clear; but with loss of a large part of that speed for which she was known, and which had been among Decatur's chief reasons for preferring her to the new "Guerrière."[462] The "Macedonian" was in company.

The British blockading division was under the command of Captain John Hayes, of the razee[463] "Majestic," and consisted, besides that ship, of the forty-gun 24-pounder frigate "Endymion," and the thirty-eight-gun 18-pounder frigates "Pomone" and "Tenedos"; the latter of which had joined on the 13th. The vessels were driven off shore by the violence of the gale; but Hayes, reasoning as a seaman, anticipated both Decatur's sailing that night and his probable course. After clearing the bar, the "President" steered nearly due east, along the south shore of Long Island, for fifty miles, when she headed off, southeast by east, for the open sea. At 5 A.M. three of the British squadron were seen ahead on the new course; the fourth, the "Tenedos," being then out of sight to the southward, either detached for a wider sweep of watchfulness, or separated by the gale.

The "President," on seeing the enemy, hauled up again along shore, and a stern chase began, which lasted till near nightfall of the 15th; the "Endymion" leading the British squadron. The "Tenedos" being sighted soon after daybreak, Hayes detached the "Pomone" to ascertain what ship it was; a step which for the time threw the "Pomone," as well as the "Tenedos," out of the running. At 5 P.M. the "Endymion" had got well within point-blank shot of the "President." It must be appreciated that, with the whole hostile squadron at her heels, the American frigate could not delay, or turn her side with its battery towards an assailant behind; for to do so enabled the others to gain on her. On the other hand, the pursuer could so deflect—yaw—at frequent intervals, and having the greater speed could continually recover the ground thus lost. This was what Captain Hope of the "Endymion" did, with sound judgment. He took a position on the off-shore quarter of the "President," where neither her broadside nor stern guns could bear upon him, so long as she held her course. Thence, yawing continually, the "Endymion" poured in her successive broadsides, practically unopposed, mistress of the situation.

Decatur endured this for a time; but it was the military merit of his antagonist's conduct that it must eventually force him to turn aside, and so convert the stern chase of the British squadron to the more hopeful attempt to cut him off on a new course. After half an hour the "President's" helm was put to port, and the ship headed abruptly south, threatening to cross the "Endymion's" bow, and rake. The British frigate had to follow this movement of her opponent, and the two ran off on parallel lines, exchanging broadsides. The object of Decatur was to dismantle this enemy, strip him of his motive power, and so increase his own chance of escape. In this he was successful. After two hours and a half, between 8 and 8.30 P.M., the "Endymion's" sails were stripped from the yards. She dropped astern, and the "President" again steered east, bringing the other enemy's ships once more in her wake,—a stern chase.

At 11 P.M. the "Pomone" and "Tenedos" overtook her. These were of the class of the "Guerrière," "Macedonian," and "Shannon," very much lighter, singly, than the "President," which had a heavier battery than the "Constitution." Had the American ship retained her normal speed, she probably would have escaped; but the "Pomone," the first to arrive, outsailed her without using studdingsails, which the "President" was still able to carry alow and aloft, despite her engagement with the "Endymion." This fresh British ship luffed to port, and fired her starboard broadside. The "President" imitated the manœuvre, heading up to north; but she did not fire. At this point the historian is met by a direct contradiction of evidence. Decatur says that the "Pomone" was now on the port bow, within musket-shot,[464] the "Tenedos" five hundred yards astern, "taking up a raking position on our quarter, and the rest (with the exception of the 'Endymion') within gunshot."[465] These statements are confirmed by the sworn testimony before the American Court of Inquiry. The log of the "Pomone," published with intention, reads that the "Tenedos" was not more than three miles off,—a distance to which no gun on shipboard of that day could carry,—and the "Endymion" and "Majestic" so far away that they did not come on the scene until 12.45 and 3 A.M., respectively, of the 16th. The "Pomone" fired a second broadside, and hauling still further to port was about to discharge a third, from a raking position ahead, when the "President" struck. She had not fired a gun at either the "Pomone" or the "Tenedos." The log of the "Pomone" is clear on this point, and Decatur's elaborate report makes no mention of having done so. The witnesses before the Court of Inquiry are equally silent.

Between the "Endymion" and the "President," in point of battery, the proportion of force was as four to three, in favor of the American ship. Against that must fairly be weighed the power of the "Endymion" to maintain for half an hour a quartering and raking position, owing to the necessity to escape laid on the "President." A quantitative estimate of this advantage would be largely guess; but it may safely be said that the disproportion of killed and wounded[466] can probably be laid to this, coupled with the very proper endeavor of Decatur to throw off his immediate enemy by aiming at her spars. After two and a half hours' fighting, the sails of the "Endymion" were "stripped from the yards," Captain Hayes reported; while the "President," by the "Pomone's" log, "continued to stand east under a press of sail," all studdingsails set, from lower to royal. This result accounts for where the "President's" shot went, and under the circumstances should have gone, and for why the "Endymion" lost fewer men; and it was not the sole reason for the last. There is, in the writer's judgment, no ground whatever for the assumption that the "Endymion" did, or singly would, have beaten the "President." The disparity of material force was counterbalanced by the circumstance that the "President" had the other vessels to take into account. From the legal point of view ships merely in sight contribute, and are therefore entitled to prize money. In the present instance they necessarily affected the manœuvring and gunnery of the "President."

There is a good deal of human nature, and some food for quiet entertainment, in the British accounts. There were several to share, and apparently the glory was not quite enough to go round. With Admiral Hotham, not present in the action, but in immediate command of the station during Cochrane's absence at New Orleans and Cockburn's in Georgia, it was "the force which I had collected off the bar of New York." Captain Hayes had much to say on his calculations of the enemy's movements: "What is a little singular, at the very instant of arriving at the point of the supposed track of the enemy, Sandy Hook west-northwest fifteen leagues, we were made happy by the sight of a ship and a brig, not more than two miles on the weather bow." The published report of Captain Hope, of the "Endymion," is simple and modest; but some of his followers apparently would have all the glory. The "Endymion" had done the whole business. This drew forth the publication of the "Pomone's" log, concerning which the Naval Chronicle remarks, "It appears that some differences have taken place between the British frigates engaged, as to the honor of having captured the 'President.'"[467]

Had Decatur appreciated at the moment that his speedy surrender to the "Pomone" would be attributed to the subjection to which the "Endymion" was supposed to have reduced his ship, he very probably would have made a second fight of it. But he was convinced that ultimate escape was impossible. "Two fresh," though much weaker, ships of the enemy at hand, his own having fought for two hours and a half; "about one fifth of my crew killed and wounded, my ship crippled, and a more than fourfold force opposed to me, without a chance of escape left, I deemed it my duty to surrender." Physical and mental fatigue, the moral discomfiture of a hopeless situation, are all fairly to be taken into account; nor should resistance be protracted where it means merely loss of life. Yet it may be questioned whether the moral tone of a military service, which is its breath of life, does not suffer when the attempt is made to invest with a halo of extraordinary heroism such a resistance as Decatur made, by his own showing. Unless the "President" was really thrashed out by the "Endymion," which was the British assertion,[468] she might have put one of his Majesty's thirty-eight-gun frigates, the "Pomone," out of commission for a long time; and that, in addition to the "Endymion,"—the two fastest British vessels,—would have been no light matter in the then state of the New York blockade. If the finding of the American Court of Inquiry,[469] that "the 'Endymion' was conquered, while the 'President' in the contest with her had sustained but little injury," be admitted, there seems no reply to the comment that the "President" surrendered within musket-shot of a thirty-eight-gun frigate which with three or four broadsides she should have nearly annihilated. She was out to destroy commerce and enemy's cruisers, and she struck before her powers in that respect—by the Court's finding— were exhausted. Escape was impossible; one object of her cruise—the enemy's commerce—had become impracticable; was it justifiable to neglect the last opportunity for the other? Decatur's personal gallantry is beyond question; but, if the defence of the "President" is to be considered "glorious," and "heroic," it is difficult to know what term can be applied to that of the "Essex." War is violence, wounds, and death. Needless bloodshed is to be avoided; but even more, at the present day, is to be deprecated the view that the objects of a war are to be sacrificed to the preservation of life.

After a long detention, through the closeness of the Boston blockade, the "Constitution," still commanded by Captain Charles Stewart, effected her escape to sea towards the end of December. On February 20, 1815, two hundred miles east-northeast from Madeira, she fell in with two British ships of war, the "Cyane," and the "Levant," then on their way from Gibraltar to the Azores, and thence to the American coast. The "Cyane," a frigate-built ship, carried a battery of carronades: thirty 32-pounders, two 18-pounders. She had also two long 9-pounders; making a total of thirty-four guns, throwing a broadside weight of five hundred and seven pounds.[470] The "Levant" was a sloop of war, of the American "Hornet" class, carrying eighteen 32-pounder carronades and two long 9-pounders; giving two hundred and ninety-seven as her broadside weight. Between the two they therefore threw eight hundred and four pounds of metal. The "Constitution's" broadside was seven hundred and four pounds; but of this three hundred and eighty-four were in long 24-pounders. Supposing both parties willing to fight under such circumstances, the game would be all in the "Constitution's" hands. Her problem rather was so to conduct the contest that neither enemy should escape. Captain Stewart, in reporting his success, dwelt upon the advantages derived by the enemy "from a divided and more active force, as also their superiority in the weight and numbers of guns." One cannot but feel the utmost diffidence in differing from a seaman of the time, and one so skilful as Stewart; but the advantage of a divided force is as difficult to see as the superiority in battery power.

Though consorts, the enemy when first seen were separated by a distance of ten miles; and were sighted successively between 1 and 2 P.M. The wind was easterly and light. The "Constitution" was unable to prevent their junction, which was effected at 5.45. They then formed in line on the starboard tack, the "Levant" leading; with an interval between them of three hundred feet. At six the "Constitution" drew up on the weather side of the "Cyane," and five minutes later the action began at a distance of three hundred yards. After a quarter of an hour, noting the enemy's fire to slacken, Stewart stopped his own, to allow the smoke to lift. When he could see, he found the "Constitution" abreast the "Levant," with the "Cyane" astern, luffing up for his port quarter. He gave his port broadside to the "Levant," then braced aback his after-sails, and so went astern towards the "Cyane," bringing her abeam under cover of the renewed cannonade. At 6.35—about ten minutes later—the enemy's fire again weakened, and the "Levant" was seen to be bearing up before the wind. Stewart made sail ahead, raked her twice from astern with the port guns, and then saw the "Cyane" also wearing. The "Constitution" immediately wore short round, and caught this opponent before she had completed her manœuvre, so that she raked her also from astern with the starboard battery. The "Cyane" then came to the wind on the port tack, and fired that broadside, to which the "Constitution," having reloaded after raking, was about to reply, when, at 6.50 this enemy struck, and fired a lee gun,—the signal of submission. A prize crew, with a party of marines to guard prisoners, was hastily thrown on board, and at eight the "Constitution" made sail again after the "Levant." At 8.30 this plucky little ship was met returning to the conflict. At 8.50 the two passed on opposite tacks, and exchanged broadsides, after which the "Constitution" kept away under the enemy's stern and raked again. The "Levant" could now run with a clear conscience. Whatever argument can be based on the united batteries of the two British ships, and the advantage of divided force, eighteen 32-pounder carronades were no match for the

"Constitution." The "Levant" took to her heels, but at 10 P.M. was overtaken and surrendered.[471]

The losses as reported by Stewart were: "Constitution," killed three; wounded twelve; "Cyane," killed twelve; wounded twenty-six; "Levant," killed twenty-three; wounded sixteen. Captain Stewart's management of his vessel was strikingly clever and prompt. The advantages which he attributed to the enemy, an aggregate of guns, slightly superior in total weight, divided between two smaller ships, the author has never been able to recognize.[472]

The sloops of war "Hornet," Commander James Biddle, and "Peacock," Commander Lewis Warrington, and the brig "Tom Bowline," which were waiting their opportunity in the lower bay of New York when the "President" sailed, got to sea five days after her, January 20. When two days out, the "Hornet" separated in chase. The vessels had a rendezvous at the lonely island of Tristan d'Acunha, in the South Atlantic, some fifteen hundred miles west of the Cape of Good Hope. The "Hornet" arrived first, and was about to anchor, at 10.30 in the morning of March 23, when a sail was seen to the southeast, steering west. As it soon passed behind the island, the "Hornet" made sail to the westward, and the two shortly came within sight. The stranger was the British sloop of war "Penguin," Captain Dickinson. By the report of Captain Biddle, based on examination after the action, she carried sixteen 32-pounder carronades, two long 12-pounders in broadside, and one long twelve on a pivot, fighting either side. The "Hornet" had eighteen 32-pounder carronades, and two long twelves.

The wind being south-southwest, the "Penguin" was to windward, and bore up to close. At 1.40 P.M., being nearly within musket-shot, she hauled to the wind on the starboard tack, a movement which the "Hornet" at once imitated, and the battle began; the "Hornet" to leeward, the two running on parallel courses,—an artillery duel. The "Penguin" drew gradually nearer, and at 1.55 put her helm hard up, to run her antagonist on board. The American crew were called to repel boarders, and so were on hand when the enemy's bowsprit came in between the main and mizzen rigging; but, while ready to resist an attempt to board, the course of the action had so satisfied Biddle of the superiority of his ship's gunnery that he would not throw his men away in a hand-to-hand contest upon the enemy's decks. The small arms men and marines, however, distributed along the "Hornet's" side kept up a lively musketry fire, which the British endured at great disadvantage, crowded upon the narrow front presented by a ship's forecastle. The "Penguin" finally wrenched clear with the loss of her foremast and bowsprit, and in this crippled state surrendered immediately. From the first gun to hauling down the flag was twenty-two minutes. The British ship had lost fourteen killed and twenty-eight wounded, her captain being among the slain. The "Hornet" had one killed and ten wounded. The comparative efficiency of the two vessels is best indicated by the fact that the "Hornet" had not a single cannon-ball in her hull, nor any serious injury even to her lower masts; yet that her rigging and sails were very much cut proves that her opponent's guns were active. By the ready skill of the seamen of that day she was completely ready for any service forty-eight hours later. The "Penguin" was scuttled.

The action between the "Hornet" and "Penguin" was the last naval combat of the War of 1812. The day after it, March 24, the "Peacock" and "Tom Bowline" arrived, in time to see the "Penguin" before her captor sunk her. The brig "Macedonian," which had sailed in company with the "President," but escaped her fate, also came to Tristan d'Acunha, which would seem to have been intended as a fresh starting point for some enterprise in common.

FOOTNOTES:

[394] Memoirs and Correspondence of Lord Castlereagh. Series iii. vol. ii. pp. 86-91.

[395] Castlereagh Memoirs, series iii. vol. ii. pp. 86-91.

[396] Castlereagh to Liverpool (Prime Minister), Aug. 28, 1814. Ibid., pp. 100-102.

[397] Wellington to Liverpool, Nov. 9, 1814. Castlereagh Memoirs, series iii. vol. ii. pp. 186-189.

[398] Canadian Archives, C. 680, p. 46. The date is Sept. 10, 1813.

[399] Letter of Captain Evans, commanding N.Y. Navy Yard, Aug. 6, 1813.

[400] Canadian Archives, C. 679, pp. 348, 362.

[401] Izard says two. Official Correspondence of the Department of War with Major-General Izard, 1814 and 1815, p. 7.

[402] British Court Martial Record.

[403] Confidence.

[404] Account of the Public Life of Sir George Prevost, p. 136.

[405] Prevost to Bathurst, July 12, 1814. Report on Canadian Archives, 1896. Lower Canada, p. 31.

[406] Prevost to Bathurst, Aug. 5, 1814. Ibid., p. 35.

[407] Prevost to Bathurst, Aug. 27.

[408] Official Correspondence of General Izard with the Department of War, pp. 56, 57. Philadelphia, 1816.

[409] Ridout, Ten Years in Upper Canada, p. 282.

[410] Niles' Register, vol. vi. p. 357.

[411] June 8, 1814. Navy Department MSS.

[412] Macomb's Report, Brannan's Military and Naval Letters, p. 415. Izard (Correspondence, p. 98) says, "There were at or about the works at Plattsburg not less than three thousand regulars, of whom fifteen hundred

were fit for duty in the field. In the number were three companies of artillery."

[413] General Benjamin Mooers, who was in command of the New York State militia during these operations, in a letter to Governor Tompkins, dated Sept. 16, 1814 (Gov. Tompkins MSS. vol. ix. pp. 212-217, State Library, Albany, N.Y.), claims that Macomb was here less than just to the militia, "many of whom stood their ground as long as it was tenable" during the first day. In a general order issued by him Sept. 8 (Niles' Register, vol. vii. p. 70), he spoke of some "who fled at the first approach of the enemy, and afterwards basely disbanded themselves, and returned home." Macomb himself wrote that after the first day, when the army had retired to the works, "the militia behaved with great spirit."

[414] For copies of these letters, and of Macdonough's reply and endorsement, I am indebted to Mr. Rodney Macdonough, the Commodore's grandson. Cochran's is dated March 22, and Colden's June 26, 1815; Macdonough's reply July 3. It is well to note that all these preceded the British naval court martial, held in Portsmouth, Aug. 18-21, 1815, where the testimony that the squadron was within range was unanimous and accepted by the Court.

[415] The first lieutenant of the "Confiance" in his evidence said that it was not more than ten minutes after the ship rounded Cumberland Head that the enemy began firing at her, and that the shot at first fell short. As far as it goes, this would show that the American squadron was over a mile from the Head; and, if so, scarcely more than a mile from the batteries.

[416] For information as to ranges, the author applied to Professor Philip R. Alger, U.S. Navy, whose intimate acquaintance with questions of ordnance and gunnery is known throughout his service.

[417] Vol. viii. p. 70, April 1, 1815.

[418] These two letters of Macomb are given in the "Account of the Public Life of Sir George Prevost," p. 165.

[419] Izard's Correspondence, p. 98.

[420] Yeo to the Admiralty, Sept. 24, 1814. From a copy in the Court Martial Record.

[421] In his Narrative, submitted to the Court Martial, Captain Pring stated that Prevost wished a joint attack, because, in the advance along the head of Cumberland Bay, the left flank of the army, when crossing Dead Creek, had been much annoyed by the American gunboats. He feared the same in crossing the Saranac to the assault of the works, and wanted the navy to draw off the gunboats.

[422] Robertson's Narrative before the Court Martial.

[423] The correspondence between Prevost and Downie, Sept. 7-10, is in the Canadian Archives, M. 389.6. pp. 176-183.

[424] This letter of Major Coore, published in a Canadian paper, Feb. 26,

1815, is to be found in the Canadian Archives MSS., M. 389.6. p. 287.

[425] Court Martial Evidence.

[426] Evidence of Pring, and of Brydone, master of the "Confiance," before the Court Martial. Robertson in his narrative is equally positive and explicit on this point.

[427] Robertson's Narrative.

[428] Robertson's Narrative.

[429] Macdonough's Report.

[430] Pronounced "wynd."

[431] Robertson's Narrative.

[432] A spring is a rope taken from the stern of a ship to the anchor, by hauling on which the ship is turned in the direction desired.

[433] Brydone's Evidence.

[434] Evidence of Sailing Master Brydone.

[435] Macdonough's Report.

[436] For the battle of Lake Champlain much the most complete and satisfactory evidence is the Record of the British Court Martial. There having been no dispute on the American side, as between Perry and Elliott at Lake Erie, there has not been the same output of conflicting statements, tending to elucidate as well as to confuse. Commander Henley of the "Eagle" was apparently dissatisfied with Macdonough's report, as the Commodore (apparently) was with his action. This drew from him a special report. Navy Department MSS. Niles' Register, vol. vii. Supplement, p. 135, contains this letter with many verbal changes, which do not materially affect its purport.

[437] Cochrane arrived at Bermuda March 6; but, despite his urgency and evident annoyance, Warren, who was senior, and had had ample notice of his supersession, took his own leisurely time about giving over the command, which he did not do till April 1, sailing for England April 8.

[438] Bathurst to Ross, Sept. 6, 1814. War Office, Entry Book.

[439] Pigot's Report to Cochrane, June 8, 1814. Admiralty In-Letters MSS.

[440] Cochrane to the Admiralty, June 20, 1814. Admiralty In-Letters MSS.

[441] Admiralty to Cochrane, Aug. 10, 1814. The reference in the text depends upon a long paper near the end of vol. 39, British War Office Records, which appears to the writer to have been drawn up for the use of the ministry in parliamentary debate. It gives step by step the procedure of the Government in entering on the New Orleans undertaking.

[442] Bathurst to Ross, Sept. 6, 1814. British War Office Records.

[443] Naval Chronicle, vol. xxxiii. p. 429.

[444] American State Papers, Foreign Relations, vol. iii. p. 397.

[445] Ibid., p. 572.

[446] Niles' Register, vol. iii. p. 182.

[447] Ibid., vol. vii. pp. 133-135.

[448] Cochrane to the Admiralty, Oct. 3, 1814. Admiralty In-Letters.

[449] Ibid.

[450] Neither Cochrane nor Lockyer gives the number of the British boats; but as there were three divisions, drawn from five ships of the line and three or four frigates, besides smaller vessels, Jones' count was probably accurate. He had ample time to observe.

[451] The gunboats of Jefferson's building had no names, and were distinguished by number only.

[452] Jones' Report of this affair is found in Niles' Register, vol. viii. p. 126; those of Cochrane and Lockyer in the Naval Chronicle, vol. xxxiii. pp. 337-341.

[453] So styled in Cochrane's Report, which also speaks of it as Bayou Catalan. The name does not appear on the map of Major Latour, chief of engineers to Jackson, who in his report calls the whole bayou Bienvenu.

[454] Gleig, Narrative of the Campaign of Washington, Baltimore, and New Orleans, pp. 282-288.

[455] Gleig, pp. 308-309.

[456] Gleig's Narrative, p. 321. Cochrane's Report, Naval Chronicle, vol. xxxiii. p. 341. Report of Major C.R. Forrest, British Assistant Quarter-master-General, War Office Records.

[457] Thornton's Report. James' Military Occurrences of the War of 1812, vol. ii., p. 547.

[458] James' Military Occurrences, vol. ii. p. 547.

[459] Niles' Register, vols. vii. and viii., gives a large number of the official reports, as well British as American, concerning the New Orleans Expedition. So also does James in his "Military Occurrences" and "Naval Occurrences" of the War of 1812. Regarded in outline, as is attempted in the text, the operations are of a simple character, presenting no difficulties.

[460] Captains' Letters. Navy Department MSS.

[461] Ibid., Sept. 26, 1814.

[462] Decatur to Navy Department, April 9, 1814. Captains' Letters.

[463] A razee is a ship cut down, and reduced from her original rate. The "Majestic" had been a seventy-four, and probably was the same vessel which under that name and rate took part in the battle of the Nile. The expedient of razeeing had been adopted by the British Government, in order rapidly to prepare vessels superior to the American forty-fours, yet less costly in crews than ships of the line. These razees were rated as carrying fifty-six guns.

[464] Deposition of Commodore Decatur at Bermuda. Naval Chronicle, vol. xxxiii. p. 371.

[465] Decatur's Report. Niles' Register, vol. viii. p. 8. In his deposition Decatur says "the 'Tenedos' did not fire at the time of such surrender."

[466] The loss of the "President" was twenty-four killed, fifty-five wounded.

(Decatur's Report.) That of the "Endymion," eleven killed and fourteen wounded. (Naval Chronicle, vol. xxxiii. p. 262.)

[467] Naval Chronicle, vol. xxxiii. p. 370.

[468] Captain Hayes' Report. Niles' Register, vol. viii. p. 175. Naval Chronicle, vol. xxxiii. p. 261.

[469] Niles' Register, vol. viii. p. 147.

[470] The armament of the "Cyane" is that reported by Lieut. Hoffman, U.S. Navy, who brought her to the United States. Niles' Register, vol. viii. p. 134.

[471] The "Cyane" reached a United States port, but the "Levant" was recaptured by a British squadron. Both names remained in the United States Navy till the Civil War. A "Levant," built in succession to the one captured, was lost at sea in 1860—never heard from.

[472] The account given in the text depends upon Stewart's "minutes of the action" (Niles' Register, vol. viii. p. 219), compared with the "Constitution's" log (Navy Department MSS.), of which the minutes are a development.

THE PEACE NEGOTIATIONS

The Government of the United States had been honestly loath to declare war in 1812, and had signalized its reluctance by immediate advances looking to a restoration of peace. These were made through Jonathan Russell, the chargé d'affaires in London when hostilities began. To use the expression of Monroe, then Secretary of State, "At the moment of the declaration of war, the President, regretting the necessity which produced it, looked to its termination, and provided for it."[473] The two concessions required as indispensable, in the overture thus referred to, dated June 26, 1812, were the revocation of the Orders in Council, and the abandonment of the practice of impressing from American merchant ships. Should these preliminary conditions be obtained, Russell was authorized to stipulate an armistice, during which the two countries should enter upon negotiations, to be conducted either at Washington or in London, for the settlement of all points of difference.

Russell made this communication to Castlereagh August 24, 1812. Before this date Admiral Warren had sailed from England for the American command, carrying with him the propositions of the British Government for a suspension of hostilities, consequent upon the repeal of the Orders in Council.[474] In view of Warren's mission, and of the fact that Russell had no powers to negotiate, but merely to conclude an arrangement upon terms which he could not alter, and which his Government had laid down in ignorance of the revocation of the Orders, Castlereagh declined to discuss with him the American requirements. "I cannot, however," he wrote, "refrain on one single point from expressing my surprise, namely, that as a condition preliminary even to a suspension of hostilities, the Government of the United States should have thought fit to demand that the British Government should desist from its ancient and accustomed practice of impressing British seamen from the merchant ships of a foreign state, simply on the assurance that a law shall hereafter be passed to prohibit the employment of British seamen in the public or commercial service of that state."[475] "The Government could not consent to suspend the exercise of a right upon which the naval strength of the empire mainly depends," until fully convinced that the object would be assured by other means. To a subsequent modification of the American propositions, in form, though not in tenor, the British minister replied in the same spirit, throwing the weight of his objections upon the question of impressment, which indeed remained alone of the two causes of rupture.[476]

Commendable as was its desire for peace, the American Government had made the mistake of being unwilling to insure it by due and timely preparation for war. In these advances, therefore, its adversary naturally saw not magnanimity, but apprehension. Russell, in reporting his final interview, wrote, "Lord Castlereagh once observed somewhat loftily, that if the American Government was so anxious to get rid of the war,[477] it would have an opportunity of doing so on learning the revocation of the Orders in Council." The American representative rejoined with proper spirit; but the remark betrayed the impression produced by this speedy offer, joined to the notorious military unreadiness of the United States. Such things do not make for peace. The British ministry, like a large part of the American people, saw in the declaration of war a mere variation upon the intermittent policy of commercial restrictions of the past five years; an attempt to frighten by bluster. In such spirit Monroe, in this very letter of June 26 to Russell, had dwelt upon the many advantages to be derived from peace with the United States; adding, "not to mention the injuries which cannot fail to result from a prosecution of the war." In transcribing his instructions, Russell discreetly omitted the latter phrase; but the omission, like the words themselves, betrays consciousness that the Administration was faithful to the tradition of its party, dealing in threats rather than in deeds. Through great part of the final negotiations the impression thus made remained with the British ministers.

On September 20, 1812, the Chancellor of the Russian Empire requested a visit from the American minister resident at St. Petersburg, Mr. John Quincy Adams. In the consequent interview, the next evening, the Chancellor said that the Czar, having recently made peace and re-established commercial intercourse with Great Britain, was much concerned that war should have arisen almost immediately between her and the United States. Hostilities between the two nations, which together nearly monopolized the carrying trade of the world, would prevent the economical benefits to Russia expected from the recent change in her political relations. The question was then asked, whether a proffer of Russian mediation would be regarded favorably by the United States. Adams had not yet received official intelligence even of the declaration of war, and was without information as to the views of his Government on the point suggested; but he expressed certainty that such an advance would be cordially met, and he could foresee no obstacle to its entertainment. The proposal was accordingly made to the President, through the customary channels, and on March 11, 1813, was formally accepted by him. James A. Bayard and Albert Gallatin were nominated commissioners, conjointly with Mr. Adams, to act for the United States in forming a treaty of peace under the mediation of the Czar. They sailed soon afterwards.

The American acceptance reached St. Petersburg about June 15; but on that day Adams was informed by the Chancellor that his despatches from London signified the rejection of the Russian proposition by the British Government, on the ground that the differences with the United States involved principles of the internal government of Great Britain, which could not be submitted to the discussion of any mediation.[478] As the Russian Court was then in campaign, at the headquarters of the allied armies, in the tremendous operations of the summer of 1813 against Napoleon, much delay necessarily ensued. On September 1, however, the British ambassador, who was accompanying the Court in the field, presented a formal letter reaffirming the unwillingness of his Government to treat under mediation, but offering through the Czar, whose mediatorial advance was so far recognized, to nominate plenipotentiaries to meet those of the United States in direct consultation. In the backward and forward going of despatches in that preoccupied and unsettled moment, it was not till near November 1 that the British Foreign Office heard from the ambassador that the American commissioners were willing so to treat, and desirous to keep their business separate from that of the continent of Europe; but that their powers were limited to action through the mediation of Russia. Castlereagh then, on November 4, addressed a note to the United States Government, offering a direct negotiation. This was accepted formally, January 5, 1814;[479] and Henry Clay with Jonathan Russell were added to the commission already constituted, raising the number of members to five. The representatives of Great Britain were three: Admiral Lord Gambier, Henry Goulburn, and William Adams. Ghent was fixed upon for the place of meeting.

The instructions issued to the American commissioners were voluminous. They contained not only the requirements of the Government, but arguments from every point of view, and alternatives of several descriptions, to meet anticipated objections. Such elaboration was perhaps necessary when negotiation was to take place so remote from communication with home. On one point, however, as originally issued in contemplation of Russian mediation, demand was peremptory. Impressment must cease, by stipulation. "If this encroachment of Great

Britain is not provided against, the United States have appealed to arms in vain." At that moment, April 15, 1813,[480] the flush of expectation was still strong. "Should improper impressions have been taken of the probable consequences of the war, you will have ample means to remove them. It is certain that from its prosecution Great Britain can promise to herself no advantage, while she exposes herself to great expenses and to the danger of still greater losses." Nine months later, looking to direct negotiation, the same confident tone is maintained. "On impressment, the sentiments of the President have undergone no change. This degrading practice must cease.... No concession is contemplated on any point in controversy;"[481] and three weeks afterwards, February 14, 1814, "Should peace be made in Europe, it is presumed that the British Government would have less objection to forbear impressment for a specified term, than it would have should the war continue. In concluding a peace, even in case of a previous general peace in Europe, it is important to obtain such a stipulation."[482] On June 27, the note was lowered. "If found indispensably necessary to terminate the war, you may omit any stipulation on the subject of impressment." This was in pursuance of the Cabinet determination of June 27, already quoted.[483] It abandoned the only ground for war that had existed since August, 1812, when the Orders in Council were known to have been repealed. The commissioners were indeed to do their best to obtain from the British Government the demanded concessions, not in the matter of impressment only, but on the whole subject of irregular blockades, which underlay the Orders in Council, as well as on other maritime questions in dispute; but in pressing such demands they were under orders to fall back before resistance. From the opening of the colloquy they were on the defensive.

Quite different was the position assumed at first by the British Government and people. The events of the critical year 1813, both in Europe and America, had changed the entire outlook. Alexander Baring, whose general attitude towards the United States was friendly, wrote to Gallatin, October 12, 1813, "We wish for peace, but the pressure of the war upon our commerce and manufactures is over. They have ample relief in other quarters; indeed, the dependence of the two countries on each other was overrated." He was positive that there would be no concession on impressment. Again, on December 14, "The pressure of the war is diminished. Commerce is now abundantly prosperous."[484] Gallatin himself had occasion to spend some time in London during the succeeding spring,—1814. Quotation from his observations has been made already.[485] In a letter of April 21,—after Napoleon's abdication,—"The prosecution of war with the United States would afford a convenient pretext for preserving a more considerable standing force."[486] This would be a useful element in the troublesome diplomacy to be foreseen, in settling the disturbed affairs of Europe; and the Government stood in need of reasons for maintaining the pressure of taxation, which was already eliciting, and later in the year still more elicited, symptoms of great discontent and dangerous Parliamentary opposition. Yet in its conduct towards America the Cabinet had the people behind it. Two months later, Gallatin wrote to the Secretary of State, "You may rest assured of the general hostile spirit of this nation, and of its wish to inflict serious injury on the United States; that no assistance can be expected from Europe; and that no better terms will be obtained than the status ante bellum."[487]

At the time of this writing, June 13, the British Foreign Secretary, Lord Castlereagh, returned from Paris, where he had been spending the two months succeeding the first abdication of Napoleon. During this period formal peace with France had been established, and the Bourbons reseated on her throne. His instructions to the British commissioners at Ghent, issued July 28, were framed on lines which showed consciousness of mastery.[488] The question of abandoning the practice of impressment would not be so much as entertained. The Rule of 1756 should "rest on its own clear and well established authority."[489] The commissioners were not even to discuss it. Equally decisive was the position taken with regard to questions of irregular blockades, and of compensation for seizures under the Orders in Council. When these were presented by the American commissioners, the first was waived aside, as one on which there was no difference of abstract principle; while as to the second, "you cannot be too peremptory in discouraging, at the outset, the smallest expectation of any restitution of captures made under the Orders in Council."[490]

Military and naval weakness, combined with the changed conditions in Europe, made the United States powerless when thus confronted with refusal. The British Secretary stood on far less sure ground, as to success, when he began to formulate his own demands. These were essentially two: suitable arrangements for the Indians, and a rectification of the frontiers. There was a third question, concerning the fisheries on the Great Banks of Newfoundland. As to these, the general right of all nations to frequent the Banks, being open sea, was explicitly admitted; but the subjects of a foreign state had no right to fish within the maritime jurisdiction of Great Britain, much less to land with their catch on coasts belonging to her. The provisions of the Treaty of 1783 therefore would not be renewed, unless for an equivalent.

As regarded the Indians, an adequate arrangement of their interests was a sine quâ non of peace; nor would a full and express recognition of present limits by itself alone fulfil this demand. There must be security for its future observance. The particular method by which this observance should be maintained was not made indispensable; but it was plainly stated in the instructions that the best means was "a mutual guarantee of the Indian possessions, as they shall be established upon the peace, against encroachment on the part of either State." The suggestion, in its logical consequence and in its intent, went to establishing the communities of Indians as a sovereign state, with boundaries guaranteed by Great Britain and the United States,—a most entangling alliance. In support of this, Castlereagh alleged that such a barrier of separation possessed a distinct advantage over a line of contact between the two guaranteeing states, such as now existed in their common boundary. The collisions incident to intercourse between red and white men were easily transferred from side to side of such a conventional line, causing continual disputes. The advantages of a buffer state, to use the modern term, would be secured by the proposed arrangement. Writing to the prime minister, the Earl of Liverpool, he said, "The question is one of expediency; and not of principle, as the American commissioners have endeavored to make it. It does not follow, because, in the year 1783, the two States, not perhaps very justly, took a common boundary, thereby assuming a sort of sovereignty over the Indians, that they may not mutually recede from that boundary, if a frontier conterminous with that of the Indians is preferable to one with each other."[491]

However plausible reasoning based upon such premises might seem to the party advancing it, it could not qualify the fact that it required from the United States a large cession of territory, to be surrendered to the Indians under British guarantee. Such a demand was a dangerous diplomatic weapon to put within reach of a commission, of which Adams and Gallatin were members. In presenting it, also, the British representatives went beyond the letter of their instructions, issued by Castlereagh on July 28, and enlarged August 14. Not only was the inclusion of the Indians in the peace to be a sine quâ non, but they wrote, "It is equally necessary" that a definite boundary be assigned, and the integrity of their possessions mutually guaranteed.[492] This paper was submitted to Castlereagh as he passed through Ghent to Paris, on his way to the Vienna Conference. "Had I been to prepare the note given in on our part, I should have been less peremptory;" but, like many superiors, he hesitated to fetter the men in immediate charge, and "acquiesced in the expression, 'It is equally necessary, etc.,' which is very strong."[493] The prime minister was still more deprecatory. He wrote Castlereagh, "Our commissioners had certainly taken a very erroneous view of our policy. If the negotiations had been allowed to break off upon the two notes already presented, ... I am satisfied the war would have become popular in America."[494]

The American commissioners could see this also, and were quick to use the advantage given by the wording of the paper before them, to improve the status of the United States in the negotiation; for one of the great weaknesses, on which Great Britain reckoned, was the disunion of

American sentiment on the subject of the war. Of their reply, dated August 24, Castlereagh wrote, "It is extremely material to answer the American note, as it is evidently intended to rouse the people upon the question of their independence."[495] Besides the Indian proposition, the British note of August 19 had conveyed also the explicit views of the ministry as to rectification of frontier. Stated briefly, the chain of the Great Lakes was asserted to be a military barrier essential to the security of Canada, as the weaker community in North America. To assure it, no territorial cession was required; but the lakes should be in the sole military tenure of Great Britain. The United States might use them freely for commercial purposes, but should maintain on them no ship of war, nor build any fortification on their shores, or within a certain distance, to be fixed by agreement. In addition to this, on the side of the lower St. Lawrence, there was to be such a cession of the northern part of Maine as would establish a direct communication between Quebec and Halifax. The American reply of August 24[496] discussed these questions, patiently but instructively. The matters involved were made plain for the American reader, and the paper closed with the clear intimation that before such terms were accepted there must be a great deal more fighting. "It is not necessary to refer such demands to the American Government for instructions. They will only be a fit subject of deliberation when it becomes necessary to decide upon the expediency of an absolute surrender of national independence." So far as the British proposals went, the question was military, not diplomatic; for soldiers and seamen to decide, not for negotiators.

So it stood, and so in the solution it proved. The American commissioners held firm to this ground; while on the part of the British there was thenceforth a continual effort to escape from a false position, or to temporize, until some favorable change of circumstances might enable them to insist. "The substance of the question," wrote Castlereagh to the prime minister, "is, are we prepared to continue the war for territorial arrangements. If not, is this the best time to make peace, or is it desirable to take the chances of the campaign and then to be governed by circumstances?"[497] "If our campaign in Canada should be as successful as our military preparations would lead us to expect," ... replied Liverpool, "if our commander does his duty, I am persuaded we shall have acquired by our arms every point on the Canadian frontier, which we ought to insist on keeping."[498]

By these considerations the next British note was dictated, and presented September 4.[499] It simply argued the question, with dilatory design, in a somewhat minatory tone. "I think it not unlikely," Liverpool had written with reference to it, "that the American commissioners will propose to refer the subject to their Government. In that case, the negotiation may be adjourned till the answer is received, and we shall know the result of the campaign before it can be resumed." But the Americans did not refer. They too needed time for their people to learn what now was the purpose of hostilities, which the British envoys had precipitately stated as an indispensable concession, and to manifest the national temper under the changed circumstances; but they did not choose that the matter should be stated as one open to discussion. They knew well enough the harassment of maintaining a land warfare three thousand miles from Great Britain, as well as the dangers threatening the European situation and embarrassing the British ministry. They in turn discussed at length, scrutinizing historically the several arguments of their opponents; but their conclusion was foregone. The two propositions—first, of assigning "a definite boundary to the Indians living within the limit of the United States, beyond which boundary they [the United States] should stipulate not to acquire any territory; secondly, of securing the exclusive military possession of the lakes to Great Britain—are both inadmissible. We cannot subscribe to, and would deem useless to refer to our Government, any arrangement containing either of these propositions." The British Government was not permitted any subterfuge to escape from the premature insistence upon cession of territory made by their envoys, which would tend to unite the people in America; nor was it to be anticipated that prolonged hostilities for such an object would be acceptable in Great Britain.

The pre-eminence given to the Indian question by Great Britain in these negotiations was due to the importance attached by British local officials to the aid of the savages in war, and to a sensitive conviction that, when thus utilized, they should not be abandoned in peace. Their military value was probably over-estimated. It consisted chiefly in numbers, in which the British were inferior, and in the terror produced by their cruelties; doubtless, also, in some degree to their skill in woodcraft; but they were not dependable. Such as it was, their support went usually to the weaker party; not because the Indian naturally sided with the weaker, but because he instinctively recognized that from the stronger he had most to fear. Therefore in colonial days France, in later days Great Britain, in both cases Canada, derived more apparent profit from their employment than did their opponent, whose more numerous white men enabled him to dispense with the fickle and feebler aid of the aborigines.

Before the firm attitude of the note of September 9, the British Government again procrastinated, and receded from demands which sound policy should from the first have recognized as untenable, unless reposing upon decisive military success and occupation. On September 19, their commissioners replied[500] that while the exclusive military possession of the lakes would be conducive to a good understanding, without endangering the security of the United States, it had not been advanced as a sine quâ non. A final proposition on the subject of the Canadian boundaries would be made, when the Indian question was settled. Concerning this, they were "authorized distinctly to declare that they are instructed not to sign a treaty of peace, unless the Indian nations are included in it, and restored to all the rights, privileges, and territories, which they enjoyed in the year 1811," by treaties then existing. "From this point the British plenipotentiaries cannot depart." They were instructed further to offer for discussion an article establishing Indian boundaries, within which the two countries should bind themselves not to make acquisitions by purchase during a term of years. To the absence of Lord Castlereagh, and consequent private correspondence between him and his colleagues in London, we owe the knowledge that the question of purchasing Indian lands, and the guarantee, would no longer be insisted on; and that the military control of the lakes was now reduced in purpose to the retention of Forts Michilimackinac and Niagara.[501] The intention remained, however, to insist upon the Indian provisions as just stated.

On September 26, the American commission replied that, as thus presented, there was no apparent difference in the purposes of the two nations as regarded the substantial welfare of the Indians themselves. The United States meant towards them peace, and the placing them in the position in which they stood before the war. "The real difference was" in the methods proposed. Great Britain "insisted on including the Indians, as allies, in the treaty of peace between her and the United States." But the Indians concerned dwelt within the acknowledged bounds of the United States, and their political relations towards her were no concern of Great Britain; nor could any arrangement be admitted which would constitute them independent communities, in whose behalf Great Britain might hereafter claim a right to interfere. The error underlying the British demand was the assumption that the Indian tribes were independent; whereas, in their relation to foreign countries, they were merely dwellers in the United States, who had made war upon her in co-operation with Great Britain. The upshot was a mutual agreement, drawn up by the British plenipotentiaries, that upon the conclusion of peace each state would put an end to hostilities in which it might be engaged with the Indians, and would restore them to the rights enjoyed before 1811. The Americans accepted this, subject to ratification at home, on the ground that, while it included the Indians in the peace, it did not do so as parties to the treaty, and left the manner of settlement in the hands of each Government interested. The agreement thus framed formed one of the articles of the treaty.

On September 27 the Gazette account of the capture of Washington was published in London. Lord Bathurst, who in the absence of Castlereagh was acting as Foreign Secretary, despatched the news the same day to the commissioners at Ghent, instructing them to assure the Americans that it made no difference in the British desire for peace, nor would modify unfavorably the requirements as to frontier, as yet unstated.[502] Liverpool wrote coincidently to Castlereagh, suggesting that he should communicate to the sovereigns and ministers at Vienna the moderation with which the Government was acting, as well as the tone assumed by the American commissioners, "so very different from what their situation appears to warrant." "I fear the Emperor of Russia is half an American, and it would be very desirable to do away any prejudices which may exist in his mind, or in that of Count Nesselrode, on this subject."[503] The remark is illuminating as to the reciprocal influence of the American contest and the European negotiations, and also as to the reasons for declining the proposed Russian mediation of 1813. The continent generally, and Russia conspicuously, held opinions on neutral maritime rights similar to those of the United States. Liverpool had already[504] expressed his wish to be well out of the war, although expecting decided military successes, and convinced that the terms as now reduced would be very unpopular in England; "but I feel too strongly the inconvenience of a continuance not to make me desirous of concluding it at the expense of some popularity."

It was in this spirit, doubtless, that Bathurst instructed the envoys that, if the Americans wished to refer the very modified proposals, or to sign them conditional upon ratification at home, either proposition would be accepted; an assurance repeated on October 5.[505] Were neither alternative embraced as to the Indian settlement, the negotiation should be closed and the commission return to England. British military anticipation then stood high. Not only was the capture of Washington over-estimated, but Ross and Cochrane had impressed their Government with brilliant expectations. "They are very sanguine about the future operations. They intend, on account of the season, to proceed in the first instance to the northward, and to occupy Rhode Island, where they propose remaining and living upon the country until about the first of November. They will then proceed southward, destroy Baltimore, if they should find it practicable without too much risk, occupy several important points on the coast of Georgia and the Carolinas, take possession of Mobile in the Floridas, and close the campaign with an attack on New Orleans."[506] This was a large programme for a corps of the size of Ross', after all allowance made for the ease with which Washington had fallen. It is probably to be read in connection with the project of sending to America very large re-enforcements; so numerous, indeed, that Lord Hill, Wellington's second in the Peninsula, had been designated for the command. This purpose had been communicated to Ross and Cochrane; and at the time of the capture of Washington they had not received the letters notifying them that "circumstances had induced his Majesty's Government to defer their intention of employing so considerable a force in that quarter."[507] For this change of mind America doubtless was indebted to European considerations. Besides the expectations mentioned, the British Government had well-founded reasons to hope for control of Lake Ontario, and for substantial results from the handsome force placed at the disposal of Sir George Prevost, to which the triumphant expedition of Cochrane and Ross had been intended only as a diversion.

Under these flattering anticipations were formulated the bases upon which to treat, now that the Indian question was out of the way. On October 18 and 20 Bathurst instructed the commissioners to propose, as a starting point, the principle that each party should hold what it had, subject to modifications for mutual accommodation. "Considering the relative situation of the two countries, the moderation evinced by his Majesty's Government in admitting this principle, (thereby surrendering claim to the future conquests), in the present state of the contest, must be manifest." When this was accepted, but not before, the mutual accommodations were to be suggested. The present captured possessions were stated to be: British, Fort Michilimackinac, Fort Niagara, and all the country east of the Penobscot; the American, Fort Erie and Fort Malden. Upon the surrender of the two latter, Great Britain would restore the forts at Castine and Machias. She would retain Mackinac and Fort Niagara, the latter with a surrounding strip of five miles of territory; and in exchange (apparently) for "all the country east of the Penobscot," would accept that part of Maine which lies north of the Aroostook River, thus insuring between Quebec and Halifax a direct communication, wholly under British jurisdiction.

There were some further minor matters of detail, unnecessary to mention; the more so that they did not come formally before the American commissioners, who immediately rejected the proposed principle of uti possidetis, and replied, October 24, that they were not empowered to yield any territory, and could treat only on the basis of entire mutual restitution. This Liverpool testily likened to the claim of the French revolutionary Government[508] that territory could not be ceded because contrary to the fundamental law of the Republic. In the American case, however, it was substantially an affirmation that the military conditions did not warrant surrender. Meanwhile, on October 21, the news of Macdonough's victory reached London from American sources. Although the British official accounts did not arrive until some time later, Liverpool, writing to Castlereagh on that day, admitted that there could be no doubt of the defeat of the flotilla.[509] Despite this check, the Cabinet still cherished hopes of further successes, and were unwilling yet to abandon entirely the last inches of the ground heretofore assumed. "Had it not been for this unfortunate adventure on Lake Champlain," wrote Bathurst to Castlereagh, "I really believe we should have signed a peace by the end of this month. This will put the enemy in spirits. The campaign will end in our doing much where we thought we should have done little, and doing nothing where we expected everything."[510] He announced the intention to send Pakenham in Ross' place for the New Orleans expedition, and to increase his force in the spring, should the war last till then. Meanwhile, it might be well to let the Powers assembled at Vienna understand that, whatever the success in Louisiana, the inhabitants would be distinctly told that in no case would the country be taken under British protection. They might be granted independence, but preferably would be urged to place themselves again under the Spanish Crown; but they must know that, in treating with the United States, neither of these solutions would be made by Great Britain a sine quâ non. The Government had probably taken a distaste to that peremptory formula by the unsatisfactory result of the proposition about the Indians.

This care concerning the effect produced upon the course of events at Vienna appears forcibly in the letters of Liverpool. After the receipt of the American commission's refusal to accept the basis of the uti possidetis, he wrote to Castlereagh, October 28, that he feared it put an end to any hopes of bringing the American war to a conclusion. The expectation of some favorable change in the aspect of affairs, however, decided the ministry to gain a little more time before bringing the negotiation to a close; and the envoys at Ghent were therefore to be instructed to demand a full projet of all the American conditions before entering on further discussion. The same day Liverpool sent a second letter,[511] in which he said distinctly that, in viewing the European settlement, it was material to consider that the war with America would probably be of some duration; that enemies should not be made in other quarters by holding out too long on the questions of Poland, Naples, and Saxony, for he was apprehensive that "some of our European allies will not be indisposed to favor the Americans; and, if the Emperor of Russia should be desirous of taking up their cause, we are well aware from some of Lord Walpole's late communications that there is a most powerful party in Russia to support him. Looking to a continuance of the American war, our financial state is far from satisfactory. We shall want a loan for the ensuing year of £27,000,000 or £28,000,000. The American war will not cost us less than £10,000,000, in addition to our peace establishment and other expenses. We must expect, therefore, to have it said that the property tax is continued for the purpose of securing a better frontier for Canada." Castlereagh himself had already spoken of the financial conditions as "perfectly without precedent in our financial history."[512]

The renewal of the European war, avowedly dreaded by Liverpool,[513] was thought not impossible by Castlereagh and Wellington; while conditions in France already threatened an explosion, such as Bonaparte occasioned in the succeeding March. "It is impossible," wrote Wellington, "to conceive the distress in which individuals of all descriptions are. The only remedy is the revival of Bonaparte's system of war and plunder; and it is evident that cannot be adopted during the reign of the Bourbons."[514] Neither he nor Castlereagh doubted the imminence of the danger. "It sounds incredible," wrote the latter, "that Talleyrand should treat the notion of any agitation at Paris as wholly unfounded."[515] A plot was believed to exist, which embraced as one of its features the seizing of the Duke, and holding him as a hostage. He himself thought it possible, and saw no means in the French Government's hands adequate to resist. "You already know my opinion of the danger at Paris.... The event may occur any night, and if it should occur, I don't think I should be allowed to depart. My safety depends upon the King's;"[516] but he was characteristically averse to any step which bore the appearance of precipitate withdrawal.

While the American negotiators were drawing up the projet which they had decided to present in response to the British demand, the combination of circumstances just stated led the British ministry to resolve on removing Wellington from Paris on some pretext, lest his services should be lost to them in the emergency now momentarily dreaded. The urgency for peace with America co-operated to determine the ostensible reason, which was almost a true one. The American command was offered to him. "The Duke of Wellington would restore confidence to the army, place the military operations on a proper footing, and give us the best chance of peace. I know he is very anxious for the restoration of peace with America, if it can be made upon terms at all honorable. It is a material consideration, likewise, that if we shall be disposed for the sake of peace to give up something of our just pretensions, we can do this more creditably through him than through any other person."[517] Liverpool voiced the conclusions of the Cabinet, and it would be difficult for words to manifest more forcibly anxiety to escape from a situation. Wellington himself drew attention to this. "Does it not occur to your lordship that, by appointing me to go to America at this moment, you give ground for belief, all over Europe, that your affairs there are in a much worse situation than they really are? and will not my nomination at this moment be a triumph to the Americans, and their friends here and elsewhere?"[518] Conditions were alarming, but the action resembled panic.

The offer, which was really a request, brought Wellington by a side wind into the American negotiations, and enabled him to give the Government the weight of his name and authority in concluding a peace otherwise than on their "just pretensions." The war, he said, has been honorable to Great Britain; meaning doubtless that, considering the huge physical mass and the proximity of the United States, it was well done to have escaped injury, as it was militarily disgraceful to the American Government, with such superiority, to have been so impotent. But, he continued, neither I nor any one else can achieve success, in the way of conquests, unless you have naval superiority on the lakes. That was what was needed; "not a general, nor general officers and troops. Till that superiority is acquired, it is impossible, according to my notion, to maintain an army in such a situation as to keep the enemy out of the whole frontier, much less to make any conquest from the enemy, which, with those superior means, might, with reasonable hopes of success, be undertaken.... The question is, whether we can obtain this naval superiority on the lakes. If we cannot, I shall do you but little good in America; and I shall go there only to prove the truth of Prevost's defence, and to sign a peace which might as well be signed now." This endorsed not only Prevost's retreat, but also the importance of Macdonough's victory. The Duke then added frankly that, in the state of the war, they had no right to demand any concession of territory. He brushed contemptuously aside the claim of occupying the country east of the Penobscot, on the ground of Sherbrooke's few companies at Castine, ready to retreat at a moment's notice. "If this reasoning be true, why stipulate for the uti possidetis?"[519] Penned November 9, the day before the American negotiators at Ghent handed in their requested projet, this letter may be regarded as decisive. November 13, Liverpool replied that the ministry was waiting anxiously for the American projet, ... and, "without entering into particulars, I can assure you that we shall be disposed to meet your views upon the points on which the negotiation appears to turn at present;" the points being the uti possidetis, with the several details of possession put forward by Bathurst. The American paper was in London before the 18th, when Liverpool wrote to Castlereagh, "I think we have determined, if all other points can be satisfactorily settled, not to continue the war for the purpose of obtaining, or securing, any acquisition of territory. We have been led to this determination by the consideration of the unsatisfactory state of the negotiations at Vienna, and by that of the alarming situation of the interior of France." "Under such circumstances, it has appeared to us desirable to bring the American war, if possible, to a conclusion."[520] The basis of the status quo ante bellum, sustained all along by the American commission, was thus definitely accepted, and so stated formally by Bathurst.[521]

This fundamental agreement having been reached, the negotiations ran rapidly to a settlement without further serious hitch; a conclusion to which contributed powerfully the increasing anxiety of the British ministry over the menacing aspect of the Continent. The American projet,[522] besides the customary formal stipulations as to procedure for bringing hostilities to a close, consisted of articles embodying the American positions on the subjects of impressment and blockade, with claims for indemnity for losses sustained by irregular captures and seizures during the late hostilities between France and Great Britain; a provision aimed at the Orders in Council. These demands, which covered the motives of the war, and may be regarded as the offensive side of the American negotiation, were pronounced inadmissible at once by the British, and were immediately abandoned. Their presentation had been merely formal; the United States Government, within its own council chamber, had already recognized that they could not be enforced. The projet included the agreement previously framed concerning the Indians; who were thus provided for in the treaty, though excluded from any recognition as parties to it, or as independent political communities. This was the only demand which Great Britain can be said fairly to have carried, and it was so far a reduction from her original requirement as to be unrecognizable. An American proposition, pledging each of the contracting parties not again to employ Indians in war, was rejected.

The remaining articles of the projet, although entirely suitable to a treaty of peace, were not essentially connected with the war. The treaty merely gave a suitable occasion for presenting them. They provided for fixing, by mixed commissions, the boundary lines between the British possessions and the United States. These the Treaty of 1783 had stated in terms which had as yet received no proper topographical determination. From the mouth of the St. Croix River, and the islands within it and in the adjacent sea, around, north and west, as far as the head of Lake Superior, the precise course of the bounding line needed definition by surveyors. These propositions were agreed to; but when it came to similar provision for settling the boundary of the new territories acquired by the Louisiana purchase, as far as the Rocky Mountains, difficulties arose. In the result it was agreed that the determination of the boundary should be carried as far as the most northwestern point of the Lake of the Woods, "in conformity with the true intent of the said Treaty of Peace of one thousand seven hundred and eighty-three." The treaty was silent on the subject of boundary westward of the Lake of the Woods, and this article of the projet was dropped. It differed indeed from its associates, in providing the settlement for a new question, and not the definition of an old settlement. In conclusion, the British commissioners obtained the adoption of an agreement that both parties "would use their best endeavors to promote the entire abolition of the slave trade." In Great Britain the agitation for this measure had reached proportions which were not the least among the embarrassments of the ministry; and at this critical juncture the practical politicians conducting affairs found themselves constrained by a popular demand to press the subject upon the less sympathetic statesmen of the Cabinet.

The American commissioners had made a good fight, and shown complete appreciation of the factors working continuously in their behalf. To the end, and even more evidently at the end, was apparent the increasing anxiety of the British Government, the reasonable cause for it in European conditions, and the immense difficulty under such circumstances of accomplishing any substantial military successes in America. The Duke of

Wellington wrote that "all the American armies of which I ever read would not beat out of a field of battle the troops that went from Bordeaux last summer;"[523] but still, "his opinion is that no military advantage can be expected if the war goes on, and he would have great reluctance in undertaking the command unless we made a serious effort first to obtain peace, without insisting upon keeping any part of our conquests."[524] On December 23, Liverpool sent a long and anxious letter to Castlereagh, in reply to his late despatches. The fear of a renewal of war on the Continent is prominent in his consideration, and it was recognized that the size of the European armaments, combined with the pecuniary burden of maintaining them, tended of itself to precipitate an outbreak. Should that occur, France could scarcely fail to be drawn in; and France, if involved, might direct her efforts towards the Low Countries, "the only object on the continent which would be regarded as a distinct British interest of sufficient magnitude to reconcile the country to war," with its renewed burden of taxation. "We are decidedly and unanimously of opinion that all your efforts should be directed to the continuance of peace. There is no mode in which the arrangements in Poland, Germany, and Italy, can be settled, consistently with the stipulations of the Treaty of Paris, which is not to be preferred, under present circumstances, to a renewal of hostilities between the Continental Powers." Coincidently with this, in another letter of the same day, he mentions the meetings which have taken place on account of the property tax, and the spirit which had arisen on the subject. "This, as well as other considerations, make us most anxious to get rid of the American war."[525]

The Treaty of Ghent was signed December 24, 1814, by the eight commissioners. The last article provided for its ratification, without alteration, at Washington, within four months from the signature. A chargé d'affaires to the United States was appointed, and directed to proceed at once in a British ship of war to America, with the Prince Regent's ratification, to be exchanged against that of the President; but he was especially instructed that the exchange should not be made unless the ratification by the United States was without alteration, addition, or exclusion, in any form whatsoever. Hostilities were not to cease until such action had taken place. The British Government were apparently determined that concessions wrung from them, by considerations foreign to the immediate struggle, should not be subjected to further modification in the Senate.

Mr. Baker, the British chargé, sailed in the British sloop of war "Favorite," accompanied by Mr. Carroll bearing the despatches of the American commissioners. The "Favorite" arrived in New York on Saturday, February 11. The treaty was ratified by the President, as it stood, by and with the advice and consent of the Senate, on the 17th of February, 1815.

A year after the conclusion of peace, a weighty opinion as to the effect of the War of 1812 upon the national history was expressed by one of the commissioners, Mr. Albert Gallatin. For fifteen years past, no man had been in closer touch with the springs of national life, national policy, and national action; as representative in Congress, and as intimate adviser of two consecutive Presidents, in his position as Secretary of the Treasury. His experience, the perspicuity of his intellect, and his lucidity of thought and expression, give particular value to his conclusions; the more so that to some extent they are the condemnation, regretfully uttered, of a scheme of political conduct with the main ideas of which he had been closely identified. He wrote: "The war has been productive of evil and of good, but I think the good preponderates. Independent of the loss of lives, and of the property of individuals, the war has laid the foundations of permanent taxes and military establishments, which the Republicans[526] had deemed unfavorable to the happiness and free institutions of the country. But under our former system we were becoming too selfish, too much attached exclusively to the acquisition of wealth, above all, too much confined in our political feelings to local and state objects. The war has renewed and reinstated the national feelings and character which the Revolution had given, and which were daily lessening. The people have now more general objects of attachment, with which their pride and political opinions are connected. They are more Americans; they feel and act more as a nation; and I hope that the permanency of the Union is thereby better secured."[527]

Such, even at so early a date, could be seen to be the meaning of the War of 1812 in the progress of the national history. The people, born by war to independence, had by war again been transformed from childhood, absorbed in the visible objects immediately surrounding it, to youth with its dawning vision and opening enthusiasms. They issued from the contest, battered by adversity, but through it at last fairly possessed by the conception of a national unity, which during days of material prosperity had struggled in vain against the predominance of immediate interests and local prepossessions. The conflict, indeed, was not yet over. Two generations of civic strife were still to signalize the slow and painful growth of the love for "The Union"; that personification of national being, upon which can safely fasten the instinct of human nature to centre devotion upon a person and a name. But, through these years of fluctuating affections, the work of the War of 1812 was continuously felt. Men had been forced out of themselves. More and more of the people became more Americans; they felt and acted more as a nation; and when the moment came that the unity of the state was threatened from within, the passion for the Union, conceived in 1812, and nurtured silently for years in homes and hearts, asserted itself. The price to be paid was heavy. Again war desolated the land; but through war the permanency of the Union was secured. Since then, relieved from internal weakness, strong now in the maturity of manhood, and in a common motive, the nation has taken its place among the Powers of the earth.

FOOTNOTES

[473] Monroe to Russell, Aug. 21, 1812. American State Papers, Foreign Relations, vol. iii. p. 587.
[474] Ante, vol. i. p. 390.
[475] American State Papers, Foreign Relations, vol. iii. p. 590.
[476] Correspondence between Russell and Castlereagh, Sept. 12-18, 1812; and Russell to Monroe, Sept. 17. American State Papers, Foreign Relations, vol. iii. pp. 591-595.
[477] Russell's italics.
[478] The correspondence relating to the Russian proffer of mediation is to be found in American State Papers, vol. iii. pp. 623-627.
[479] American State Papers, vol. iii. pp. 621-622.
[480] Ibid., pp. 695-700.
[481] American State Papers, Foreign Relations, vol. iii. p. 701.
[482] Ibid., p. 703.
[483] Ante, p. 266, and note.
[484] Writings of Albert Gallatin, edited by Henry Adams, vol. i. pp. 586, 592.
[485] Ante, p. 332.
[486] Writings of Albert Gallatin, vol. i. p. 603.
[487] Ibid., vol. i. p. 629.
[488] A similar consciousness appears to the writer discernible in a letter of Wellington to Castlereagh, of May 25, 1814. To procure "the cession of Olivenza by Spain to Portugal, we could promise to bind North America, by a secret article in our treaty of peace, to give no encouragement, or countenance, or assistance, to the Spanish colonies" (then in revolt). Memoirs and Correspondence of Lord Castlereagh, series iii. vol. ii. p. 44. The italics are mine.
[489] Castlereagh to the British commissioners, July 28, 1814. Castlereagh's Memoirs and Correspondence, series iii. vol. ii. p. 69.
[490] Ibid., Aug. 14, 1814, pp. 88, 89.
[491] Castlereagh to Liverpool, Paris, Aug. 28, 1814. Castlereagh Memoirs, p. 101.
[492] Note of the British commissioners, Aug. 19, 1814. American State Papers, Foreign Relations, vol. iii. p. 710. My italics.
[493] Castlereagh to Liverpool, Aug. 28, 1814. Castlereagh Memoirs, series iii. vol. ii. p. 100.

[494] Liverpool to Castlereagh, Sept. 2, 1814. Castlereagh Papers MSS.
[495] Castlereagh Memoirs, etc., series iii. vol. ii. p. 101.
[496] American State Papers, Foreign Relations, vol. iii. pp. 711-713.
[497] Castlereagh to Liverpool, August 28. Memoirs, etc., series iii. vol. ii. p. 102.
[498] Liverpool to Castlereagh, September 2, Castlereagh Papers MSS.
[499] American State Papers, Foreign Relations, vol. iii. p. 713.
[500] American State Papers, Foreign Relations, vol. iii. p. 717.
[501] Bathurst to Castlereagh, Sept. 16, 1814. Castlereagh Papers MSS.
[502] Castlereagh Memoirs, series iii. vol. ii. p. 138.
[503] Liverpool to Castlereagh, September 27. Castlereagh Papers MSS.
[504] September 23. Ibid.
[505] Castlereagh Memoirs, series iii. vol. ii. p. 148.
[506] Liverpool to Castlereagh, Sept. 27, 1814. Castlereagh Papers MSS.
[507] Ante, p. 385; and 384, note.
[508] Liverpool to Castlereagh, Oct. 28. Castlereagh Papers MSS.
[509] Liverpool to Castlereagh, Oct. 21, 1814. Ibid.
[510] Bathurst to Castlereagh, Oct. 21, 1814. Castlereagh Papers MSS.
[511] Castlereagh Papers MSS.
[512] Castlereagh to Sir H. Wellesley, Sept. 9, 1814. Memoirs, series iii. vol. ii. p. 112.
[513] Liverpool to Castlereagh, Nov. 2, 1814. Castlereagh Papers MSS.
[514] Wellington to Liverpool, Nov. 9, 1814. Castlereagh Memoirs, series iii. vol. ii. p. 187.
[515] Castlereagh to Wellington, Nov. 21, 1814. Castlereagh Memoirs, series iii. vol. ii. p. 205.
[516] Wellington to Liverpool, Nov. 7 and 9, 1814. Ibid., pp. 186, 190.
[517] Liverpool to Castlereagh, Nov. 4, 1814. Castlereagh MSS.
[518] Wellington to Liverpool, Nov. 18, 1814. Castlereagh Letters, series iii. vol. ii. p. 203.
[519] Wellington to Liverpool, Nov. 9, 1814. Castlereagh Memoirs, series iii. vol. ii. p. 189.
[520] Liverpool to Castlereagh, Nov. 18, 1814. Castlereagh MSS.
[521] Bathurst to the commissioners, Dec. 6, 1814. Castlereagh Memoirs, series iii. vol. ii. p. 214.
[522] American State Papers, Foreign Relations, vol. iii. p. 735.
[523] Castlereagh Memoirs, series iii. vol. ii. p. 188.
[524] Liverpool to Castlereagh, Nov. 18, 1814. Castlereagh MSS.
[525] Ibid., Dec. 23, 1814. Castlereagh MSS.
[526] The contemporary name of the political party to which Jefferson, Madison, and Gallatin belonged.
[527] Writings of Gallatin, May 7, 1816, vol. i. p. 700.

ALFRED THAYER MAHAN

CPSIA information can be obtained
at www.ICGtesting.com
Printed in the USA
LVHW02s1056170818
587285LV00021BA/1891/P